OCR Ancient History

AS AND A LEVEL

COMPONENT 2

OCR Ancient History

AS AND A LEVEL

COMPONENT 2:
Rome

ROBERT CROMARTY
JAMES HARRISON
STEVE MATTHEWS

GENERAL EDITOR:
JAMES RENSHAW

Bloomsbury Academic
An imprint of Bloomsbury Publishing Plc

B L O O M S B U R Y
LONDON · OXFORD · NEW YORK · NEW DELHI · SYDNEY

Bloomsbury Academic

An imprint of Bloomsbury Publishing Plc

50 Bedford Square	1385 Broadway
London	New York
WC1B 3DP	NY 10018
UK	USA

www.bloomsbury.com

BLOOMSBURY and the Diana logo are trademarks of Bloomsbury Publishing Plc

First published 2018

© Robert Cromarty, James Harrison, Steve Matthews, 2018

Robert Cromarty, James Harrison and Steve Matthews have asserted their right under the
Copyright, Designs and Patents Act, 1988, to be identified as Author of this work.

British Library Cataloguing-in-Publication Data
A catalogue record for this book is available from the British Library.

ISBN:	PB:	978-1-3500-1527-2
	ePDF:	978-1-3500-1529-6
	ePub:	978-1-3500-1528-9

Library of Congress Cataloging-in-Publication Data
A catalog record for this book is available from the Library of Congress.

Cover design by Terry Woodley and Olivia D'Cruz
Cover image © Getty/Digitaler Lumpensammler

Typeset by RefineCatch Limited, Bungay, Suffolk
Printed and bound in India

To find out more about our authors and books, visit www.bloomsbury.com. Here you
will find extracts, author interviews, details of forthcoming events and the option
to sign up for our newsletters.

ACKNOWLEDGEMENTS

The authors divided the text between them as follows:

Ch 1: The Julio-Claudian Emperors, 31 BC–AD 68 by Robert Cromarty and
   James Harrison
Ch 2: The Breakdown of the Late Republic, 88–31 BC by Steve Matthews
Ch 3: The Flavians, AD 68–96 by Robert Cromarty
Ch 4: Ruling Roman Britain, AD 43–*c*. 128 by James Harrison

The authors would like to thank the many anonymous reviewers at universities, schools
and OCR who read and commented on drafts of this text. All errors remain their own.

CONTENTS

Contents

INTRODUCTION

Welcome to your textbook for OCR AS and A Level Ancient History.

This book has been created to support the Roman half of the OCR AS and A Level specifications for first teaching from September 2017. It contains the compulsory Period Study 'The Julio-Claudian Emperors, 31 BC–AD 68' as well as the three Depth Study options, one of which you will study: 'The Breakdown of the Late Republic, 88–31 BC', 'The Flavians, AD 68–96' and 'Ruling Roman Britain, AD 43–c. 128'.

Through your reading of this textbook and your wider study in class, you will be able to gain a broad understanding of military, political, religious, social and cultural aspects of the history of the ancient world. You will read and analyse ancient source material, and study certain debates by modern scholars related to this material. This will enable you to develop the skills to formulate coherent arguments about key issues and concepts.

The specification requires you to respond to the prescribed source material and assess its content through analysis and evaluation. The box features (see pp. ix–x) are designed to build up your skills and knowledge, while exam tips, practice questions, and chapters on assessment will prepare you for taking your final examinations.

A Companion Website, available at www.bloomsbury.com/anc-hist-as-a-level, supports this textbook with further information, resources and updates. If you have any suggestions for improvement and additional resources please get in touch by writing to contact@bloomsbury.com.

HOW TO USE THIS BOOK

The layout and box features of this book are designed to aid your learning.

ICONS

The Prescribed Source icon **PS** flags a quotation or image that is a source prescribed in the specification.

The Stretch and Challenge icon **S&C** indicates that an exercise extends beyond the core content of the specification.

The Companion Website icon **CW** highlights where extra material can be found on the Bloomsbury Companion Website: www.bloomsbury.com/anc-hist-as-a-level.

BOX FEATURES

In the margins you will find feature boxes giving short factfiles of key events, individuals and places.

Other features either **recommend** teaching material or highlight **prescribed** content and **assessment** tips and information.

Recommended teaching material is found in the following box features:

- Activities
- Debates
- Explore Further
- Further Reading
- Study Questions
- Topic Reviews

Prescribed content and assessment-focused tips and information are found in the following box features:

- Exam Overviews
- Exam Tips
- Practice Questions
- Prescribed Debates
- Prescribed Sources

Note that Prescribed Source boxes are not repeated after their first occurrence, even if the source is used in subsequent timespans or topics.

Material that extends beyond the specification is found in the Stretch and Challenge box features. Remember that the specification requires you to study extra sources and material not listed in the specification, so **S&C** information and exercises will be a good place for you to start.

A NOTE ON QUESTIONS

Discussion prompts found in Topic Review boxes and Study Question boxes are not worded in the form that you will find on the exam papers. They should encourage investigation and revision of the material, but do not reflect the questions you will answer in the exam. Practice Questions at the end of each topic, and the questions found in the 'What to Expect in the Exam' chapters, do mirror the format and wording used in the exam.

GLOSSARY

At the back of the book you will find a full glossary of key words. These words are also defined on pages in margin features.

Spellings of names and texts are formatted in line with the OCR specification.

On the Companion Website you will find a colour-coded glossary that highlights which components the words come from.

IMAGES

Illustrations give you the opportunity to see the ancient visual material you are required to study, flagged with the **PS** icon, but also show other relevant aspects of the ancient world.

COMPANION WEBSITE

Resources will include:

- links to the text of Prescribed Literary Sources
- further images and information on Prescribed Visual/Material Sources
- annotated further reading
- links to websites that give useful contextual material for study
- quizzes on key topics and themes
- worksheets to supplement Activity box features in the book.

DON'T FORGET

Look out for cross references to other pages in the book – these will help you to find further information and to link concepts or themes.

ATLANTIC
OCEAN

BRITANNIA

GERMANIA

LOWER
GERMANY

BELGICA

LUGDUNENSIS

Rhine

Danube

RAETIA

NORICUM

AQUITANIA

UPPER
GERMANY

Lugdunum
(Lyons)

ALPES
POENINAE

ALPES COTTIAE

ALPES
MARITIMAE

NARBONENSIS

Bononia
(Bologna)

ITALIA

TARRACONENSIS

Massilia
(Marseilles)

CORSICA

Rome

LUSITANIA

Neapolis
(Naples)

BALEARES

Pompe

SARDINIA

BAETICA

Carthage

SICILY

MAURETANIA
TINGITANA

MAURETANIA
CAESARIENSIS

AFRICA
PROCONSULARIS

NUMIDIA

AFRICA PROCONSULARIS (TRIPOLITANIA

The extent of the Roman empire by 44 BC

The extent of the Roman empire by AD 14

The extent of the Roman empire by AD 96

- - - Boundary of the Roman empire

——— Povinicial boundary

• Povinicial capital

0   100   200   300   400 km

0   100   200   300 miles

**PART 1
PERIOD STUDY:
THE JULIO-CLAUDIAN
EMPERORS, 31 BC–AD 68**

Introduction to The Julio-Claudian Emperors, 31 BC–AD 68

Half of your AS and a quarter of your A Level in Ancient History involve a Roman Period Study. This component covers the years 31 BC–AD 68, focusing on the establishment of the system of government known as the principate.

The period begins with the ending of a Roman civil war that itself came at the end of nearly a century of civil unrest as the Roman Republic strained under the pressure of trying to govern an expanding multicultural empire. After two Triumviral periods, to say nothing of the dictatorship of Julius Caesar, the fate of Rome was to be dictated by the outcome of the Battle of Actium on 2 September 31 BC, where Octavian – Julius Caesar's adopted son – defeated the forces of Mark Antony (Julius Caesar's former colleague) and Cleopatra, the last Pharaoh of Egypt. Octavian's victory and then his rulership of Rome set the stage for the development of a new system of governance that tried to balance the need for firm leadership with Rome's resentment of monarchy. The constant challenge of Octavian's – or Augustus', as he came to be called – reign was to provide the governing guidance that Rome required without offending the sensibilities of the Romans themselves: he was to walk this tightrope for some forty-five years.

The course then goes on to examine the extent to which he left a stable state to his successor, Tiberius, and the other members of the Julio-Claudian family who sat on the imperial throne, and how these individuals continued to shape the principate and the Roman world. Their characters and the political demands of each of their reigns, along with the actions of those around them, make for a dynamic period of history: one that still resonates with European and world politics. In short, this Period Study revolves around study of the nature of power itself.

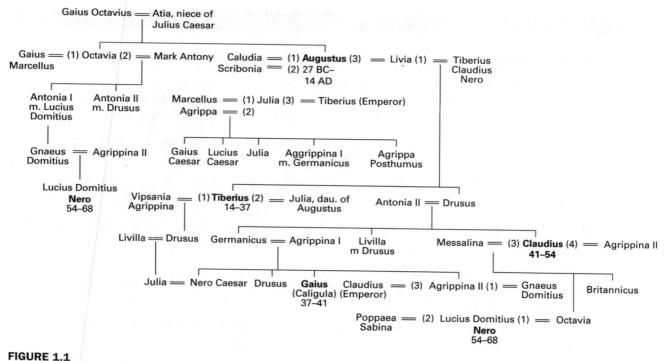

FIGURE 1.1
The family tree of the Julio-Claudian dynasty.

       H007/02

Your assessment for the Period Study option will be:

       50% of the AS Level   1 hr 30 mins   60 marks

15 marks will test AO1: demonstrate knowledge and understanding of the key features and characteristics of the historical periods studied.

15 marks will test AO2: analyse and evaluate historical events and historical periods to arrive at substantiated judgements.

30 marks will test AO3: use, analyse and evaluate ancient sources within their historical context to make judgements and reach conclusions about:

- historical events and historical periods studied
- how the portrayal of events by ancient writers/sources relates to the historical contexts in which they were written/produced.

EXAM OVERVIEW: A LEVEL   H407/21, H407/22, H407/23

Your assessment for the Period Study option will be found in Section A of your exam paper. It comprises:

25% of the A Level

1 hr 20 mins
out of 2 hrs 30 mins
for the whole paper

50 marks
out of 98 marks
for the whole paper

10 marks will test AO1: demonstrate knowledge and understanding of the key features and characteristics of the historical periods studied.

10 marks will test AO2: analyse and evaluate historical events and historical periods to arrive at substantiated judgements.

15 marks will test AO3: use, analyse and evaluate ancient sources within their historical context to make judgements and reach conclusions about:

- historical events and historical periods studied
- how the portrayal of events by ancient writers/sources relates to the historical contexts in which they were written/produced.

15 marks will test AO4: analyse and evaluate, in context, modern historians' interpretations of the historical events and topics studied.

1.1 Augustus, 31 BC–AD 14

- Coins (identified by references in LACTOR 17)
  - aurei (H18, H21, H33, J41, N15, N24, J58)
  - denarii (H27, N31, L1, L10, N5)
  - as (J24)

- Edicts of Cyrene
- Inscription from Nikopolis
- Laudatio Agrippae
- Triumphal Arch, Rome.

---

principate the new system of government created by Augustus in 27 BC, essentially an autocracy framed in the traditions of the Republic

princeps the name adopted to define Augustus' role in his new system of government, first used in 27 BC

Republic the system of government that had existed in Rome since 509 BC

magistrate an elected official in the Roman Republic and principate

cursus honorum the 'course of offices', the path through successive magisterial offices that senators followed

KEY INDIVIDUAL

Octavian/Augustus
Dates: 63 BC–AD 14
Great-nephew and adopted heir of Julius Caesar who became sole ruler of the Roman world after the battle of Actium, and was given the name Augustus in 27 BC.

Augustus began a new era in Rome. As a young man, named Octavian, he was the eventual victor in civil wars that had dominated the first century BC. His long reign as Rome's first **princeps**, from 27 BC to AD 14, established the model of government, the **principate**, against which all subsequent emperors were judged. Ostensibly, this model was based on the centuries-old system of government known as the **Republic**, in which executive **magistrates** of the state were all elected for just one year and always with colleagues, so that no individual could have sole authority. A political career proceeded along a series of positions of increasing importance, the **cursus honorum** (for important context to Augustus' reforms, see pp. 86–87 on this system in the Republic).

THE PRESENTATION OF AUGUSTUS' VICTORY AT ACTIUM

The battle of Actium on 2 September in 31 BC ended the civil war between the two last great rivals in Rome, Mark Antony – the former general of Julius Caesar – and Octavian – Julius Caesar's adopted son (later named Augustus by the Roman people). These two former allies had spent the period 34–31 BC embroiled in a political rivalry that had eventually spilled over into armed conflict. Its outcome would settle the dominion of the Mediterranean (Suetonius, *Augustus* 17–18 **PS**). Octavian commanded the forces of the western Roman Empire, aided by the skilled admiral Marcus Agrippa. Mark Antony allied himself with his consort Cleopatra, Queen of Egypt, and commanded the forces of the eastern empire and Egypt.

In many ways, the battle was anticlimactic: Cleopatra and Antony fled before the outcome was settled and, although they did not commit suicide until 30 BC, Actium effectively ended the conflict and established Octavian as the 'last man standing' after nearly a century of unrest. Unsurprisingly, Octavian immediately tried to exploit the propaganda value of his victory and continued to do so throughout his lifetime. He founded a new town near the battle site (Suetonius, *Augustus* 18 **PS**), Nikopolis ('Victory City'), where a huge monument was set up overlooking the sea. Its inscription survives **PS**. At a nearby temple to Apollo, he also dedicated a victory offering of ten ships (Strabo *Geography* 7.7.6 **PS**).

PRESCRIBED SOURCE

Inscription from Nikopolis

Date: 29 BC

Location: Nikopolis, northwest Greece

Significance: Victory monument celebrating the Battle of Actium

Read it here: H10 in LACTOR 17: The Age of Augustus (London: KCL, 2003)

PRESCRIBED SOURCE

Title: *Geography*

Author: Strabo

Date: During Tiberius' reign (AD 14–23)

Genre: Encyclopaedia

Significance: An account of the Roman world, based on the work of others intermixed with Strabo's own views

Prescribed sections: 7.7.6, 5.3.7, 17.3.5, 4.3.2, 3.2.15, 5.3.8

Read it here: LACTOR 17: The Age of Augustus (London, KCL, 2003)

KEY INDIVIDUAL

Agrippa
Dates: 63–12 BC

The closest ally of Augustus for the first half of his reign and commander of his fleet at Actium.

KEY EVENT

Battle of Actium
Date: 2 September 31 BC

Mark Antony, Cleopatra and their combined forces were defeated by Octavian and Agrippa in a naval battle off the western coast of Greece.

Senate the council of ex-magistrates which advised the magistrates and the people

PRESCRIBED SOURCE

Title: *Aeneid*

Author: Virgil

Date: 29–19 BC

Genre: Epic poetry

Significance: A twelve-book poem commissioned by Augustus, which details the foundation of the Roman race by the mythical hero Aeneas, and looks forward to the Augustan age as a 'Golden Age'

Prescribed sections: 1.257–1.296; 6.752–6.806; 8.671–8.731

Read it here: LACTOR 17: The Age of Augustus (London: KCL, 2003)

Octavian also used literature to popularise his message that victory at Actium marked the beginning of peace and stability for the Roman world. The poets Virgil (*Aeneid* 8.671–731 **PS**) and Horace (*Ode* 1.37 **PS**) both emphasise the defeat of a specifically foreign enemy, Cleopatra, rather than a fellow Roman, Mark Antony. These poets reflect the 'official' presentation of Actium, which sought to portray Octavian as the leader of the Roman **Senate** and People: even the *Res Gestae* **PS**, Augustus' catalogue of his own achievements set up after his death, claims that 'the whole of Italy of its own accord . . . demanded [Octavian] as its commander for the war in which [he] conquered at Actium' (25 **PS**). These sources, separated by the forty-three years of his reign, reinforce the lasting legacy that this victory bequeathed to the man in both his guises: Octavian and Augustus.

The propaganda success of this presentation of Actium may explain why Augustus faced relatively few significant moments of opposition and remained generally popular. Velleius Paterculus (*History of Rome* 2.89.1 **PS**) notes that he was greeted in Rome by 'huge crowds and universal acclaim' when he returned from Actium and subsequent campaigns in Egypt and Dalmatia. Actium was hugely significant as the keystone of Augustus' public image.

PRESCRIBED SOURCE

Title: *Odes*

Author: Horace

Date: *c.* 30–13 BC

Genre: Poetry

Significance: Four books of poems written during Augustus' reign, many referring to Augustus, his family or his achievements

Prescribed *odes*: 1.2 on Rome's need for Augustus; 1.37 on the suicide of Cleopatra; 3.6 on the problems facing the Romans after the civil war; 4.15 on the achievements of Augustus

Read it here: LACTOR 17: The Age of Augustus (London: KCL, 2003)

PRESCRIBED SOURCE

Title: *Res Gestae*

Author: Augustus

Date: *c.* AD 14

Genre: Biography

Original location: Set up outside his mausoleum upon his death

Current location: Extant versions from the province of Galatia survive today

Significance: A catalogue of achievements compiled by Augustus himself

Read it here: LACTOR 17: The Age of Augustus (London: KCL, 2003)

PRESCRIBED SOURCE

Title: *History of Rome*

Author: Velleius Paterculus

Date: AD 30

Genre: History

Significance: An eye-witness senatorial account of events during the reigns of Augustus and Tiberius, though biased because Velleius owed his political career to them

Prescribed sections: 88.1–91.4, 93.1–100.1, 103.1–104.1, 121.1–123.2

Read it here: LACTOR 17: The Age of Augustus (London: KCL, 2003)

AUGUSTUS' MILITARY ACHIEVEMENTS

> **triumph** a public parade of celebration for a successful military commander who had achieved a notable victory

Although the Battle of Actium did not end the civil war, when Octavian eventually returned to Rome in 29 BC, he held a **triumph** on an unprecedented scale: the Triple Triumph. This celebrated victories in Dalmatia, Actium and Alexandria (Suetonius, *Augustus* 22 **PS**; Dio 51:21 **PS**) and served to cement Octavian's image as Rome's supreme military authority. Indeed, its significance was further reinforced by the creation of a memorial in Rome: a triumphal triple arch. Although the original arch does not survive, copies were established throughout the wider empire, spreading Octavian's message at the outset of his reign.

PRESCRIBED SOURCE

Title: *Life of Augustus*

Author: Suetonius

Date: Early second century AD

Genre: Biography

Significance: Written by the emperor Hadrian's secretary, who consciously ignores chronology, and focuses on Augustus' character rather than the politics of his reign

Prescribed sections: 8.1, 17–23, 26–28, 30–31, 34–37, 39–40, 64–66, 93, 98–101

Read it here: *Suetonius: The Twelve Caesars*, trans. R. Graves (Harmondsworth: Penguin, 1957)

PRESCRIBED SOURCE

Title: *Roman History*

Author: Dio Cassius

Date: *c.* AD 212–*c.* 223

Genre: History

Significance: A detailed account of Augustus' reign written from a senatorial perspective in the third century AD; fictionalised speeches probably reflect the politics of Dio's own day

Prescribed sections: 51:21; 52:4; 53:11–13, 16–17

Read it here: *Cassius Dio: The Roman History: The Reign of Augustus*, trans. I Scott-Kilvert (Harmondsworth: Penguin, 1987)

FIGURE 1.2
The Augustan Arch at Rimini with its inscription.

The arch was also emblazoned with an inscription that left the viewer in no doubt as to the danger from which Octavian had rescued the Roman state:

> The Senate and People of Rome [set this up] in honour of Imperator Caesar, son of the Deified, consul five times, designated **consul** for a sixth time, imperator seven times, to commemorate the preservation of the state.

> **consul** one of two annually elected senior magistrates, by whose names the Romans dated their years (see p. 87)

Pax Augusta 'Augustan Peace': the concept of the stability and safety that Augustus brought to the Roman world

Similarly, throughout his reign Augustus was careful to commemorate his military successes on coinage. This began with the Triple Triumph itself (see Fig 1.3).

The visual rhetoric of both arch and coinage reinforced the military might of Octavian. It is revealing that such a militaristic presentation lessened during his reign, as the constitutionally ratified Augustus sought to distance himself from his younger self, whose power was won at the point of a sword. However, military success remained a source of national pride and was not entirely disregarded: coins in 27 BC and 20/19–18 BC respectively commemorate the capture of Egypt and the annexation of Armenia (Figs 1.4 and 1.5).

These campaigns established the **Pax Augusta**. The Romans viewed themselves as having a divine mandate to bring peace and stability to the world. Augustus himself in the *Res Gestae* records a series of military successes, but his key point comes in Chapter 13 **PS**, where he notes that the doors of the Temple of Janus Quirinus were closed three times during his reign. This symbolised peace throughout the Empire and Augustus is at pains to state that 'before [he] was born', the doors had only been closed twice. His claim

denarius a small silver coin worth 4 sestertii

FIGURE 1.3
Denarius of Augustus.

PRESCRIBED SOURCE

Capture of Egypt denarius (Figure 1.4)

Date: 27 BC

Obverse: Augustus, head bare; 'Caesar Son of the Deified, consul for the seventh time'

Reverse: Crocodile; 'Egypt captured'

Significance: Celebrates Octavian's capture and annexation of Egypt in 30 BC

View it here: N31 in LACTOR 17: The Age of Augustus (London: KCL, 2003)

PRESCRIBED SOURCE

Capture of Armenia aureus (Figure 1.5)

Date: 20/19–18 BC

Obverse: Augustus, head bare

Reverse: Victory cutting the throat of a bull; 'Armenia captured'

Significance: Celebrates the capture of Armenia and its establishment as a client kingdom (cf. *Res Gestae* 27)

View it here: N24 in LACTOR 17: The Age of Augustus (London: KCL, 2003)

FIGURE 1.4
'Capture of Egypt' denarius. PS

FIGURE 1.5
'Capture of Armenia' aureus. PS

aureus the highest value coin, made in gold and equivalent to 100 sesterces

is that his birth marked a new age of peace. This message also emerges strongly in two prophetic passages in Virgil's *Aeneid* (1.257–96 PS and 6.752–806 PS), which both promote the idea that Augustus had been predestined to rule.

Suetonius (*Augustus*, 22.1 PS) repeats this claim about the doors of the Temple of Janus, as does the construction – proposed by the Senate – of the Ara Pacis Augustae (Altar of Augustan Peace) on 4 July 13 BC (dedicated 30 January 9 BC). These references to peace highlight its importance to Augustus, effectively justifying all other actions because he brought stability and order. Velleius Paterculus, in a passage praising the emperor's achievements (*History of Rome* 2.89.1–91.4 PS), records the established view of Augustus' achievements:

> . . . the civil wars were now dead and buried, and the limbs of the body politic torn apart by the wounds inflicted by so long a series of conflicts were healing back together.

Velleius Paterculus, *History of Rome*, 2.90.1 (LACTOR 17, E)

---

auctoritas 'influence', that is the ability of an individual to affect socio-political circumstances without the need for specific official power

potestas official political power, typically held by senators occupying positions on the cursus honorum

---

KEY EVENT

First Constitutional Settlement
Date: 27 BC

Augustus' first attempt to codify his power as princeps.

Curia the assembly house of the Senate

Praetorian Guard the cohorts of soldiers who protected the emperor and who were some of the only troops allowed inside the city itself. They enjoyed preferential treatment compared with the rest of the army

---

Velleius was deeply pro-Augustan, but his remark nevertheless captures something of the attitude of a Rome wearied by war which found respite under Augustus. A similar tone is found in an ode by Horace (4.15 **PS**).

THE CONSTITUTIONAL SETTLEMENTS OF 27 AND 23 BC

As the figure of Octavian gradually morphed into that of Augustus, his image as grand military victor, while useful in the short term, became an unwelcome reminder of civil war. His image needed to be changed to show how he now held constitutionally ratified power, balanced between **auctoritas** and **potestas**.

The need for such a balance cannot be overestimated, as Romans had a hatred of power in the hands of one person: the city had expelled its last king in 510 BC and Julius Caesar's seizure of titles and powers had led to his assassination in 44 BC. Dio affirms Augustus' understanding of this in the speech which he gives to Marcus Agrippa (52.4 **PS**).

The would-be princeps faced the problem that Rome needed firm leadership and guidance, but inherently resented that need. Augustus needed a formal allocation of powers by the Senate, on behalf of the people, to prevent any possible resentment. He did so by ensuring the Senate offered him autocratic powers in light of the need for strong governance, feigning rejection of these powers, and then accepting them on the Senate's insistence. This was engineered through the First Constitutional Settlement of 27 BC.

Augustus was anxious to suggest that, far from seizing power, he was shouldering the burden of guiding the Roman state at the request of both Senate and People. His speech to the Senate, when seeking approval for such powers, tellingly begins by asserting '[his] power to rule over [them] for life' was evident (Dio 53.4), but he was stepping aside to preserve the Republic for which he had fought so hard.

The effect was as desired: there was an outcry in the **Curia** against such a "selfless" rejection of power. Dio (53.11 **PS**) informs us that some senators knew his intentions, while others were suspicious and concerned. Unsurprisingly the Senate 'were compelled either to believe him or else pretend that they did' and pleaded for monarchical government, pushing Augustus to accept absolute powers.

Dio's account is very useful and its tone is telling. He explains that in this process, the power of both People and Senate was wholly transferred into Augustus' hands, and that thereafter, although it would be most truthful to describe the political situation as a monarchy (53.17.1 **PS**), the emperors could argue that all their powers had come with the consent of Senate and People. This was little more than a facade of republicanism. Dio informs us that Augustus immediately pushed through a vote that his personal bodyguard – the **Praetorian Guard** – should be paid twice the rate of normal troops, so that he might be reliably guarded, and sarcastically notes, 'this shows how sincere had been his desire to lay down the monarchy' (53.11.5 **PS**).

The First Constitutional Settlement marks the beginnings of the principate, so it is important to understand its components. First, it was not a formal voting of powers, but rather a collection of honours and grants of prestige that acknowledged Augustus' supremacy. Indeed, the very name that he was now given as a title – Augustus ('revered one') – affirms this. The name was as unprecedented as his position: Dio (53.16.7) tells us that he toyed with the name of Romulus, the legendary founder of Rome, as an alternative, but its associations with kingship were too problematic.

Secondly, the First Constitutional Settlement gave Augustus the following honours (*Res Gestae* 34 **PS**; Dio 53.16.1–17.6 **PS**): that his doorposts could be decorated with laurel; the award of the Civic Crown; the award and display of the Shield of Virtue; and the recognition of his auctoritas. These honours were commemorated on Augustus' coinage, reinforcing their propaganda value.

One aspect of real (not honorific) power that the First Settlement *did* give Augustus was the redistribution of the provinces. Although Augustus claimed that the state was again controlled by the Senate and People (*Res Gestae* 34.1 **PS**), this is only true in the sense that constitutional governance by consuls resumed. In reality, Augustus controlled key provinces, notably those with military presence. One was a 'super-province' comprising Gaul, Spain and Syria (Dio 53.12 **PS**). The others were designated 'public' provinces, and were administered by the Senate (Strabo, *Geography* 17.3.25 **PS**). Augustus justified this by claiming that his areas still needed pacification and that he wished to reduce the workload of the Senate. Dio, however, notes that Augustus' real aim was 'that the senators should be unarmed and unprepared for war, while he possessed arms and controlled troops' (53.12 **PS**).

With control of the army, his position as consul and control over public funds (Dio 53.16 **PS**), Augustus was essentially confirmed in supreme command. However, even here he was subtle, as this authority was granted just for ten years (Dio 53.13 **PS**). Time-limited power was typically Republican, when autocracy had been controlled by limited tenures in office: the First Settlement continued this idea. Thus Augustus could declare that he 'excelled everyone in influence (auctoritas), but had no more power (potestas) than . . . [his] colleagues in each magistracy' (*Res Gestae* 34.3 **PS**). This

EXPLORE FURTHER
Using your sources and other resources, research each of these awards and understand the significance of them to Augustus at this stage of his principate.

FIGURE 1.6
Aureus of Augustus depicting the 'civic crown'. **PS**

PRESCRIBED SOURCE

Aureus depicting the 'Civic Crown' of Augustus (Figure 1.6)

Date: 27 BC

Obverse: Augustus, head bare; 'Caesar, consul for the seventh time, for saving the lives of the citizens'

Reverse: Eagle, wings spread, standing on an oak-wreath; two laurel branches behind; 'Augustus, by decree of the Senate'

Significance: The eagle (signifying Augustus' supreme position in the state) grasps the Civic Crown awarded (here to Augustus) for saving the life of a citizen in war

View it here: H21 in LACTOR 17: The Age of Augustus (London: KCL, 2003)

KEY EVENT

Second Constitutional Settlement

Date: 23 BC

Augustus' second and more formal collation of his powers as princeps, better reflecting the day-to-day necessities of being emperor.

imperium proconsulare maius literally 'power greater than that of a proconsul': power confirmed that Augustus had the ability to overrule any provincial governor

imperium general Latin term meaning 'command', 'power' or 'ability to lead', frequently then sub-categorised to reflect the roles of specific magistracies

pomerium the sacred boundary of the city of Rome

tribunicia potestas nominally the power of one of the ten annually elected tribunes, an office created to protect the interests of the people (see p. 87)

might explain why Velleius Paterculus (*History of Rome* 2.89.3–4 **PS**) can claim that the ancient form of the Republic was brought back. Velleius' statement is much discussed, but he probably means that the Republican machinery of state and organs of government were maintained.

Ultimately, the First Constitutional Settlement was unsuitable and a **Second Constitutional Settlement** was agreed in 23 BC. The problems included the fact that by monopolising one of two consulships, Augustus was snubbing the senators and damaging his relationship with them. Moreover, he could not leave the loose collection of titles and honours to a successor. There is enough evidence to suggest that even by 23 BC, Augustus was considering the issue of succession and recognised that the powers of his new position as princeps needed to be codified. Thus, in the Second Constitutional Settlement, the two key powers of an emperor were created.

The first power was **imperium proconsulare maius**. It reaffirmed the princeps as the head of the Roman army (Dio 53.32.5), enabling Augustus to overrule any provincial governor's authority. This power was necessary because in the Second Settlement Augustus gave up his consulship, yet required **imperium** ('command') over the army. Moreover, unlike consular imperium over the army, he did not need to lay it down when crossing the **pomerium**, i.e. when returning to Rome. This power effectively created a lifelong control over the army, and its constitutional nature meant that it could be inherited.

However, the second power was more significant: **tribunicia potestas**. Tacitus described it as 'the expression of the supremacy of [the emperor's] position' (*Annals*, 3.65 **PS**).

Augustus himself highlights the importance of tribunicia potestas (*Res Gestae* 10.1 **PS**). Through it he could pass legislation (such as his morality laws in 18 BC: *Res Gestae* 6.2 **PS**). That it was the supreme power of the emperor can be seen from the fact that it was used to date Augustus' reign, and used to indicate potential successors

---

PRESCRIBED SOURCE

Title: *Annals*

Author: Tacitus

Date: Early second century AD

Genre: History

Significance: Focusing on Rome and the Empire from the death of Augustus in AD 14 to the later years of Nero's reign, there is very little focus on the principate of Augustus but Tacitus does give us a summary of his reign at the beginning of Book 1 of the *Annals*.

Prescribed sections: 1: 2.1–4.5, 6.1–15.3; 4:37; 3:56; 3:29; 4:57; 6:10–11; 12:23; 2:59; 8:1; 3:24; 2:27

Read it here: LACTOR 17: The Age of Augustus (London: KCL, 2003)

(see p. 25). Tribunicia potestas granted the right to call the Senate and put forward an item for discussion, and the power to veto legislation.

These two powers confirmed Augustus, and every subsequent emperor, as an authority beyond the normally constituted Roman government. They became codified as imperial powers, and were bestowed on every emperor from Gaius onward upon their accession. These powers perhaps account for Tacitus' observation that Augustus 'rose up gradually and drew to himself the responsibilities of senate, magistrates and laws' (*Annals*, 1.2.1 **PS**). But equally, because of their super-constitutional nature, Velleius Paterculus' observation that 'force was restored to the laws, authority to the courts, majesty to the Senate' (*History of Rome*, 2.89.3 **PS**) is not invalid. Augustus' supremacy was all but complete: by 23 BC the facade of republican governance was in place, but Augustus had ensured that he existed on a power level above it.

Study question
How complete were Augustus' powers following the Second Constitutional Settlement?

Use your sources and other resources to compile a list of offices, powers and titles that Augustus acquired after 23 BC.

THE RESTORATION OF THE REPUBLIC AND THE REVIVAL OF TRADITIONAL ROMAN VALUES AND PRACTICES

Whether Augustus restored the Republic was disputed, and depended more on interpretation of the evidence than to anything else; thus Tacitus and Velleius Paterculus are diametrically opposed in their treatment of the same facts. Perhaps the safest conclusion is that Augustus restored the organs and practices of the Republic, but ensured that he retained ultimate control of these elements.

However, the idea of restoration was fundamental for Augustus. The need for social and moral restoration is clearly highlighted in contemporary poetry, e.g. Horace's *Ode* 3.6 **PS**. The implication is clear: Rome had become corrupt and decadent; Augustus could portray himself as Rome's saviour.

This attitude and presentation, designed to preserve the facade of republicanism, is still clear on much of Augustus' coinage. Both coins referred to here (below/right and overleaf)

FIGURE 1.7
Aureus of
Augustus of 28 BC. **PS**

PRESCRIBED SOURCE

Aureus of Augustus (Figure 1.7)

Date: 28 BC

Obverse: Laureate head of Octavian; 'Commander Caesar, Son of the Deified, consul for the sixth time'

Reverse: Octavian, seated on magistrate's chair wearing toga, holding scroll in right hand; magistrate's document container on ground to left; 'He has restored to the Roman People their laws and rights'

Significance: Proclaims the restoration of the Republic in 28 BC

View it here: H18 in LACTOR 17: The Age of Augustus (London: KCL, 2003)

---

laureate wearing a laurel wreath

PRESCRIBED SOURCE

Lost aureus showing Augustus raising a fallen *Res Publica*

Date: 12 BC

Obverse: Augustus, head bare; AVGVSTVS

Reverse: Augustus wearing a toga extends his right hand to a kneeling personification of the Roman state

Significance: Augustus literally raises a fallen state from its knees, almost twenty years after ending civil war

View it here: H33 in LACTOR 17 The Age of Augustus: (London: KCL, 2003); Zanker, P. (1990), *The Power of Images in the Age of Augustus*, Ann Arbor: University of Michigan Press: Figure 74 **CW** (page 91)

---

lustrum the formal purificatory ritual that officially marked the ending of the census

dictator originally a magistrate elected during a time of crisis with supreme authority (see pp. 98–100 and 129–30)

---

confirm the impression that Augustus wished to be seen as a restorer, not only of the Republic, but also of the day-to-day values and privileges of a Roman. Likewise, Virgil's *Aeneid* (6.792–3 **PS**) refers to Augustus as he 'who shall bring back again / the age of gold to Latium'. The volume of evidence presenting Augustus as a saviour is enormous, though unsurprising. By preserving the 'best of the old', he made his more innovative political changes more palatable, disguising them within a programme of revival. His building programme (see p. 20) and his attitude towards religion (see p. 17) show that he was doing this, but it is also evident elsewhere.

Suetonius tells us that Augustus had a severe attitude toward moral and social purity, not wishing 'native Roman stock to be tainted with foreign or servile blood' (*Augustus*, 40 **PS**). This focus on the legitimacy of offspring is echoed in two key pieces of Augustan legislation, the 'Julian Law on the duties of husbands' and the 'Julian Law on constraining adultery'. Known as Augustus' moral reforms, these were passed in 18 BC using his tribunician power (*Res Gestae* 6.2 **PS**). Both laws were designed to promote legitimate offspring among Rome's upper classes, but equally they indicate adultery was common among them. Although the laws were thoroughly unpopular with the senatorial and equestrian classes, they nevertheless reinforced Augustus' desire to promote what he saw as traditional family values. The poet Ovid seems to praise the reforms in a passage that compares Augustus favourably with Romulus (*Fasti* 2.119–44 **PS**).

Among Augustus' other revivals, the *Res Gestae* records that he carried out the first official census of the Roman people in 42 years (8.2 **PS**). Indeed, he completed three such **lustra** in 28 BC, 8 BC and AD 14, each with a corresponding increase in the total citizen population. No other piece of governmental business so utterly communicates the Augustan focus on renewal, stability and increase as the census does: its data indisputably argues that under Augustus, Rome is flourishing.

Augustus' focus on traditionalism is perhaps most overt in his handling of his own offices and titles. In the *Res Gestae* (6.1 **PS**), he claims that he took no office that contravened ancestral customs. Similarly, Velleius Paterculus relates how Augustus refused to become **dictator** despite being offered it repeatedly (*History of Rome*

PRESCRIBED SOURCE

Title: *Fasti*

Author: Ovid

Date: *c.* AD 17

Genre: Poetry

Significance: Written under Augustus, about the Roman religious calendar

Prescribed sections: 1.1–14; 2.55–66; 5.140–158, 2.119–144

Read it here: LACTOR 17: The Age of Augustus (London: KCL, 2003)

89.5 (PS)). But who defined 'traditional'? Here, Augustus sets himself up as the judge of traditionalism. This is exemplified when, having attained the office of **Pontifex Maximus** in 12 BC, Augustus collected and destroyed 2,000 volumes of prophetic verse (Suetonius, *Augustus* 31 (PS)), even editing the Sibylline Books themselves. Augustus quite literally rewrote tradition to fit his own ideals and endeavours.

> **Pontifex Maximus** Chief Priest in Roman religion, assumed by Augustus in 12 BC when the previous incumbent died, as was the tradition

AUGUSTUS' ATTITUDE TOWARDS RELIGION, INCLUDING THE IMPERIAL CULT INSIDE AND OUTSIDE OF ROME

Religion was key for Augustus in underlining his role as helmsman of the ship of state. Contemporary literature emphasised the restoration of Roman religion and the divine support for Augustus. In an almost unique statement among our sources, in *Ode* 1.2 (PS) (from the earliest years of the principate), Horace even depicts Augustus as a god incarnate.

Inevitably, religion features heavily in Augustus' propaganda. The *Res Gestae* tells us that he held seven simultaneous priesthoods (7.2–3 (PS)), and four are commemorated on a denarius (PS) which predates Augustus' election to the position of Pontifex Maximus.

The Romans would have had little difficulty in attributing past problems to abandonment by the gods, and thus the emergence of a golden age was easily seen as a reconciliation brought about by the emperor. Claims are always more believable when there is physical evidence, and Augustus' restoration of the neglected temples of Rome suggested a religion similarly brought back to life. Augustus records the number of restored shrines as eighty-two (*Res Gestae* 20.4 (PS)); Virgil mentions 300 (*Aeneid* 8.716 (PS)). Ovid focuses on this in his second book of the *Fasti* (2.55–66 (PS)).

Almost as soon as Egypt had been added to the Roman Empire, the eastern provinces petitioned to worship their new emperor as a living god. Those states traditionally

FIGURE 1.8
Augustus as Pontifex Maximus.

FIGURE 1.9
Denarius of Augustus.

PRESCRIBED SOURCE

Denarius which shows symbols of four priesthoods held by Augustus (Figure 1.9)

Date: 16 BC

Obverse: Bust of Venus

Reverse: Four symbols of priesthoods; 'Imperator Caesar Augustus, consul for the eleventh time'

Significance: Directly associates Augustus with traditional Roman religious symbols

View it here: L1 in LACTOR 17: The Age of Augustus (London: KCL, 2003)

imperial cult the worship
of the emperor or his
family as divine

numen the divinity of a
person

genius the spirit of a
person or place

PRESCRIBED SOURCE

**Altar to numen of
Augustus**

Date: AD 12–13

Location: Narbo in Gaul

Significance: Shows the
devotion of provincial
citizens to the emperor
through the imperial
cult

Read it here: L17 in
LACTOR 17: The Age
of Augustus (London:
KCL, 2003)

PRESCRIBED SOURCE

**Augustan Lares
inscription**

Date: Possibly 7 BC

Location: Rome

Significance: Augustus
introduced the cult
of his own protective
spirits (Augustan
Lares) at crossroads
between districts

Read it here: L12 in
LACTOR 17: The Age
of Augustus (London:
KCL, 2003)

---

worshipped their rulers. Suetonius (*Augustus* 93 **PS**) tells us that Augustus was respectful to long-established religions, but considered the worship of a living individual dangerous, especially in Rome and the west. The **imperial cult** could thus be tolerated only in the east.

The people of Pergamum in Asia Minor successfully petitioned Octavian to build a temple to him and Rome in 29 BC. Tacitus (*Annals* 4.37 **PS**) tells us that he did not stand in their way: the imperial cult could successfully bind all peoples of the vast empire under imperial rule (see Strabo, *Geography* 4.3.2 **PS**).

The Romans believed that everyone had a divine aspect called the **numen** and worship was permitted of the numen of Augustus as well as of his **genius**. Thus, Augustus could accrue the benefits of worship without being accused of claiming to be more than human. The man was mortal, but his spirit divine. The imperial cult was quickly adopted at both geographical extremes of the Empire. Western evidence comes from an inscription on an altar to the numen of Augustus dated AD 12–13 from Narbo in Gaul **PS**. The fact that it was originally established for Augustus' intercession into a legal matter in Narbo reinforces the personal (if not paternal) interest that the princeps took in the administration of the empire, linking his 'worship' to that idea.

There is similar evidence that aspects of Augustus were being worshipped closer to home: Ovid's *Fasti* (5.140–158 **PS**) mentions the divine spirit of Augustus being worshipped at crossroads. Similarly an inscription from Rome around 7 BC **PS** records priests of the cult of the Augustan Lares chosen from freedmen. This form of worship allowed people to focus on Augustus' divinity indirectly and was less controversial.

However, although the imperial cult was a source of prestige for Augustus, it could also be used to question the extent to which Augustus actually restored traditional Roman religion:

> There were no honours left for the gods, now that Augustus chose to be worshipped with temples and godlike images by flamines and priests.
>
> Tacitus, *Annals*, 1.10.6 **PS**

ADMINISTRATIVE CHANGES TO ROME AND THE PROVINCES

Inevitably with a new form of government, administrative changes are necessary. Some of these innovations illuminate Augustus' relationship with the various groups of Roman society (see pp. 21–3).

Perhaps the most fundamental administrative overhaul was Augustus' division of Rome into thirteen districts, placing them under the control of magistrates chosen annually by lot, and then subdividing these into wards under locally elected supervisors (Suetonius, *Augustus* 30 **PS**). This bold move may be seen as his administration in microcosm, ensuring careful control of all elements. Indeed, through the acquisition of new territories for the Empire (*Res Gestae* 26–7 **PS**), Augustus could even extend the boundary of Rome's pomerium itself (Tacitus, *Annals* 12.23 **PS**), thereby setting a precedent for subsequent emperors (e.g. see pp. 58 and 175). He also instituted a fire brigade for the city and regulations to prevent fires (Suetonius *Augustus* 30 (PS); Strabo, *Geography* 5.3.7 (PS)).

Suetonius also remarks on Augustus' diligence in revising and expanding laws (*Augustus*, 34 (PS)), while Velleius Paterculus (*History of Rome*, 2.89.4 (PS)) affirms that these laws were for the general advantage. We have already commented on Augustus' redistribution of the provinces themselves in 27 BC and his new moral legislations. Here was a man looking to overhaul and amend nearly every aspect of the day-to-day administration of the Roman world.

One of the most overt sets of administrative changes that Augustus made concerned the Senate itself. In *Res Gestae* (8.2 (PS)), he states that he revised the senatorial roll three times (probably in 29, 18 and 11 BC). The Senate had reached a peak of 1,000 members under Julius Caesar, so when in *Res Gestae* 25.3 (PS) Augustus claims that 700 senators served him at Actium, as many as 300 may have sided with Mark Antony or remained undecided. Such disloyalty could not be endured, so Augustus imposed severe property qualifications upon this group: he more than doubled the minimum property requirement from 400,000 sesterces to 1 million and made senatorial status hereditary. A total of 190 senators were removed in the first revision; by 18 BC the total had dropped to 600.

However, other Augustan administrative changes seem designed to appease this same body. He banned the publication of the 'Proceedings of the Senate' (Suetonius, *Augustus* 36 (PS)); he created new offices for the upkeep of public buildings, roads and aqueducts, and for grain distribution (*Augustus* 37 (PS)); two new offices of **praetor** were created beyond the existing eight (Velleius Paterculus, *History of Rome* 2.89.3 (PS)); and leading senators could serve as the newly created **praefectus urbi** (Prefect of the City) (Tacitus, *Annals* 6.10–11 (PS)).

The full catalogue of changes implemented or encouraged by Augustus is very long, but all the evidence conveys the impression of a man dedicated to his task as head of state. The personal degree of his involvement is highlighted by the Edicts of Cyrene (PS). They concern jury composition and citizenship in the province of Cyrene and are striking evidence of Augustus controlling elements of provincial administration and jurisdiction.

> **praetor** one of eight to sixteen magistrates elected annually; mainly responsible for the administration of justice (see pp. 86–7)
>
> **praefectus urbi** a role created by Augustus to deal with the day-to-day administration of the city of Rome

---

PRESCRIBED SOURCE

Edicts of Cyrene

Date: 7/6 BC

Location: Cyrene in North Africa

Significance: Evidence for Augustus controlling business in provinces himself

Read it here: M60 in LACTOR 17: The Age of Augustus (London: KCL, 2003)

Indeed, it is perhaps in this personal relationship with the inhabitants of the wider Empire that the most drastic administrative change of the principate is reflected. Instead of dealing with a faceless bureaucracy, or a regularly changing Republican leadership, the existence of the princeps enabled everyone in the Empire to appeal directly to the head of state. Throughout his reign, Augustus exercised this personal authority unrelentingly, and one passage of Strabo (*Geography* 3.2.15 **PS**) shows how Romanised locals (here, in the province of Baetica) could become at this time.

AUGUSTUS' BUILDING PROGRAMME

In parallel with his overhaul of the political and social spheres, Augustus reshaped the physical environment of Rome. A colossal building programme was undertaken. His purpose is clearly outlined by Suetonius as creating a Rome that was architecturally worthy of being the capital of the Empire. He records the famous statement that Augustus 'found a Rome built of bricks' but left one 'clothed in marble' (*Augustus*, 28 **PS**). This process spoke of the reinvention of Rome, a city defined and modelled by Augustus, communicating civic well-being and power.

Res Gestae 18–21 details the massive scope of these building projects, centred around the Augustan Forum with its Temple of Mars Ultor. But the works also included restorations of earlier buildings, in keeping with Augustus' public image. *Res Gestae* 20.1 **PS** is at pains to point out that he did not put his own name on those buildings he restored, preserving those of the original builders. Once again, renewal and respect for the past marched hand-in-hand. An important feature was the construction of and improvements to public aqueducts (Strabo, *Geography* 5.3.8 **PS**), a project that had been overseen by Marcus Agrippa since as early as 33 BC (Pliny, *Natural History* 36.121 **PS**).

EXPLORE FURTHER

Using *Res Gestae* 18–21 and Suetonius *Augustus* 29–30, research the major building projects of Augustus and come to an understanding of their political and social significance. You may also wish to refer to Zanker, P. (1990), *The Power of Images in the Age of Augustus*, Ann Arbor: University of Michigan Press.

PRESCRIBED SOURCE

Title: *Natural History*

Author: Pliny

Date: 77–9 AD

Genre: Encyclopaedia

Significance: 7.147–150 discusses several misfortunes and tragedies which befell Augustus; 36.121 describes Agrippa's waterworks of 33 BC

Prescribed sections: 7.147–50; 36.121

Read it here: LACTOR 17: The Age of Augustus (London: KCL, 2003)

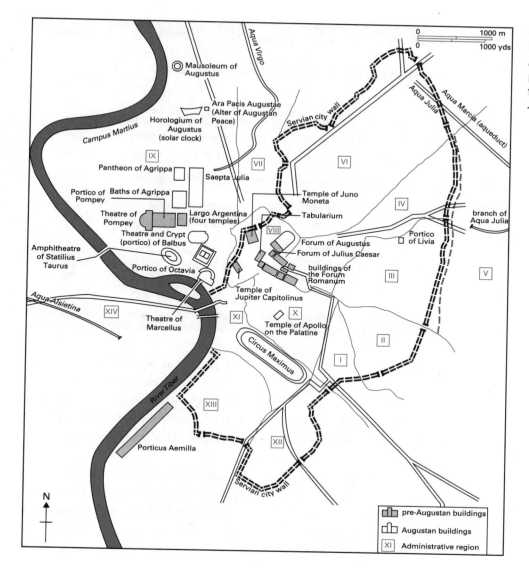

FIGURE 1.10
Map of Rome showing Augustus' building programme and new fourteen districts.

Legend:
- pre-Augustan buildings
- Augustan buildings
- XI Administrative region

RELATIONS WITH THE SENATE, EQUESTRIANS AND ORDINARY PEOPLE OF ROME

The **plebs** of Rome are often forgotten because our sources are all written by upper-class men. However, Augustus understood that Rome was the 'mob' and, since democracy was being replaced by autocracy, he also understood the need to court favour with it. His success in doing so may be seen in the public inscriptions commemorating vows for his safety (e.g. the denarius described on p. 22 **PS**). Such public monuments were intended to reflect the significance of Augustus to the state for all Romans.

Augustus used two key methods to ensure the loyalty of the plebs: entertainment and **largesse**. In doing so, he created a model for all future emperors, which would later be satirised by Juvenal in the claim that all the Roman People needed was 'bread and circuses'. This is also echoed by Tacitus (*Annals* 1.2.1 **PS**), who states that Augustus 'seduced the soldiery with gifts, the people with corn, and everyone with the delights of peace'.

> **plebs** commoners, the ordinary people of Rome

> **largesse** great generosity, often lavish gifts of goods or money

PRESCRIBED SOURCE

Denarius displaying public vows for Augustus' safety

Date: 16 BC

Obverse: Inscription within oak-wreath; 'To Jupiter Greatest and Best, the Senate and People of Rome took vows for the safety of Imperator Caesar because through him the State is in a more expansive and peaceful condition'

Reverse: Pillar inscribed 'To Imperator Caesar Augustus by common consensus'

Significance: An abbreviated version of an honorary inscription erected in Rome to show the vows made by the senate and people of Rome for Augustus' safety

View it here: L10 in LACTOR 17: The Age of Augustus (London: KCL, 2003)

Study question

Based on what we have read so far, make a list of the various actions that Augustus had taken that would have potentially alienated members of the Senate.

---

congiarium (pl. congiaria) money (or tokens exchanged for money) given to the plebs, typically at events such as accessions, imperial birthdays or victories

equestrians (Latin: *equites*) members of the second rank of the nobility in Rome, for which there was a wealth qualification. Originally they served as the cavalry of Rome, but eventually took significance as the professional or business class of the Roman world

---

Augustus' success in gaining the support of the plebs may be seen in the fact that in 22 BC, the first year he had not served as consul, the people rioted when there was a corn shortage, demanding that Augustus be appointed dictator to deal with the crisis (*Res Gestae* 5.1–2 **PS**). His swift resolution of the emergency has led some to speculate that he engineered the shortage by stockpiling grain precisely in order to be able to solve a shortage he had himself created.

The management of the grain supply was vital, since the poorest Romans were given a set amount of corn (known as the 'corn dole'), and Augustus set up a formal management system after further shortages in AD 6–7. In addition, frequent handouts (**congiaria**) bolstered his popularity. The *Res Gestae* gives many examples of such gifts, such as 400 sesterces each in 24 BC (15.1 **PS**), as well as Augustus adding to public treasuries with his own money (17.1 **PS**).

However, probably Augustus' readiest means of gaining plebeian support was that of mass public entertainment. Again, the *Res Gestae* gives much information about the scale of these events (22–3 **PS**). For the Roman plebs, Augustus must have seemed to be the messianic figure of Virgil's *Aeneid* bringing peace and plenty back to their lives.

The **equestrians** are perhaps the most interesting class to look at under the principate, as they were very much promoted to political significance by the emperors, with Augustus doing much to make them a distinct political group (see Suetonius, *Augustus* 39–40 **PS**), including creating some exclusively equestrian political roles, such as governor of Egypt.

However, it is with the Senate that Augustus had his most interesting and changeable relationship, which is unsurprising, as his rise to power had effectively rendered it unneeded for political policy-making. Its new position as little more than a bureaucratic rubber-stamp must have alienated at least some senators, although as Tacitus remarks (*Annals* 1.3.7 **PS**), by the end of Augustus reign in AD 14: 'How many remained who had seen the republic?'

EXPLORE FURTHER

Aside from the reference to Suetonius above, none of the prescribed sources formally discusses the equites under Augustus.

For more on the interesting developments regarding this group, read:

Pflaumer, J. (2008), 'Augustus and the Equites: Developing Rome's Middle Class' in *John Wesley Powell Research Conference Publications 2007–2008*. Paper 7.

Millar, F. (1992), *The Emperor in the Roman World*, 2nd Edition, London: Bloomsbury Academic, 279–84.

Sources T30–3 in LACTOR 17.

KEY INDIVIDUAL

Livia

Dates: 58 BC–AD 29

Married Octavian in 38 BC, while pregnant with her second son Drusus. She was renowned for her beauty, dignity and intelligence.

But to retain the republican image that he had so carefully fostered, Augustus needed to placate the Senate to a degree. He gave money to individual senators (Macrobius, *Saturnalia* 2.4.23 **PS**; Tacitus *Annals* 2.27 **PS**); the lower ranks of the cursus honorum were expanded to allow for more senators to gain political experience (Suetonius, *Augustus* 37 **PS**); we could even argue that the purges of the Senate made the order more exclusive (Suetonius, *Augustus* 35 **PS**). Nevertheless, it could not have been lost on the Senate that they were no longer the preeminent political body. Augustus' banning senators from the province of Egypt (Tacitus, *Annals* 2.59 **PS**), his creation of a virtual privy council (the **consilium principis**), and his imposition of a 5 per cent inheritance tax on senators in AD 6 to fund the military treasury all reinforced his supremacy. For a senator to prosper, he now had to be an advocate of the principate. There was little scope for opposition.

consilium principis a council set up by Augustus to prepare the agenda for the senate, comprising Augustus, the two consuls and fifteen senators; it was reconstituted every six months

CHALLENGES TO HIS RULE, INCLUDING CONSPIRACIES

Pliny (*Natural History* 7.147–50 **PS**) lists numerous challenges Augustus faced, although other sources report little formal opposition to his rule. Velleius Paterculus

---

PRESCRIBED SOURCE

Title: *Saturnalia*

Author: Macrobius

Date: 5th century AD

Genre: Dialogue

Significance: Section 1.11.21 mentions the 'plot' of Caepio against Augustus; 2.4.23 narrates an anecdote of an ungrateful senator for whom Augustus had settled debts

Prescribed sections: 1.11.21; 2.4.23

Read it here: LACTOR 17: The Age of Augustus (London: KCL, 2003)

PRESCRIBED SOURCE

Title: *Life of Tiberius*

Author: Suetonius

Genre: Biography

Significance: Episode early in Tiberius' career where he brings a successful charge against Fannius Caepio for high treason against Augustus

Prescribed section: 8.1

Read it here: P10 in LACTOR 17, The Age of Augustus (London, KCL, 2003)

PRESCRIBED SOURCE

Title: *On Clemency*

Author: Younger Seneca

Date: AD 55–6

Genre: Philosophical treatise

Significance: Describes Augustus' clemency to Cinna after his assassination plot

Prescribed sections: 1.9.2–1.9.12

Read it here: LACTOR 17: The Age of Augustus (London: KCL, 2003)

Study question

Use your sources to investigate the following examples of 'opposition'. How significant were they?

- 'Conspiracy' of Caepio and Murena
- Egnatius Rufus
- Cinna's 'assassination plot'
- Gallus' actions as Governor of Egypt

You may wish to begin with: Tacitus *Annals* 1.2; Suetonius *Augustus* 19, *Tiberius* 8.1; Macrobius *Saturnalia* 1.11.21; Seneca *On Clemency* 1.9.2–12; Velleius Paterculus *History of Rome* 2.91.1–4.

refers to a conspiracy at the start of his reign (*History of Rome* 2.88.1–3 **PS**), while Suetonius mentions a number of conspiracies (*Augustus* 19, 66 **PS**), one of which is a supposed plot by Fannius Caepio and Varro Murena of *c.* 23 BC (see also Suetonius, *Tiberius* 8.1 **PS**). Although this plot was also mentioned by Velleius Paterculus (2.91.2 **PS**) and Macrobius (*Saturnalia* 1.11.21 **PS**), ancient and modern writers have been unable to decide whether it actually happened, or whether Augustus invented it in order to remove individuals. Another conspiracy story is presented by Seneca (*On Clemency* 1.9.2–12 **PS**), in which Augustus follows the advice of his wife Livia and reacts mercifully to a plot by Cinna in 16 BC. Seneca suggests that this bound Cinna to Augustus for the rest of Cinna's life and ended conspiracies against him.

However, Tacitus warns us against contemporary accounts of the reign of Augustus, saying the culture was increasingly one of flattery towards the emperor (*Annals*, 1.2.1–2 **PS**). He presents Augustan society as duplicitous, and his main criticism is reserved not for Augustus but for his fellow aristocracy. Therefore we can only question whether the allegations of 'opposition' and 'conspiracy' are valid.

THE ESTABLISHMENT OF THE DYNASTY AND ISSUES OF SUCCESSION

Undoubtedly Augustus' greatest challenge was the creation of a hereditary dynasty within a society which hated sole power. Mindful of the expulsion of the kings in 510 BC and Julius Caesar's assassination 466 years later in 44 BC for monarchic aspirations, Augustus walked a fine line between increasing his power and offending either the Roman mob or the aristocracy.

Velleius Paterculus (2.103.4–5; 2.121.1–123.2 **PS**) presents the accession of Augustus' stepson Tiberius as seamless and appropriate, having outlined the claims of the various candidates and their eventual ends (93.1–100.1, 103.1–104.1 **PS**). Augustus, knowing that he was dying, apparently called Tiberius to him and died in his arms, comforted by the fact that Tiberius would take over all aspects of his principate. Writing in the reign of Tiberius, Velleius could hardly have told the real story: that Tiberius was far from Augustus' ideal successor and nowhere near his first choice.

KEY INDIVIDUALS

Tiberius
Dates: 42 BC–AD 37

Stepson and successor to Augustus; emperor AD 14–37.

Marcellus
Dates: 42–23 BC

Augustus' nephew, he married Julia in 25 BC and became **aedile** in 23 BC before his sudden death later that year.

aedile one of six magistrates elected annually; responsible for city maintenance, markets and public games

Tacitus (*Annals* 1.3–1.4 **PS**) gives a brief assessment of the attempts made by Augustus to establish a successor. First, Augustus (who had no son) married his daughter Julia to his nephew Marcellus and accelerated Marcellus' career. However, Marcellus' sudden death in 23 BC was the first of many setbacks. In this year, Augustus acquired tribunician power, which he used to designate candidates for the succession (Tacitus, *Annals* 3.56 **PS**).

After the death of Marcellus, Augustus married his daughter Julia to his closest ally, Marcus Agrippa. In fact, Julia was married three times to potential successors: Marcellus, Agrippa and Tiberius, and produced three male heirs: Gaius, Lucius and Agrippa Postumus before being exiled in 2 BC for adultery (Tacitus, *Annals* 3.24 **PS**; Suetonius, *Augustus* 65 **PS**).

A denarius **PS** from 13 BC is crucial in understanding the role played by Agrippa in the early principate of Augustus. Agrippa was granted tribunician power in 18 BC and then again in 13 BC (Suetonius, *Augustus* 27 **PS**; *Laudatio Agrippae* **PS**), and is featured with Augustus on the coin, showing that the power of both men was almost identical and clearly indicating the preferred succession should Augustus die. However, Agrippa died in 12 BC.

KEY INDIVIDUAL

Julia

Dates: 39 BC–AD 14

Augustus' daughter from his first marriage, she was exiled in 2 BC for adultery, and died from starvation in AD 14 after her father's death.

PRESCRIBED SOURCE

Title: *Laudatio Agrippae*

Date: 12 BC

Location: Fayum, Egypt

Significance: A papyrus fragment of part of Augustus' funeral speech for Agrippa

Read it here: T14 in LACTOR 17: The Age of Augustus (London: KCL, 2003)

PRESCRIBED SOURCE

Denarius of Augustus and Agrippa as tribunes (Figure 1.11)

Date: 13 BC

Obverse: Augustus, head bare; CAESAR AVGVSTVS

Reverse: Augustus and Agrippa wearing togas seated on a tribune's bench; C SVLPICIVS PLATORIN (name of monetary magistrate)

Significance: Commemorates Agrippa's second grant of tribunician power. The impression given is that Augustus shares power with colleagues according to republican tradition

View it here: H27 in LACTOR 17: The Age of Augustus (London: KCL, 2003)

FIGURE 1.11
Denarius of Augustus and Agrippa as tribunes.

quaestor one of twenty magistrates who served as treasurers (see pp. 86–87)

legate a Roman official placed in charge of a province or region on behalf of the emperor, or a deputy to such an official

Velleius (2.93.1–100.1 **PS**) glosses over Agrippa's death, choosing to focus on Tiberius' rise to power, firstly as **quaestor** in Rome in 23 BC (Tacitus, *Annals* 3.29 **PS**) and then as **legate** abroad. An aureus **PS** from 15–12 BC illustrates Tiberius (and his brother Drusus) presenting Augustus with triumphal branches in recognition of the victory.

Tacitus (*Annals* 1.3.2 **PS**) tells us that the Senate decreed that the grandsons of Augustus, Agrippa and Julia's eldest two sons, Gaius and Lucius, should each be known

PRESCRIBED SOURCE

Aureus of Augustus receiving triumphal branches (Figure 1.12)

Date: 15–12 BC

Obverse: Augustus, head bare; 'Augustus, son of the Deified'

Reverse: Augustus seated on platform, receiving branches from two men in military dress; 'Hailed victorious for the tenth time'

Significance: Probably commemorates Tiberius and Drusus' conquest of Raetia in the summer of 15 BC. It shows Augustus' position as supreme commander of all armies

View it here: N15 in LACTOR 17: The Age of Augustus (London: KCL, 2003)

FIGURE 1.12
Aureus of Augustus.

PRESCRIBED SOURCE

Aureus of Gaius and Lucius as principes iuventutis (Figure 1.13)

Date: 2 BC–AD 11

Obverse: Augustus, laureate; 'Caesar Augustus, Son of the Deified, Father of the Fatherland'

Reverse: Gaius and Lucius Caesar standing, veiled, with shields, spears and priestly symbols between them; 'Gaius and Lucius Caesar, Sons of Augustus, Consuls designate, Leaders of the Younger Generation'

Significance: Commemorates the awarding of the title of princeps iuventutis and consul-designate to Gaius and Lucius Caesar by the Senate

View it here: J58 in LACTOR 17: The Age of Augustus (London: KCL, 2003)

FIGURE 1.13
Aureus of Gaius and Lucius.

as **princeps iuventutis** ('leader of the youth') and both be made consuls designate at the age of fifteen, clearly demarking both as potential successors despite their youth (see also Suetonius, *Augustus* 26, 64 **PS**). The historians' accounts can be compared to Augustus' own version in the *Res Gestae* (14 **PS**) and is supported by a commemorative aureus **PS**.

After the deaths of Gaius and Lucius (Suetonius, *Augustus* 65 **PS**), Augustus adopted Tiberius, who had been away from Rome in self-imposed exile due to his discontent with the promotion of Gaius and Lucius. As before, Augustus highlighted his final choice of successor on contemporary coinage (Aureus of Tiberius **PS**).

At this point, it is also important to mention Augustus' formidable wife, Livia, mother of Tiberius and Drusus. It is impossible to discuss adequately her significance to Augustus' reign, both good and bad. She was a constant presence at his court, often seen to be acting behind the scenes. Tacitus alleges that Livia had a hand in the deaths of Gaius and Lucius (*Annals* 1.3.3 **PS**) in order to promote her own son Tiberius in the succession. Yet she is also seen as a positive influence in the case of Augustus' dealing with Cinna (see p. 24). For our sources, Livia is a polarising figure; their treatments of her often reveal more about their own biases and preconceptions. Tacitus' opinion is clear when he describes her as being as much a burden on the state as she was on Augustus' own family (*Annals* 1.10.5 **PS**).

---

princeps iuventutis
'leader of the youth': a title given to both Gaius and Lucius Caesar by Augustus to indicate their potential as successors

---

KEY INDIVIDUALS

Gaius and Lucius
Dates: 20 BC–AD 4 and 17 BC–AD 2

Grandsons of Augustus from the marriage of Agrippa and Julia. Earmarked for succession at a young age, Gaius was adopted by Augustus in 17 BC on the birth of his brother Lucius.

EXPLORE FURTHER

Examine these prescribed sources:

- Suetonius *Augustus* 40, 99, 101;
- Tacitus *Annals* 1.3.3, 1.6.2, 1.8.1, 1.10.5; and
- Seneca the Younger, *On Clemency* 1.9.2–12.

Complement them with Tacitus *Annals* 1.5 and Sources J26–8 in LACTOR 17. What conclusions may we draw about Livia's role in the principate?

PRESCRIBED SOURCE

Aureus of Tiberius (Figure 1.14)

Date: AD 13–14

Obverse: Augustus, laureate; 'Caesar Augustus, Son of the Deified, Father of the Fatherland'

Reverse: Tiberius, head bare; 'Tiberius Caesar, Son of Augustus, Tribunician power for the fifteenth time'

Significance: From the final year of Augustus' life, illustrating in no uncertain terms that Tiberius will be Augustus' successor

View it here: J41 in LACTOR 17: The Age of Augustus (London: KCL, 2003)

FIGURE 1.14
Aureus of Tiberius.

KEY INDIVIDUAL

Germanicus

Dates: 15 BC–AD 19

Nephew of Tiberius, who adopted him in AD 4. By the age of fourteen, Germanicus was an important general in command on the Rhine. He died in suspicious circumstances in AD 19.

It seems that Augustus was not just concerned about the immediate succession: Tacitus (*Annals* 1.3.5) tells us that Tiberius adopted his nephew Germanicus in AD 4, which created an ongoing line of succession (*Annals* 4.57 **PS**; Ovid, *Fasti* 1.1–14 **PS**). The ramifications of this adoption would not be felt until well into Tiberius' reign (see pp. 34–6).

Thanks perhaps to the difficulties he faced securing a successor, Augustus' coinage never stops depicting him as youthful and vigorous (see Fig 1.15 **PS**). The health and image of the princeps had become virtually synonymous with the state of the Roman world, as well as the unique nature of his position: as long as Augustus was in good health, the situation was secure.

Ultimately, Augustus had to bequeath his principate, the state that he had shaped, to an individual he had never fully favoured (Suetonius provides a moving account of his final days, death and legacy: *Augustus* 98–101 **PS**). Tacitus provides a pithy assessment of this situation:

> He had not even appointed Tiberius as his successor from affection or from concern for the republic but because, when he looked at his arrogance and cruelty, he hoped that the odious comparison would redound to his own greater glory.
>
> Tacitus, *Annals* 1.10.7

PRESCRIBED SOURCE

As of Augustus aged 73 (Figure 1.15)

Date: AD 11–12

Obverse: Augustus, head bare; 'Imperator Caesar Augustus, Son of the Deified, hailed victorious general twenty times'

Reverse: SC (by decree of the Senate); 'Pontifex Maximus, Tribunician power for the thirty-fourth time'

Significance: The image of Augustus on coins remains youthful and unchanging throughout his long reign.

View it here: J24 in LACTOR 17: The Age of Augustus (KCL, 2003)

FIGURE 1.15
As of Augustus. **PS**

as (pl. asses) low-denomination coin for everyday expenditures, equivalent to $1/16$ sestertius

PRESCRIBED DEBATE: THE EXTENT TO WHICH AUGUSTUS ACTUALLY RESTORED THE REPUBLIC

This is a key issue in the reign of Augustus, with modern scholars and ancient authors alike often failing to reach any consensus. We may even ask whether the concept of 'the Republic' is misguided, based more upon the nostalgia of authors such as Tacitus. Augustus himself tried to popularise the idea that the Republic had been restored, but Suetonius (*Augustus* 28.1 **PS**) claims that Augustus 'seriously thought about restoring the Republic twice', but never actually did so. What truth there may be is often shrouded in the bias of sources, such as may be seen in *Annals* 1.9–10 **PS** where Tacitus recounts the debates that occurred on Augustus' legacy following his death.

Try to read as widely as possible about this issue. You might like to start with the following reflections by modern scholars:

Rich (1990), *The Augustan Settlement*, Warminster: Aris & Phillips, pp. 23–35 and pp. 43–9 cover Dio 53.

Wallace-Hadrill, A, (2018), *Augustan Rome*, Second Edition, London: Bloomsbury Academic, chapter 2.

Millar, F. (1992), *The Emperor in the Roman World*, Second Edition, London: Bloomsbury Academic.

Syme, R. (1939), *The Roman Revolution*, Oxford: Oxford University Press, chapter 22.

Zanker, P. (1990), *The Power of Images in the Age of Augustus*, Ann Arbor: University of Michigan Press, 89–100.

TIMESPAN REVIEW

- Assess how the period 31–27 BC is characterised by the sources.
- Evaluate the importance of the First and Second Constitutional Settlements.
- Discuss how Augustus used propaganda to promote himself and his achievements.
- Consider who the key successors to Augustus were.

Further Reading

Cooley, A.E. (2009), *Res Gestae Divi Augustae*, Cambridge: Cambridge University Press.

Favro, D. (1996), *The Urban Image of Augustan Rome*, Cambridge: Cambridge University Press.

Shotter, D. (2005), *Augustus Caesar*, Abingdon: Routledge..

Wallace-Hadrill, A. (1998), *Augustan Rome*, London: Bloomsbury Academic.

Zanker, P. (1988), *The Power of Images in the Age of Augustus*, Ann Arbor: University of Michigan Press.

PRACTICE QUESTIONS

AS Level

1. Read Horace *Odes* 3.6 **PS**.

On the basis of this passage and other sources you have studied, how consistent is the portrayal of the period after Actium but before the First Constitutional Settlement? [20]

A Level

1. Read the interpretation below.

Augustus' transformation of Rome was a long and gradual process: the full 45 years of his reign were spent discovering the consequences for Rome of the victory at Actium, experimenting and working out implications. It should not be imagined that Augustus had a blue-print, and knew in advance what sort of a system he was likely to create. On the contrary, we see him again and again forced to change his mind and reverse earlier initiatives. It may seem obvious to us that a system of imperial government, with more or less the features that were to remain constant for the next couple of centuries, would be developed. But it was not obvious to Augustus or to the Romans now looking to him for a solution. That helps to explain the paradox that he set about creating a new system by restoring the old one. From different viewpoints, we may see this 'restoration' as a devious and cynical piece of political manipulation, or as a false start that later required drastic modification. Actium placed the victorious leader in a dilemma. He had led the 'senate and people' of Rome to war (a staggering 700 senators crossed the seas in display of solidarity), on their urging, so he claimed, to free Rome from threat and preserve the traditions Rome stood for.

Andrew Wallace-Hadrill, (2017), *Augustan Rome*

How convincing do you find Wallace-Hadrill's interpretation that Augustus' restoration of the republic in 27 BC was a 'devious and cynical piece of political manipulation'?

You must use your knowledge of the historical period and the ancient sources you have studied to analyse and evaluate Wallace-Hadrill's interpretation. [20]

1.2 Tiberius, AD 14–37

TIMESPAN OVERVIEW

- The views of classical authors on Tiberius' reign
- Tiberius' relationships with Germanicus and Sejanus
- Conspiracies and challenges to his reign, including mutinies and revolts
- The treason trials
- Tiberius' attitude towards religion, including the imperial cult inside and outside Rome
- Relations with the Senate, equestrians and ordinary people of Rome.

The prescribed sources for this timespan are:

- Dio Cassius, *Roman History*, 58:4.1–4, 5, 6–7.3, 8.4–11
- Suetonius, *The Twelve Caesars, Life of Tiberius*, 23–24, 26–27, 29–33, 36, 39–41, 47–48, 61–63, 65, 75
- Tacitus, *The Annals of Imperial Rome*, 1.6.1–1.15.3; 1.16–1.18; 1.21–1.25; 1.28–1.35; 1.38–1.43; 1.46–1.47; 1.49; 1.52; 1.61–1.62; 1.72; 2.52–3; 2.55; 2.57; 2.59–2.60; 2.69–2.71; 2.73; 3.20–3.21; 3.32; 3.50; 3.55; 3.65; 3.70; 3.73–3.74; 4.1–4.3; 4.20; 4.30–4.31; 4.39–4.41; 4.74; 6.18–6.19
- Velleius Paterculus, *History of Rome* 2:125.1–130.5
- Younger Seneca, *On Benefits* 3.26.1–2

- Sestertius (K4) (identified by reference in LACTOR 19)
- Inscription about Emperor Worship at Gytheion
- Inscription about *Genius* of Tiberius, Rome

Tiberius was an outstanding military general and key player in the complex succession to Augustus, eventually winning over others either dead, disgraced or too inexperienced. With one exception, the sources present him as a cryptic ruler who made no real attempt to win the support of the lower and upper classes.

THE VIEWS OF CLASSICAL AUTHORS ON TIBERIUS' REIGN

The sources on Tiberius vary hugely: some find qualities to admire while others highlight his hypocrisy, cruelty and perversity.

Tacitus portrays Tiberius in the worst possible light. However, his account is not first-hand, but based on documents he had access to as a senator, existing literary accounts and unverifiable rumours. His Tiberius is cryptic, harsh, perverted, reticent and cold; the emperor is inscrutable to the Senate. He stands in stark contrast to Augustus and is presented as an unworthy successor (*Annals* 1.10.7 **PS**). Tacitus writes as a senator and often portrays events in the context of the relationship between emperor and senators. However, he also claims that he is writing to teach moral lessons (*Annals* 3.65 **PS**). Thus he highlights failings so that they are not repeated. The account from the later historian Dio Cassius is broadly similar, based also on common traditions and documents, although using the *Annals* as his main source. Suetonius, however, acknowledges that Tiberius was at first respectful and courteous to senators (*Tiberius* 27, 29–32 **PS**), before a change after his son's death in AD 23* (*Tiberius* 33 **PS**).

Conversely, Velleius Paterculus gives a highly positive view of Tiberius' reign (e.g. 2.126.1–4 **PS**; 2.129.1–4 **PS**), and we shall see just how differently he interprets events. For example, while Suetonius (*Tiberius* 47 **PS**) claims that 'no magnificent public works' took place under Tiberius, Velleius Paterculus (2.130.1–2 **PS**) describes his 'magnificent public buildings'. Regardless of whether Tiberius needed a building programme following Augustus' extensive works, the disparity between the two sources is marked and should caution us about being over-credulous.

PRESCRIBED SOURCE

Title: *Life of Tiberius*

Date: *c.* AD 120–5

Author: Suetonius

Genre: Biography

Significance: Anecdotal biography of Tiberius from birth to death

Prescribed sections: 23–24, 26–27, 29–33, 36, 39–41, 47–48, 61–63, 65, 75

Read it here: *Suetonius: The Twelve Caesars*, trans. R. Graves (London: Penguin, 1957, 2007)

PRESCRIBED SOURCE

Title: *Annals*

Author: Tacitus

Date: Early second century AD

Genre: History

Significance: Presents Tiberius in a negative light alongside the Praetorian Prefect Sejanus

Prescribed sections: See Timespan Overview at the start of this topic

Read it here: LACTOR 17: The Age of Augustus (London: KCL, 2003); *Tacitus: The Annals of Imperial Rome*, trans. Michael Grant (London: Penguin, 1956, 1996)

---

* From this point on, AD will not be given in the main text unless needed for clarity.

PRESCRIBED SOURCE

Title: *Roman History*

Author: Dio Cassius

Date: Third century AD

Genre: History

Significance: A detailed, secondary account of Tiberius' reign, part of which survives only in the summaries provided by Xiphilinus and Zonaras

Prescribed sections: 58:4.1–4, 5, 6–7.3, 8.4–11

Read it here: LACTOR 19: Tiberius to Nero (London: KCL, 2002)

PRESCRIBED SOURCE

Title: *History of Rome*

Author: Velleius Paterculus

Date: AD 30

Genre: History

Significance: A very flattering account of Tiberius' reign by a contemporary senator

Prescribed sections: 2:125.1–130.5

Read it here: LACTOR 19: Tiberius to Nero (London: KCL, 2002)

Nowhere is this disparity more marked than in the accounts of Tiberius' accession (Tacitus, *Annals* 1.6–8 **PS**, 1.11–15 **PS**; Suetonius *Tiberius* 23–24 **PS**). When Augustus died there was no precedent of succession for Tiberius to follow. Although Augustus had made him his heir, given him proconsular imperium equal to his own, and clearly groomed him in public as his successor, he could do no more. The auctoritas that Augustus had acquired through his long pre-eminence and particular personality died with him. It was this that Tiberius lacked. Immediately he had to be seen to exercise power, while at the same time appearing to the Senate unwilling to do this, so that they might confer upon him the authority to exercise that power. By trying not to offend the Senate, he laid himself open to Tacitus' charge of blatant hypocrisy.

Tiberius was hampered by the rebellion of the Pannonian legions (Tacitus, *Annals* 1.16–18 **PS**) and a second mutiny from the German legions at Mainz (*Annals* 1.28–35). Neither of these were 'political' in nature (although the German legions preferred Germanicus for emperor), but were motivated by the fact that many soldiers had been underpaid or had exceeded their terms of service, yet had not been released. This highlights the fact that during periods of accession and transfer of power, the opportunity for crisis was far greater.

Tiberius, who had already irked the Senate (Tacitus, *Annals* 1.11–12 **PS**) despatched Drusus (the Younger) to deal with the Pannonian rebellion, while Germanicus subdued the German legions. Tacitus' account is very long and detailed, covering some thirty-seven chapters of Book 1 of the *Annals* (including the Prescribed Sources 1.16–18; 1.21–5; 1.38–43; 1.46–7; 1.49; 1.52). He uses it to highlight character traits of both Tiberius and Germanicus. For example, in 1.46 **PS** Tiberius appears highly ineffective to his contemporaries; while in 1.52 **PS**, when the mutinies are eventually suppressed, his delight is mixed with concern that Germanicus has now become too popular with the soldiery.

KEY INDIVIDUAL

Drusus the Younger

Dates: 13 BC–AD 23

The legitimate son of Tiberius. He received tribunician power in 22, marking him out for succession, but was murdered the following year.

Velleius Paterculus' account of the mutinies (2.125.1–5 **PS**) by contrast presents the accession as seamless. Tiberius seems to deal with the mutinies almost overnight by his 'long experience as an army commander' (2.15.3 **PS**).

These accounts and others reinforce the need for a critical understanding of the reliability of our sources and their agendas.

TIBERIUS' RELATIONSHIPS WITH GERMANICUS AND SEJANUS

Given Tacitus' moralistic agenda, it is perhaps unsurprising that most of his characters are very black and white, being 'heroes' and 'villains'. This is particularly marked for Germanicus and Sejanus, two key figures under Tiberius. Dio also gives an account of Sejanus' rise and fall (58:4.1–4, 5–7.3, 8.4–11 **PS**), and in particular he highlights the way Sejanus' power overrides the political system.

Forced into adopting Germanicus in AD 4 by Augustus, Tiberius was clearly expected to further the young man's career as a potential successor. But as Tiberius already had a son, this was inevitably problematic. Moreover, Germanicus was a capable military leader who inspired the loyalty of his troops, as revealed by their desire to make him emperor (Tacitus, *Annals* 1.35.3 **PS**; Velleius Paterculus 2.125.1 **PS**). This popularity clearly perturbed Tiberius and, according to Tacitus (e.g. *Annals* 1.62.2 **PS**), made him see Germanicus as a threat.

An opportunity came in 17 when problems arose in the eastern provinces, in particular Judaea and Syria. Tiberius suggested that Germanicus settle matters. This had the advantage of seeming to utilise his capabilities, but separated him from the region of his military support. Tiberius also simultaneously replaced the governor of Syria with Gnaeus Calpurnius Piso.

According to Tacitus, Piso believed he was in Syria to curb Germanicus' hopes. Tacitus highlights how groups within the imperial court attached to different possible successors: people flocked to Germanicus because Tiberius seemed unfriendly.

In 18, on his way east (*Annals* 2.53; 2.55 **PS**), Germanicus was welcomed and lauded everywhere he stopped. Yet Piso, travelling behind, stopped in all the same places and undermined him (2.55 **PS**). Piso overtook Germanicus at Rhodes and arrived in Syria first, where he began to turn the legions to his side through 'lavishness and favouritism' (2.55 **PS**). The two men finally confronted one another and parted in open hatred (2.57 **PS**).

The year 19 begins with Germanicus visiting the province of Egypt, but without the permission of Tiberius (*Annals*, 2.59–60 **PS**). Tiberius saw this as a serious challenge to his authority, and indeed his permission was needed, in keeping with the Augustan practice. While Germanicus was away, Piso continued to undermine his activities (*Annals*, 2.69.1 **PS**) and on Germanicus' return to Syria, Piso elected to leave. However, at this point Germanicus fell seriously ill and died. He was convinced that he had been poisoned by Piso (*Annals*, 2.69–71 **PS**), and that Tiberius was involved: in his dying words to his wife Agrippina (the Elder), Germanicus warned her not to anger those in power.

Piso was brought back for trial in Rome, but the main charge was that of stirring up civil war in the province of Syria. Piso committed suicide when he realised that Tiberius would not assist him. The Senate still passed a series of judgements over him and his two sons, but we get the impression that Tiberius was trying to resolve the matter as quickly as possible.

Tacitus uses this episode to highlight Tiberius' cruelty, and his disconnection from the plebs. When news of Germanicus' illness reached Rome, the people grieved hugely, speculating that Tiberius was partly responsible. Tiberius refused even to meet Agrippina when she returned with Germanicus' ashes, and limited the public honours, encouraging the people to stop grieving. Tiberius appears cold and distant, and Tacitus suggests no real grief for the loss of his adopted son.

Velleius Paterculus' version (2.130.3–130.5 **PS**) glosses over Germanicus' death as merely one of Tiberius' misfortunes, with the real issue being the 'sorrow, fury, and shame' that he was forced to endure because of the subsequent hostility of Agrippina and her sons.

If, for Tacitus, Tiberius is the villain, then Sejanus is very much his right-hand man. His character is blackened like no other in the *Annals*. He is accused of being sexually perverse (4.1 **PS**), corrupt and power-hungry (4.1 **PS**), and able to manipulate Tiberius to a tremendous degree (4.1 **PS**). Sejanus is the prime example of a political opportunist who prospered under the principate. When power rests in an individual's hands, it can easily be abused. That was Sejanus' aim.

As commander of the Praetorian Guard, whose significance he immediately began to promote (Tacitus *Annals* 4.2 **PS**), Sejanus had privileged access to Tiberius. He quickly exploited this for his own ends, engineering himself into the succession. Tiberius' trust may be explained by his lack of alternatives: at the outset of his reign, he begged the Senate for colleagues to assist him (*Annals*, 1.11.1 **PS**), but no one volunteered.

Velleius Paterculus, whose history was published before Sejanus' eventual downfall, is glowing about him (2.127.1–128.4 **PS**), calling him a 'distinguished assistant', who enjoyed the 'long-standing regard' of both people and emperor, and saying that he 'shared the burdens of the imperial office'. Here we see once again the sycophancy of the Senate towards the powerful. Dio (*Roman History*, 58.4.1 **PS**) affirms this, claiming that Sejanus was treated 'as if he were actually emperor', and that Tiberius called him the 'Sharer of my Cares'.

The rise of Sejanus encompassed some particularly unpleasant deeds, from the (alleged) murder in 23 of Tiberius' son Drusus, his rival for the throne (*Annals* 4.3 **PS**), to the seduction of Drusus' wife Livilla, and his attempts to convince Tiberius to allow him to marry her (4.39–40 **PS**), given how he could benefit the state.

Tiberius' refusal was Sejanus' first real impediment. He therefore contrived to convince Tiberius to leave Rome, first to Campania in 25, and thence to Capri in 26 (*Annals*, 4.41 **PS**; Suetonius, *Tiberius* 39–41 **PS**). Tiberius' consent may seem surprising, but he had frequently left Rome during Augustus' reign, and must now have tired of being princeps, having always claimed he was unsuitable.

Following Tiberius' withdrawal, Sejanus was effectively the centre of power. Dio (58.5.1 **PS**) summarises the situation: 'it was he who appeared to be emperor and Tiberius

KEY INDIVIDUAL

Agrippina the Elder
Dates: 14 BC–AD 33
Wife of Germanicus, mother of the future emperor Gaius and granddaughter of Augustus.

EXPLORE FURTHER
Read the full account of the Germanicus and Piso episode in Tacitus' *Annals* 2.53–61; 2.69–3.18 (which includes some prescribed sources).

Highlight where Tacitus makes very clear his opinions on the characters of Tiberius, Germanicus, and Piso, and the relationships between them.

Compare the above with the *Senatorial Decree concerning Gnaeus Calpurnius Piso* (SCPP; LACTOR 19, P3). This record from AD 20 gives a different account of the trial and punishment of Piso from Tacitus'.

Study question
Examine:
- Dio 58.4.1–4 **PS** and 58.5.1–7 **PS**;
- Velleius Paterculus 2.127.1–128.4 **PS**; and
- Suetonius 61–3 **PS**.

How much agreement in these sources is there on the relationship between Tiberius and Sejanus?

a kind of off-shore monarch.' The senators are particularly sycophantic towards Sejanus, highlighting yet again that they were politically impotent. But in 31, a change overtakes Tiberius, which he claimed was prompted by Sejanus' persecution of Germanicus' sons, Nero and Drusus (Suetonius, *Tiberius* 61.1 **PS**), who as other potential successors were clear targets for Sejanus. Some reports also suggest that Sejanus' abandoned wife, Apicata, informed Tiberius of Sejanus' part in the death of Tiberius' son Drusus.

Sejanus' end was sudden (see Dio 58.8.4–10.8 **PS**; Suetonius *Tiberius* 65 **PS**). The Senate and people, who had previously fawned over him, quickly abandoned him, vilifying the man in the same breath as they revealed their own hypocrisy (Dio 58.10.7 **PS**). He and his children were executed, in a particularly brutal fashion (Dio 58.11.5 **PS**), and the career of the arch-political opportunist ended in ignominy.

CONSPIRACIES AND CHALLENGES TO TIBERIUS' REIGN, INCLUDING MUTINIES AND REVOLTS

In addition to the mutinies of 14 discussed above, the only other revolts of Tiberius' reign were those of an auxiliary deserter called Tacfarinas in the province of Africa between 15 and 24.

Tacitus (*Annals* 2.52 **PS**, 3.20–21 **PS**, 3.32 **PS**) tells of the struggle of four successive governors against the rebel group who launched raids on Roman territory which seriously threatened to interrupt the grain supply. Tacfarinas' troops, despite outnumbering the Romans, were comprehensively defeated by Furius Camillus in 17, but Tacfarinas escaped. He continued to ransack villages and eventually recorded a victory against a cohort from the Third Legion, which was subsequently decimated by the proconsul Lucius Apronius for retreating against an enemy (3.20–21 **PS**).

Tacitus records Tiberius' outrage when Tacfarinas wrote demanding a settlement of land for himself and his rebel troops, threatening war if the emperor refused (3.73–74 **PS**). Knowing that a decisive end to this war was necessary, Tiberius appointed Quintus Junius Blaesus as commander. He routed Tacfarinas' men, having won over large numbers through the offer of an amnesty. Eventually Publius Cornelius Dolabella, knowing that violence against Rome would only cease with Tacfarinas' death, successfully orchestrated an unexpected early-morning attack on the insurgents' camp where Tacfarinas was killed.

Tacitus' detailed description of this prolonged war allows us to see the problems which Tiberius had to deal with during his early reign in bringing stability to the empire. This, as well as the mutinies in Pannonia and Germany, shows how much Tiberius relied on others to solve crises.

maiestas a charge of treason against the workings of the Roman state, tried in the Senate; the usual punishment was death and confiscation of property

THE TREASON TRIALS

One of the most controversial and critical aspects of Tiberius' reign is the return of treason or **maiestas** trials.

PRESCRIBED SOURCE

Title: *On Benefits*

Author: Younger Seneca

Date: *c.* AD 56–62

Significance: One of a series of moral essays used to educate the young emperor Nero. The implication is that Tiberius' actions are not to be emulated

Read it here: T1 in LACTOR 19: Tiberius to Nero (London: KCL, 2002)

Tacitus introduces the concept with his usual style of **sent-entia**, whereby a seeming positive remark on Tiberius is immediately undercut by a negative observation. Having described how Tiberius rejected the title of *pater patriae* (Father of the Fatherland) in an effort to look 'citizen-like', Tacitus immediately introduces the term maiestas. This is the most politically loaded word in the *Annals*, as Tacitus uses it to highlight the tyrannical power of the emperors. He is particularly aggrieved by the maiestas trials, as they were predominantly directed against senators and were seen as the suppression of free speech. Tacitus' bias derives from his experience of similar maiestas trials under Domitian during the 90s. In total, Tacitus details about eighty treason trials under Tiberius (including Prescribed Sources *Annals* 2.73, 3.50, 3.70, 4.20, 4.30–1, 6.18–19 **PS**).

Suetonius agrees that Tiberius enforced the law most savagely. Similarly, the Younger Seneca highlights that 'treason trials became so commonplace that they amounted to a form of national madness', and records an attempted false allegation (*On Benefits* 3.26.1–2 **PS**). This madness was exacerbated by the rise of professional informants, **delatores**, who personally profited from making accusations.

TIBERIUS' ATTITUDE TOWARDS RELIGION, INCLUDING THE IMPERIAL CULT INSIDE AND OUTSIDE ROME

Something which perhaps shows Tiberius' reticence to engage with public life is his repeated vetoing of divine honours for himself. By his accession, both Julius Caesar and Augustus had been deified (see Fig 1.16 **PS**; also Suetonius, *Tiberius* 40 **PS**) and so the imperial cult was now part of religious life in the empire.

Various cities competed to worship Tiberius, presumably to signify allegiance. As with Augustus, there is evidence that aspects of this worship were tolerated in Rome (see the genius of Tiberius inscription at Rome **PS**). We also have an inscription from the citizens of Gytheion **PS** in the Greek Peloponnese from 15 asking permission to offer divine honours to Tiberius and the imperial family. Tiberius is quite firm in his rejection

Study questions
Examine:

- Younger Seneca, *On Benefits* 3.26.1–2 **PS**;
- Tacitus, *Annals* 2.73, 3.50, 3.70, 4.20, 4.30–1, 6.18–19 (all **PS**);
- Suetonius, *Tiberius* 55–66 (including some **PS**);
- Tacitus *Annals* 1.73–5, 2.27–32, 3.49, 4.34–6, 6.9, 6.14, 6.23–7, 6.29–30, 6.38–9 (not **PS**, but key evidence for Tacitus' presentation of the treason trials); and
- Velleius Paterculus, *History of Rome* 2.126.1–4 **PS**; 2.129.1–4 **PS**.

1. To what extent is there agreement on the nature of the maiestas trials in Tiberius' reign?

2. What may we learn about Tiberius' reign from this evidence?

sententia a particular style of Tacitus', where his opinion comes at the end of a section

delatores informants in Tiberian Rome, drawn from any social class, and rewarded with a quarter of the value of the property of those convicted of treason

FIGURE 1.16
Sestertius of Tiberius. **PS**

PRESCRIBED SOURCE

Sestertius of Tiberius (Figure 1.16)

Date: AD 34/35

Obverse: Chariot drawn by four elephants with statue of Augustus; 'To the Divine Augustus from the Senate and People of Rome'

Reverse: 'Augustus, son of Divus Augustus, pontifex maximus, in his 36th year of tribunician power (by the decree of the Senate)'

Significance: Emphasises the political and religious significance of Tiberius' close relationship to the Divine Augustus

View it here: K4 in LACTOR 19: Tiberius to Nero (London: KCL, 2002)

PRESCRIBED SOURCE

Genius of Tiberius inscription

Date: AD 27

Location: Rome

Significance: Evidence of the worship of Tiberius' genius by a leading citizen in Rome.

Read it here: L6 in LACTOR 19: Tiberius to Nero (London: KCL, 2002)

PRESCRIBED SOURCE

Emperor-worship inscription

Date: AD 15

Location: Gytheion, Greece

Significance: A petition to Tiberius from the people of Gytheion detailing arrangements for an eight-day festival in honour of members of the imperial family and Tiberius' response declining all divine honours

Read it here: L4 in LACTOR 19: Tiberius to Nero (London: KCL, 2002)

---

of such honours. This supports the claims in Suetonius (*Tiberius* 26 **PS**) that Tiberius refused all decrees asking for temples and priesthoods to be set up in his honour.

RELATIONS WITH THE SENATE, EQUESTRIANS, AND ORDINARY PEOPLE OF ROME

It is clear that Tiberius did not enjoy particularly good relations with any ranks of society. Despite efforts to work with the Senate, from the very outset the relationship was full of difficulty. Tacitus remarks (*Annals* 3.65 **PS**) that Tiberius viewed them as 'Men primed for slavery!' The Senate as a body seems sycophantic (*Annals* 4.74 **PS**), but ultimately of limited political significance. Tiberius had sought collegiality, but either through unwillingness or inability, the Senate had failed to deliver. His exasperation with them as a group becomes clear throughout his reign.

Similarly, his relations with the plebs were never strong. A virtually reclusive princeps who was cautious with money did not sit well with a populace conditioned to the generosity of Augustus. Suetonius informs us that large-scale generosity was rare (*Tiberius* 47–8 **PS**), while Tacitus notes that he took steps against luxury (*Annals* 3.55 **PS**). However, this meant that he had funds to deal with fires in Rome as well as provide earthquake relief and tax remission for the province of Asia. His successor Gaius inherited a cash surplus. Although Velleius Paterculus would have us believe that Tiberius was very generous (2.129.3 **PS**), the contemporary perspective of him was not positive. Suetonius (*Tiberius* 75 **PS**) records the unbridled joy when news of his death reached Rome, accompanied by cries of 'To the Tiber with Tiberius!'

However, Tiberius' portrayal is perhaps unfairly biased. He probably was an unpopular emperor, but anyone who followed Augustus would have suffered by the comparison. Tiberius was a competent administrator and a careful financier. He even attempted to seem modest, such as through his refusal of the title of 'Father of the Fatherland' (Tacitus *Annals* 1.72 **PS**). However, he suffered from his inability to play the role of princeps in the same way as Augustus.

> **Study question**
> Examine the prescribed sources opposite and:
> - Suetonius, *Tiberius* 26, 36 **PS**;
> - Tacitus, *Annals* 4.37–8
>
> What may we learn about Tiberius' attitude to religion?

> **Study question**
> Based on your reading up to this point, how would you assess the principate of Tiberius overall?

PRESCRIBED DEBATE: THE CHARACTER OF TIBERIUS

Tacitus portrays Tiberius as a cryptic emperor, inscrutable to most around him. Read the Prescribed Sources for his reign and consider what we can learn from his relationships with the senators and equestrians as well as the people and those closest to him. How effective was he at dealing with problems during his reign and how far do the sources present a consistent view of Tiberian Rome?

The following reflections by modern scholars should be read when considering these central issues:

Alston, R. (2014), *Aspects of Roman History 31 BC–AD 117*, Abingdon: Routledge, pp. 93–128.
Levick, B. (1999), *Tiberius the Politician*, Abingdon: Routledge.
Seager, R. (2008), *Tiberius*, Oxford: Wiley-Blackwell.

TIMESPAN REVIEW

- Discuss Tiberius' behaviour when he first accedes to the imperial throne.
- Examine how effectively the mutinies in Pannonia and Germany are dealt with.
- Analyse the relationship between Tiberius and Germanicus and that of Tiberius with Sejanus.
- Evaluate the reliability of the sources for this period.

Further Reading

Alston, R. (2014), *Aspects of Roman History 31 BC–AD 117*, Abingdon: Routledge.

Levick, B. (1999), *Tiberius the Politician*, Abingdon: Routledge.

Martin R. (1994), *Tacitus Rev. ed.,* Bristol: Bristol Classical Press.

Seager, R. (2008), *Tiberius*, Oxford: Wiley-Blackwell.

Woodman, AJ. (2009), *The Cambridge Companion to Tacitus*, Cambridge: Cambridge University Press.

PRACTICE QUESTIONS

AS Level

1. Explain Tiberius' attitude towards the imperial cult. [10]

A Level

1. To what extent do the sources help us understand Tiberius' relationship with the Senate and ordinary people of Rome?

   You must use and analyse the ancient sources you have studied as well as your own knowledge to support your answer. [30]

1.3 Gaius, AD 37–41

TIMESPAN OVERVIEW

- The presentation of Gaius' character and personality as emperor by the ancient sources
- Administrative changes to Rome
- Relations with the Senate, Equestrians and ordinary people of Rome
- His attitude towards religion, including the imperial cult inside and outside Rome
- The assassination in AD 41.

The prescribed sources for this timespan are:

- Dio Cassius, *Roman History* 59.3.1–5.5; 59.9.4–7; 59.16.1–11; 59.26.5–27.1; 59.28.1–11; 59.29.1–30.3
- Josephus, *Jewish Antiquities* 19.1–3; 19.4–11; 19.17–27; 19.100–14; 201–11
- Pliny the Elder, *Natural History* 36.122–3
- Seneca the Younger, *On Anger* 3.19.1–5
- Seneca the Younger, *On Consolation to Polybius* 17.3–5
- Seneca the Younger, *On Firmness of Purpose* 18.3
- Suetonius, *Gaius* 13–14, 18–20, 22, 27–33, 37, 56–9

- Coins (identified by references in LACTOR 19)
  - Denarius (J7n)
  - Quadrans (J19h)

Gaius' reign was brief, and this timespan focuses in particular on his associations with the imperial cult, which tended towards megalomania. It also examines the most significant event of his reign: his assassination, which indicated that murder had effectively now become a viable political tool.

THE PRESENTATION OF GAIUS' CHARACTER AND PERSONALITY AS EMPEROR BY THE ANCIENT SOURCES

Perhaps the most striking observation about Gaius is by Suetonius (*Gaius* 22 **PS**): 'So much for Gaius the Emperor; the rest of this history must needs deal with Gaius the Monster.'

PRESCRIBED SOURCE

Title: *Life of Gaius*

Author: Suetonius

Genre: Biography

Significance: Compelling biography of Gaius which delights in the vagaries and perceived tyrannies of his reign

Prescribed sections: 13–14, 18–20, 22, 27–33, 37, 56–9

Read it here: *Suetonius: The Twelve Caesars*, trans. R. Graves (Penguin, 1957, 2007)

This exemplifies Suetonius' desire to divide imperial reigns into good and bad parts, but is also very appropriate. Although Gaius' reign was brief, it is certainly easily divisible in two. Other sources echo Suetonius in separating an initially promising period (prior to an illness in October/November 37) from subsequent tyrannical cruelty and megalomania.

There was much potential in the opening months of Gaius' reign, as he consciously sought to distance both himself and his policies from the unpopular Tiberius. Although he had no political or military experience, Gaius was savvy enough to grasp that he should make overtures to the Roman people. Suetonius (*Gaius* 13–14 **PS**; 18–20 **PS**) calls it 'a dream come true'. Gaius strengthened his popularity by every possible means, in particular by:

- holding a series of games;
- recalling all exiles and dismissing criminal charges that were pending from under Tiberius; and
- making a public statement of reunifying the imperial household not only through his adoption of Tiberius Gemellus, but also by honouring his grandmother with the title of Augusta (Dio, *Roman History* 59.3.4 **PS**).

He even sailed in person to Pandataria and the Pontian islands to bring the remains of his mother and brother back to the Mausoleum of Augustus (59.3.5 **PS**).

These early actions seem to have been designed to enthral the mob, although Gaius was also careful to begin his reign with the support of the army. Here he could play upon his descent from the beloved Germanicus. The coin in Fig 1.17 **PS**, clearly linking Gaius and Germanicus, was designed to transfer some of the glamour of Germanicus' military glory onto Gaius himself, thereby securing the loyalty of the troops.

PRESCRIBED SOURCE

Title: *History of Rome*

Author: Dio Cassius

Date: Third century AD

Genre: History

Significance: Retrospective history from a senatorial perspective. Note that some of these prescribed sections only survive in the summaries provided by Xiphilinus

Prescribed sections: 59.3.1–5.5; 59.9.4–7; 59.16.1–11; 59.26.5–27.1; 59.28.1–11; 59.29.1–30.3

Read it here: LACTOR 19: Tiberius to Nero (London: KCL, 2002)

Despite Gaius' early courting of the people, the sources pass over such details quickly, using them as little more than evidence to show how far and how quickly Gaius descended into maniacal tyranny (see Dio *Roman History*, 59:3.1–5.5 **PS**; Josephus, *Jewish Antiquities* 19.1–3 **PS**; 19.4–11 **PS**; Seneca, *On Consolation to Polybius* 17.3–5 **PS**). Dio perhaps gives us the most carefully considered account, but he too is struck by the divided nature of Gaius' personality, and frequently gives examples. Moreover, the 'illness' that prompts Gaius' madness was perhaps merely a convenient and easy way of explaining how an emperor who promised so much at the outset of his reign could so completely fail to deliver.

PRESCRIBED SOURCE

Denarius of Gaius (Figure 1.17)

Date: AD 37

Mint: Lugdunum

Obverse: Head of Gaius Caligula; 'Gaius Caesar, Augustus, Germanicus, pontifex maximus, with tribunician power'

Reverse: Head of Germanicus; 'Germanicus Caesar, father of Gaius Caesar Augustus Germanicus'

Significance: Minted by Gaius to celebrate Germanicus

View it here: J7n in LACTOR 19: Tiberius to Nero (London: KCL, 2002)

FIGURE 1.17
Denarius of Gaius.

43

Title: *Jewish Antiquities*

Author: Josephus

Date: *c.* AD 94

Genre: History

Significance: The earliest surviving testimony of the events described, which used at least one contemporary record as a source. As both a Jewish author and a court historian to the Flavian emperors, Josephus is perhaps doubly likely to be critical of Gaius

Prescribed sections: 19.1–3; 19.4–11; 19.17–27; 19.100–14

Read it here: LACTOR 19: Tiberius to Nero (London: KCL, 2002)

Title: *On Consolation to Polybius*

Author: Seneca the Younger

Date: Certainly after AD 41; most probably 55–9

Genre: Philosophical/didactic treatise

Significance: A damning analysis of Gaius' character and rule, possibly to ingratiate Seneca (in exile) with Claudius through contrast

Prescribed sections: 17.3–5

Read it here: J22e in LACTOR 19: Tiberius to Nero (London: KCL, 2002)

ADMINISTRATIVE CHANGES TO ROME

Given the brevity of his reign, and his subsequent unpopularity, it is perhaps unsurprising that Gaius left little impact upon Rome from an administrative perspective. Yet at times he shows a real understanding of the demands placed on an emperor, especially with regard to placating the masses.

The **quadrans** PS in Fig 1.18 dates to 39 (after Gaius' supposed 'madness') and commemorates his removal of the 0.5 per cent auction tax. This is clearly designed to generate goodwill, although suggesting that it is a freedom from slavery (using the **pileus**) is a great exaggeration. Using a low-value quadrans shows that this was decidedly populist in design.

> **quadrans** the lowest denomination (value) of coin
>
> **pileus** a cap worn by freed slaves

PRESCRIBED SOURCE

Quadrans of Gaius (Figure 1.18)

Date: AD 39

Mint: Rome

Obverse: Pileus between SC; 'Gaius Caesar Augustus, grandson of Augustus, by decree of the senate'

Reverse: RCC (Remission of the 1/200 tax); 'pontifex maximus, in his 3rd year of tribunician power, father of the fatherland, designated consul for the 3rd time'

Significance: Commemorates Gaius' tax remission

View it here: J19h in LACTOR 19: Tiberius to Nero (London: KCL, 2002)

FIGURE 1.18
Quadrans of Gaius.

However, this popularity would not last. When Gaius had burned through Tiberius' surplus – according to Dio (*Roman History* 59.2.6 **PS**), he squandered 575,000,000 denarii in under a year – he introduced new and more severe taxation measures (Dio, *Roman History* 59.28.11 **PS**). This resulted in the plebs storming the Circus Maximus.

Pliny the Elder (*Natural History*, 36.122–3 **PS**) notes that Gaius began work on various aqueducts, including the Anio Novus, that were later completed by Claudius. Since Pliny praises practical building programmes and condemns private projects, his attribution of such works to Gaius is interesting, and at odds with the majority of our sources: we know of a bridge of boats at Baiae (Suetonius, *Gaius* 19 **PS**) and pleasure barges on Lake Nemi.

PRESCRIBED SOURCE

Title: *Natural History*

Author: Pliny the Elder

Date: AD 77–9

Genre: Encyclopaedia

Significance: Pliny mentions Gaius instituting work on various aqueducts, reflecting Pliny's attitude to the importance of practical building programmes

Prescribed section: 36.122–3

Read it here: K24 in LACTOR 19: Tiberius to Nero (London: KCL, 2002)

Suetonius notes that Gaius:

- lifted the censorship on various Augustan orators and historians;
- published imperial budgets;
- gave magistrates full authority over court cases;
- revised the list of equites;
- created a fifth judicial division to spread the workload more evenly; and
- reorganised the rulership of several buffer regions.

These are the actions not of a tyrant or madman, but of an emperor working for the good of the empire. Likewise Dio (*Roman History*, 59.9.4–7 **PS**) records commendable acts, particularly revisions to and expansion of the equestrian class.

Dio is far less understanding on policies that seemed to return political power to the people, such as the undoing of Tiberius' AD 14 measures that made popular assemblies unable to do anything other than ratify senatorial recommendations for magistracies. Dio says that this 'distressed sensible people' (59.9.7 **PS**), revealing his own highly conservative and senatorial perspective. Perhaps the label of 'madness' betrays the inability of our sources to understand the logic of some of Gaius' decisions, which were clearly designed to speak towards specific elements of the Roman population.

RELATIONS WITH THE SENATE, EQUESTRIANS, AND PLEBS

Given Gaius' rather unpredictable nature, it is unsurprising that his relationship with various groups is inconsistent. Perhaps his most curious is that with the Senate. Both Dio (*Roman History*, 59.3.1–2 **PS**) and Suetonius (*Gaius* 14.1 **PS**) record the speed and ease with which the Senate imparted all of the imperial titles and powers onto Gaius. Indeed Gaius' accession set the precedent for those that followed. Yet his was even more remarkable since at the time of his accession, he held no official position and had to be gifted with both imperium proconsulare maius and tribunicia potestas. This pandering by the Senate at the outset of his reign never lessened.

Dio recounts a speech of Gaius in 39 (59.16.1–11 **PS**) in which Tiberius advises him to 'show neither affection nor mercy' and 'take thought only for [his] own pleasure and safety'. This led to the reintroduction of maiestas trials. The Senate could have reacted more forcibly, but it was cowed by long servitude. Senators' personal prosperity depended on pleasing the princeps, so they 'reassembled and made many speeches praising Gaius as a most sincere and pious ruler, since they were most grateful to him for not having put them to death'. They also approved an annual sacrifice to commemorate his clemency, a golden image of him on the Capitoline Hill and the celebration of a lesser triumph, as if he had defeated a foreign enemy.

Perhaps we should not judge the Senate too harshly, given Gaius' atrocities. But this assumes that our accounts are true. Suetonius (*Gaius* 27–33 **PS**) gives numerous instances of his cruelty, revelling in compiling this catalogue of outrages, but what is decidedly lacking everywhere is evidence of the reliability of his sources. Allegations are

---

PRESCRIBED SOURCE

Title: *On Anger*

Author: Seneca the Younger

Date: Certainly after AD 41; most probably 55–9

Genre: Philosophical/didactic treatise

Significance: A presentation of Gaius' cruelties in the context of the socio-political dangers of excessive savagery and anger

Prescribed section: 3.19.1–5

Read it here: T6 in LACTOR 19: Tiberius to Nero (London: KCL, 2002)

---

vague and anecdotal at best, perhaps telling us more about Suetonius' bias as a source than anything else. Yet Suetonius is not alone in his presentation of Gaius as shockingly cruel. Seneca (*On Anger* 3.19.1–5 **PS**) provides much the same catalogue, with the observation that 'there is nothing surprising in all this. Gaius was a mad beast, and such brutalities were his daily bread and butter.'

As for the other classes of society, our evidence for their relationship with Gaius is similarly anecdotal. Josephus (*Jewish Antiquities* 19.24 **PS**) does suggest that Gaius would make decisions to please the plebs and gain popularity, but he goes on to describe Gaius' brutal treatment of protesting citizens (19.25–6 **PS**). Suetonius (*Gaius* 30 **PS**) tells us that the *equites* constantly displeased him, but this does not tally well with the fact that he revised and expanded the order. Both here in Suetonius and in Seneca (*On Anger* 3.19.2 **PS**, perhaps Suetonius' source), we find the infamous remark that Gaius wished 'all you Romans had only one neck!'

The major problem for understanding Gaius' relations with Rome is the limited evidence: the majority of sources are upper-class authors who wish to cast Gaius as the mad tyrant. Our most contemporary authors are biased. Josephus had a Jewish anti-Gaius perspective, and as *the* Flavian historian, he needed to reflect that dynasty's condemnation of Gaius as a poor model of emperor. Seneca's treatises were largely designed to guide the young Nero in a sensible path of governance.

GAIUS' ATTITUDE TOWARDS RELIGION, INCLUDING THE IMPERIAL CULT INSIDE AND OUTSIDE ROME

The aspect of Gaius' reign given the most attention in the sources is his attitude towards the imperial cult. Indeed, his opinion of his own divinity becomes the defining characteristic of his reign, again in complete contrast with his predecessor (see Dio 59.26.5–27.1 **PS**; 59.28.1–11 **PS**). This was perhaps a result of his desire to be seen as different from Tiberius, who, as Tacitus states, spurned worship of himself. It was also perhaps a natural extension of the flattery Gaius received from all quarters on his accession. But other explanations must be considered, including the fact that it was a useful substitute to pre-existing power for a princeps who had no background in politics or the military, and therefore needed another way to acquire Augustan auctoritas.

But while Augustus had established a double system where it was legitimate for a living emperor to be worshipped in the provinces, as a means of control and Romanisation, but not in Rome other than through the worship of Augustus' genius (guiding spirit) as the bringer of peace and stability (see p. 18), Gaius' reign is characterised by a drive to do away with this duality. Yet even this was not immediate, since Dio (*Roman History* 59.4.4 **PS**) notes that at the start of his reign, Gaius forbade the setting up of any images of him, and once refused to sanction a vote that sacrifices be conducted to his Fortune. (This importantly reminds us that Roman state imperial cult policy was frequently formed by the cooperative efforts of all Rome's governing bodies, rather than the princeps himself.)

Our sources suggest that Gaius made numerous efforts to promote his own divinity, although this is presented with such bias that it is difficult to know the truth. He was certainly 'interested in doing only the impossible' (Suetonius, *Gaius* 37 **PS**), with his entire lifestyle being one of excess and indulgence. Likewise Dio (59.26.8 **PS**) states that 'in every respect he wanted to appear more than just a human being and an emperor'. But the terms 'impossible' and 'like an emperor' here are very revealing, being characteristically Roman in perspective, whereas for an eastern monarch, such behaviour would be quite commonplace. Gaius' behaviour is explicable if we conjecture that he was trying to convert the principate into more of an absolute monarchy, smashing the republican facade that Augustus had created and Tiberius preserved. Thus his promotion of the imperial cult brings it more in line with Egyptian pharaonic worship or that of Near Eastern god-kings.

Nor was there much actual contemporary condemnation of his behaviour. Dio (59.28.2 **PS**) tells us that the Senate granted a temple for Gaius on the Palatine, although he had to fund it himself. Suetonius (*Gaius* 22 **PS**) informs us that all of the richest citizens tried to gain priesthoods therein. Thus we should observe that although Gaius was dressing up as various deities (Dio 59.26.5–6 **PS**) and 'claiming from his subjects honours no longer appropriate for mortal men' (Josephus, *Jewish Antiquities* 19.4 **PS**), he was actually being indulged by both Senate and people.

Perhaps it is better to say that the condemnation of Gaius' divine pretensions is actually due to the individual biases of the sources. The imperial cult is probably where Gaius acquires the most contempt, as it manifestly communicated the omnipotence of the emperor, transforming the role from civilis princeps (citizen-commander) to overt monarch.

THE ASSASSINATION OF AD 41

The key sources on Gaius' assassination are Josephus (*Jewish Antiquities* 19.17–27 **PS**, 19.100–114 **PS**), Suetonius (*Gaius* 56–9 **PS**) and Dio (*Roman History* 59.29.1–30.3 **PS**).

S & C
On the basis of the sources you have studied under Augustus and Tiberius, and your wider reading, what was the attitude towards the imperial cult in Rome by the time of Gaius' accession?

Study question
Read Suetonius *Gaius* 22 **PS**, Dio, *Roman History* 59.26.5–27.1; 59.28.1–11 **PS**, and Josephus, *Jewish Antiquities* 19.4–11 **PS**.
What specific examples do these authors give of Gaius' actions relating to the imperial cult?

The murder would seem to be the best possible evidence for the condemnation of his reign and its excesses, but again the picture is not black and white, as the conspirators are drawn from a very limited cohort. Although Josephus claims that there were three different assassination plans (*Jewish Antiquities* 19.17 (PS)), this does not tally with his own subsequent account, nor with what we are told in Dio (59.29.1 (PS)). Josephus appears to be trying to create a sense of mass opposition to Gaius.

Josephus places Cassius Chaerea at the head of the assassination conspiracy. Dio (59.29. (PS)) tells us that the conspirators included Cornelius Sabinus (another Praetorian tribune), Callistus (an imperial freedman) and Marcus Arrecinus Clemens (the Praetorian Prefect). Josephus (*Jewish Antiquities* 19.18 (PS)) adds Lucius Annius Vinicianus as a senatorial presence.

After much procrastination, Gaius' end came at a festival on the Palatine Hill. Dio (59.29.5 (PS)) tells us that even the consul at the time was bending over to kiss Gaius' feet – again reinforcing the idea of the majority still pandering to him. Josephus, Dio and Suetonius all give versions of Gaius' final moments. Although the details differ slightly between each account, all three agree on its brutality: Dio goes so far as to say that 'everybody kept stabbing him savagely, even though he was dead: some even tasted his flesh' (59.29.7 (PS)).

The motivations for the assassination may seem obvious, but the sources do not give us any real explanation. One unanimous observation is that Chaerea was in part motivated by Gaius' constant insults towards him for effeminacy. Seneca (*On Firmness of Purpose* 18.3 (PS)) seems to make this the ultimate trigger for Chaerea.

Ultimately, this murder was not born of some grand ideal about the restoration of the republic, as may be seen from the aftermath (see pp. 52–5), nor was it a mass conspiracy of the oppressed. Chaerea and Sabinus seem to have been motivated at least partly by self-preservation, Callistus by a desire to guarantee his own future and Vinicianus by his own imperial ambitions. They were not idealists, but rather opportunists.

KEY INDIVIDUAL

Cassius Chaerea
Dates: Died AD 41

In AD 41, a tribune in the Praetorian Guard and a leading player in Gaius' assassination. He was executed on Claudius' accession.

EXPLORE FURTHER

Read Josephus *Jewish Antiquities* 19.28–99 (LACTOR 19, E7–E15) on the conspiracy of Chaerea and his associates.

PRESCRIBED SOURCE

Title: *On Firmness of Purpose*

Author: Seneca the Younger

Date: Certainly after AD 41; most probably 55–9

Genre: Philosophical/didactic treatise

Significance: Seneca records Chaerea's personal motivation for the assassination of Gaius

Prescribed section: 18.3

Read it here: P6b in LACTOR 19: Tiberius to Nero (London: KCL, 2002)

It is certain that, despite the vagaries of the sources, Gaius tried to do too much too soon: he tried to be an absolute monarch when the expectation for an emperor was very different. Josephus (*Jewish Antiquities* 19.202 **PS**), as part of a useful (if biased) summation of Gaius' personality and reign (*Jewish Antiquities* 201–10 **PS**), concludes that 'He aspired to be, and to be seen to be, superior to the laws of god and man'.

PRESCRIBED DEBATE: THE CHARACTER OF GAIUS

Trying to understand the character and personality of Gaius as emperor is difficult. The sources are wholly hostile and it is impossible for us to verify anecdotes from Dio and Suetonius regarding his cruel and unpredictable behaviour. The central question when assessing the reign of Gaius is the extent to which his behaviour can be put down to insanity. How can we as modern historians assess the sanity of someone who lived over 2,000 years ago?

The following reflections by modern scholars should be read when considering this central issue:

Alston, R. (2014), *Aspects of Roman History 31 BC–AD 117*, Abingdon: Routledge, pages 129–47.
Barrett, A. (1989), *Caligula: The Corruption of Power*, London: Batsford.
Winterling, A. (2015), *Caligula: A Biography*, Oakland: University of California Press.

TIMESPAN REVIEW

- Assess how the senate and the people react when Gaius becomes emperor.
- Analyse how Gaius displays his cruelty during the second part of his reign.
- Evaluate the evidence there is to show that Gaius thought himself to be a living god.
- Discuss how the assassination is presented by the sources.

Further Reading

Barrett, A. (1989), *Caligula: The Corruption of Power*, London: Batsford.
Katz, R.S. (1972), 'The Illness of Caligula', in *The Classical World* Vol.65, No. 7: 223–5.
Simpson, C.J. (1981), 'The Cult of the Emperor Gaius', in Latomus T.40. Fasc. 3: 489–511.
Winterling, A. (2015), *Caligula: A Biography*, Oakland: University of California Press.

PRACTICE QUESTIONS

AS Level

1. How far do the sources show that Gaius was universally unpopular during his reign?

You must use and analyse the ancient sources you have studied as well as your own knowledge to support your answer. [30]

A Level

1. Read the interpretation below.

Gaius' assumption of divinity was an extreme reaction to his problems, but it was not, in itself, the act of a madman. His religious representation may be seen as a means of displaying authority. We must remember that Gaius numbered among his ancestors Venus, Mars, Romulus, Hercules, Divus Julius and Divus Augustus. When interpreted in the context of contemporary religious practice and attitudes towards the imperial position, Gaius' policy may have been misconceived, but it was not revolutionary.

Richard Alston, *Aspects of Roman History, 31 BC–AD 117*

How convincing do you find Alston's interpretation of Gaius' divine pretensions?

You must use your knowledge of the historical period and the ancient sources you have studied to analyse and evaluate Alston's interpretation. [20]

1.4 Claudius, AD 41–54

TIMESPAN OVERVIEW

- The difficulties of the accession
- The presentation of Claudius' role in, and motives for, the invasion of Britain
- The importance of his wives and freedmen
- Claudius' relationship with Nero and Britannicus
- The events surrounding his death
- Administrative changes to Rome
- Relations with the Senate, Equestrians and ordinary people of Rome

The prescribed sources for this timespan are:

- Dio Cassius, *Roman History* 60.3.1.7, 6.1–7.4, 14.1–16.4, 17.8–18.4
- Josephus, *Jewish Antiquities* 19.158–64, 227–36, 254–62; 20.148, 151–2
- Pliny the Elder, *Natural History* 36.124, 36.122–3, 33.134
- Seneca the Younger, *On the Shortness of Life* 18.5–6
- Suetonius, *Claudius* 10–14, 17–18, 20–2, 25, 29, 36, 44–5
- Tacitus, *Annals* 3.65; 11.24; 12.25–6; 12.41; 12.65–9

- Cippus inscription on the Claudian extension to the pomerium
- Coins (identified by references in LACTOR 19)
    - Aurei (J3b; J12b; N22)
    - Dupondius (K13);
- Inscription from Claudius' harbour AD 46
- Inscription on the Freedman Procurator of Ostia;
- Letter of Claudius to the Alexandrians

KEY INDIVIDUAL

Claudius
Dates: 10 BC–AD 54

The uncle of Gaius; Roman Emperor 41–54

Claudius' reign highlights various themes and issues within the principate. One fundamental issue was that Rome required an autocratic ruler, but one who constantly had to mollify an urban aristocracy. Claudius' reign also highlights the issues with source bias, as he is seemingly unfairly treated by most of the later sources.

THE DIFFICULTIES OF THE ACCESSION

The murder of Gaius on 24 January 41 was unprecedented, but established assassination as a viable political tool. It also caused a constitutional crisis. After the death of the princeps without an heir, the question was: 'What happens now?'

The key sources for Claudius' accession are Suetonius (*Claudius* 10–11 (PS)), Dio (60.3.1–7 (PS)) and Josephus (*Jewish Antiquities* 19.158–64 (PS), 227–36 (PS), 254–62 (PS)). Perhaps the most striking aspect is that, in the initial stages at least, the man himself did not play an active role. Suetonius (*Claudius* 10 (PS)) calls Claudius' accession 'an extraordinary accident'. While the sources disagree on location, all agree that Claudius was discovered hiding after Gaius' assassination. The Praetorian Guard discovered him, the significance of which cannot be overstated. Suetonius also recalls that once Claudius had decided to accept the principate, he 'promised every [Praetorian Guard] 15,000 sesterces, which made him the first of the Caesars to purchase the loyalty of his troops'.

PRESCRIBED SOURCE

Title: *Life of Claudius*

Date: *c.* AD 120–5

Author: Suetonius

Genre: Biography

Significance: Characterised by anecdotal stories and gossip, nevertheless it is a compelling source on popular attitudes

Prescribed sections: 10–14, 17–18, 20–2, 25, 29, 36, 44–5

Read it here: *Suetonius: The Twelve Caesars*, trans. R. Graves (London: Penguin, 1957, 2007)

PRESCRIBED SOURCE

Title: *History of Rome*

Author: Dio Cassius

Date: Third century AD

Genre: History

Significance: A detailed, secondary account of Claudius' reign, part of which survives only in the summaries provided by Xiphilinus and Zonaras

Prescribed sections: 60.3.1.7, 6.1–7.4, 14.1–16.4, 17.8–18.4

Read it here: LACTOR 19: Tiberius to Nero (London: KCL, 2002)

PRESCRIBED SOURCE

Title: *Jewish Antiquities*

Author: Josephus

Date: *c.* AD 94

Genre: History

Significance: Earliest surviving testimony to the events described, which also used at least one contemporary record, most likely the account of Marcus Cluvius Rufus

Prescribed sections: 19.158–64, 201–11, 227–36, 254–62; 20.148, 151–2

Read it here: LACTOR 19: Tiberius to Nero (London: KCL, 2002)

PRESCRIBED SOURCE

Aureus of Claudius (Figure 1.19)

Date: AD 41–5

Obverse: Laureate head of Claudius; 'Tiberius Claudius Caesar Augustus, pontifex maximus, with tribunician power'

Reverse: Claudius wearing a toga, clasping the hand of a long-haired soldier with shield and legionary eagle; 'With the praetorians having been received'

Significance: Claudius' relationship with the soldiers is stressed, reinforcing the basis for his power

View it here: J12b in LACTOR 19: Tiberius to Nero (London: KCL, 2002)

FIGURE 1.19
Aureus of Claudius.

The commemoration of this event on Claudian coinage ensured that it would not be forgotten, and reinforced Claudius' reliance on the loyalty of the military. But note that on the *aureus* in Fig 1.19 the Praetorians are portrayed as 'being received' by the new princeps rather than proclaiming him themselves. This is an important distinction, but ultimately unconvincing.

The Senate in particular must have recognised that the army, for so long the guarantee of the power of the princeps, was now the real political force in the Roman world. Indeed this moment more than any other highlights that the Senate was now a spent force: the military effectively settled the matter of the succession while the Senate dithered.

Study question
Examine the earlier Timespans on pp. 8–30, 31–40 and 41–51. Where else have the military been seen to be flexing their political muscles?

PRESCRIBED SOURCE

Title: *Annals*

Author: Tacitus

Date: Early second century AD

Genre: History

Significance: Fullest account of this latter period of Claudius' reign. However, we need to be aware of Tacitus' own bias as a late-first-century AD senator with decidedly republican sentiments

Prescribed sections: 11.24; 12.25–6; 12.41; 12.65–9

Read it here: LACTOR 19: Tiberius to Nero (London: KCL, 2002)

Dio (*Roman History* 60.1.1 (PS)) records how 'many different views were expressed'. Some advocated a return to the Republic. Others continued the idea of a principate, with different factions suggesting their own candidates. Not the least of these was Vinicianus, betraying his motivation for plotting Gaius' assassination. The lack of unity and agreement within the senatorial body is striking and supports the Tiberian assertion that they were 'men fit to be slaves' (Tacitus, *Annals* 3.65 (PS)).

Faced with the determined action of the Praetorians, the Senate had little choice but to give in. Josephus remarks that 'a return to senatorial government was totally unrealistic' (*Jewish Antiquities* 19.225) and this indeed seems to be the case as he presents the matter, with soldiery and plebs keen to maintain the principate (19.228 (PS)). Despite the Senate's bravado (19.230 (PS)), it is clear they actually had very little influence (19.234 (PS)).

After two days of uncertainty, Claudius was established as princeps. He swiftly obliterated the records that a new constitution had been considered during these forty-eight hours (Suetonius, *Claudius* 11 (PS)) and established a general amnesty. This was sensible, but was also designed to convey immediately his avoidance of tyrannical attitudes. Nevertheless, although Claudius may have wished for an era of moderation, the circumstances of his accession cast a shadow over his entire reign. His military backing put an end to the princeps being seen as first among equals. This did irreparable damage to Claudius' relationship with the Senate, even though he did much to present himself as attempting to return to the model of Augustus. This is seen particularly in his attitude towards the imperial cult, as exemplified by his letter to the Alexandrians in 41 (PS) where he deliberately refuses to be acknowledged as a god. We may suggest that this was a sound policy for an emperor keen to reinforce his parity with the Senate, even though the circumstances of his accession made clear this was a facade.

PRESCRIBED SOURCE

Letter of Claudius to the Alexandrians

Author: Claudius

Date: AD 41

Significance: Claudius rejects the notion that he should be worshipped as a god, marking a deliberate break with the policy of Gaius

Read it here: L17 in LACTOR 19: Tiberius to Nero (London: KCL, 2002)

THE PRESENTATION OF CLAUDIUS' ROLE IN, AND MOTIVES FOR, THE INVASION OF BRITAIN

The campaign against Britain in 43 is inextricably linked with the events of the preceding year, in particular the revolt of Camillus Scribonianus. Following the execution of Gaius Appius Silanus (Dio 60.14.1–16.4 **PS**; Suetonius *Claudius* 13 **PS**), who was accused of plotting Claudius' death and executed on spurious evidence, Camillus was encouraged by Vinicianus to turn his troops against Claudius. The revolt was short-lived, lasting no more than five days, as Camillus could not convince sufficient forces to support his cause. Dio states that his soldiers 'refused to listen to him any longer' (*Roman History* 60.15.3 **PS**). Camillus' suicide after his failure was hastily followed by his denouncement as a public enemy.

While the revolt was fruitless, it nevertheless reduced Claudius to a state of great terror. His immediate response was to bestow the titles 'Claudian', 'Loyal' and 'Patriotic' on the Seventh and Eleventh Legions, which had remained faithful to him. But he needed the loyalty of the army as a whole, and thus sought a quick campaign that would give the army both plunder and glory. In truth there had not been a significant campaign for many years, not since that of Drusus, Claudius' father, in Germany in 12–9 BC, the continued significance of which may be seen in the Claudian coinage commemorating those victories (Fig 1.20 **PS**).

The significance of his connection with Drusus, and also his brother Germanicus, had been a major factor in securing the loyalty of the army during his early reign. Claudius' campaign against Britain would now ensure military credentials of his own. No one had attempted an invasion of Britain since Julius Caesar in 54 BC, and the military triumph that would follow a successful campaign would strengthen Claudius' position.

FIGURE 1.20
Aureus of Drusus.

> **PRESCRIBED SOURCE**
>
> **Aureus of Drusus (Figure 1.20)**
>
> **Date:** AD 41–5
>
> **Obverse:** Laureate head of Drusus; 'Nero Claudius Drusus Germanicus, Commander'
>
> **Reverse:** Two shields crossed, with two pairs of crossed spears and trumpets, in front of standard; 'Over Germany'
>
> **Significance:** Claudius is stressing his connection with his father as a means of ensuring the loyalty of the troops
>
> **View it here:** J3b in LACTOR 19: Tiberius to Nero (London: KCL, 2002)

However, not all our sources praise this campaign: Suetonius describes it as 'of no great importance' (*Claudius* 17 **PS**). However, the preparations were meticulous and four legions set out under the command of Aulus Plautius in the summer of 43. The campaign was primarily directed against the anti-Roman Catavellauni, who were expanding their territory and influence under the rule of the two sons of the recently deceased Cunobelinus, Togidumnus and Caratacus. The actions of the Catavellauni, while no real threat to Roman interests, were nevertheless a useful justification for the campaign.

Plautius advanced to the river Medway, ably assisted by Flavius Vespasianus (the future emperor Vespasian), commander of the Second Legion Augusta. Following a decisive Roman victory here, the British tribes withdrew to the Thames where, even with Togidumnus dead, they rallied, preventing Plautius from crossing the river. The Roman commander chose to consolidate his position and sent for Claudius himself for the final stages of the campaign.

Claudius' crossing to Britain was swiftly achieved, although Suetonius (*Claudius* 17 **PS**) suggests that he was nearly wrecked twice en route to Massilia (modern Marseilles). However, Dio makes no mention of these hardships, which suggests that Suetonius may have included the allegation because it fits into his overall presentation of Claudius as a bumbling incompetent.

In Britain, Claudius took command of the legions, crossed the Thames, defeated the enemy and captured Camulodunum (modern Colchester), which had served as Cunobelinus' capital. Although Dio highlights the campaign's speed and efficiency, we must question the degree of opposition which the British tribes could have offered against a Roman force now approaching 40,000 men.

However, the campaign certainly achieved Claudius' immediate goal of military glory. The Senate granted him (and his son) the title of 'Britannicus', and offered him the

> **KEY INDIVIDUAL**
>
> **Britannicus**
> **Dates:** AD 41–55
>
> Son of Claudius and his third wife Messalina. His accession was derailed by Agrippina and her promotion of Nero.

PRESCRIBED SOURCE

Aureus of Claudius (Figure 1.21)

Date: AD 46–7

Obverse: Laureate head of Claudius; 'Tiberius Claudius Caesar Augustus, pontifex maximus, in his 6th year of tribunician power, hailed as victorious commander 11 times'

Reverse: Triumphal arch surmounted by an equestrian statue between two trophies; 'Over Britain'

Significance: Celebration of the British triumph

View it here: N22 in LACTOR 19: Tiberius to Nero (London: KCL, 2002)

FIGURE 1.21
Aureus of Claudius. **PS**

PRESCRIBED SOURCE

Cippus inscription on the Claudian extension to the pomerium

Date: AD 49

Location: Southeast of Monte Testaccio in Rome

Significance: Formal commemoration of Claudius' right to extend Rome's sacred boundary

Read it here: N24 in LACTOR 19: Tiberius to Nero (London: KCL, 2002)

EXPLORE FURTHER

Read Tacitus' account of Caratacus' treatment in Rome at *Annals* 12.35–37. How is Claudius presented here?

honour of celebrating a triumph. Claudius celebrated this triumph in 44, after perhaps six months' absence from Rome (Suetonius, *Claudius* 17 **PS**), although he may himself have been in Britain for as little as sixteen days.

The triumph was particularly splendid (Suetonius, *Claudius* 17 **PS**). It is clear that both this and the campaign were continuing sources of legitimacy and glory from coins minted between 46 and 50. These commemorated the invasion and his triumphal arch (itself not completed until 51).

Similarly, Claudius in 49 took advantage of an archaic ceremony, last used by Augustus, that the extension of the empire should be mirrored by extending the pomerium. Its commemorative inscription **PS** extols his official titles and the benefit his campaign brought Rome.

Finally, in 50, after a series of further battles, Caratacus was captured and brought to Rome as a prisoner. Thus the British invasion had achieved perhaps more than even Claudius could have hoped: a solid military campaign, carried out efficiently, resulting in opportunities for political praise. Suetonius' lukewarm assessment of the campaign is, therefore, curious, but can be understood if we consider that even the success of this campaign could not overshadow the perceived shortcomings in Claudius' reign.

THE IMPORTANCE OF CLAUDIUS' WIVES AND FREEDMEN, INCLUDING THEIR ROLE IN AFFECTING THE RELATIONSHIPS BETWEEN CLAUDIUS, NERO AND BRITANNICUS

A key criticism of Claudius surrounded the role ascribed to, and the treatment of, his wives and freedmen. Suetonius (*Claudius* 25 **PS**) gives the standard view of the imperial court:

> One might say that everything Claudius did throughout his reign was dictated by his wives and freedmen: he practically always obeyed their whims rather than his own judgement.

Dio also speaks caustically of the offences of wives and freedmen alike (*Roman History* 60.17.8 **PS**).

The sources' opinions on the freedmen and wives are almost universally negative: they were perceived as being the real powers behind the throne, accruing enormous importance and wealth (e.g. Pliny the Elder, *Natural History* 33.134 **PS**) and promoting themselves well above their (perceived) station. In a principate that had begun with a poor relationship between princeps and Senate, this meant that the rift never healed.

The demands of running the empire had long exceeded the capacity of a single individual. Claudius acknowledged this and utilised his freedmen effectively as a civil service: an imperial secretariat. While he did not create this bureaucratic body, he

PRESCRIBED SOURCE

Title: *Natural History*

Author: Pliny the Elder

Date: Published *c.* AD 77

Genre: Encyclopaedia

Significance: Contemporary perspective on significant events in the late Julio-Claudian and early Flavian periods

Prescribed sections: 36.124, 36.122–3, 33.134

Read it here: K24, K21, S25 in LACTOR 19: Tiberius to Nero (London: KCL, 2002)

institutionalised it, with his individual freedmen becoming political figures of huge significance. Our sources highlight three pre-eminent members of the group:

- Callistus, who was in charge of petitions;
- Narcissus, Chief Secretary, in charge of correspondence; and
- Pallas, treasurer and chief accountant.

Inevitably perhaps, given their positions, and the fact that they fulfilled administrative roles historically held by the Senate, these individuals are vilified by our senatorially sympathetic sources. There was great resentment at the wealth they gathered, which Dio states was partly due to their 'offering for sale and peddling not merely citizenships and military commands and procuratorships and provincial governorships, but everything else as well' (*Roman History* 60.17.8 **PS**). Their political influence and privileged access to the emperor were also disliked. Suetonius (*Claudius* 29 **PS**) lists a series of Claudius' actions carried out at the behest of his freedmen, though the most telling is the execution of thirty-five senators and 300 equites. The incorporation of this detail links these murders implicitly with the influence of the freedmen.

Although the role of the freedmen was later a reason to criticise Claudius, the contemporary Senate do not seem to have been averse to courting their favour: both Tacitus and Pliny the Younger record that the Senate authorised a bronze statue of Pallas on 23 January 52. We need to remember that this imperial secretariat was created to make up for the shortcomings of the Senate. Moreover, the Claudian administration was incredibly effective, and characterised by long-term planning and an overhaul of fundamental infrastructures in which the freedmen must have played a role. The criticisms of the Senate (and later sources) about the rapacity of the freedmen are rather examples of 'the pot calling the kettle black': Josephus records that the plebs and provincials favoured a sole princeps because he acted as 'a curb to the rapacity of the Senate' (*Jewish Antiquities* 19.228 **PS**).

Turning to Claudius' wives, his first two marriages – to Plautia Urgulanilla and Aelia Paetina – produced little of political significance, aside from Paetina giving birth to a healthy daughter, Claudia Antonia. Indeed, the casting aside of these women shows just how transient marriages could be in the political crucible of the principate.

However, Claudius' third marriage to Valeria Messalina was far more significant. Although she produced two children, Claudia Octavia and, in 48, a son Tiberius Claudius (later renamed Britannicus), Messalina was a cause of humiliation and discord for Claudius, according to our sources. Her name became a byword for sexual excess (e.g. Dio 60.17.8–18.4 **PS**).

Official messages presenting the unity of the imperial family (see 'Explore Further' left) may be nicely contrasted with the presentation of Messalina in the later sources. Suetonius mentions her 'disgraceful crimes' and her affairs, while the satirist Juvenal delights in cataloguing her numerous adulteries. Tacitus records the most damning evidence against her: an affair with Gaius Silius culminating in their bigamous 'marriage', while Claudius is away at Ostia. Tacitus suggests that the pair wish to usurp the imperial position, but are prevented by Narcissus, who has Claudius informed of the outrage and then leads soldiers to end the attempted coup.

Messalina was executed. Although she was not mourned, she had to be replaced. Each freedman suggested their own choice: Tacitus declares that this 'wrenched apart the princeps' household'. The woman eventually selected was Pallas' candidate, Agrippina the Younger, Claudius' own niece. Agrippina had distinct advantages – blood relative of Augustus, daughter of Germanicus, and with a young son who was also a Julian. Thus her name held powerful political associations.

For more on the political significance of this marriage, see pp. 69–70; here we may focus on her impact on Claudius' reign. Her key influence was the promotion of her own son ahead of the princeps' own son Britannicus (Tacitus, *Annals* 12.25–6 **PS**). The precedence that Claudius gave him on his adoption in 50 (see Tacitus *Annals* 12.41 **PS**), when he changed his name to Nero to reflect his entry into the Claudian family, showed how much influence Agrippina now exerted at court.

Eventually, in 54, the year of his death, Claudius began to hint that he was growing weary of Agrippina's activities. Narcissus also seems to have actively opposed Agrippina and her promotion of Nero (*Annals* 12.65 **PS**), highlighting the factionalism within the imperial court. Agrippina's concern over Claudius' possible reprisals led to an acceleration of her actions, suggesting that her entire relationship with Claudius was designed solely for achieving the pre-eminence of Nero. Both Tacitus (*Annals* 12.66–7 **PS**) and Suetonius (*Claudius* 44–5 **PS**) allege Agrippina's involvement in poisoning Claudius. Thus Claudius' fourth wife certainly seems to have been the cause of his downfall.

ADMINISTRATIVE CHANGES TO ROME

Thus far the positives of Claudius' reign are somewhat hidden. However, there is much to commend in Claudius' principate, as it is characterised by a distinct focus on administration and infrastructure (e.g. Suetonius, *Claudius* 18 **PS**; Dio 60.6.1–7.4 **PS**), as well as a healthy understanding of the value that the Romans placed on traditionalism (Suetonius, *Claudius* 22 **PS**).

The urgency of such a focus is exemplified by the fact that upon Claudius' accession there was only seven or eight days' food supply remaining (Seneca, *On the Shortness of Life* 18.5–6 **PS**). The deprivations and excesses of Gaius had virtually bankrupted Rome, as he squandered Tiberius' accrued funds of 2,700 million sesterces within a year (see p. 45). Claudius' desire to secure and maintain the grain supply is recorded on a series of coins (e.g. Fig 1.22 **PS**).

The low denomination of the coin in Figure 1.21 shows that this message was primarily for the urban plebs who received the corn dole. Claudius' focus on the day-to-day necessities of urban life is also evidenced in his development of the harbour at Ostia.

PRESCRIBED SOURCE

Inscription from Claudius' harbour

Date: AD 46

Location: Ostia

Significance:
Commemoration of Claudius' construction of the new harbour at Ostia

Read it here: K16 in LACTOR 19: Tiberius to Nero (London: KCL, 2002)

PRESCRIBED SOURCE

Title: *On the Shortness of Life*

Author: Seneca the Younger

Date: AD 49

Genre: Philosophical/didactic treatise

Significance: Seneca describes the shortage of grain reserves at the accession of Claudius

Prescribed sections: 18.5–6

Read it here: K12 in LACTOR 19: Tiberius to Nero (London: KCL, 2002)

PRESCRIBED SOURCE

Dupondius of Claudius (Figure 1.22)

Date: Uncertain

Obverse: Head of Claudius; 'Tiberius Claudius Caesar Augustus, pontifex maximus, with tribunician power, hailed as victorious commander'

Reverse: Ceres, veiled and draped, sitting on an ornamental throne, holding two ears of corn in her right hand and long torch in her left; 'Augustan goddess of corn'

Significance: Claudius commemorates his supervision of Rome's corn supply

View it here: K13 in LACTOR 19: Tiberius to Nero (London: KCL, 2002)

FIGURE 1.22
Dupondius of Claudius.

This was a key pillar of his infrastructural overhaul, as commemorated in its monumental inscription **PS**. It is also telling that he appointed an imperial freedman to administer the harbour (see **PS** below left), again reinforcing the significance of the project, as he wished to oversee the harbour directly through his de facto civil service.

This extensive engineering project was not completed until perhaps 64, but it reinforces Claudius' long-term planning and his desire to ensure that Rome was well-supplied beyond his reign. A similar strategy is shown in Claudius' completion of Gaius' aqueducts Anio Novus and Aqua Claudia (Pliny the Elder, *Natural History* 36.122–3 **PS**). These almost doubled Rome's supply, bringing water to all fourteen Augustan districts. The security that such developments guaranteed for Rome again shows Claudius' intention to ensure that Rome would not be in difficulty even after his own death. In this respect, Claudius' building programme and administration may be said to have been more practical and effective than Augustus', which perhaps addressed needs more cultural and 'spiritual'.

Not all of Claudius' projects were so successful, however. His development of the Fucine Lake area as an agricultural hot-spot was, according to Tacitus, carelessly completed. However, it was well intentioned, designed to secure Rome's food supplies, while simultaneously reducing the dependence on Egyptian corn, and Pliny the Elder (*Natural History* 36.124 **PS**) is far more positive. Suetonius (*Claudius* 20 **PS**) is impressed by the sheer scale of the works, using some 30,000 men, which shows the organisational capacity of Claudius' administration.

Beyond his infrastructural innovations, Claudius' prime concern seems to have been the legal system, where he took a keen personal interest, frequently judging cases himself (Suetonius, *Claudius* 14 **PS**). However, the sources turn this into another criticism: an unhealthy passion for passing judgement. His unpredictability is most remarked upon, which brought widespread contempt. However, Suetonius was biased against Claudius, easily exploiting his concern for law and legal procedure to demonstrate his 'tyrannical zeal'.

Finally, we must acknowledge Claudius' role as **censor**, a position which Suetonius notes had lapsed for thirty-four years. This again emphatically recollects the reign of Augustus, who used the lustra as a means of demonstrating the prosperity of the Empire under the Augustan settlement (*Res Gestae* 8.2–4 **PS**).

Claudius' concern for the welfare of the empire is marked by his pronouncement in 48 that 5,984,072 citizens were registered under his lustrum, a notable increase on the final Augustan quota of 4,937,000 in AD 14. This desire for stability and progress is also behind Claudius' proposal to alter the make-up of the Senate by admitting Gauls (Tacitus, *Annals* 11.24 **PS**). This had several advantages:

- It introduced new blood into a Senate no longer fit for purpose.
- It made the Senate a more representative body for the wider Empire.
- It reaffirmed the princeps' willingness to continue to work with the Senate.

Although in fact it did not heal the rift with that body, there were now individuals who owed their senatorial rank to Claudius himself.

PRESCRIBED SOURCE

Inscription on the Freedman Procurator of Ostia

Date: Unknown

Location: Ostia

Significance: A short inscription that reiterates Claudius' use of his imperial freedmen to oversee key areas of administration

Read it here: K17 in LACTOR 19: Tiberius to Nero (London: KCL, 2002)

---

censor a magistrate responsible for updating and maintaining the census of Roman citizens

Compare and contrast Tacitus' version of the speech delivered by Claudius (*Annals* 11.24 **PS**) with the original, preserved as an inscription upon a bronze tablet at Lugdunum (LACTOR 19, M11). What can we learn of the character of Claudius from his own words? What does this also highlight about Tacitus' writing?

RELATIONS WITH THE SENATE, EQUESTRIANS AND ORDINARY PEOPLE OF ROME

It is argued that the Senate, overall, had a poor relationship with Claudius, but although our sources suggest sufficient aspects to his governance that would have led to objections from the Senate, they give little evidence of formal opposition (Suetonius, *Claudius* 13, 36 **PS**). Despite Claudius' efforts with the Senate, it is clear that his relationship with them was never easy. He seemed to enjoy greater success with the other classes of Roman society.

Certain privileges were extended to the equestrians, such as the right of admission to the imperial presence, identified by wearing a golden ring decorated with an image of the princeps. However, given the allegation that 300 equestrians were executed in his reign, combined with other vague anecdotes in Suetonius, it seems the class was not entirely favoured.

It was perhaps with the plebs that Claudius enjoyed his strongest relationship, aside from the army. His securing of the grain and water supplies were popular measures not to be overlooked. Claudius lavished largesse and entertainment upon the people (Suetonius, *Claudius* 21 **PS**). Dio also surveys Claudius' treatment of the various sections of society (60.6.1–7.4 **PS**), highlighting not only his eye for detail, but his concern that the city should be well administered.

His popularity with the plebs is clear from the rumour (attested by Suetonius) of public dismay when he was reported to have been killed on the Ostia road (*Claudius* 12 **PS**). This affection from the people was a natural result of the degree of care and patronage that he had extended to the city and people. He fully embedded the role of princeps as effectively being the *pater familias* to the entire Roman people, a role which subsequent emperors would honour or abuse in equal measure.

Study question
Read Suetonius *Claudius* 21 **PS**. How many different forms of entertainment provided by Claudius for the people are mentioned?

THE EVENTS SURROUNDING CLAUDIUS' DEATH

Claudius' death, on 13 October 54, is frequently cited as being symbolic of the vicissitudes that blighted the Julio-Claudian dynasty. Suetonius and Tacitus assign Agrippina a key role stage-managing the situation to allow for the supremacy of Nero to be established (*Claudius* 44–5 **PS**; *Annals* 12.65–9 **PS**; see also Josephus *Jewish Antiquities* 20.148; 151–2 **PS** and p. 69). Claudius' rather ignominious end drew the curtain on a reign which perhaps more than any other highlights the bias of our sources, requiring us to be particularly cautious in our treatment of them.

EXPLORE FURTHER

The *Apocolocyntosis* (see LACTOR 19, section F) is one of the most interesting sources on Claudius' reign. The text is ascribed to Seneca, Nero's tutor, and seems to have been a piece of 'after-dinner entertainment' for the young emperor and his cronies. It is a vicious satire of Claudius and his reign, which may in some degree be due to the fact that Seneca was exiled by Claudius in 41.

PRESCRIBED DEBATE: THE CHARACTER OF CLAUDIUS

Some earlier scholars suggest that Claudius is little more than a befuddled old man, completely in thrall to the influence of his wives and freedmen. Others interpret Claudius as being a fine example for a princeps – indeed Vespasian (the first Flavian emperor) certainly modelled much of his activity on Claudian precedents.

Try to read as widely as possible about this issue. You might like to start with the following reflections by modern scholars:

Dickison, S.K. (1977), 'Claudius: Saturnalicius Princeps', in Latomus, T. 36, Fasc. 3 (JUILLET–SEPTEMBRE 1977), pp. 634–47.
Levick, B. (1993), *Claudius*, Abingdon: Routledge.
Ramage, E.S. (1983), 'Denigration of Predecessor under Claudius, Galba, and Vespasian', in Historia: Zeitschrift für Alte Geschichte, Bd. 32, H. 2 (2nd Qtr., 1983), pp. 201–14.
Weaver, P.R.C. (1965), 'Freedmen Procurators in the Imperial Administration', in Historia: Zeitschrift für Alte Geschichte, Bd. 14, H. 4 (Oct., 1965), pp. 460–9.

TIMESPAN REVIEW

- Evaluate the extent to which Claudius conforms to the impression that Suetonius gives us of his being a confused old man.
- Discuss the extent to which Claudius' reign can be seen as a restoration.
- Explain how limited we are in our ability to understand the plebeian attitude towards Claudius.
- Assess the reliability of the source accounts of this period.

Further Reading

Alston, R. (2014), *Aspects of Roman History 31 BC-AD 117* (Routledge): pp. 148–72.
Garzetti, A. (1974), *From Tiberius to the Antonines* (Methuen &Co: London): pp. 106–45.
Levick, B. (1993), *Claudius* (Routledge).

PRACTICE QUESTIONS

AS Level

1. Explain why the circumstances of Claudius' accession are complicated.

[10]

A Level

1. Read the interpretation below.

> As to [Claudius'] conscious aims and achievements, the material . . . yields the portrait of an emperor who began his usurping reign with a heroic double effort, in conciliating the nobility, above all in invading Britain, to secure his position. Both proved inadequate against the resentment that his usurpation caused, and in 48 fissures developing amongst his own supporters weakened his political position still further. At no stage did Claudius dare to give up manipulation as his main political weapon or to assume the full weight of the Principate as he had helped to make it.

B. Levick, *Claudius* p.196

How convincing do you find Levick's interpretation of Claudius' reign?
You must use your knowledge of the historical period and the ancient sources you have studied to analyse and evaluate Levick's interpretation.

[20]

1.5 Nero, AD 54–68

TIMESPAN OVERVIEW

- The presentation of Nero as emperor by the ancient sources
- The early part of his reign and the changing role of Agrippina
- The importance of his wives
- Piso's conspiracy in AD 65
- Tacitus' and Suetonius' accounts of the Great Fire of Rome in AD 64
- The achievements of Corbulo in Armenia
- The revolt of Vindex
- The death of Nero and the accession of Galba
- Nero's attitude towards religion, including the imperial cult inside and outside Rome
- Administrative changes to Rome
- Relations with the Senate, Equestrians and ordinary people of Rome

The prescribed sources for this timespan are:

- Dio Cassius, *Roman History* 63.22.1–26.1, 63.26.3–27.1, 63.27.2–29.3
- Pliny, *Natural History* 34.45–6, 36.111
- Suetonius, *Nero* 10–11, 20–3, 26–7, 31–2, 34, 38, 40–9, 53
- Tacitus, *Annals* 12.41, 12.65–9, 14.1–16, 15.37–44, 15.48–74

- Coins (identified by references in LACTOR 19)
  - Aurei (J21b, J30a, L25)
  - Denarii (P13b, P13f)
  - Sestertii (N51, Q14)
  - As (Q13)

Nero marks the end of the Julio-Claudian dynasty and his reign has come to epitomise the excesses of the principate. Care is needed to separate fact from fiction, and balance the hostility of the sources against the (albeit few) positive aspects of Nero's governance.

THE PRESENTATION OF NERO AS EMPEROR BY THE ANCIENT SOURCES

The presentation of Nero in the sources is rarely positive, but various authors at least allow him a **quinquennium aureum**, five 'golden years', at the start of his reign (e.g. Suetonius, *Nero* 10–11 **PS**). In this period he seems to do what is expected, such as deifying his adopted father Claudius (see Fig 1.23 **PS** and Tacitus *Annals* 12.69 **PS**), as Augustus did Julius Caesar.

One consistent criticism of Nero is his **philhellenism**: love of all things Greek. Far from being a compliment, this implied a disregard for Roman values. His love of music and theatre, highlighted in Suetonius (*Nero*, 20–3 **PS**) becomes perhaps the defining characteristic of his reign. He even toured Greece for two years, performing in the

> **quinquennium aureum** 'A Golden Five Years', typically applied to the opening of Nero's reign
>
> **philhellenism** the love of Greek culture

PRESCRIBED SOURCE

Aureus showing Claudius' deification (Figure 1.23)

Date: AD 54

Obverse: Laureate head of Claudius; 'Divine Claudius Augustus'

Reverse: Ornamental four-horse chariot surmounted by miniature set of four horses flanked by Victories; 'By decree of the Senate'

Significance: Demonstrates the filial piety of Nero, also giving him further auctoritas as emperor

View it here: L25 in LACTOR 19: *Tiberius to Nero* (London: KCL, 2002)

FIGURE 1.23
Aureus showing Claudius' deification.

PRESCRIBED SOURCE

Title: *Life of Nero*

Date: *c.* AD 120–5

Author: Suetonius

Genre: Biography

Significance: Although characterised by anecdotal stories and gossip, Suetonius' biography is a compelling source on popular attitudes

Prescribed sections: 10–11, 20–3, 26–7, 31–2, 34, 38, 40–9, 53

Read it here: *Suetonius: The Twelve Caesars*, trans. R. Graves (London: Penguin, 1957, 2007)

various festivals. Such behaviour, coupled with his interest in chariot-racing, infuriated the traditional moral conservatism of authors such as Tacitus:

> It was an old desire of his to stand in the racer of a four-horse team, and a no less foul enthusiasm to sing to the lyre as if at the games.

Tacitus, *Annals* 14.14

Tacitus here reveals his snobbery towards activities considered beneath the dignity of the Roman elite. Indeed, he seems to delight in describing the 'outrages' of Nero, presenting him as a corrupting influence upon Roman society (e.g. *Annals* 14.15, 15.37 **PS**). A picture of the young princeps emerges: drawn to unsuitable activities; keen on a foreign culture; and actively inciting others to join in his 'shame'. Suetonius and Dio also highlight the social, religious, and sexual excesses of Nero (e.g. Suetonius *Nero*, 26–7, 30, 53 **PS**). Nero himself openly celebrated his sense of being cultured, such as on the *as* of 62 **PS**, where he portrayed himself as a lyre-player. While for Nero it may have spoken of sophistication, such images would have merely fuelled the source authors' hostility to him.

The most unusual of Nero's excesses is the so-called Colossus. This immense bronze statue of Nero was placed near the centre of the city (Suetonius *Nero*, 31 **PS**). Pliny the Elder (*Natural History*, 34.45–6 **PS**) states that Nero would have been prepared to pay for casting the statue in silver or gold. Thus the Colossus becomes a by-word for self-indulgence, a symbol of Nero's desire for immortality in the arts.

It must be remembered that none of these sources is balanced or objective. While Nero was certainly unpopular at the time of his death, it is interesting that in 69, Otho could draw support by citing his Neronian connections. Dio also reports that a pseudo-Nero (an imposter), Terentius Maximus, gathered followers in the east during the reign of Titus (*Roman History* 66.19.3). If, over a decade after his death, Nero's name could still attract popular support, any loathing of him cannot have been 'universal'.

THE EARLY PART OF NERO'S REIGN AND THE CHANGING ROLE OF AGRIPPINA

Nero was sixteen when he ascended to the throne in 54. The transfer of power was stage-managed by key figures in the imperial household: Agrippina, Burrus and Seneca. Nero was presented to the Praetorian Cohorts (see Tacitus, *Annals* 12.65–9 **PS**) and Claudius' own son, Britannicus, was delayed in the palace by Agrippina (12.68 **PS**). From the outset this presents him as a usurper, despite his blood relationship to Augustus.

It is clear that Agrippina was instrumental to her son's acquisition of power, and her marriage to Claudius seems to have been designed solely for that end (see Tacitus, *Annals* 12.41 **PS**, on the early promotion of Nero). This behaviour is consistent with her wider portrayal in the sources (e.g. Tacitus, *Annals* 14.2 **PS**), though the allegation that she had poisoned Claudius (Suetonius, *Claudius* 44 **PS**) is perhaps more the result of hostility than proof. Yet the speed with which Nero was rushed to the Praetorian Camp, assisted by Burrus, does indicate the political intrigue which allowed Nero, an adopted son, to replace Britannicus. The use of soldiers to endorse Nero also highlights the significance that the army now enjoyed in determining who ruled.

In the early years of Nero's reign, Agrippina clearly remained a powerful influence over him, as the aureus in Fig 1.24 **PS**, dated within months of his accession, suggests. It highlights the special relationship between mother and son: although other imperial women had featured on coinage, none had featured so prominently as Agrippina here.

Seneca and Burrus quickly found themselves in opposition to Agrippina as factions competed to guide the young princeps. Agrippina was not easily removed. Tacitus (*Annals*, 14.2 **PS**) alleges that she used sex as a means to control Nero. This may have been prompted by the emergence of an independent and ruthless streak within Nero, one that matched if did not exceed Agrippina's own. Seneca actively exploited the situation to lessen the influence of Agrippina. Agrippina even threatened to support Britannicus' claim to the throne as he was now approaching the age of maturity, but all this achieved was the murder of Britannicus by Nero at a banquet in 55.

PRESCRIBED SOURCE

Title: *Natural History*

Author: Pliny the Elder

Date: *c.* AD 77

Genre: Encyclopaedia

Significance:
Contemporary perspective on events in the late Julio-Claudian and early Flavian periods

Prescribed sections: 34.45–6, 36.111

Read it here: LACTOR 19: Tiberius to Nero (London: KCL, 2002)

KEY INDIVIDUAL

Sextus Afranius Burrus
Dates: AD 1–62

A favourite of Agrippina, through whose influence he was appointed as sole Praetorian Prefect by Claudius in 51. He retained the post under Nero, to whom he was a leading advisor.

KEY INDIVIDUAL

Lucius Annaeus Seneca
Dates: 4 BC–AD 65

A very learned man, in 49, Seneca was appointed Nero's tutor. After the death of Agrippina in 59, the relationship with Nero became strained and he was eventually forced to commit suicide.

FIGURE 1.24
Aureus of Nero.

 PS

Agrippina's desire to be 'the power behind the throne' ultimately came to nothing. Tacitus (*Annals* 14.3–11 PS) gives a rich account of the plots to kill her, with Suetonius (*Nero*, 34 PS) providing his own abbreviated version. Her removal in 59 coincides with the end of Nero's quinquennium, not because she was a positive influence, but thereafter Nero seems to ignore all his advisors. The actions of Burrus and, in particular, Seneca in removing the 'threat' of Agrippina thus actually set a precedent for their own removal.

THE IMPORTANCE OF NERO'S WIVES

Nero's marriages have perhaps been underplayed in many accounts of his reign, but they reveal much about both his character and the nature of the principate at this time. Sources often present imperial women as either paragons of virtue or personifications of evil. The women in Nero's life are no exception, in particular his first wife Octavia, daughter of Claudius, and his third wife Statilia Messalina.

The marriage in 53 between Nero and Octavia established Nero's legitimacy, but it was far from happy. The Claudian credentials of Octavia were all that Nero required from her and once his reign was established he quickly supplanted her with his freedwoman Acte. His removal of Octavia, however, was particularly objectionable: Nero accused her of sexual outrages, exiling her to Pandateria and then having her murdered in 62.

Nero's next affair and marriage was with the infamous Poppaea Sabina. This marriage came hard upon the execution of Octavia: a daughter, Claudia, was born on 21 January 63. The sources allege that both Octavia and Agrippina were removed to facilitate this relationship with Poppaea, at her encouragement (see Tacitus, *Annals* 14.1 PS).

By contrast, both the coinage and the account of Josephus suggest that Poppaea was a competent and interested political figure, presenting her far more positively than do Dio and Tacitus, who described her as among the emperor's most intimate counsellors in his moments of rage (*Annals*, 15.61 PS). Yet Poppaea's influence over Nero was brief. She

S & C Octavia is commemorated in a *fabula praetexta*, a play on a historical theme. While its date and authorship are uncertain, it is unmistakeably sympathetic to Octavia. Read the *Octavia* and evaluate how Nero and Octavia are presented.

died in 65, following her own daughter Claudia, who had died aged only four months. Nero deified both of them, exceeding even the precedent of Gaius' deification of his sister Drusilla in 38. The deification seems to have been motivated by genuine affection, although guilt may have played a part, as Tacitus records that Poppaea's death was linked to Nero's attacking her while she was pregnant.

Nero took a third wife, Statilia Messalina, a great-great-granddaughter of Augustus' general Statilius Taurus, who had twice been consul and won a triumph. The choice was likely to have been motivated by a desire to appear conventional and respectable to the wider Roman public, although Suetonius states that Nero first had to murder Statilia's husband, Atticus Vestinus. Their wedding in June 66 was Statilia's fifth, and in fact she outlived her husband to marry twice more.

Nero's wives, while themselves interesting characters, are perhaps more useful for reflecting our sources' presentation of Nero and his principate: Octavia is the abused innocent; Poppaea the partner-in-crime; Statilia the political convenience. Each becomes a mirror to Nero.

THE PISONIAN CONSPIRACY IN 65

Given his excesses, there was unsurprisingly opposition to Nero, the most significant being that of the Pisonian Conspiracy of 65. Our fullest account is by Tacitus (*Annals*, 15.48–74 **PS**), who is very clear about the motivations of the various conspirators. The figurehead was Gaius Calpurnius Piso.

Tacitus makes it clear that the conspiracy was widespread, with 'senators, equestrians, soldiery, and even females' involved (*Annals*, 15.48 **PS**, repeated at 15.54 **PS**). To call it 'Piso's conspiracy' is rather a misnomer. Tacitus' description portrays an affable character rather than a political firebrand, suggesting that Piso was exploited by his co-conspirators (15.48 **PS**).

It seems that the initial conspirators were looking more to capitalise on circumstances than engineer them themselves, and that 'agitation about the time and place for the slaughter' (15.50 **PS**) only took place once Faenius Rufus, the Praetorian co-Prefect came on board. However, the conspirators were prone to indecision, suggesting that many were not inclined to bloodshed at first.

They were also concerned about would follow Nero's removal. The turmoil of 69 shows how valid these concerns were. One issue was that Piso's party was not the only faction: Tacitus mentions the worry that another senator, Lucius Silanus, might assume 'a command which would be readily offered to him by people whom the conspiracy had not touched' (15.52 **PS**).

Piso and his associates waited about four months, until the festival of Ceres (12–19 April). Flavius Scaevinus emerged as the would-be primary assailant. He was to stab Nero, with a specially procured dagger, while Piso readied himself with Antonia, Claudius' surviving daughter. Tacitus acknowledges that the details surrounding Antonia's involvement are somewhat suspect, citing the elder Pliny as his source (15.53 **PS**). However, if it is true, it is a good example of the importance of blood legitimacy, and the use of imperial women to acquire it.

KEY EVENT

The Pisonian Conspiracy
Date: AD 65

The earliest conspicuous formal opposition to Nero. An assassination plot headed by several senators and prominent equestrians.

KEY INDIVIDUAL

Gaius Calpurnius Piso
Dates: died AD 65

A senator who became the figurehead of an assassination plot against Nero in 65.

Yet the extent that this conspiracy was a serious threat to Nero is somewhat undermined by the ease with which it was dealt. A freedman of Scaevinus, Milichus, betrayed the plot (15.54 **PS**). Scaevinus' rapid arrest led to others being named, including Seneca, although there is no real evidence of his involvement: he was perhaps included to please Nero (15.56 **PS**). The speed with which those arrested gave up their comrades is condemned by Tacitus (15.57 **PS**), but may simply indicate that events had escalated beyond the capabilities of those involved. Despite being urged by some to make a play for power by heading for the Praetorian Camp and attempting to win their loyalty, Piso actually locked himself in his home, eventually taking his own life when soldiers arrived to arrest him (15.59 **PS**).

Nero used the conspiracy as an excuse to execute dozens of senators and equestrians. Not only was this a highly visible means of reasserting his authority, the confiscated property provided much-needed funds. Tacitus lists the victims of this purge (15.60–4 **PS**); of these, Seneca is particularly notable. He was Nero's guiding hand for a long time, and his death thus symbolises Nero's entire principate, revealing the emperor's inconsistencies and declining morality.

THE GREAT FIRE OF ROME IN 64

Perhaps the most infamous event of Nero's reign is the Great Fire of Rome, which broke out on 18–19 July 64 (see Tacitus, *Annals*, 38–44 **PS**; Suetonius, *Nero*, 38 **PS**). It caused mass destruction, with only four of the fourteen Augustan districts left untouched, and three districts utterly levelled.

While the scale of the fire is indisputable, what is by no means clear is the level of Nero's involvement in its outbreak. Tacitus states that various authors attributed it to both chance and the princeps' cunning (15.38 **PS**). Suetonius (*Nero*, 38 **PS**) is staunchly in the latter camp:

> . . . pretending to be disgusted by the drab old buildings and narrow winding streets of Rome, he brazenly set fire to the city . . .
>
>
>
> Suetonius, *Nero* 38

Suetonius then claims that Nero entered a tower in the Gardens of Maecenas and sang about the fall of Troy. This account fits well into the evolution of Suetonius' Nero, coming at the climax of a catalogue of outrages against his family, the Senate, and the people. Thus his final crime is against Rome herself, as his metaphoric destruction of Rome becomes a literal one.

Tacitus is more measured, focusing on the susceptibility of Rome to fire and the panic and selfishness of the people during the event. He states that Nero was actually at Antium when the fire broke out, only returning to Rome when the Palatine Hill itself was threatened. Here, he opened up his private gardens to accommodate the refugees and brought in supplies from Ostia. However, Tacitus also records the rumour that spread about Nero's singing of Troy's destruction, and at times Tacitus' narrative is suspicious of Nero's part in the affair, suggesting that, while Nero may not have brought about the

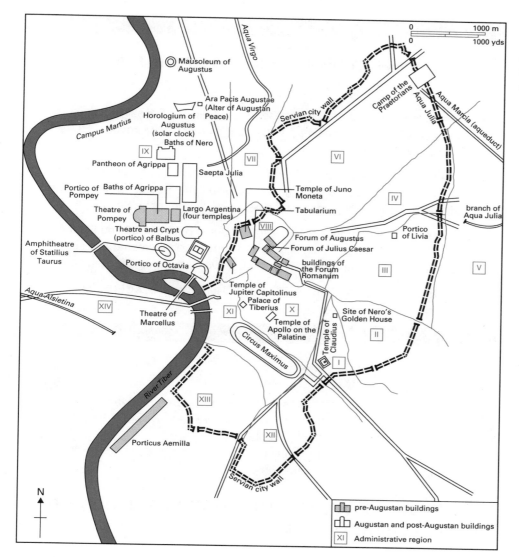

FIGURE 1.25

Map of Rome including buildings by Nero after the Great Fire.

fire personally, he may have allowed it to clear areas of Rome which he hoped to redevelop in the construction of his great project: the Domus Aurea ('Golden House').

Undoubtedly, following the fire, Nero sought to re-design Rome according to his own tastes. The majority of this rebuilding was centred on the Domus Aurea ('Golden House', a term coined by Pliny (*Natural History*, 36.111 PS; see also Suetonius, *Nero* 31 PS). To call it a palace is somewhat inaccurate, as it was really a sprawling series of connected structures. It would also be unfair to say that Nero's rebuilding work did not benefit Rome in general terms. Tacitus notes that the new building regulations and the order that Nero imposed on the city were welcomed for their practicality as well as for bringing lustre and reminders of martial glory to the city, for example the Triumphal Arch (see on Fig 1.26 PS). But even this is problematic as Nero assumed the glory due to the general Corbulo, although his intention was again to mirror Augustus (compare Fig 1.2). In many ways, the Great Fire of Rome facilitated the building projects of later emperors, so although it was a tragedy at the time, it brought about the Rome that would endure for centuries.

KEY PLACE

Domus Aurea

Nero's 'Golden House' which he had built in the centre of Rome in the aftermath of the great fire.

FIGURE 1.26
Sestertius showing
Nero's triumphal
arch.

PRESCRIBED SOURCE

Sestertius showing Triumphal Arch of Nero (Figure 1.26)

Date: *c.* AD 64

Obverse: Laureate head of Nero (obese); 'Nero Claudius Caesar Augustus
Germanicus, *pontifex maximus*, with tribunician power, victorious
commander, father of the fatherland'

Reverse: Ornate triumphal arch, seen from left. Nero in four horse chariot on
top, accompanied by Victory (right) and Peace (left). Figure of Mars in niche
on side of arch, holding spear and shield; 'By decree of the Senate'

Significance: Commemorates Nero's arch (erected between 58 and 62) for
Corbulo's Armenian campaigns; though Corbulo was the commanding
general, the glory transfers to Nero as the overall commander of the army

View it here: N51 in LACTOR 19: Tiberius to Nero (London: KCL, 2002)

EXPLORE FURTHER

To find out more about Corbulo's campaign in Armenia, read Tacitus, *Annals*
13.5–9, 34–41; 14.23–6; 15.1–17, 24–31. Dio (*Roman History* 63.16.1–17.6)
also briefly treats the death of Corbulo.
  In particular, focus on the moral qualities with which the authors imbue
Corbulo, seeing him as a contrast to Nero.

THE REVOLT OF VINDEX; THE DEATH OF NERO AND THE ACCESSION OF GALBA

The second half of Nero's reign saw a number of Roman provinces exhibiting signs of
discontent with Roman rule (Dio 63.22.1 **PS**): areas of Britain had rebelled under Boudicca
in 61 (with further uprisings in late 68 and early 69; see p. 160); Judaea rebelled in 66 (in an
uprising that really lasted until 73 when Masada fell). But perhaps the most terrifying from
the Roman perspective was that in Gaul, headed by Gaius Julius Vindex. This ultimately led
to Nero's downfall and death. Unfortunately, the *Annals* breaks off in 66, so we do not have
Tacitus' record of the rebellion and its consequences. We have to rely on the summaries in
Dio Cassius (63.22.1–26.1 **PS**, 63.26.3–27.1 **PS**) and Suetonius (*Nero* 40–9 **PS**).
  Suetonius (*Nero*, 40 **PS**) sees the revolt as divine retribution for Nero's mismanagement
of the empire. Vindex himself is also presented as a suitably heroic figurehead:

> . . . a man strong in physique and shrewd in intelligence, skilled in warfare and
> not lacking in courage to meet any big challenge. He also had a passionate love
> of freedom and boundless ambition.

Dio Cassius, *Roman History* 63.22.1

KEY INDIVIDUAL

**Gnaeus Domitius
Corbulo**

Dates: *c.* AD 7–67

Perhaps the leading
Roman general of the
Claudian and Neronian
periods, renowned for
both military and
diplomatic skills, as
well as being a strict,
old-fashioned
disciplinarian. Between 54
and 63, Corbulo
campaigned in Armenia
and Syria to deal with
rebellions and political
issues. He was ordered to
commit suicide in 67 by
Nero, who was allegedly
concerned by his success
and popularity.

Since our sources consider the removal of Nero as a blessing, despite the following year of intense civil war, Vindex becomes the antithesis to Nero: a barbarian who has adopted Roman culture becomes its champion to remove a philhellene emperor who has betrayed his people. The impassioned speech which Dio gives to Vindex (*Roman History*, 63.22.3–6 (PS)), unusually for Dio rendered as direct speech, reiterates many of Dio's earlier criticisms of Nero, turning Vindex into a spokesperson for judgement and retribution.

The final words, 'Rescue yourselves and rescue the Romans as well! Liberate the entire world!' (63.22.6 (PS)), present Vindex as acting for the common good. Indeed his own coinage, issued at the time of the revolt (valuable propaganda as ever), makes similar claims, as Fig 1.27 (PS) illustrates.

The coin's inscription communicates two key ideas about Vindex's revolt: first, that it was motivated by a desire for freedom from oppression; and secondly his claim to have acted for the Senate and People of Rome. The latter suggests that the revolt was about the nature of governance rather than nationalism, though Suetonius' constant use of the term 'Gallic' does not agree (e.g. *Nero*, 41, 43 (PS)).

Nero was in Neapolis when the revolt started (Suetonius, *Nero* 40 (PS)) and did nothing for eight days. However, on the surface at least, Vindex's rebellion may not have seemed that serious: Vindex was governor of a Gallic province without a legionary garrison and Nero had no reason to doubt the loyalty of the local urban cohorts at Lugdunum or the nearest legions, in Upper Germany under the newly appointed Lucius Verginius Rufus. In fact Nero even seems to have welcomed the rebellion as it offered a ready-made excuse to levy fines and order executions (Dio Cassius, *Roman History* 63.26.3 (PS); Suetonius, *Nero* 40 (PS)). Evidently, either through his lack of foresight or his over-confidence, Nero was seemingly untroubled by the 'call to freedom' from Gaul – according to Dio he chose this moment to announce his development of a new type of water organ (63.26.5 (PS)).

However, this changed when Servius Sulpicius Galba, legate of Hispania Tarraconensis since 60, was declared emperor by his soldiers on 9 June 68, following Vindex's request

PRESCRIBED SOURCE

Denarius of Vindex (Figure 1.27)

Date: AD 68

Obverse: Victory standing on a globe, with a wreath in her right hand and a palm in her left; 'Salvation of the human race'

Reverse: Oak wreath; 'Senate and people of Rome'

Significance: Vindex presents his rebellion as being for the benefit of the whole Roman world

View it here: P13b in LACTOR 19: Tiberius to Nero (London: KCL, 2002)

FIGURE 1.27
Denarius of Vindex.

Denarius of Galba

Date: *c.* AD 68

Obverse: Female bust with hair in a small knot above neck; 'Liberty to the Roman people'

Reverse: Pileus between two daggers; 'Restored'

Significance: Demonstrates the justification for his rebellion in the need for restoring liberty to the Roman people. Nero is thus by implication a tyrant

View it here: P13f in LACTOR 19: Tiberius to Nero (London: KCL, 2002)

for help from him. Dio notes that Vindex was not after supreme power, but supported Galba (63.23.1 **PS**). The news of this shocked Nero (Suetonius *Nero*, 42 **PS**; Dio 63.27.1 **PS**). He now desperately needed to take action. Suetonius (*Nero*, 44 **PS**) alleges that he merely packed up his stage equipment and selected concubines. Such parody in Suetonius (and Dio) nevertheless has a kernel of truth that Nero did little of practical value in the aftermath of the revolt.

Verginius Rufus, on the other hand, gathered the forces of Upper Germany and advanced into Gaul as far as Vesontio. Despite planning to meet with Vindex, the ill-discipline and aggressive nature of Rufus' soldiers won out and they fell upon Vindex's army (Dio Cassius, *Roman History* 63.24.3 **PS**). The slaughter that resulted, with 20,000 of Vindex's men being killed, prompted Vindex's suicide.

This should have settled the matter for Nero, but his lack of determined action left the way clear for Galba. Rufus refused his troops' suggestion that he become emperor himself, referring the matter of who should govern to 'the Senate and People of Rome' (Dio 63.25.2 **PS**). The Senate now chose to endorse Galba officially and declared Nero a public enemy (63.27.2b **PS**), doubtless justifying this with the popularity of Vindex's rebellion and the deep resentment of Nero (Suetonius, *Nero* 45 **PS**). Certainly Galba saw himself as a liberator, a man restoring Rome to her true self, as revealed in his coinage (see denarius left **PS**; also see the Flavian Depth Study, p. 175), which evokes the coinage minted by the assassins of Julius Caesar who dubbed themselves 'Liberators' (see Late Republic Depth Study, pp. 132–134).

Nero, stripped of all support, elected to flee Rome. Dio presents his final moment in a suitably theatrical manner: Nero assumes a tragic role (*Roman History*, 63.28.5 **PS**) with the notorious final words 'Jupiter, what an artist perishes in me!' (63.29.2 **PS**). Thus, while Vindex's rebellion in itself achieved little, it was the initial domino in the cascade that led to Nero's final downfall and the end of the Julio-Claudian dynasty.

NERO'S ATTITUDE TOWARDS RELIGION INCLUDING THE IMPERIAL CULT INSIDE AND OUTSIDE ROME

Our primary sources rarely mention any occasion of Nero exploiting the imperial cult. Although Neronian court poets such as Calpurnius Siculus praise Nero as a god and may suggest he believed he was a god, this is more literary convention in the mode of the Augustan poets than evidence.

However, although Nero seems to have been uninterested in the imperial cult, he was certainly intolerant of non-traditional religions. His formal introduction into the priestly colleges (see Fig 1.28 **PS**), echoing Augustus (see p. 17), partly justified this outlook. Tacitus (*Annals* 15.44 **PS**) emphasises how Nero scapegoated Christians following the Great Fire of 64. But this may simply have been expedient: blaming an already marginal group within Roman society would remove any culpability for the fire from himself, and it was not necessarily a religiously motivated choice.

PRESCRIBED SOURCE

Aureus of Nero (Figure 1.28)

Date: AD 50–54

Obverse: Draped bust of Nero; 'Nero Claudius Caesar Drusus Germanicus, leader of the younger generation'

Reverse: Ladle above tripod to left; augur's wand above dishes (used in sacrifices) to right; 'Co-opted as an additional member of every college of priests, by decree of the senate'

Significance: Nero is being established as a worthy successor to Claudius, through associations with traditional Roman cult practice

View it here: J30a in LACTOR 19: Tiberius to Nero (London: KCL, 2002)

FIGURE 1.28
Aureus of Nero.

ADMINISTRATIVE CHANGES TO ROME

Given what has been said thus far about Nero's decadent lifestyle, it is perhaps surprising that he did also enact administrative amendments. Although, especially in Suetonius, it is difficult to pinpoint chronology, we may speculate that many date to his quinquennium. Thereafter the sources highlight his self-indulgent behaviour, while the maintenance of the empire was handed over to his subordinates. This allowed the emperor the time for the important thing in life to him: pleasure. Overall, he did not fundamentally alter the mechanisms of the government or administration.

RELATIONS WITH THE SENATE, EQUESTRIANS AND ORDINARY PEOPLE OF ROME

Our sources are primarily senatorial (or identified with that class) and as such would sympathise with the Senate's humiliation at Nero's hands. Their stories of such offences, for example how descendants of noble families forced to perform on stage (Tacitus, *Annals* 14.14 **PS**), clearly reveal this bias. However, Nero's attitude does seem to change during the course of his reign, with early pandering to the Senate replaced by a viciousness that the sources revel in recording.

Study questions

1 Examine the prescribed sources for Nero and identify aspects that may relate to his use of the imperial cult.

2 One academic interpretation of Nero's opinion towards the imperial cult is summed up by Griffin: 'There is little evidence for the notion that Nero introduced important innovations in ruler cult.' Would you agree with this interpretation?

EXPLORE FURTHER

Examine the following sources:

- Suetonius, *Nero* 15–16; 24; 30;
- Tacitus *Annals*, 13.1; 13.31; 13.50–1; 15.32;
- Dio, *Roman History* 63.11–12;
- Pliny the Elder, *Natural History* 33.47.

What can they tell us about Nero's attitude to administration at Rome?

Despite everything, the Senate remained remarkably compliant with Nero throughout his reign, even coming to meet him in 'festive garb' following the announcement of Agrippina's death (*Annals* 14.13 (PS)). One senatorial figure, however, requires particular study: Thrasea Paetus, who features in Tacitus with an unusual voice of opposition. His willingness to speak out marks the beginning of a phenomenon which is usually called 'Stoic' opposition (which would continue under the Flavians – see p. 177).

Paetus is used by Tacitus as the model of senatorial virtue. For example, when Nero announces the death of Agrippina, Paetus stands and pointedly exits the Senate (*Annals*, 14.12 (PS)). However noble this gesture, even Tacitus acknowledges that it merely 'provided grounds for danger to himself, but did not present the others with an entry to freedom'. His death is marked in an extended passage of the *Annals* (16.21–35).

While individual equestrians fared little better, as a class Nero did perhaps see them as a useful alternative to the Senate. Equestrians featured heavily among his entourage of paid 'fans', and specially trained applauders earned 400,000 sesterces a performance (Suetonius, *Nero*, 20 (PS)). Nor should we forget the most prominent equestrian under Nero: Gaius Ofonius Tigellinus, the joint commander of the Praetorian Guard from 62 to 68.

Tacitus is scathing in his treatment of Tigellinus, claiming that he corrupted Nero and introduced him to every kind of depravity before finally deserting him when his fall became inevitable. Tigellinus is another example of how the ambitious and unscrupulous individual could prosper under the principate. However, his universal condemnation after his suicide, also highlights the hatred such individuals received, especially in our sources.

Ultimately, however, it was with the plebs that Nero found the adulation he so craved. Tacitus is typically judgemental of the plebs in this (*Annals*, 14.14 (PS)), but Nero clearly understood how to win their affection. Suetonius records that Nero provided an immense variety of entertainments (*Nero*, 11 (PS)). Nero also made a point of being generous through the practice of largesse, as had all the Julio-Claudians before him.

Fig 1.29 (PS), the *sestertius* of 64 depicting the corn dole, suggests that Nero wished such actions to be celebrated, reminding the public of his generosity after the event.

With Nero's frequent entertainments, in particular his love of chariot-racing (Suetonius, *Nero* 22 (PS)), and his large-scale handouts, it is telling that in our sources it is only at the very end of his reign that the people begin to turn against him. Suetonius notes the popular resentment about his profiteering in grain (*Nero*, 45 (PS)), yet even with this Nero was still sufficiently popular that, several years after his death, pretenders impersonating Nero still had people flock to their banners (e.g. see Tacitus, *Histories* 2.8–9).

Ultimately, Nero was a populist emperor, and as much as he victimised the upper classes, the urban plebs and the majority of the provincials continued to revel in the benefits provided by their pleasure-driven princeps.

S & C Read Tacitus' account of the death of Paetus at *Annals* 16.21–35. How does he contrast the characters of Nero and Paetus?

PRESCRIBED SOURCE

Sestertius of Nero (Figure 1.29)

Date: AD 64

Obverse: Laureate bust of Nero wearing aegis; 'Nero Claudius Caesar Augustus Germanicus, pontifex maximus, with tribunician power, victorious commander, father of the fatherland'

Reverse: Nero in a toga on a platform with the prefect of the corn dole behind him. An attendant in the centre hands a token to a standing citizen in a toga. Minerva stands behind with owl and spear in hand, beside the flat roof of a building; 'He gives a second handout to the people' ·

Significance: Commemorates Nero's grants of the corn dole

View it here: Q14 in LACTOR 19: Tiberius to Nero (London: KCL, 2002)

FIGURE 1.29
Sestertius of Nero.

PRESCRIBED DEBATE: THE CHARACTER OF NERO

Perhaps more than any other emperor, Nero is a polarising figure. Some scholars argue that Nero was little more than a monster, who should never have sat upon the imperial throne. More recent scholarship has highlighted positive aspects of his reign, noting that, with the urban plebs at least, he was rather popular. The situation is inevitably complex, with much depending on both the attitude and politics of the sources and scholarly interpretations.

Try to read as widely as possible about this issue. You might like to start with the following reflections by modern scholars:

Champlin, E. (2005), *Nero*, Cambridge: Harvard University Press.

Griffin, M.T. (2000), *Nero: The End of a Dynasty*, Abingdon: Routledge.

Scullard, H.H. (1982), *From the Gracchi to Nero: History of Rome from 133 B.C. to A.D. 68*, Abingdon: Routledge.

Shotter, D. (2004), *Nero*, Abingdon: Routledge.

Warmington, B.H. (1969), *Nero: Reality and Legend*, Chatto and Windus: London.

PRESCRIBED DEBATE: THE BENEFITS OF IMPERIAL RULE FOR THE INHABITANTS OF ROME

The relative benefits of imperial Rome for its inhabitants is a debate of considerable interest and complexity. The principate provided much-needed stability for the urban population, and the civil wars that preceded Augustus and followed Nero's death showcase the grim alternative. However, while the urban plebs certainly enjoyed benefits from the system, some of their formal political outlets were suppressed.

Try to read as widely as possible about this issue. You might like to start with the following:

Ewald, B.C. and Norena, C.F. (eds.) (2015), *The Emperor and Rome: Space, Representation and Ritual*, Cambridge: CUP.

Favro, D. (1992), 'Pater urbis: Augustus as City Father of Rome,' *JSAH* 51.61–84.

Garzetti, A. (1974), *From Tiberius to the Antonines: A History of the Roman Empire*, Methuen & Co.; London (especially pp. 3–181).

Millar, F. (1977), *The Emperor in the Roman World*, London: Bloomsbury Academic.

Rostovtzeff, M. (1957), *The Social and Economic History of the Roman Empire*, Oxford: Oxford University Press.

Yavetz, Z. (1988), *Plebs and princeps*, 2nd ed., Oxford: Oxford University Press.

TIMESPAN REVIEW

- Assess Suetonius' view that Nero's reign was characterised by 'follies and crimes' (*Nero* 19).
- Discuss how far Nero advocated a new form of government.
- Outline the limitations to understanding the wider context of the empire under Nero.
- Compare the reliability of the source accounts of this period.

Further Reading

Champlin, E. (2005), *Nero*, Cambridge: Harvard University Press.
Griffin, M.T. (2000), *Nero: The End of a Dynasty*, Abingdon: Routledge.
Scullard, H.H. (1982), *From the Gracchi to Nero: History of Rome from 133 B.C. to A.D.68*, Abingdon: Routledge.
Shotter, D. (2004), *Nero*, Abingdon: Routledge.
Warmington, B.H. (1969), *Nero: Reality and Legend*, Chatto and Windus: London.

PRACTICE QUESTIONS

AS Level

1. Read Suetonius *Nero* 10 **PS**. On the basis of this passage and other sources you have studied, how consistently does Nero seem to follow the model of Augustus?

[20]

A-Level

1. 'The failings of Nero's principate were the result of bad advice, rather than his own mistakes.' To what extent do you agree with this statement?

   You must use and analyse the ancient sources you have studied as well as your own knowledge to support your answer.

[30]

PART 2
DEPTH STUDIES

Introduction to the Depth Study options

One quarter of your A Level in Ancient History involves the study of a substantial and coherent short time span.

OCR offers the choice between three options:

The Breakdown of the Late Republic, 88–31 BC	H407/21
The Flavians, AD 68–96	H407/22
Ruling Roman Britain, AD 43–128	H407/23

The following pages of this textbook guide you through the content of all three of these options, but you will only study one.

All three Depth Studies develop what you have learned in the Period Study about Rome under the Julio-Claudian emperors.

- The events studied in 'The Breakdown of the Late Republic' precede the events of the Period Study and allow you to understand the backdrop for the shift to imperial rule.
- In 'The Flavians' you will study the emperors who took the helm after the Julio-Claudians following the Civil War and the Year of the Four Emperors.
- In 'Ruling Roman Britain', you will learn about the way an empire was ruled by focusing on one province.

EXAM OVERVIEW	H407/21, H407/22, H407/23

Your assessment for the Depth Study option will be found in Section B of your exam paper. It comprises

25% of the A Level	1 hr 10 mins out of 2 hrs 30 mins for the whole paper	48 marks out of 98 marks for the whole paper

12 marks will test AO1: demonstrate knowledge and understanding of the key features and characteristics of the historical periods studied.

12 marks will test AO2: analyse and evaluate historical events and historical periods to arrive at substantiated judgements.

24 marks will test AO3: use, analyse and evaluate a range of ancient source material within its historical context to:

- reach conclusions about historical events and historical periods studied; and
- make judgements about how the portrayal of events by ancient writers/sources relates to the social, political, religious and cultural contexts in which they were written/produced

DEPTH STUDY 1

The Breakdown of the Late Republic, 88–31 BC

Introduction to The Breakdown of the Late Republic, 88–31 BC

Although the Roman Republic came to an end in 31 BC, the process had begun at least a century before, when Rome had expanded its empire rapidly. The Roman Constitution that had originally well served the needs of a small farming community in central Italy was ill-equipped to deal with provincial territories and protracted overseas wars. There was a tension between those who sought to preserve the existing order and those who sought to use the power of the common people to their own ends. Politicians used a combination of legal and illegal methods to bring about their goals: oratory, corruption, largesse, corn doles, bribery, intimidation, street violence and ultimately civil war.

This Depth Study focuses on the use of these methods, and the interplay between the social and economic factors that prompted change. The different parts of the specification content for this component interrelate. After an overview of the constitution in Topic 2.1, the specification requirements for 'The Challenges to the Constitution' and 'The means by which politicians achieved success' are broken down into five topics (2.2–2.6), pairing aspects from each section. Throughout, it is evident that politicians used various methods to try to influence events. Their actions are interrelated with the social and economic pressures on Roman society, and students are encouraged to look at Topics 2.2–2.6 as a narrative that will provide examples for the final two sections of the specification content, 'Social and economic relationships' and 'The importance of individuals'. Although these are outlined together in Topic 2.7, much of the whole of this Depth Study will explore these themes.

EXAM OVERVIEW	H407/21 SECTION B

Your examination for the Roman Republic, in Section B of your paper, will require you to show knowledge and understanding of the material you have studied. This component is worth 48 marks – 12 based on AO1 skills, 12 on AO2 and 24 on AO3.

In this section, you will answer two questions:

- a 12-mark stimulus question focusing on an issue relating to a historical event or situation, where you will need to assess the source's utility; and
- one of two essay questions, each worth 36 marks. The questions will require you to use, analyse and evaluate source material to address issues in the question. The essays will target one or more of the themes listed.

2.1 The Form of the Constitution

TOPIC OVERVIEW

The form of the Constitution

- The makeup, role and responsibilities of:
  - the Senate, including Senatus Consulta
  - assemblies (*comitia centuriata, comitia plebis tributa, consilium plebis, comitia populi tributa*) including law-making
  - magistrates, including the cursus honorum and the Electoral Process
  - the tribunes of the plebs.

- The place of the courts, including quaestiones perpetuae and extraordinary courts in the political process.
- The background to the problems in 88 BC, including an overview of the issues stemming from the Gracchi and Marius.

The means by which politicians achieved success and their importance in the breakdown of the Republic

- Factions including optimates and populares.

The prescribed sources for this topic are:

- Cicero, *pro Sestio* 96–105
- Cicero, *de lege agraria* II.7–10
- Plutarch, *Caesar* 6

The official title of the Roman state, senatus populusque Romanus (SPQR), translates as the Senate and the people of Rome. There was also a third group, the magistrates, who formed the executive. This topic will consider the makeup of the Roman constitution and the division of duties between these groups: law making, elections and the courts as political mechanisms. It will also examine why this system was not functioning well by 88 BC, and the precedents established by the Gracchi and then Marius that highlighted a need for change.

THE SENATE INCLUDING SENATUS CONSULTA

Rome had evolved from an agrarian society where the people had trusted in a benevolent aristocracy who directed the state through an assembly, the Senate. The members of the Senate held in turn the chief magistracies of the state for a single year. The state had survived for 400 years in this form because senators looked after the interests of their clients, people who originally worked for them or lived close to them. There was an unspoken principle that leadership was incumbent on the elite who freely gave public service. By the late Republic, after Sulla's reforms as dictator, the Senate numbered 600 members. These members had all served the state in an administrative or military capacity as elected magistrates, and were therefore well placed to debate issues of state and issue advice to both magistrates and the people. There were some standing functions that the Senate had assumed, chiefly concerning foreign affairs, so they appointed governors to provinces and received foreign embassies. The Senate also controlled state expenditure.

> **senatus consultum (pl. senatus consulta) (SC)** an opinion of the senate arrived at after a debate that directed magistrates or people to follow a particular course of action

A decision of the Senate, a **senatus consultum (SC)**, was not a law; rather it was an opinion or a piece of advice. However, an SC usually carried enough authority to sway the voting people to approve it as a law, or for a magistrate to take the advice and to act upon it. It was in the magistrates' interest to maintain the prestige of the body to which they belonged. Therefore, magistrates tended to abide by senatorial opinion and be conservative in outlook. Within the 600 senators, a few powerful families formed temporary and shifting factions to keep power to themselves. Those who had a consul in their family tree considered themselves noble. These families tended to support their own relatives to the top positions.

MAGISTRATES AND THE CURSUS HONORUM

The executive magistrates were elected for just one year and always with colleagues, so that no individual could have sole authority. They carried rather more real authority under the Republic than after Augustus' principate. The career of a politician proceeded along a series of positions of increasing importance – the cursus honorum:

1. Quaestor (twenty elected annually, minimum age thirty). The position gained entry into the Senate for an individual. Two remained at Rome in charge of the treasury, the remainder served abroad as deputies to provincial governors.
2. Aedile (four elected annually, minimum age thirty-six). They were responsible for the public buildings, streets markets, the food supply to Rome and certain games. This was not an essential step in the cursus honorum, but it was a useful one, especially because of the connection with food distributions and games, as these allowed aediles to practise largesse towards the urban poor.
3. Praetor (eight elected annually, minimum age thirty-nine). Their primary function was judicial, presiding over the standing law courts. They also possessed imperium – the power to command, both militarily, but also to impose the law. They could command troops and preside over assemblies. On completion of their term in

office, most went on to to govern a province where, within the confines of their province, they retained their imperium, as pro-praetore – in the place of a praetor.

4. Consul (two elected annually, minimum age forty-two). The chief magistrates of the land, whose chief function was to preside over senatorial debate and some public assemblies. They possessed imperium and could command armies in times of crisis. On completion of their term in office, most governed a province with proconsular imperium. Ex-consuls were very influential within the Senate.

It was thought best to gain office at the earliest possible date. If individuals were unsuccessful after a couple of attempts, most accepted that their political advancement had ceased, although they remained a senator. Therefore, politicians tended to compete with the same individuals from year to year, with progressively more dropping out. The electoral process will be examined in greater detail in Topic 2.3 with reference to Cicero's campaign (see p. 108).

TRIBUNES

There were also ten tribunes. These had to be **plebeian** (see p. 92). Often aspiring politicians would hold the post as a way of getting themselves known to the poor. Traditionally the post had been responsible for defending the people against the excesses of magistrates. To enable a tribune to intervene on behalf of citizens, their person was sacrosanct and therefore they could not be physically intimidated. The tribunes also had the right to veto proposed laws. As dictator, Sulla curbed the authority of the tribunes so that they were no longer permitted to propose legislation to the people or hold any further political office. As a result, the position became unattractive for the ambitious. Sulla's changes were not permanent; the ban on further office was soon overturned and full powers were restored within a decade.

THE PEOPLE

There were three assemblies of the people: the centuriate assembly – the **comitia centuriata** and two tribal assemblies – the **comitia populi tributa** and **comitia plebis tributa** (also called the consilium plebis). The distinctions came down to the organisation of the people into voting blocks and their functions.

> **comitia centuriata** the assembly that elected senior magistrates
>
> **comitia plebis/populi tributa** the assemblies that passed laws and elected junior magistrates

1. The comitia centuriata was organised into 193 centuries of voters, subdivided into seven classes according to wealth. At the top sat the senators and equestrians, then five classes of decreasing wealth until a seventh class with insufficient property to be assessed, who were simply counted according to their person. The number of centuries within each class was unequal. There were eighteen equestrian centuries and seventy of the next richest property class. These people voted first, so that they represented eighty-eight of 193 centuries and almost had a majority before the less well-off got to vote. This would have allowed them to dominate voting if

they agreed. However, competition between rich members of the Senate made this uncommon and required rich politicians to gain the favours of the masses. The less well-off were gathered into fewer voting centuries per class with each successive drop in wealth. The seventh class were all enrolled in a single century, so that the poorer members were effectively disenfranchised. Within each century, one man had one vote and then the century brought forward its majority vote. This assembly was mostly concerned with electing senior magistrates, the consuls and praetors, although a few special laws were passed through it.

2. The other assemblies were the comitia populi tributa and the comitia plebis tributa (concilium plebis). The latter excluded members of the patrician order (see p. 92) and was presided over by a tribune; the former was presided over by a consul or a praetor. Otherwise the two were so similar that it is not always clear which is being discussed in the ancient sources, the only clue being the status of the presiding officer, if that was recorded. These bodies elected the quaestors, aediles and the tribunes themselves. More importantly they were the main forums through which laws were passed. Often laws were debated and drafted by the Senate and presented to a comitia as an SC, where the people were required actually to vote them into law. Every tribesman voted within his tribe. There were thirty-five tribes in total: four urban and thirty-one rural. Because an individual had to be present in the forum at Rome to vote, relatively few country people could swing their tribe's vote, but many more city dwellers were needed to control the four urban tribes. A tribesman was expected to support his patron within the tribe, and as such the rich could still influence the voting in these assemblies, although not as directly as in the comitia centuriata. It was acceptable for an individual to remind his fellow tribesmen of their obligations by gifts of dinners and money – this was legal largesse. If an individual distributed gifts to members of another tribe, that was considered bribery.

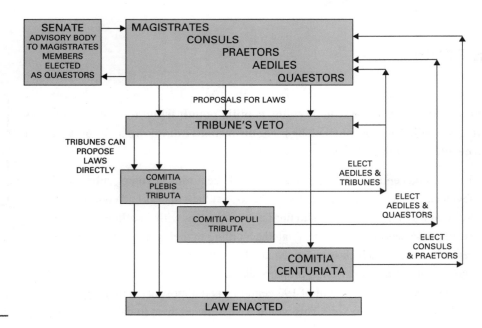

FIGURE 2.1
Functions of the Roman constitutional bodies.

Overall there should have existed a balance of power between all three elements of the Roman constitution. When it worked properly, the Senate would consider issues through debate and issue an SC that would advise a magistrate on a course of action. Magistrates could also make decisions according to precedent. However, if an issue was controversial, a magistrate would take an SC onto the popular assemblies to gain the People's approval of a law that justified a particular course of action. Tribunes could also directly propose laws.

FACTIONS, INCLUDING OPTIMATES AND POPULARES

The prestige of holding office was such that individuals coveted the top jobs. With provincial conquest, the opportunity for military prestige and wealth to be exacted from defeated foes increased. As a result, some individuals sought to achieve more power or hold onto power longer that the system ought to have allowed. They might do this through nepotism so that a successful politician would sponsor a succession of sons and nephews to the higher offices that he had already held. Additionally, or alternatively, senatorial friends and families grouped together and formed alliances (**amicitiae**) or **factiones** (factions). These alliances were often temporary and changing in both membership and purpose. Individuals might come together for the purpose of a single election campaign or a single issue. One amicitia might be at odds with another, and a politician would often have to balance conflicting amicitiae. However, amicitiae were also sometimes the product of normal patron–client relationships, and might extend across the generations. Romans tended to use amicitia in a positive manner and factio in a negative sense.

Beyond factions, there were two much looser groupings: the **optimates** – literally the 'best people' – and the **populares**. It is not uncommon to see these referred to as factiones, but it is better to see them as individuals who, in the case of the optimates, had a common outlook and, in the case of the populares, sought to be popular with the People, and use the people's power to their own advantage. The problems of definition stem from a speech of Cicero's that has been subject to extensive discussion.

> **amicitia (pl. amicitiae)** a political alliance to serve a particular purpose
>
> **factio (pl. factiones)** synonymous with amicitia
>
> **optimate (pl. optimates)** literally 'the best people', individuals who saw themselves as the defenders of the established order
>
> **popularis (pl. populares)** those politicians who played to the needs and wants of the poor in order to secure their political support

PS

There have always been two groups of men in this state who have been eager to be involved in affairs of state and to play a pre-eminent part in them; of these groups one wanted themselves to be considered and to be populares, the other optimates. Those who wanted what they did and what they said to be pleasing to the crowd (populus) were considered populares, while those who acted in such a way that their policies found favour with the best people (optimi) were considered optimates. Who, then, are all these best people? Optimates are all those who are not guilty of crime, who are not evil by nature, who are not raving mad, who are not encumbered in their domestic affairs.

Cicero, *pro Sestio* 96–7 (LACTOR 7, L7)

EXPLORE FURTHER

Read Cicero *Commentariolum Petitionis* 2–7, 27–38.

Write a relative hierarchy of which amicitiae were most important to cultivate.

PRESCRIBED SOURCE

Title: *Pro Sestio*

Author: Cicero

Date: 56 BC

Genre: Speech

Significance: Made in defence of P. Sestius on a charge of violence. The prescribed section deals with Cicero's view of the positive merits of the optimate stance

Prescribed sections: 96–105

Read it here: L7 in LACTOR 7: *Late Republican Rome, 88–31 BC* (London: KCL, 2017)

Ostensibly in this passage the matter seems quite straightforward: all right-minded individuals should consider themselves optimates; only bad people would be populares. However, Cicero was speaking against his nemesis, the popularis Clodius, while defending an associate Sestius on a charge of violence. It was to his advantage to polarise politics into two camps, and he is therefore not necessarily speaking truthfully. Outside of this passage, the use of optimates and populares as antithetical terms is so rare that scholars have debated how far the groups ever really existed. There certainly was no defined membership of either group. There was a common purpose among many of the senatorial order to preserve the status quo and their own privileged position. However, competition within the elite also meant that co-ordinated action was rare. These individuals might consider themselves as optimates; we might consider one or more individuals optimate, but ought not to consider all optimates a faction.

Other individuals intent on political power but lacking the elite connections of those who had most influence in the Senate sometimes appealed directly to the people for support in gaining the magistracies and power. These were the populares. To gain this support, the populares normally offered something to the people's advantage: for example, land redistribution, debt cancellation or hand-outs of corn, in order to secure votes. This does not necessarily imply any genuine concern for the plight of the poor. Despite his arguments in *pro Sestio*, elsewhere Cicero talks in terms of good or true populares and those who simply sought to use the people:

> Nor should those who promise lands to the Roman people, whether they are plotting some secret scheme while they are putting it forward with hope and specious pretence, be reckoned populares.

Cicero, *de lege agraria* ll.10 (LACTOR 7, L5)

PRESCRIBED SOURCE

Title: *De Lege Agraria*

Author: Cicero

Date: 63 BC (written up before 60 BC)

Genre: Speech

Significance: One of three speeches by Cicero, denouncing Rullus' proposed land bill of 63 BC. This section looks to persuade the people to trust in the wisdom of Cicero as their representative and not be tempted by largesse from the populares

Prescribed sections: II.7–10

Read it here: L5 in LACTOR 7: *Late Republican Rome, 88–31 BC* (London: KCL, 2017)

DEBATE

Some historians couch a history of this period as a struggle between the two camps of optimates and populares. This goes back as far as Plutarch (*Caesar* 6 **PS**). It is accepted by all that optimates and populares were not political parties, but what the terms actually did mean is still debated. Read the entries by M. Robb on optimates and populares in *The Encyclopedia of Ancient History* (Malden, 2012) pp. 4911–14.

PRESCRIBED SOURCE

Title: *Caesar*

Author: Plutarch

Date: *c.* AD 100

Genre: Biography

Significance: Plutarch paired Greek and Roman statesmen seeking to exhibit common traits between them. He was selective of his material and sometimes compresses or conflates events. However, he can be cross referenced with sources closer to events, in particular Cicero's letters after 65 BC. He is generally hostile to Caesar, seeing him as being responsible for the fall of the Republic

Prescribed section: 6

Read it here: OCR source booklet

Despite the debate, for the purposes of the following topics, members of the establishment elite who oppose change will often be referred to as optimates. Those people who harnessed the power of the poor will be referred to as populares. Among those individuals who were optimate in outlook or popularis in action, there were also factiones. For instance, Caesar refers to a small factio that opposed him in the run-up to the civil war.

The individuals concerned were optimates, but not all optimates were within that particular factio.

THE LAW COURTS, INCLUDING QUAESTIONES PERPETUAE

quaestiones perpetuae seven courts established by Sulla that oversaw cases in seven types of crime

The law was a private matter in Rome. This meant that if an individual was wronged, he brought the alleged wrongdoer to court. Rich patrons represented the interests of their clients, but these were often reasonably well-off clients. The poor had little representation. Sulla reorganised the law, establishing seven standing courts – **quaestiones perpetuae**, each one normally presided over by a praetor. These tried cases according to particular crimes: provincial extortion (something which had become a major problem as provincial territory grew), murder and poisoning, violence, treason, electoral bribery, embezzlement and fraud. These crimes were generally political: provincial maladministration, treason and electoral bribery very clearly so. The accusation of violence also had political uses. There were a couple of occasions when extraordinary proceedings were carried out, outside of the quaestiones perpetuae, such as the trial of Rabirius on the charge of activity hostile to the state and the prosecution of Clodius on the religious charge of sacrilege.

THE SOCIAL ORDERS

patricians originally the aristocracy, the title was passed down by birth

plebeians originally the labouring classes, by the Late Republic the distinction was mostly gone; it was more a question of status

plebs urbana the plebs, or urban poor

HS abbreviation for **sestertius**

sestertius (pl. sestertii) a Roman coin. Ancient wealth is very difficult to compare, but a poor man may have only earned HS 1–2 a day, while an equestrian could expect at least HS 20,000 a year

Roman society was stratified. In the distant past, **patricians** had governed while **plebeians** had worked. The plebeians had been barred from holding public offices and the two orders had not been allowed to intermarry. By the Late Republic there was little difference between the two orders, except for a few positions and access to the comitia plebis tributa, which was still dependent upon being plebeian. Members of the Senate could be either patrician or plebeian. There were, strictly speaking, only 600 senators. Although the wider family might see itself as senatorial, sons were not senators until they were elected. Below the senatorial order were the equestrians, from whom the senators technically came. These were the richer members of society. An individual required HS 400,000 in assets to be of equestrian status. However, the vast majority of the population (80–90 per cent) were poor. Outside of Rome, these citizens were mostly engaged in agriculture. At Rome, with a population of about 1 million, the urban poor were often reliant on hand-outs from the rich and the state. They became an important political force and are generally referred to as the **plebs urbana**, as opposed to the plebeians, who could be rich or poor, labourer or magistrate.

The poor were connected to the rich, equestrians and senators through the bounds of patronage: a reciprocal relationship whereby richer patrons offered protection to poorer clients in exchange for services. This system pervaded Roman society; the protection might be legal support in the courts or representation of their interests in the **Senate**; clients often worked the land in the community from which the patron originated. Patrons expected a morning visit from their clients. This was in turn rewarded with a small daily gift of sustenance, money or food. At Rome these daily hand-outs from the important political families bought the services of the poor in canvassing for political office.

THE GRACCHI AND MARIUS

As Rome had expanded through the Italian peninsula, it had confiscated large tracts of land that were designated public land – **ager publicus**. Roman citizens had the right to use ager publicus but not own it. However, once a family was in possession of this public land, it tended to be passed from generation to generation, with money and labour being invested in it. With wars of conquest around the Mediterranean, poor citizen farmers were called up to serve in the army and spend long periods away from home. Now the richer land owners began appropriating the land, both that which was owned and the ager publicus which was in the possession of their poor neighbours. They did this through purchase – which in the case of ager publicus was not technically possible – or through intimidation.

Complementing this acquisition of land by the rich, there was a huge influx of slaves taken as prisoners of war. The richer landowners used these slaves to farm their expanding estates, which were called **latifundia**. Also with overseas conquest came imported grain. The tribute from first Sicily and then Sardinia and Africa was a 10 per cent tithe on their grain production, which had the effect of further reducing the profitability of farming in Italy. The large land owners turned to olives and vines, both of which were labour intensive, and required the use of slaves to be profitable. All this competition made farming for the poor unattractive and many citizens, those returning to a dilapidated farm from overseas wars, or able to sell up because of rising land values, or simply pushed out by the rich, migrated to Rome. This caused a demographic shift, a crisis in the countryside that began in the second century BC and continued into the study timespan. In the late second century, the actions of the two brothers Tiberius and Gaius Gracchus looked to alleviate this crisis.

> **ager publicus** public land owned by the state often worked by Roman citizens

> **latifundium (pl. latifundia)** large estates owned by the rich and staffed with slaves

S & C See N. Rosenstein, 'Aristocrats and Agriculture in the Late Republic' in *The Journal of Roman Studies* Vol 98 (2008) for a calculation of the agricultural needs of the urban population.

1 What is Rosenstein's conclusion about the scale of land ownership?
2 What is Rosenstein's conclusion about the wealth of the senatorial order?
3 What flaws are there in Rosenstein's arguments? **CW**

DEBATE

The depiction of the crisis in the countryside is the standard view, which has been increasingly challenged since the 1970s. The idea of latifundia rests on the literary record, but the archaeological evidence, specifically slave barracks, has not been forthcoming. Recent work has pointed to the needs of Rome not being so significant that widespread latifundia would have been required. Notwithstanding these views, there was net migration in the second and first century and Roman politicians did bring land bills that were intended to settle urban poor back in the countryside. See N. Rosenstein, *Rome and the Mediterranean 290–146 BC: The Imperial Republic* (Edinburgh: Edinburgh University Press 2012) for a more complex interpretation of the crisis in the countryside.

The Gracchi

possessores those in possession of and working ager publicus but not actually owning it

In 133, a tribune called Tiberius Gracchus proposed to redistribute ager publicus occupied, but not owned, by **possessores**. He reaffirmed an old and ignored 500 iugera limit, plus 250 iugera for each of two sons, on possession of this land. One iugerum of land was equivalent to 0.25 hectare (50 m × 50 m). Because these were low limits, Tiberius' proposal would have taken land mostly from the rich. Although the proposal would alleviate the suffering of the poor, Tiberius' uppermost concern was to ensure enough recruits to the army upon which the Roman state relied. Despite having support among the Senate, he took the decision straight to the comitia plebis tributa to enact a law. People poured into Rome to vote on this measure: both the poor who were in favour because they stood to gain, and the rich together with their clients (many of whom stood to lose out by the reforms) to vote against it.

Another tribune, Octavius, representing the rich, vetoed the proposals. In response, Tiberius proposed a law to depose Octavius; in so doing he was infringing a tribune's right to veto legislation. Tiberius justified his actions as protecting the will of the people. When the land law was passed, Tiberius sought the funds to pay for it from the recently bequeathed kingdom of Attalus of Pergamum. This impacted on a traditional sphere of the Senate's interests: foreign affairs. Then when he sought re-election as tribune, something that was not illegal but unconventional, he was charged with seeking to make himself king, a title hateful to the Romans. Tiberius was attacked by a party of senators and killed.

Ten years later in 123, Tiberius' brother Gaius Gracchus became tribune. He looked for support beyond the rural poor to include the plebs urbana and the equestrian order. He was re-elected for a second term, leaving him also open to charges of wanting to gain absolute power. He passed a series of laws that sought to continue social reform and avenge his brother's death, among which were bills as follows:

Latin status municipal rights that allowed individuals to trade and marry with Romans. Originally confined to the area close to Rome, by the late Republic this was a way of elevating a community above that of provincials in the case of Sicily and Transalpine Gaul. Further afield individual towns might enjoy Latin municipal rights. Magistrates in these communities gained Roman citizenship

senatus consultum ultimum (SCU) the last decree of the senate, empowering all magistrates to do whatever they deemed necessary for the preservation of the state

1. Re-affirming the right of the individual to trial by the people in cases carrying the death penalty, something his brother had been denied.
2. Establishing a corn dole, a distribution of grain at a subsidised price to the poor.
3. Establishing contracts for the collection of the Asian taxes – tax farming. This would be within the traditional role of the Senate.
4. Instigating public works, i.e. roads and granaries, acts of large-scale largesse.
5. Changing the composition of the juries to include equestrians in the court for provincial extortion, so buying equestrian support.
6. Establishing overseas colonies, to relocate the poor.
7. Proposing that citizenship be extended to the Latin people, and **Latin status** be granted to the rest of Italy.

These last two points brought widespread condemnation and senatorial opposition such that Gaius failed to be re-elected tribune a third time. Opponents proposed a law to stop the colonisation of Carthage, which caused Gaius to take up arms. The Senate passed for the first time a decree known thereafter as the last decree of the Senate – the **senatus consultum ultimum (SCU)**. This empowered all magistrates to take up arms to defend the state. Gaius and many of his supporters were killed by magistrates acting under the

KEY INDIVIDUALS

Tiberius Sempronius Gracchus
Dates: Died 133 BC

Tribune in 133 BC who proposed a limit on the quantity of ager publicus that could be possessed by a family, and a redistribution of the surplus to poor citizens. When seeking re-election as tribune, he was attacked and killed by representatives of the rich.

Gaius Sempronius Gracchus
Dates: 154–121 BC

Tribune in 123 and 122 BC, who continued his brother Tiberius' land-redistribution. He also set many popular precedents in relation to corn doles, largesse and the Roman franchise that would be used again by politicians in the last decades of the Republic. He was killed by senators acting under the authority of the SCU, which had been passed for the first time.

authority of the SCU. The land redistribution petered out, the colonisation programme was abandoned and the corn dole was reduced.

Marius

Marius was an accomplished soldier with an undistinguished early political career who, against the wishes of his patron, the influential Q. Caecilius Metellus, successfully gained the consulship in 107 BC. He was a new man, a **novus homo** in both senses. Stung by the lack of support from his patron, Marius took the unprecedented step of persuading the comitia plebis tributa to pass a law appointing him to the command of the war against the African king Jugurtha, which at that time was being directed by Metellus. In so doing, Marius was challenging not only Metellus but the traditional role of the Senate in deciding overseas commands. Marius is also credited with recruiting soldiers from the lowest property classification, who had previously been exempt from military service. It is now thought that he simply formalised a practice that had gone on for some time. This would have achieved what Tiberius Gracchus had sought to do with land reform: provide sufficient troops to continue overseas expansion.

Having defeated Jugurtha, in the face of a threat to Italy by nomadic German tribes, Marius was re-elected as consul an unprecedented further six times. During his sixth consulship of 100 BC, Marius formed an amicitia with L. Appuleius Saturninus, a popularis tribune. Saturninus proposed a land bill that would have benefited Marius' veterans. He also increased the number of recipients of the grain dole. Saturninus used street gangs to force through his proposals. The establishment countered gangs with gangs. In the ensuing violence, a candidate for the consulship was killed. Marius could not ignore the lawlessness. After an SCU was passed, he arrested Saturninus and his followers, holding them in the Senate House. However, he was unable to prevent a mob breaking in via the roof and pelting them to death with roof tiles. After this inglorious event, Marius retired.

novus homo 'new man': the first member of a family to gain entry into the Senate. Additionally the first member of a family to gain the consulship

KEY INDIVIDUAL
Gaius Marius
Dates: 157–86 BC

Consul seven times, and a notable general, he is perhaps best known for his reforms of the Roman army.

TOPIC REVIEW

- Discuss why Rome was ready for change in the early first century.
- Explain whether or not the Gracchi should be considered reformers.
- Assess whether or not the Roman constitution was fit for purpose.

Further Reading

Brunt. P.A. (1982), *Social Conflicts in the Roman Republic*, London: Chatto & Windus.

Lintott. A. (1999), *The Constitution of the Roman Republic*, Oxford: Oxford University Press.

Robb. M. (2012), 'optimates, populares' in *The Encyclopaedia of Ancient History*, ed. Roger S. Bagnall, Kai Brodersen, Craige B. Champion, Andrew Erskine, Oxford: Wiley-Blackwell, pp. 4911–14.

Rosenstein. N. (2008), 'Aristocrats and Agriculture in the Late Republic' in *The Journal of Roman Studies* Vol 98, pp. 1–26.

Rosenstein. N. (2012), *Rome and the Mediterranean 290–146: The Imperial Republic*, Edinburgh: Edinburgh University Press.

Taylor L.R. (1949), *Party Politics in the Age of Caesar*, Berkeley: University of California Press.

PRACTICE QUESTIONS

1. Read Cicero *pro Sestio* 105 **PS** and Plutarch, *Life of Caesar* 6 **PS**

How useful are these passages for our understanding of the motivation and actions of amicitiae, factions, optimates and populares in the Late Republic?

[12]

2.2 Sulla and the 70s

The challenges to the Constitution

- The reforms of Sulla as dictator
- The undoing of Sulla's reforms through the 70s leading to Pompey and Crassus as consuls in 70 BC
- The role of the tribunes.

The means by which politicians achieved success and their importance in the breakdown of the Republic

- Factions including optimates and populares
- Land bills and largesse
- Intimidation during trials and elections
- Violence and corruption
- The military commands of Pompey
- The threat of military action
- Veteran support
- Rhetoric/oratory.

The roles and importance of individuals in the breakdown of the Republic

- Sulla
- Lepidus
- Pompey
- Crassus

The prescribed sources for this topic are:

- Cicero, *in Verrem* I.1.35–47
- Sallust *Histories* [2.82] {2.98M}, [3.34] {3.48M}
- Plutarch, *Sulla* 7–10, 31
- Plutarch, *Pompey* 14–15, 20

- Denarius of Sulla 84–83 BC
- Denarius of Sulla 82

In this topic, we consider how Sulla, as a dictator, attempted to re-adjust the constitution to become better suited to the needs of the day, and how this was opposed. Sulla first rose to prominence serving under Marius, in the Jugurthine War, where he is said to have stolen the glory for the capture of the African king Jugurtha and so incurred Marius' hostility.

THE REFORMS OF SULLA AS DICTATOR

KEY INDIVIDUAL

L. Cornelius Sulla Felix
Dates: *c.* 138–78 BC

Consul in 88, but ousted from Rome by the tribune Sulpicius. He took the unprecedented step of marching on Rome to re-secure his command and his authority. He was later outlawed while absent fighting Mithridates, but returned in 83 to wage and win the Civil War. He was appointed dictator, but resigned *c.* 79 and died the next year.

From 91 to 87, Rome's Italian allies fought with Rome for the right of Roman citizenship; this was called the Social War. At the same time the king of Pontus, Mithridates, fostered revolution in the Roman province of Asia. On the back of his successes in the Social War and with the sponsorship of the powerful noble family the Metelli, Sulla gained the consulship of 88. As consul he clashed with the popularis tribune P. Sulpicius Rufus about how to allocate the newly enfranchised allies into the Roman voting tribes. Sulpicius employed a 3,000-strong street gang and had gained the support of Marius, now old but still keen for glory, by transferring the Mithridatic command away from Sulla to Marius (Plutarch, *Sulla* 7–8 **PS**). Sulpicius forced Sulla to flee from Rome, but Sulla took the unprecedented, although not unreasonable, move of marching on Rome. Sulpicius was killed, but Marius escaped (Plutarch, *Sulla* 9–10 **PS**). As consul, Sulla presided over the elections for 87. When the popularis L. Cornelius Cinna was elected, Sulla secured promises of fidelity before departing for the Mithridatic War as originally planned.

The popularis consul, Cinna, with Marius' support, clashed with his optimate colleague for 87, Octavius. Street fighting degenerated into civil war, in which Octavius was killed. Cinna with Marius retook Rome and Marius behaved savagely, killing any perceived opposition, not ceasing until he died (of natural causes). Thereafter Cinna held the

---

PRESCRIBED SOURCE

Title: *Lives of Sulla and Pompey*

Author: Plutarch

Date: *c.* AD 100

Genre: Biography

Significance: Plutarch paints Sulla in a negative light, dwelling on the butchery of the proscriptions which cast a shadow over the period. He is sometimes hostile to Pompey, seeing him as being partly responsible for the fall of the Republic

Prescribed sections: *Sulla* 7–10, 31; *Pompey* 14–15, 20

Read it here: OCR source booklet

consulship with Cn. Papirius Carbo and for five years they headed a popularis regime at Rome; they declared Sulla a public enemy in absentia. After securing a peace with Mithridates, Sulla returned to Italy in 83 and fought and won the Civil War. Throughout this period, individual commanders minted coins to pay their soldiers. It was very normal for them to use these as pieces of everyday visual propaganda to legitimise their rule. Sulla did so before returning to Rome.

PRESCRIBED SOURCE

Denarius of Sulla (Figure 2.2)

Date: 84–83 BC

Obverse: Head of Venus right, wearing diadem; on right, Cupid holding palm-branch Inscription Sull(a)

Reverse: Two trophies; between, jug and lituus; above Inscription Imper(ator) iterum

Significance: This coin celebrates Sulla's success over Mithridates' forces in Greece. The jug and lituus (a crooked wand) are the symbols of the officer of augur. Seemingly he was trying to solemnise his claim to the victories

View it here: 359.2.1 in Ghey, Leins, Crawford, *Roman Republican Coins in the British Museum* (online catalogue: http://www.britishmuseum.org/research/publications/online_research_catalogues/rrc/roman_republican_coins.aspx) **CW**

FIGURE 2.2
Denarius of Sulla, 84–83 BC. **PS**

PRESCRIBED SOURCE

Denarius of Sulla (Figure 2.3)

Date: 82 BC

Obverse: Helmeted head of Roma Inscription L·MANLI(us) T(orquatus) the man who actually minted the coin

Reverse: Triumphator, crowned by flying Victory, in quadriga Inscription L. Sulla Im(perator)

Significance: This coin makes a claim to victory prior to Sulla re-taking Rome.

View it here: 367.3.1 in Ghey, Leins, Crawford, *Roman Republican Coins in the British Museum* (online catalogue: http://www.britishmuseum.org/research/publications/online_research_catalogues/rrc/roman_republican_coins.aspx) **CW**

FIGURE 2.3 **PS**
Denarius of Sulla, 82 BC.

The victorious Sulla was in need of money and came up with the novel idea of posting proscriptions of outlawed men, with a price on their heads. Their property was seized and sold on to raise cash (Plutarch, *Sulla* 31 **PS**). At least forty senators and 1,600 equestrians were proscribed; their sons and grandsons were barred from holding future magistracies. Soon, however, the violence spread and people were killed because of personal feuds and their names posthumously added to the lists.

The bonds between commander and army were such that soldiers expected rewards, normally land, for service. When Sulla demobilised up to 120,000 troops he gave them land seized from those communities that had opposed him in the Civil War, especially Etruria in the north and Campania in the south. The social upheaval must have been enormous. A great many Italians would have lost their homes. Many would have drifted to Rome and increased the problems of the plebs at Rome (Appian, *The Civil War* 1.95–6). The violence and arbitrary nature of Sulla's proscriptions would cast a long shadow over the Late Republic.

Sulla was appointed dictator for the purpose of writing laws and re-establishing the Republic. He was not an ardent traditionalist, certainly not born into the optimate elite, but he was supported by the Metelli. In coming into conflict with first Marius then the popularis regimes of Cinna and Carbo, he naturally sided with optimate sentiment. At this time, political opinion tended to be polarised. Moderates do not do well in times of crisis. As dictator, Sulla acted as an agent not of change but of retrenchment, bolstering the authority of the Senate in seeking to prevent continual unrest through a series of political reforms, in which he:

1. increased the size of the Senate to 600; this answered the political ambitions of the equestrians and bought personal loyalty;
2. re-affirmed the age requirements of the cursus honorum and instigated a ten-year interval between consulships;
3. increased the number of praetors to eight so that the number of magistrates equated to the number of provinces, thereby preventing the need to extend provincial commands;
4. increased the number of quaestors to 20 and made this the route into the Senate;
5. established seven permanent courts, the quaestiones perpetuae, staffed from the now increased Senate; the equestrians were no longer to serve on the juries;
6. abolished the corn dole; the plebs urbana would be dependent on the aristocratic households once again;
7. removed the tribunes' power to propose legislation to the comitia plebis tributa; and
8. banned tribunes from holding further office and so made the position a political dead end.

Overall, Sulla aimed to protect the Republic by strengthening the position of the Senate. He did this most effectively by curbing the authority of the tribunes to bring laws to the popular assemblies. He also prevented aspiring politicians, such as Sulpicius who had opposed him in 88 BC and Saturninus who had caused unrest in 100 BC, from gaining further office on the back of popular renown won while they were tribunes. However, the tribunes retained their powers to defend Roman citizens and probably to veto legislation (see **CW**). Having confirmed the authority of the Senate, Sulla stood down. It is unclear why he did not stay on to ensure that his reforms were upheld, but it can be seen that they were not well received by the almost immediate calls for them to be overturned.

THE UNDOING OF SULLA'S REFORMS

The first to challenge Sulla's reforms was the consul for 78, M. Aemilius Lepidus, a popularis who had belatedly sided with Sulla during the Civil War. Lepidus proposed the recall of those exiled through the proscriptions and the return of their land to their families, together with a new corn dole and restoration of the powers of the tribunate (Plutarch, *Pompey* 15 **PS**). As a direct result of Lepidus' proposals, a revolt broke out at Faesulae in Etruria against a colony of Sulla's newly settled veterans. The Senate dispatched both consuls, Q. Lutatius Catulus and – despite him being the author of the revolt – Lepidus himself, to quell the uprising. When he arrived in Etruria, Lepidus, probably simply out of a sense of duty, took command of the revolt. The Senate was unsure of Lepidus' position and was slow to damn him until he actually marched on Rome in 77. Only then was the SCU passed. Lepidus was defeated by Catulus and escaped to die in Sardinia.

Tribunes in 76, 75, 74 and 73 campaigned for a full restoration of their powers. In 75 the consul C. Aurelius Cotta, a supporter of Sulla, removed the ban on tribunes holding further office. The authority of the tribunate had become the political cause of the 70s. This was partly because Sulla had diminished the importance of the peoples' defender, although he had not actually removed that role from them. More importantly, many aspiring politicians looked to the tribunate to kick-start their political career, hence Cotta's decision to remove the ban on holding further office. Furthermore the ability to pass legislation through the comitia plebis tributa which was much quicker than the comitia centuriata, and the ability to veto legislation was felt to be useful for all. Therefore many sought to restore all the tribune's former powers. Our evidence comes chiefly from Sallust's last work, the fragmentary Histories. In these is a speech supposedly given by the tribune C. Licinius Macer in 73 agitating for the full restoration of the tribunes' powers. In this speech the previous attempts to restore the powers of the tribunate through the 70s are catalogued (Sallust, *Histories* 3.34 {3.48M} **PS**).

ACTIVITY

Read Sallust *Histories* 3.34 {3.48M} **PS**

1. Compile a timeline of the occasions when individuals sought to restore the powers of the tribunate.
2. What is Macer's argument for the restoration of the tribunate?

KEY INDIVIDUAL

M. Aemilius Lepidus
Dates: Died *c.* 77 BC

A popularis politician. Consul in 78, he proposed overturning Sulla's reforms and headed up a revolution in northern Italy. Defeated in 77, he died soon after.

PRESCRIBED SOURCE

Title: *Histories*

Author: Sallust

Date: Late 40s early 30s BC

Genre: History beginning 78 BC, only fragments survive

Significance: The closest source for the events of the 70s

Prescribed sections: [2.82] {2.98M}, [3.34] {3.48M}

Read it here: B33 and B37 in LACTOR 7: *Late Republican Rome, 88–31 BC* (London: KCL, 2017)

POMPEY'S MILITARY COMMANDS

When Sulla fought the civil war from 83, he was joined by several aspiring politicians, including Crassus, Catiline and Pompey, the last bringing a private army with him. After Sulla was secure in Italy, the young Pompey went first to Sicily and then Africa with pro-praetorian imperium. He was nicknamed the teenage butcher, because of the manner in which he executed Carbo and his associates. On his return, Pompey argued for a triumph, which he eventually received, and the title Magnus – the great (Plutarch, *Pompey* 14 **PS**). When Lepidus had headed up the uprising in Etruria, Catulus' military credentials were questioned and the Senate at the behest of a L. Marcius Philippus next authorised Pompey with pro-praetorian imperium to deal with the rebellious elements in Cisalpine Gaul. Now Pompey's authority was increasing so far that he refused to disband his forces awaiting a further command. The Senate, again with the urging of Philippus, agreed to send him, this time with proconsular imperium, to Spain to augment the efforts of Q. Caecilius Metellus Pius, who was fighting against Q. Sertorius, a former supporter of Cinna and Carbo. Metellus had previously asked for reinforcements, but none had come.

By 75 there was deadlock and Pompey sent a challenge to the Senate demanding reinforcements and suggesting that if his request were not granted, he would bring his army back to Rome (Sallust, *Histories* 2.82 {2.98M} **PS**; Plutarch, *Pompey* 20 **PS**). Pompey was clearly supremely confident. He had raised an army on his own initiative when first meeting Sulla, he had shown no scruples about dealing with popularis opponents, he had refused to disband his forces after Cisalpine Gaul, and now he threatened violence in Italy unless he received what he wanted. The consuls of 74, L. Licinius Lucullus and M. Aurelius Cotta, were keen to grant Pompey's wishes so that they could embark on a fresh campaign against Mithridates and thus gain glory and prestige equal to Pompey's. Over the next two years, Pompey pushed Sertorius back. Sertorius was finally assassinated by a subordinate called M. Perperna; Pompey subsequently easily defeated Perperna (Plutarch, *Pompey* 20 **PS**).

POMPEY AND CRASSUS AS CONSULS

Despite starting out as Sulla's henchman, as the 70s progressed, Pompey drifted towards popularis policies. Ever the opportunist, he was looking for a political career on the back of his military credentials. Crassus sought power where he could get it and had connections both in the Senate and among the equestrians. There was personal rivalry – Pompey especially never tolerated an equal. Yet Plutarch reports they agreed to each other's candidacy for the consulship. For Pompey this was illegal, as he was not even a senator, having never been elected to any magistracy. However, he had served with pro-praetorian imperium twice in Sicily and Africa, and again in Cisalpine Gaul. He had also held proconsular imperium in Spain. It is easy to see why he believed that his status warranted the consulship. Once in office the two men did not get on, and Plutarch is dismissive of their achievements. He does so to diminish the importance of their reforms that followed. Pompey and Crassus may not have liked each other, but both could see the political benefit to completing the removal of Sulla's reforms. Pompey restored the tribunes' power to bring laws before the comitia plebis tributa. This, along with the earlier restoration of their right to hold further office, meant that the tribunate was once again an important way for an aspiring politician to gain renown among the voters. There was no optimate opposition (Cicero, *in Verrem* I.1.45 **PS**).

Since Sulla's reforms, the equestrians had been deprived of the right of sitting on juries. Most contentiously in the court for provincial maladministration that tried pro-magistrates who had impacted upon the business interests of the equestrian order in the provinces. In 70 a delegation of Sicilians asked Cicero to prosecute C. Verres, the former governor of Sicily, who had systematically robbed the Sicilians of their wealth, their belongings, and their lives. Verres was not necessarily that unusual, a provincial governor was entitled to take the needs of his household from the resources of his province. Over time, pro-magistrates looked at their provincial command as an opportunity to reimburse themselves for the costs of the election campaign that had secured them high office and the subsequent provincial command. If Cicero's reports of Verres' crimes are even only half correct, his guilt was certain.

In Cicero's introduction to the case (Cicero *in Verrem* I.1.40–1 **PS**), he made it quite clear that the whole legal system was on trial. The speech showed the scale of provincial extortion and illustrated the prejudices of the senatorial order towards the provincials. Then Cicero called witnesses and enumerated the crimes in a sufficiently damning manner for Verres to abandon his defence and flee Rome. The jury despite probable bribes were left with no alternative but to find Verres guilty. On the back of this celebrated case, the senatorial order lost their monopoly of the law courts that Sulla had imposed and the equestrians were able to look out for their business interests once again. It was a praetor, L. Aurelius Cotta, who changed the law, but it is generally accepted that he was acting with the support of Pompey and Crassus.

After his consulship, Pompey held no immediate command, as opponents did not want to allow him further glory. He subsequently harnessed the support of tribunes to propose fresh overseas commands. First, against the pirates, who presented a perennial problem, and then to replace Lucullus in command of the war against Mithridates, who fled to the Crimea and soon committed suicide. Pompey re-founded Greek cities and redrew the map of provinces. In so doing, he increased his personal clientele. He also massively increased the public revenues of Rome through taxation. When Pompey returned from the east, he might have thought that he could claim to be the leading man of the state. However, never the most accomplished politician, he would find that events had passed him by. He had been gone from Rome too long.

PRESCRIBED SOURCE

Title: *in Verrem*

Author: Cicero

Date: After the trial in 70 BC

Genre: Prosecution Speech

Significance: In the prescribed section Cicero challenges the *Senate's* indifference to the provincials and their acceptance of bribery in the law courts

Prescribed sections: I.1.35–47

Read it here: G42 in LACTOR 7: *Late Republican Rome, 88–31 BC* (London: KCL, 2017)

ACTIVITY

Read *in Verrem* I.1.35–47 **PS**. According to Cicero's speech, how widespread can we believe bribery in the courts to have been?

TOPIC REVIEW

Refer to Plutarch's *Lives* and Sallust's *Histories*.

- Discuss what Sulla hoped to achieve with his reforms.
- Consider the reasons that the optimates allowed Pompey's extraordinary commands in the 70s.
- Assess why the Senate granted Pompey's demand for extra troops in Spain.
- Consider why so many politicians were keen to undo Sulla's reforms.

Further Reading

Keaveney, A. (2005), *Sulla*, Abingdon: Routledge.
Seager, R. (2002), *Pompey the Great*, 2nd edition, Oxford: Wiley-Blackwell.
Southern, P. (2002), *Pompey the Great*, Stroud: Tempus.

2.3 The Catilinarian Conspiracy

The challenges to the Constitution

- The Catilinarian conspiracy.

The means by which politicians achieved success and their importance in the breakdown of the Republic

- Factions including optimates and populares
- Land bills
- Largesse
- Intimidation during elections
- Violence
- Veteran support
- Rhetoric/oratory.

The roles and importance of individuals in the breakdown of the Republic

- Cicero
- Catiline
- Caesar

The prescribed sources for this subheading are:

- Cicero, Selected Letters No 3 (*ad Atticum* 1.1
- Cicero, *in Catilinam* II.17–23, *in Catilinam* IV.7–10, 20–2
- Cicero, *de lege agraria* II.7–10
- Q. Cicero *Commentariolum Petitionis* 13–24
- Sallust, *The Catiline Conspiracy* 10–16, 18–19, 20–1, 33–9, 51–4
- Plutarch, *Caesar* 7

Pompey and Crassus had shown that one need not be of the optimate elite to achieve the highest office. In the mid–60s, following their example, other aspiring politicians attempted to gain great political prestige within the confines of a constitution that could not accommodate them all. Among these were the aristocratic Julius Caesar and Catiline and, coming from outside the establishment, Cicero.

CATILINE

Catiline had served under Sulla and had been actively involved in the proscriptions. He was very well connected and seems to have taken a traditional path along the cursus honorum and was prosecuted for provincial extortion upon his return from a pro-praetorian governorship of Africa.

Towards the end of 66, the consuls elect for 65 were prosecuted for electoral bribery. According to Sallust (*Bellum Catilinae* 18–19 **PS**), Catiline was involved in an attempted assassination of their replacements, L. Aurelius Cotta and L. Manlius Torquatus. Catiline's motivation was that he was prevented from standing as a replacement because of his pending court case for provincial extortion. He apparently joined with one of those who had been condemned for electoral bribery, P. Autronius Paetus, and together with a quaestor, Cn. Calpurnius Piso, plotted to murder the new consuls on 1 January, their first day of office. Autronius and Catiline were to seize the consulships and Piso was to govern Spain. Rumours of the plot surfaced, a postponement occurred, and a fresh plan was hatched to extend the murder to include most of the Senate. This also failed. As an afterword Piso, despite only being a quaestor, was sent to Spain with pro-praetorian imperium, either at Crassus' order or that of the optimates, both groups seemingly wanting to set up an alternative power to Pompey in Spain. Pompey had a strong client base in Spain after his years against Sertorius. It is evident that jealousy of Pompey's successes motivated optimate and popularis alike. Piso was in any case killed by his own men.

These events are known by modern historians as the First Catiline Conspiracy, and should be distinguished from the Catiline Conspiracy itself, which reached its head in 63. However, the truth about this event is not clear. The tradition above is taken directly from Sallust, but he qualifies his report with a disclaimer that he cannot be certain about what happened: although he was writing just twenty years later, much of the story may have been fabricated by Catiline's detractors, especially Cicero, during and after the events of the conspiracy of 63. Within eighteen months of the supposed assassination, Cicero gave a speech as consular candidate in which he made it quite clear that people now knew about the plot. It would, however, be prudent for any politician to deride an opponent during an election if there were rumours of serious misconduct. Once Catiline had been clearly shown to be attempting revolution in 63, Cicero referred repeatedly to the First Conspiracy as he tried to damage Catiline's reputation. Yet earlier, in 65, Cicero had actually considered defending Catiline on the charge of provincial extortion. Therefore we can conclude that whatever truth there was in Catiline or others seeking to kill the consuls of 65, the story was at first unknown to Cicero; but by mid–64 sufficient rumour existed for Cicero to make political capital out of it.

PRESCRIBED SOURCE

Title: *The Catiline Conspiracy* (Sallust, *Bellum Catilinae*)

Author: Sallust

Date: Mid-40s BC

Genre: Historical monograph

Significance: Sallust believed that Rome had become degenerate since the fall of Carthage and used Catiline to illustrate how bad things had become. Catiline is portrayed as a dangerous criminal who sought to overthrow the state

Prescribed sections: 10–16, 18–19, 20–1, 33–9, 51–4

Read it here: OCR source booklet

ACTIVITY

With reference to Sallust BC 18–19 **PS**, Cicero, *in Toga Candida* (LACTOR 3), *in Catilinam* 1.15, *pro Murena* 81, *pro Sulla* 11, 81 and *ad Atticum* 1.2 = SL 4 (LACTOR 3), how far do the sources let us know what happened in the so-called First Catiline Conspiracy? (Cicero's speeches can generally all be found online http://perseus.uchicago.edu/cgi-bin/philologic/search3torth?dbname=LatinAugust2012&author=^c.) **CW**

Irrespective of any involvement in the first conspiracy, Catiline was acquitted of the charge of provincial extortion and stood for election to the consulship of 63. If Sallust is to be believed, Catiline corrupted the upper-class youth of Rome and incited them to usurp their fathers (Sallust, *Bellum Catilinae* 14–16 **PS**). He had gathered a group of discontented second-rate politicians to support his bid for the consulship. Their lack of political acumen and experience was one reason why he failed in his consulship bid and the subsequent attempted revolution. Their motivation is clearly seen in a speech made by Catiline that is couched in terms of missed opportunity:

> Because of this, all influence, power, rank, and wealth are in their hands, or wherever they wish them to be; to us they have left danger, defeat, prosecutions, and poverty . . . Use me either as your leader or as a soldier in the ranks; my soul and my body shall be at your service. These very schemes I hope to help you carry out as your consul . . .

> Sallust, *Catiline Conspiracy* 20

It must be recognised that this speech was invented by Sallust. He was not there, and those present were subsequently killed. Sallust was aiming to illustrate the motivation of Catiline as he saw it and thus there is a problem of veracity. Yet it is notable that Catiline was supposedly still aiming at the consulship. He went on to promise magistracies, priesthoods, opportunities for plunder, and proscriptions, but all with him as head of state. He also promised the cornerstone of his electoral campaign, a cancellation of debts or new tablets (*novae tabulae*). The wax tablets on which debts were recorded were to be smoothed over (Sallust, *Bellum Catilinae* 21 **PS**). The cancellation of debts was sure to attract the support of those members of the upper classes who had fallen into debt, and also the masses.

During the mid-60s there was a credit crisis in Italy. This was because since Mithridates' first uprising in 89, businessmen had been unwilling to invest in Asia; but with Pompey's departure to the east, they expected stability to return. Money lenders who had been lending at lower rates to safer enterprises in Italy, including many landowners, both rich and poor, were now calling in debts. However, debt cannot be simply cancelled; if the debtors were not to pay back the money, then the money lenders would have been out of pocket, hence the naivety of such a policy. This explains equestrian and optimate opposition to Catiline. Cicero would later play on the agreement between Senate and equestrians at this time to produce what he termed concordia ordinum, a harmony of the orders, which he would go on to champion at times of future discord.

CICERO'S ELECTION CAMPAIGN

> For you, an *eques*, are seeking the highest position in the state, highest in the sense that the same office confers much more distinction on a man who is brave, eloquent, and free from crime than on others.
>
> Q. Cicero, *Commentariolum Petitionis* 13

The nature of an electoral campaign is illustrated in the *Commentariolum Petitionis*, a pamphlet apparently written by Cicero's brother, not so much to tell Cicero what he did not already know, but rather to arrange the areas of importance that he should address. Although amicitiae are to be sought in all quarters, there is a very definite hierarchy: nobles, magistrates, and especially the consuls, tribunes and other men of influence who can bring their clients with them, should be sought out. Those who Cicero may have represented in court, or will represent in the future, should also be pursued (*Commentariolum Petitionis* 13–24 **PS**).

The nature of amicitiae was very brief; an alliance could be made for a single vote if it suited both parties, but they could also be many and various, so that an amicitia with one individual or group might be contrary to an amicitia with another. Cicero illustrates the problem in a letter to Atticus where he apologises that he cannot support Atticus' uncle, who was in conflict with an associate of the powerful noble L. Domitius Ahenobarbus, whose favour Cicero sought (Cicero, *Atticum* 1.1 = SL 3 **PS**). The *Commentariolum* (55) also reports that the bribery of voters was commonplace – although there is no suggestion that Cicero should do so, simply that he should guard against it.

Notwithstanding the rumours of the First Catiline Conspiracy, popular support for Catiline's proposal of debt cancellation was growing. Crassus and Caesar were possibly supportive. Sallust reports that information concerning the conspirators' willingness to go beyond legitimate means in order to seize power was already being leaked to the optimates. They were worried, and turned to Cicero. Despite his being a novus homo, he appeared a safe bet for the consulship. Plutarch reports that both the optimates and the people were happy to elect Cicero.

PRESCRIBED SOURCE

Title: *Commentariolum Petitionis*

Author: Quintus Cicero, (Cicero's brother)

Dates: *c.* 65–64 BC

Genre: Political pamphlet

Significance: Advises Cicero how to win the electoral campaign

Prescribed sections: 13–24

Read it here: LACTOR 3: A Short Guide to Electioneering (KCL, 1968)

FIGURE 2.4
Cicero.

On taking up the consulship in 63, Cicero immediately made his allegiances known. He spoke against the proposed land bill of the tribune P. Servilius Rullus, which would have addressed the needs of the poor who were still gravitating to Rome for hand-outs and work. Rullus' proposals were wide ranging: ager publicus in Italy was to be redistributed, while newly acquired land in the provinces would be sold to pay for this. Through eloquent speaking, Cicero played on the fears of the people and persuaded the audience that he was acting in their best interest. He was a 'people's consul' guiding the plebs; the land bill was a piece of largesse that would exhaust the treasury, and the people would all be poorer for it (Cicero, *de lege agraria* II.7–10 **PS**). Incredibly, because of Cicero's persuasive speech, the people did not vote through Rullus' bill.

Study question
With reference to Q. Cicero's *Commentariolum Petitionis,* by what means did Quintus think Cicero should win the consulship?

S & C

Consider Dio, 37.26–8 and Cicero pro Rabirio Perduellionis 2–4, 20–1.

1. How is the trial procedure unusual?
2. What is Cicero's view of the SCU?
3. How does Cicero justify Rabirius' actions?
4. Why is the timing of this case interesting?

CAESAR

Despite Caesar's later achievements, it is important to recognise that until the First Triumvirate of 59, he was just another ambitious politician on the make. Caesar, together with Crassus, may have sympathised with Catiline when he began his bid for power, but they were both too clever to get dragged down by intrigue and, sometime in 63, they must have decided to let him go. Political tensions were high in 63. Caesar brought about, and was judge in, the trial of C. Rabirius for the crime of high treason, which carried the death penalty. Rabirius had been part of the body of senators who with Marius had been involved in the death of Saturninus and his supporters in 100. This was clearly a show trial, as it occurred thirty-seven years after the event. Rabirius' guilt was not in doubt; it was a test case for the validity of the SCU. The trial was ultimately abandoned, maybe at Caesar's direction, but not before the SCU as a political tool had been brought into question.

There was also a bill which argued for restoring political rights to the children of those proscribed under Sulla; Caesar is thought to have supported this. Late in 63 Caesar stood for the position of chief priest, pontifex maximus, an honorary position that carried huge prestige. The more senior figure and leading optimate Catulus, wanting the position himself, tried to bribe Caesar to stand down. In response, Caesar bribed the voters with Crassus' money and won (Plutarch, *Caesar* 7 **PS**). In so doing, Caesar was making a political statement to the optimates that he could buy prestige.

CATILINE AND CICERO

Sallust reports that Catiline was preparing for revolution through 63, but it is not easy to tell how seriously he was doing so. Sallust wanted to paint Catiline in the worst possible light. Certainly Catiline sought the consulship again in 62. Despite rumours of assassination and revolution coming through informers, Catiline was too well connected to be prosecuted. He began talking about leading the unfortunate members of society – the miseri. Cicero openly challenged him, and that brought about the response known as Catiline's threat:

> 'I see two bodies' he said, 'one thin and wasted, but with a head, the other headless, but big and strong. What is there so dreadful about it, if I myself become the head of the body which needs one?'

> Plutarch, *Cicero* 14

The inference was that the senate was weak and the people strong, but lacking a leader. Cicero presided over the consular elections, wearing a breastplate and with an extensive bodyguard of young nobles, a piece of theatre emphasising the danger that Catiline was supposed to pose. Catiline failed to get elected once more.

Only now did Catiline turn to armed uprising. He dispatched men to raise troops in the countryside. Chief among these was C. Manlius, who was sent to mobilise forces in

Etruria. There were also plans for fire-starting in the city and seizing strategic points with armed men. On receipt of letters warning prominent popularis figures of planned massacres, the Senate passed the SCU. Troops were dispatched against Manlius and to other areas of Italy where there was unrest. Of the support that Catiline engendered, it was the military forces, the veterans, that seemed most formidable. The political classes were second rate and the poor, through no fault of their own, were weak. On 6 November there was a meeting of the conspirators, where Catiline encouraged some to kill Cicero at home when he took the morning greeting the next day. Cicero thus finally had enough evidence to denounce Catiline. On 8 November he delivered the first of four speeches against Catiline. Defiantly, Catiline attempted to defend himself but he was shouted down. He left the city ostensibly for exile in Massalia, but actually joined with Manlius in Etruria. Catiline, despite Sallust's invective, was a reluctant revolutionary.

The next day Cicero delivered his second speech against Catiline before the people in the forum. He made a case for Catiline's followers being the worst members of society. He put them into six classes ordered by increasing disdain (Cicero, *in Catilinam* II 17–23): the worst group of all was made up of Catiline's friends:

> They devote their whole lives and all their waking hours to the vast labour of banqueting all night long. In this herd is found the gambler and adulterer, and all the filth of Rome. These charming and refined lads have learned not only to make love and to suffer it, to dance and sing, but also to murder with dagger or poison.
>
> Cicero, *in Catilinam* II.22–3 (LACTOR 7, B64c)

Sallust reproduces a plea from Manlius, Catiline's general in the field, that shows the motivation of the veterans, in which it is clear that debt was a very real issue:

> For we are wretched and destitute, many of us have been driven from our country by the violence and cruelty of the moneylenders, while all have lost repute and fortune. None of us has been allowed, in accordance with the usage of our forefathers, to enjoy the protection of the law and retain our personal liberty after being stripped of our patrimony, such was the inhumanity of the moneylenders and the praetor.
>
> Sallust, *Catiline Conspiracy* 33

Sallust also reproduces a letter (Sallust, *Bellum Catilinae* 35). from Catiline himself to the optimate Catulus, where he complains that he has been robbed of his just desserts, and that it is only the selfishness of a few powerful individuals that has pushed him into taking to the field. He wraps his justification up in a case of supporting the miseri; but the tone of the letter, rather like the speech to his political supporters (Sallust, *Bellum Catilinae* 20), is all about missed opportunity and honour slighted. Catiline was as selfish as those he denounced in the letter: he started a revolution because he had failed as a politician.

The manner in which the conspiracy unfolded at Rome is clear in Sallust's narrative. An emergency session of the Senate debated the fate of those conspirators arrested at Rome. The consul elect D. Iunius Silanus proposed the death penalty. All who spoke after him agreed until Caesar spoke against killing the men. His argument was that Rome had laws and the fact that these men had sought to break them did not mean that the Senate

PRESCRIBED SOURCE

Title: *in Catilinam II*

Author: Cicero

Date: Delivered 9 November 63, written up before 60

Genre: Political speech

Significance: The message of the prescribed section is that no right-minded citizen would support Catiline

Prescribed sections: 17–23

Read it here: B64c in LACTOR 7: *Late Republican Rome, 88–31 BC* (London: KCL, 2017)

PRESCRIBED SOURCE

Title: *In Catilinam IV*

Author: Cicero

Date: Delivered 5 December 63, written up before 60

Genre: Political speech

Significance: The fourth Catiline oration deals with the debate over the fate of the conspirators

Prescribed sections: 7–10, 20–2

Read it here: B76a and B76b in LACTOR 7: *Late Republican Rome, 88–31 BC* (London: KCL, 2017)

should do the same by executing them without trial. Caesar thus changed opinion, until the young noble M. Porcius Cato, who traded on the probity of the family name gained from his famous grandfather Cato the Censor, delivered a withering speech that sealed the conspirators' fate (Sallust, *Bellum Catilinae* 51–4 **PS**; Plutarch, *Caesar* 7 **PS**). Sallust's report of this debate is framed by his own admiration for both men. He was a partisan of Caesar's but also an admirer of Cato's uprightness, which he saw as a model to challenge what he perceived as the degradation of Roman society. Both men come out well:

> . . . for a long time, as when mothers are exhausted by child-bearing, no one at all was produced at Rome who was great in merit. But within my own memory there have appeared two men of towering merit, though of diverse character, Marcus Cato and Gaius Caesar.
>
> Sallust, *Catiline Conspiracy* 53

In Cicero's version of the debate (*in Catilinam* IV.7–10 **PS**, 20–2 **PS**), Cato's role is written out while Cicero's is emphasised. It is known from a later letter of Cicero's that Cato received a great deal of literary praise after the event in a panegyric by Brutus, which may have been Sallust's source. This is a cautionary tale in following Sallust too closely, he was looking to eulogise both Caesar and Cato. Although Cicero was praised in the immediate aftermath, he would later be attacked for having the conspirators executed without trial (Cicero, *in Catilinam* IV.20 **PS**).

Catiline died in battle the next year. Overall it could be argued that the Catiline Conspiracy was a 'storm in a tea cup'. His political supporters were inadequate and the poor were impotent, so that only the veteran forces were effective, although outnumbered. Seemingly Cicero worked up the scale of the threat for his own personal aggrandisement. Even though he chiefly acted out of self-interest, Catiline addressed very real social problems; debt was a millstone for many at the time. If nothing else, the Catiline Conspiracy showed popularis politicians that armed insurrection would not do; to succeed at bringing about social change, they would have to subvert the existing system.

TOPIC REVIEW

- Discuss how far the sources can be trusted for the character of Catiline.
- Assess why the Catiline Conspiracy failed.
- Consider how far the Catiline Conspiracy was ever a serious threat to Rome.

Further Reading

Everitt, A. (2001), *Cicero*, London: John Murray.
Goldsworthy, A. (2006), *Caesar*, London: Weidenfeld & Nicolson.
Stockton, D. (1971), *Cicero,* Oxford: Oxford University Press.

2.4 The 50s: A Turbulent Decade

TOPIC OVERVIEW

The challenges to the Constitution

- The First Triumvirate, its purposes and outcomes
- Unrest through the 50s BC.

The means by which politicians achieved success and their importance in the breakdown of the Republic

- Factions including optimates and populares
- Land bills, largesse and games
- Intimidation during trials and elections
- Violence, bribery and corruption
- The military commands of Pompey and Caesar
- Army and veteran support
- Rhetoric/oratory
- Political marriages and scandals.

The roles and importance of individuals in the breakdown of the Republic

- Pompey
- Crassus
- Caesar
- Cato
- Clodius

The prescribed sources for this subheading are:

- Sallust, *The Catiline Conspiracy* 37
- Cicero, Selected Letters Nos 10, 15, 16, 22, 25 (*ad Atticum* 1.16, 2.19, 2.21, 4.3, *ad Quintum fratrem* 2.3)
- Plutarch, *Pompey* 47–8.
- Plutarch, *Caesar* 13–14.

After Catiline, it was clear that if popularis politicians were to achieve personal glory, they would have to change the political landscape somehow. This happened with the First Triumvirate, the amicitia of Caesar, Pompey and Crassus that took place for Caesar's consular year of 59 and was loosely held thereafter. It was brought about because all three triumvirs had found their wants thwarted by optimate elements in the Senate. The very term 'First Triumvirate' is a modern one, applied to this union by historians. At no time was it legalised as the Second Triumvirate would be, and it was only gradually understood by the political classes.

POMPEY'S NEEDS

Pompey had returned from Asia in 62 to a rather cold welcome. He had reorganised the provinces of the east which had increased the public revenues of Rome through taxation by 70 per cent, together with an immediate booty of HS 480 million. He might have expected huge thanks for this and for having defeated Mithridates. In his eyes, land grants for his veterans would have been completely appropriate. His decisions about the eastern provinces were legitimate within the limits of his imperium. Now that he had returned, they required the Senate's ratification, but confirmation would also be expected. However, over the next two years, opposition, born out of simple jealousy, would push him into the arms of Caesar. Pompey was becoming increasingly popularis in outlook, if only because the establishment resisted his continued successes. He sent ahead a lieutenant M. Pupius Piso Frugi as candidate for the consulship of 61, and asked that elections were delayed so that he could lend his support in person. Cato swung the Senate against the request. As it happened, Piso won anyway. Once elected, Piso tried to sponsor a land bill for Pompey's veterans without success. Q. Caecilius Metellus Celer was expected to gain the consulship of 60, and Pompey could not expect any favours from him. This was not only because of Metellus' optimate stance, but also because Pompey had divorced Metellus' half-sister. Pompey therefore began bribing the electorate to get another former lieutenant L. Afranius elected as consul for 60, as Cicero reported to Atticus:

> Now elections are in prospect; into them, against the wishes of all, our Magnus is thrusting Aulus' son and in his cause he is fighting not with authority (auctoritas) and influence (gratia), but with those methods by which Philip said all fortifications could be stormed provided that a donkey laden with gold could get up to them.
>
> Cicero, *ad Atticum* 1.16 = SL 10 (LACTOR 7, L15)

The 'Magnus' here is Pompey, Aulus' son is Afranius. The bribery became notorious and Afranius was easily elected. Afranius tried to steer the approval of Pompey's eastern settlements through the Senate, but these were opposed by Lucullus, the man who Pompey had ousted from the Mithridatic command in 66 (see p. 103). He was aided by Cato and Metellus. They sought to have every one of Pompey's decisions debated, rather than gain a blanket approval for all. Pompey, having been thwarted in the Senate, used the tribune L. Flavius to propose a land bill directly to the people. Flavius clashed severely with Metellus and hauled him off to jail, as a tribune could in theory do this. Metellus as consul made a show of this, summoning the Senate to his cell, so that Flavius and Pompey were made to look ridiculous.

> Thus he learned that he did not possess any real power, but merely the name and envy resulting from his former authority, while in point of fact he received no benefit from it; and he repented of having let his legions go so soon and of having put himself in the power of his enemies.

Dio 37.50

Study question
With reference to Plutarch's life of Pompey and Dio 37.50, was Pompey politically powerful at Rome?

publicani the corporations of equestrians who managed state contracts. They had to pay a fixed price up front to the treasury for their contract. In the case of taxes, they were free to keep a percentage of the revenue collected

CRASSUS' NEEDS

Since the time of the Gracchi, the collection of provincial taxes had been delegated to corporations of business men, who were allowed to take a cut of the money collected. Equestrians made up these corporations termed the **publicani**. In 60 BC, the publicani complained to the Senate that they had overbid for their contracts in Asia and wanted to be released from a third of the cost. Crassus supported their claim because his own financial interests were linked to those of the publicani. The sources say least about this triumvir, but his wealth was prodigious; he lent freely to all classes – equestrians and senators – and gained widespread political support from doing so.

Cicero wrote to Atticus about the unpleasantness of having to speak in favour of the publicani and cajole the Senate to agree. Although he did not approve of their request, he saw the need to maintain his concept of concordia ordinum whereby the Senatorial and equestrian orders worked together to preserve the established state of things. Cato was the chief spokesman against, and the question held up other business for a while. Cato had also brought a bill about bribery in the courts explicitly making equestrians liable to prosecution, while previous laws had only allowed for the prosecution of senators. This was perceived by the equestrians as another attack on their status. By Cicero's analysis, Cato was tormenting the equestrians with high morality, rather than judgement, and living in a utopian ideal rather than Rome's pragmatic political arena.

KEY INDIVIDUAL

M. Licinius Crassus
Dates: *c.* 115–53 BC

First became rich through the proscriptions. He defeated Spartacus in the Slave War. Consul in 70 with Pompey, triumvir in 59 and consul with Pompey a second time in 55. He died during the Parthian campaign at Carrhae in 53.

CAESAR'S NEEDS

Caesar had gained sufficient military success as pro-praetorian governor of Spain in 61 to seek a triumph upon his return, but he was also looking to stand for the consulship of 59. He asked to stand in absentia and await his triumph, but the proposal was discussed at such length by Cato that it was left undecided, a process termed filibustering (Plutarch, *Caesar* 13 **PS**). Although Cato dressed this up as defending the proper order of things, his motivation was actually more personal. He was hoping to allow his son-in-law Bibulus the opportunity to gain some prestige independently of Caesar, as previously he had had to compete against and share magistracies with Caesar. Additionally, Cato was

KEY INDIVIDUAL

M. Porcius Cato
Dates: 95–46 BC

Prominent traditionalist politician. Argued decisively for the execution of Catiline's co-conspirators. As tribune in 62, he increased the number of recipients of the grain dole. He opposed the Triumvirs through the 50s. Defeated in the Civil War, he committed suicide at Utica in Africa.

always upset by his half-sister Servilia's long-standing relationship with Caesar. This personal and petty nature of politics pervades the period. If Cato had really been the moral champion he pretended to be, he might have been more conciliatory.

THE FORMATION OF THE FIRST TRIUMVIRATE

Pompey was very happy to support Caesar. Despite the failure of Piso Frugi and Afranius to gain settlement for his veterans and ratify his eastern decisions, Caesar offered a renewed, more determined approach. In the face of Caesar's expected election, the optimates resorted to bribery to ensure Bibulus was also successful, something that even Cato reportedly approved. Otherwise the optimates were largely indifferent, and one must ask why? The traditional system whereby the nobles had sufficient influence to promote their sons and nephews to the top jobs still prevailed and power normally remained within a few families, with consuls being advised by their close relatives. Although there had been a steady stream of populares radical politicians achieving high office, these individuals could only hold power for a single year; even if both consuls were cooperating as Crassus and Pompey had done in 70, the effects were transient. Thus the optimates probably felt that the occasional populares politician was just part of the political scenery. They did manage to snub Caesar with a senatorial decision that the consular provinces for the coming year would be the woods and pastures of Italy, as opposed to a more lucrative overseas command. Even if there were a need to improve rural communications, and suppress banditry, this was beneath the dignity of a consul and can only have been an insult; it would certainly not attract an army. This was only a minor irritation, to be overcome once in office. Despite Cato's ideological ranting, the optimates had become complacent.

Caesar and Pompey first joined in an amicitia, but Caesar recognised a threat to their union in Crassus. As consul elect, he sought to reconcile Pompey to Crassus. Politically they were not far apart. All three were broadly speaking populares, but in the case of Crassus and Pompey, their personal ambition and mutual animosity was getting in the way of personal success. Plutarch observed:

> For it was not the case that by getting Crassus to support Pompey or Pompey to support Crassus he made either of them greater than before; instead, by using them he made himself greater than anyone.

Plutarch, *Crassus* 14 (see also Plutarch, *Caesar* 13)

This is indicative of Caesar's political good judgement. Pompey had vast wealth and the loyalty of his veterans; this loyalty would be cemented if he could bring about land settlements. Crassus was equally wealthy, influential and very well-connected; while Pompey had fought wars, he had made business deals that pervaded all of Roman society.

Study question

With reference to Plutarch Pompey 47 **PS**, Caesar 13 **PS**, Suetonius 18, how vigorously did the establishment oppose Caesar's candidature?

CAESAR'S FIRST CONSULSHIP

Caesar's first consideration as consul was to secure land for Pompey's veterans. Within his first few days in office, he proposed a bill that a land commission be set up to settle veterans and urban poor. At first his proposals were conciliatory, and were brought before the senate for approval. They included the following:

1. The ager Campanus, where many optimates had land-holdings and which was subject to taxation was excluded.
2. The commission would comprise twenty men. The high number would diminish any individual's importance.
3. The commissioners could only purchase land that was willingly sold.
4. All previous land occupation was recognised, to prevent claims of theft.
5. The money was to come from Pompey's settlements in the east.
6. New settlers were banned from selling for twenty years, to prevent them making a quick profit and the rich buying up land soon after.

Furthermore, Caesar made it clear that he was willing to negotiate on any given point. Despite the reasonableness of these proposals, there was little support in the Senate. Cato stood up to filibuster the whole proposal. Caesar's temper broke and he threatened to arrest Cato, but this made him look foolish and he revoked the order (Plutarch, *Caesar* 14 **PS**). Although Cato had won a moral victory, Caesar, ever the pragmatist, took the bill to the comitia tributa. Before a law was voted on, preliminary hearings took place; these allowed people time to consider their position before voting. At one of these hearings, Bibulus spoke against the bill, but Caesar called upon Crassus and Pompey to support it.

> . . . And when he was opposed by his colleague Bibulus, and Cato stood ready to support Bibulus with all his might, Caesar brought Pompey on the rostra before the people, and asked him in so many words whether he approved the proposed laws: and when Pompey said he did, 'Then,' said Caesar, 'in case any resistance should be made to the law, will you come to the aid of the people?' 'Yes, indeed,' said Pompey, 'I will come, bringing, against those who threaten swords, both sword and shield.'
>
> Plutarch, *Pompey* 47

Afterwards, Pompey's veterans were everywhere in the city. Bibulus, while being accompanied to the forum with Cato, was set upon by a mob, his symbolic rods of office were broken and a bucket of dung was thrown over him (Plutarch, *Pompey* 48 **PS**, Caes 14 **PS**). It appears that the triumvirs were orchestrating this violent intimidation. The law was passed easily when it came to the vote. Bibulus did try to invoke the Senate against Caesar but to no avail, and so he ended up going home to declare the omens unfavourable. He did this because if the omens were indeed inauspicious, no public business should have been transacted. This might have been a nuisance but would never be a serious impediment; after all, Caesar was pontifex maximus and Pompey was an augur (seer), so they could discredit Bibulus' interpretations from a position of authority. Within a couple of months Caesar produced a complementary land bill in which the ager Campanus was now included to be redistributed to 20,000 urban families that had three or more children.

He took this directly to the comitia tributa. This was a direct affront to the optimates, many of whom stood to lose property by such a move. Soon after, Caesar also proposed through a tribune that Pompey's eastern decisions were confirmed. Similarly the Asian tax collectors had their contracts renegotiated to address Crassus' concerns.

It only became obvious very late that the triumvirs were, in fact, working together. Cicero wrote to Atticus in May 59 that Pompey's behaviour was perplexing and his justification contrived, so Pompey was said to be approving of the legislation but not necessarily the procedures used, or the manner in which Bibulus was treated. By July, Cicero was distraught:

> Pompey, my hero, has brought about his own ruin, a fact which causes me great pain.
>
> Cicero, *ad Atticum* 2.19 = SL 15 (LACTOR 7, B97c)

In the same letter, Cicero was far from pleased with Bibulus' ineffectual edicts. He does report that popular sentiment was turning against the triumvirs and Pompey had been publicly mocked in the theatre. Although one must take the individual events at face value, the importance that Cicero attaches to them is liable to his own conservative bias. An actor in the theatre probably did engender applause by heckling Pompey, but how far this represented popular sentiment is unclear. While the political classes may have been aghast at the triumvirs' actions, it seems unlikely that there was widespread dissatisfaction from the lowest classes, who stood to gain most from their regime.

As the year progressed Caesar looked ahead; he used the tribune P. Vatinius to propose in the comitia plebis tributa that Caesar be given control of Cisalpine Gaul and Illyricum for five years, which was an unusually long imperium. The Senate had traditionally appointed provincial commands, but it has been shown that Marius first ignored this practice, and Pompey had twice secured commands this way. In view of the Senate's proposal that Caesar be given the woods and pastures of Italy, it is easy to see why he used the comitia plebis tributa in this case. When the governor of Transalpine Gaul suddenly died, Pompey proposed that this also would be added to Caesar's imperium. This time the Senate acquiesced, seeing no value in opposition. Although the sources dwell on Vatinius' actions, it is to be noted that Cato and at least three other tribunes, otherwise unremarkable, actively sided with Bibulus to oppose the Triumvirate.

Towards the end of 59, Caesar married Calpurnia the daughter of L. Calpurnius Piso, the designated consul for 58. In doing this, he was hoping to ensure that his actions were not reversed as soon as he left office. More importantly, Caesar married his daughter Julia to Pompey, a man much older even by Roman standards. Yet this marriage was a surprising success and did much to secure cooperation between the triumvirs in the 50s (Plutarch, *Pompey* 47 (PS); *Caesar* 14 (PS)). Caesar was also looking for a replacement tribune to act in his interests. The young aristocratic but popularis radical P. Clodius Pulcher had long wanted to gain the office of tribune, but was prevented because of his patrician birth. Although Clodius was of a very noble family, the Claudii, and sought the honours of high political office, he was the youngest son, and while his brothers traded on established optimate credentials, Clodius sought renown by being controversial and ingratiating himself with the plebs.

In late 62, Clodius had been caught observing and so profaning the rites of the all-female festival of Bona Dea which was being held in the house of Caesar as pontifex maximus. This was a minor piece of upper class bravado, to sneak into an all-female ceremony and tell the tale. However it was soon blown out of all proportion. Clodius had upset a few people with his popularis stance, most especially Lucullus because he had provoked a mutiny among his troops when serving in Armenia. Now his enemies hoped to persecute him. At the trial, the bribery was notorious. Clodius was supported by Crassus who, according to Cicero, paid off debts, agreed to sponsor bills and made other political promises to various jurors, so that despite Clodius' clear guilt, he was acquitted (*ad Atticum* 1.16 = SL 10 **PS**). Cicero had provided evidence against Clodius' alibi, despite Clodius previously supporting Cicero against Catiline, and now Clodius bore a grudge.

To gain the tribunate, Clodius was seeking adoption into a plebeian family, which required the approval of the pontifex maximus – Caesar. Cicero was still sufficiently influential for Caesar to try to keep onside, so at first he refused. However, when Cicero verbally attacked the Triumvirate in court, Caesar became exasperated and agreed to the adoption. Although Clodius would represent Caesar's interests in his absence, one should not discount the ambition of Clodius himself. He was far from Caesar's puppet; he was his own man, forging an alliance with one of the pre-eminent politicians of his day. At the very end of 59, a rather shadowy episode occurred; this was known as the Vettius' affair, in which a group of nobles were implicated in an attempted assassination of Pompey. Yet the whole thing appears to have been an attempt by Caesar to keep Pompey faithful to the Triumvirate (Cicero, *ad Atticum* 2.24 **CW**).

KEY INDIVIDUAL

P. Clodius Pulcher
Dates: *c.* 92–52 BC

A popularis but aristocratic politician. He was prosecuted over the Bona Dea scandal but acquitted through widespread bribery. As tribune in 58 he made the corn dole free, used some collegia as street gangs and banished Cicero for killing the Catiline conspirators. He subsequently waged street warfare with gangs through the 50s, and was killed at Bovillae in 52.

CLODIUS AS TRIBUNE

As tribune, Clodius had the opportunity to bring bills directly to the people. He was looking to cement his own popularis credentials. He quickly passed several laws, two of which directly impacted on the plebs urbana, whose number and importance had grown in recent years:

> Besides this, the young men who had maintained a wretched existence by manual labour in the country, tempted by public and private doles had come to prefer idleness in the city to their hateful toil.

Sallust, *Catiline Conspiracy* 37

Here Sallust is exaggerating the idleness of many, but there was a growing community at Rome that relied on hand-outs from the political classes and whose support could be used for political ends. Properly all urbanites ought to have only been enrolled in the four urban tribes, but no census had been completed since 70, so many of the poor domiciled at Rome were still enrolled in rural tribes. They were much better placed to attend the comitia plebis tributa than their rural counterparts, and so the plebs urbana were able to swing the vote of rural tribes, of which there were thirty-one, and hence the comitia plebis tributa as a whole. With his first law Clodius made the corn dole free and increased the number of recipients to 320,000. This was a massive piece of largesse funded by the

Study questions
With reference to the sources:

1. Why was Pompey unable to achieve veteran settlement alone?
2. Why were the triumvirs successful where Catiline was not?
3. How important was Vatinius to the Triumvirate?
4. Outline the methods used by politicians in the late 60s and 59 to try to achieve their wishes.

> **collegium (pl. collegia)**
> clubs made up of
> individuals often living in
> close proximity. They
> fulfilled a social function,
> often seeing to burial
> needs. Under Clodius,
> some became street
> gangs.

state, but at Clodius' direction. Secondly, **collegia**, which had been suppressed as a measure against Catiline, were legalised again. These collegia were clubs that fulfilled a social function that gave the poor a sense of community. Clodius went further in that some (but by no means all) of the collegia were transformed into street gangs, to impose his will. However, many of the poor were still attached through the bonds of patronage to other political families, and so it was only a short time before opposing street gangs were being organised by other politicians. Most prominently among them were those of T. Annius Milo and P. Sestius, both of whom were backed by Pompey. Street warfare would ensue.

Cicero had been attacked by the tribune Q. Caecilius Metellus Nepos immediately after the Catiline Conspiracy for acting outside of the law when he executed the conspirators. Clodius had also been threatening Cicero, since he disproved Clodius' alibi in the Bona Dea trial (Cicero, *ad Atticum* 2.21 =SL 16 **PS**). As tribune, Clodius carried a law against those who had brought about the death of Roman citizens without trial. Cicero was not explicitly mentioned, but the law was clearly aimed at him. Cicero's response was theatrical. He put on mourning, as did large numbers of supporters, while Clodius and his gang members harangued him verbally and physically. Cicero might have expected help from the consuls of 58, Calpurnius Piso and A. Gabinius, as he had previously been on good terms with both. However, Clodius had bought their support by arranging good provinces for the following year. Nor did Cicero get any help from Pompey, who refused to meet with him. But most disappointing was the absence of optimate support; Clodius may have been popularis but he was aristocratic, while Cicero was merely a novus homo. Despite Cicero acting in the optimates' interests through his consulship, the establishment was not prepared to protect him actively against one of their own. In the end, Cicero slipped away from Rome into exile.

Cicero's supporters looked to have his exile overturned from the very beginning, but their meetings, proposals and votes for Cicero's recall frequently met with violence. The evidence for this comes chiefly from Cicero's own speech, which he later delivered in defence of P. Sestius on a charge of violence. The relevant parts of this speech are not prescribed sources, but they do indicate the increasingly violent nature of the political process at Rome.

Late in 57 Cicero was recalled, but animosity between Cicero and Clodius rumbled on. On 3 November 57, armed gangs acting under Clodius' orders attacked workers at Cicero's house, which was being restored after Clodius had demolished it during his absence. The evidence comes from a letter of Cicero's (*ad Atticum* 4.3 = SL 22 **PS**) where he reports the actions of Clodius in the worst possible light, attacking enemies openly, recruiting slaves, partaking in arson, demolishing property and showing simple recklessness.

> . . . he thinks of nothing but massacring his enemies, and goes from street to street openly offering slaves their freedom. . . . But after this orgy of wrecking, arson, and loot, his followers have left him. . . . . He sees that if he slaughters everybody he chooses in broad daylight, his case, when it comes to court, won't be a jot worse than it is already.
>
> Cicero, *ad Atticum* 4.3 = SL 22

Clodius was unrepentant. He sought the aedileship for 56, a position that would allow him further political activity and enable him to avoid any prosecution for his street fighting. The same letter reports how in response Milo, who was a tribune that year, arrived at the elections early to declare the auspices unfavourable and so postpone proceedings. This greatly annoyed the consul Metellus Nepos, who was related to Clodius through marriage. Here family prestige overrode political leanings. Clodius was supported by his brother Appius who was very much the optimate, as were the Metelli. Cicero was optimistic that Milo would bring Clodius to trial for violence before he was elected. Throughout the letter, Cicero is full of admiration for Milo and enjoying the contest between the two camps. He sees no fault in his own supporters using violence to overcome Clodius, even suggesting that Milo might just do away with Clodius himself, predicting what will indeed happen later. However, despite Cicero's optimism, Clodius was elected aedile and so avoided prosecution.

Straight away, on 2 February 56, Clodius prosecuted Milo for violence, of which he was of course equally guilty. It must be remembered that in Rome there was no police force or public prosecution; the law was a private matter where one citizen brought a case against another. As such it was the preserve of the rich and in the 50s was being used as a political tool to incapacitate rivals. Despite Milo's guilt, Cicero and Pompey both defended him. The court case descended into riot, with a two-hour shouting match between the factions:

> . . . all manner of insults ended with some highly scabrous verse to the address of Clodius and Clodia. Pale with fury, he started a game of question and answer in the middle of the shouting: 'Who's starving the people to death?' 'Pompey,' answered the gang. 'Who wants to go to Alexandria?' Answer: 'Pompey.' 'Whom do you want to go?' Answer: 'Crassus' (who was present as a supporter of Milo, wishing him no good). About 2.15 the Clodians started spitting at us, as though on a signal. Sharp rise in temperature! They made a push to dislodge us, our side counter-charged. Flight of gang. Clodius was hurled from the rostra.

Cicero, *ad Quintum fratrem* 2.3 = SL 25

PS

Cicero fully approved of these actions and exulted in the idea of Pompey moving men from the country to bolster Milo's forces and to perpetuate street fighting (Cicero, *ad Quintum fratrem* 2.3 = SL 25 **PS** **CW**). The trial was postponed several times before ultimately being shelved.

THE RE-ESTABLISHMENT OF THE TRIUMVIRATE

Although the triumvirs had initially promoted their people to the positions of authority, by 56 Caesar's consulship was becoming a memory, little more than a hiccup in the established order. The consulship was again being granted to optimate members of the established political families; maybe the complacency of 59 had been justified. Cicero was politically active once again, as he tried to dismantle the triumvir's actions by attacking Caesar's land laws in the Senate; that he could do so shows that they had not been fully enacted. He also hoped to prise Pompey away from the amicitia of the Triumvirate, which was certainly very loose, as the respective backing of street gangs by both Pompey and Crassus showed. At the same time L. Domitius Ahenobarbus, an incredibly rich optimate who had extensive landholdings and clients in Gaul, was agitating to replace Caesar in command of Gaul, which he saw as his own natural sphere of influence.

Although the Triumvirate had only been a loose amicitia, preserved through mutual distrust, it was not in Crassus' and Caesar's interest that they should lose Pompey's support completely. Pompey had been openly attacked by Clodius and tacitly by Crassus, but he was no more welcome in optimate quarters. For all three, a reassertion of their alliance made sense. Pompey travelled north to Luca in Cisalpine Gaul to meet with Caesar; Caesar had previously met with Crassus at Ravenna. When Pompey returned, he had a stern message for Cicero to back off and leave Caesar's land laws alone. All the sources report that many other prominent senators made the journey to Luca to negotiate with the triumvirs where the following terms were agreed:

1. Pompey and Crassus were to be co-consuls again in 55.
2. Pompey was to get a five-year proconsular imperium in Spain.
3. Crassus was to get a five-year proconsular imperium in Syria and an expected military victory against the Parthians to equal the other triumvirs.
4. Caesar's imperium was to be extended another five years.

Once it became known that Pompey and Crassus intended to stand for the consulship, only Ahenobarbus, with Cato's support, stood against them. Cato himself sought to be praetor. These two carried such great influence that Crassus mobilised a tribune, confusingly called C. Cato, and Clodius to foster fresh civic unrest. They managed to postpone the elections long enough for Caesar to release troops on leave back to Rome in early 55 to participate in the vote. The presence of large numbers of troops made the atmosphere even more intimidating. On election day, there was fighting, but Pompey and Crassus were elected. Their first business was the election of praetors, but to prevent Cato getting the position, they openly engaged in bribery and secured the election of Vatinius, who as tribune had supported the triumvirs in 59 instead.

Once in power, Pompey and Crassus used the by now familiar expedient of getting a tribune in C. Trebonius to bring laws to secure their overseas commands, and again the later sources report violence surrounding the vote. Pompey also engaged in large-scale largesse, putting on elaborate shows to open his new stone-built theatre. At the end of the year, Crassus went to Syria to undertake his ill-fated Parthian campaign; he died at Carrhae. Pompey governed his province of Spain through subordinates. The next year, 54, Domitius Ahenobarbus and A. Claudius Pulcher, Clodius' brother, were voted in as consuls on account of their well-established optimate credentials. Yet they were found to be as inadequate and self-serving as the triumvirs. During the elections for aedile in 53, more people were killed. Pompey was splattered with blood, and the sight of this caused his wife, Caesar's daughter, to miscarry. She died in childbirth the next year, removing one of the bonds that existed between the triumvirs; Pompey soon remarried. Violence and bribery accompanied the elections throughout these years. This culminated in the death of Clodius at the hands of Milo. In the aftermath, to restore order, Bibulus and Cato proposed that Pompey be appointed consul for 52 without a colleague. Pompey must

EXPLORE FURTHER

With reference to Plutarch's Crassus 1–14, how far can we ascertain the importance of Crassus?

have been elated. The Senate wanted order and Pompey could provide it. Milo was prosecuted and Cicero's defence proved inadequate. Yet with Pompey in charge, 52 passed into 51 peacefully at Rome.

TOPIC REVIEW

Refer to the sources you have read.

- Compile a list of the occasions when largesse was used as a political tool.
- Explain whether Clodius was any worse than Milo.
- Explain why the Senate allowed the violence to continue through the 50s.
- Consider why Pompey abandoned the Triumvirate.

Further Reading

Everitt, A. (2001), *Cicero*, London: John Murray.

Goldsworthy, A. (2006), *Caesar*, London: Weidenfeld & Nicolson.

Seager, R. (2002), *Pompey the Great*, 2nd edition, Oxford: Wiley-Blackwell.

Southern, P. (2002), *Pompey the Great*, Stroud: Tempus.

Stockton, D. (1971), *Cicero*, Oxford: Oxford University Press.

Tatum, J. (1999), *The Patrician Tribune*, Chapel Hill: University of North Carolina Press.

Taylor, D. (2013), *Cicero and Rome*, London: Bloomsbury Academic.

PRACTICE QUESTIONS

1. How far was Clodius typical of politicians of the period?

You must use and analyse the ancient sources you have studied as well as your own knowledge to support your answer.

[36]

2.5 Civil War and Caesar's Dictatorship

TOPIC OVERVIEW

The challenges to the Constitution

- The reasons for the Civil War of 49 BC
- Caesar's dictatorship and social change
- Caesar's assassination.

The means by which politicians achieved success and their importance in the breakdown of the Republic

- Land bills, largesse, games and donatives
- The threat of military action
- The military commands of Caesar
- Army and veteran support.

The roles and importance of individuals in the breakdown of the Republic

- Caesar
- Brutus and Cassius

The prescribed sources for this subheading are:

- Cicero, Selected Letters Nos 59, 67, 68, (*ad Atticum* 7.6, 8.13, C 9.7C)
- Caesar, *The Civil War* (*Bellum Civile*) 1.1–1.5, 1.7
- Plutarch, *Caesar* 29–32, 57–58
- Suetonius, *Deified Julius* 28–33, 38–43

- Denarius of Caesar 48–47 BC
- Denarius of Caesar 47–46 BC.

supplicatio (pl. supplicationes) public thanksgiving for a particular victory. The longer the supplicatio, the longer the period of celebration that the people enjoyed and the prestige that the recipient gained.

Through the 50s, Caesar had enjoyed spectacular success in Gaul. He had been fortunate that hostile tribes had moved into his area of influence as this gave him a pretext to start operations, but thereafter he contrived to fight with successive Gallic and German tribes. He was honoured three times with public thanksgivings or **supplicationes** of unprecedented length. When Gallic tribes that had previously made their peace rebelled, he was not above widespread destruction, which at times amounted to genocide. The scale of his victories, the enormous wealth that he built up and the largesse through which he was distributing it meant that he was fast eclipsing Pompey as Rome's most successful general. By the end of 51, Caesar was looking for a triumphant return to Rome and a second consulship.

THE REASONS FOR THE CIVIL WAR

Caesar was looking to gain the consulship in 48, which would conform to the ten-year gap set by Sulla. This would make it easier to have his actions in Gaul sanctioned by the Senate. He could also hope to settle his veterans; he had raised several fresh levies through the Gallic wars, including non-citizens from Cisalpine Gaul to whom he had granted citizenship. His political opponents were questioning the reason for any continued command in Gaul when, according to Caesar's own commentaries, no enemy remained. Some still harboured a desire to prosecute him over the actions of the First Triumvirate. Others, most notably Cato and Ahenobarbus, wanted to prosecute him for attacks he had made on German tribes that were considered too far outside of his already considerable imperium. The consulship would save him from the indignity of a trial and allow him to secure a new proconsular command. Yet overriding all else was his sense of honour:

> . . . Asinius Pollio's comment in his *History*. . ., where he says that Caesar, at Pharsalus, watching his enemies fly or be killed, said in these exact words: 'They chose this; they would have condemned me, Gaius Caesar, despite my victories, if I had not sought the army's help.'
>
> Suetonius, *Deified Julius* 30

At Rome, in the aftermath of Clodius' death, Pompey had briefly been sole consul, as close as he might hope to get to a dictatorship, and despite Caesar's military successes, Pompey saw himself as the pre-eminent man at Rome. The selfishness and intransigence of a few individuals, who were only a minority even among the optimates, would play on

S & C The nature of Caesar's commentaries

It is thought that Caesar's commentaries were written up at the end of each campaigning season and probably publicly recited each year at Rome. What would be the effect upon the people of Rome of such activity? See Powell & Welch *Julius Caesar as Artful Reporter* Duckworth 1998.

KEY INDIVIDUAL

C. Julius Caesar

Dates: 100–44 BC

Prominent popularis politician, who was part of the First Triumvirate in 59. Seeking re-election to consulship, he began the Civil War in 49. He carried out a massive reform programme as dictator. Assassinated 15 March 44.

PRESCRIBED SOURCE

Title: *Deified Julius*

Author: Suetonius

Date: *c.* AD 120

Genre: Biography

Prescribed sections: 28–33, 38–43

Significance: The prescribed section of Caesar's life deals with the start of the Civil War and his reforms as dictator

Read it here: OCR source booklet

Pompey's vanity and push him and Caesar into civil war. These included Cato and Ahenobarbus, and members of the Claudii Marcelli family.

Caesar used the tribunes of 52 to bring a law allowing him to stand for the consulship in absentia and remain safe in his province; at this point Pompey was in agreement. Caesar began to foster support at Rome with fresh displays of largesse. He put on games in honour of his recently deceased daughter, who had been Pompey's wife. He also privately funded a new corn dole and gave away slaves from his Gallic spoils. Later in the year, Pompey began to distance himself from Caesar. He passed a law that required a five-year interval between holding a magistracy at Rome and a provincial command. This would prevent somebody, Caesar included, going from magistracy to provincial command with no opportunity to be held accountable for their actions in office. This law resulted in a trawl of ex-consuls to be sent to provincial commands, including Cicero, who begrudgingly set off to Cilicia, where he stayed abreast of events through correspondence. A letter of October 51 to Cicero (Cicero, *ad Familiares* 8.8.4–10) reported a debate in the Senate over the question of Caesar's command. The consul for that year, M. Claudius Marcellus, proposed that the matter be decided after 1 March 50; Pompey agreed that a decision was required after that date. Pompey went further and, when asked what he would do if Caesar disobeyed the Senate, he replied, 'what if my son wants to beat me with a stick?' He was thus making a claim to seniority in the dispute and belittling Caesar as a naughty child trying to outwit his parent.

The question of when Caesar's imperium should have terminated was a contentious issue at the time, and still cannot be fully resolved now. It is fair to say that, in all likelihood, Caesar genuinely saw things differently from his optimate opponents and Pompey. That Pompey and Marcellus were prepared to discuss Caesar's recall after 1 March 50 suggests that they thought this was the proper date of the termination. The law of Vatinius, which was passed during the First Triumvirate in 59, gave Caesar imperium for five years, and was probably due to expire on 1 March 54. In 55 Pompey and Crassus prolonged Caesar's imperium by five years. Many sources make reference to the five-year extension, or of ten years in total (Cicero, *ad Atticum* 7.6 = SL 59 **PS**). Yet whether the second five years ought to run from 55, or should be added to his original command and so not lapse until 1 March 49, is the question on which Caesar and his opponents disagreed.

Certainly Caesar had no claim to keep his command until 1 January 48, the earliest date at which, under the laws of Sulla, he could legally start a second consulate. However, constitutional convention gave him security because until recently, provinces had needed to be allocated prior to a consul's election. Therefore the first magistrates who could take over from him were the consuls of 49, who would be elected in the summer of 50. These individuals would not normally leave Rome until the end of their consular year and so could not take over a province until the next year. Thus, while the legal limit of Caesar's tenure might, in his view, have been 1 March 49, he could according to normal precedent expect to retain his province until the arrival of a successor at the beginning of 48. However, Pompey's legislation, which required an interval of five years between a magistracy at Rome and a pro-magistracy in a province, changed all of this. Now any ex-consul could be allocated a province, Gaul included, and could proceed to that province immediately.

By the start of 50, Caesar had bought off the formerly establishment young noble Q. Scribonius Curio, who was tribune that year. Curio subsequently opposed repeated attempts by the consul for 50, C. Claudius Marcellus, the cousin of M. Marcellus, to strip Caesar of his command. (Plutarch, *Caesar* 29–30 **PS**). On 1 December 50, C. Marcellus proposed that Caesar should give up his command, but that Pompey should retain his. Curio reframed the question, proposing that both Caesar and Pompey should lay down their arms. Only twenty-two senators voted against Curio, while 370 were in favour of both men standing down. Therefore it is clear that the majority of the Senate favoured peace; but it was equally true that they were impotent in the face of a small minority of hardliners. Caesar now sent letters via the new tribunes for 49, Mark Antony and Q. Cassius Longinus, requesting that he retire to Cisalpine Gaul with just two legions until he could gain the consulship. This was later modified to Illyricum and one legion; Cicero, recently returned from Cilicia, apparently pushed for this and Pompey seemingly agreed (Suetonius, *Deified Julius* 29 **PS**; Plutarch, *Caesar* 31 **PS**). So according to these accounts, both Caesar and Pompey were prepared to make concessions to avoid war. However, some saw the letters as inflammatory. In Appian's account, where Curio delivered the letter, its contents were more combative, with Caesar threatening to march on Italy if his requests were not met. Q. Caecilius Metellus Scipio Nasica, who was Pompey's new father-in-law, and in Caesar's view Pompey's mouthpiece, proposed that Caesar either lay down his command or be declared a public enemy. The tribunes Mark Antony and Q. Cassius vetoed the proposal, but were threatened and together with Curio fled Rome to join Caesar (Caesar, *The Civil War* 1.1–3 **PS**; Plutarch, *Caesar* 31 **PS**). The Senate reacted as if Caesar's letter were a declaration of war; Ahenobarbus was appointed Caesar's successor in Gaul, the role he had long coveted. On 5 January 49 BC, the SCU was passed again, mobilising all magistrates to defend the state. This specifically included Pompey, who still held imperium for Spain (Caesar, *The Civil War* 1.4–5 **PS**). When the news of the SCU reached Caesar, he paraded before his men the abuse that the tribunes had suffered. He complained how the SCU was designed to deal with those who actually threatened Rome, not good honest Roman citizen soldiers such as his audience, and beseeched them to defend his dignity. That same night he crossed the Rubicon, the boundary of his province with Italy, and the limits of his legal imperium (Caesar, *The Civil War* 1.7 **PS**; Plutarch, *Caesar* 32 **PS**; Suetonius, *Deified Julius* 31–3 **PS**).

CAESAR'S MILITARY COMMAND

Civil war involves significant confusion and turmoil. In Italy people were compelled to choose one side or the other. Caesar tended to pardon those he defeated, which resulted in many Italian communities coming over to him willingly. As a policy this is explicitly recorded in a letter which survives in Cicero's correspondence, from Caesar to his political agents Oppius and Balbus (Cicero, C 9.7C = SL 68 **PS**). Cicero commented in another letter that the country people only cared about their fields and farms (*ad Atticum* 8.13 = SL 67 **PS**). It is important to recognise that the common man would have cared more about his livelihood, and so favoured Caesar, than the Republican ideals and high politics with which Cicero and the later sources are concerned.

PRESCRIBED SOURCE

Title: *The Civil War (Bellum Civile)*

Author: Caesar

Date: 49–44 BC

Prescribed sections: 1.1–1.5, 1.7

Significance: Caesar's own account of the civil war is mostly military history. The prescribed sections deal with events in the few days before the outbreak of civil war

Read it here: B142 in LACTOR 7: *Late Republican Rome, 88–31 BC* (London: KCL, 2017)

FIGURE 2.5
Denarius of Caesar
48–47.

Pompey, with no forces in Italy to oppose Caesar, had fled to Greece to muster opposition. Caesar had no navy with which to pursue him and so he looked west. In Spain, Caesar defeated Pompey's lieutenants Afranius and Petreius. In the winter of 49–48, Caesar crossed to Greece. The following summer, Pompey was defeated at Pharsalus. Pompey fled to Egypt but was killed on arrival by Egyptians, who feared that he would annex their country. Caesar followed and was delayed first in Egyptian domestic affairs and then in Pontus until the end of 47. The next year Caesar moved to Africa to confront those Pompeians who had survived his victories so far. It was here that Cato

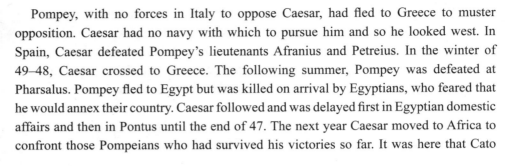

PRESCRIBED SOURCE

Denarius of Caesar (Figure 2.5)

Date: 48–47 BC

Obverse: Female head wearing oak-wreath and diadem

Reverse: Trophy with Gallic shield and carnyx; below, bearded captive seated with hands tied behind back, inscription 'Caesar'

Significance: Caesar reminds the Roman people of his Gallic successes

View it here: 452.4.1 in Ghey, Leins, Crawford, *Roman Republican Coins in the British Museum* (online catalogue: http://www.britishmuseum. org/research/publications/online_research_catalogues/rrc/roman_ republican_coins.aspx)

FIGURE 2.6
Denarius of Caesar
47–46.

PRESCRIBED SOURCE

Denarius of Caesar (Figure 2.6)

Date: 47–46 BC

Obverse: Head of Venus, wearing diadem

Reverse: Aeneas carrying palladium in right hand and Anchises on shoulder, inscription 'Caesar'

Significance: Caesar reminds the Roman people of his lineage all the way back to Aeneas

View it here: 458.1.1 in Ghey, Leins, Crawford, *Roman Republican Coins in the British Museum* (online catalogue: http://www.britishmuseum. org/research/publications/online_research_catalogues/rrc/roman_ republican_coins.aspx)

died. However, Caesar's appointed governor of Spain, the former tribune Q. Cassius, had robbed the propertied classes of Spain through systematic extortion, in part to bribe an army that with every pay-off became less and less disciplined. The mutinous army had then accepted Pompey's son Gnaeus as their commander. Therefore, despite his earlier victories, Caesar had to return to Spain in 45, and defeat the younger Pompey at Munda.

CAESAR'S DICTATORSHIP

While Roman armies fought all around the Mediterranean, most Roman citizens were still resident in Italy. Here from 49 onwards, Caesar had control. He was appointed dictator, briefly but long enough to secure his own election to the consulship of 48, the very reason for the war. He passed some administrative measures in that year that seem to have been aimed at easing the pressure of war on the city, including cancelling some debt and forbidding the hoarding of cash. As his consulship came to an end in 48 he was appointed dictator for a second time, allowing him to retain control over home affairs. Caesar faced a significant mutiny in 47 when he returned from Egypt; many of his troops had campaigned since the start of the Gallic campaigns, and had believed that they would be discharged after Pharsalus. His lieutenant, the author Sallust, was unable to quell the resentment; it took Caesar's personal presence to bring them back in line. The loyalty of the soldiers was vital to Caesar's regime, and would be for Octavian also; this incident is an early example of what would follow and how the leading individuals had to tread carefully around the wishes of the troops. Coins issued by Caesar emphasise his lineage – he was supposed to be a descendent of Aeneas, the mythical founder of Rome. Others celebrate his Gallic victories and the captives that he had provided to the people (p. 128). In 46, although re-elected consul, Caesar was also appointed dictator for a third time, and this time for ten years. He celebrated four triumphs over Gaul, Pontus, Africa and Egypt, ostensibly all foreign foes; there was some disquiet over Cato's image being displayed in the parade. Caesar was awarded a 40-day supplicatio and the opportunity for largesse on a massive scale: donatives for every male citizen, together with races, games and dinners. The plebs were very satisfied with Caesar's rule. His veterans received massive donatives equivalent to a lifetime's pay, and army pay for those still serving was doubled to HS 900 each year (Suetonius, *Deified Julius* 38–9 (PS)). At the end of 45, he abdicated from a fourth consulship and started appointing his intimates as suffect (replacement) consuls for part of the year (Plutarch, *Caesar* 58 (PS)). Between late January and mid-February 44, he was appointed dictator for life. His men had saluted him as imperator after the battle of Munda; the Senate voted this a permanent title.

Amidst all the celebration and the honours, Caesar (see Suetonius, *Deified Julius* 38–43 (PS)) undertook a wide-ranging and in part long-overdue programme of political and social reforms, among which were:

1. large increase in the membership of the Senate;
2. creation of new patrician families;
3. sons of the proscribed were allowed to stand for office;
4. an increased number of magistrates to deal with the increased number of provinces;

5. restriction on the time governors could hold a province;
6. citizen status was granted to Cisalpine Gaul;
7. doctors and teachers resident at Rome were granted citizenship;
8. Latin rights were granted to Sicily and parts of Transalpine Gaul;
9. foreign cities that had supported him were granted Latin municipal rights;
10. colonisation and resettlement of 80,000 veterans and urban poor in Italy and the provinces;
11. debt relief had begun in 48, with assessments made at pre-war values, so alleviating the effect of inflation through the war;
12. in 47 he released tenants in Rome from payments of rents up to HS 2,000 per year, those in Italy up to HS 500;
13. tribute was fixed for Transalpine Gaul, and rearranged for Asia and Sicily;
14. embarked on a large programme of public works;
15. reduced the number of recipients of the corn dole;
16. farm owners were compelled to employ at least one-third of their herdsmen as free men;
17. awarded prizes for having large families; and
18. reformed the calendar to align with the solar year.

This would have all been costly. Much of the wealth gained in the Gallic Wars would have been lost through waging the Civil War. Yet through setting tribute contributions, Caesar gained enough new income to reward his supporters and alleviate the lot of the plebs. His most expensive, but most important, actions were the colonisation and re-settlement programmes. Reducing the corn dole may appear counter-intuitive, but this was in the context of colonisation and providing work for the poor through building projects. By insisting on the employment of freeborn men in the countryside, he reduced the number of slave-run estates. Caesar was also promoting the unification of Italy, which had faltered since the Social War. He was generous with the franchise, extending it to Cisalpine Gaul and granting Latin rights to Sicily. His view was inclusive; the Roman world was expanding, as a direct result of his conquests and it would need citizens throughout.

ASSASSINATION

However, the Romans gave way before the good fortune of the man and accepted the bit, and regarding the monarchy as a respite from the evils of the civil wars, they appointed him dictator for life. This was frankly a tyranny, since the monarchy, besides the element of irresponsibility, now took on that of permanence.

Plutarch, *Caesar* 57

Later commentators like Plutarch (above) and Suetonius are critical of Caesar's assumption of powers and honorific titles. With each victory, former enemies returned to Rome, and Plutarch comments that Caesar's enemies were as happy as his supporters to see him honoured, because it gave them a reason to dislike him. Political criticism came when he failed to rise when a senatorial delegation visited him. In contrast he rebuked a tribune who failed to rise when he rode past in triumph. When some citizens were punished by a couple of tribunes for crowning his statue, he chastised the tribunes. During the Lupercalia festival, his lieutenant Anthony repeatedly tried to bestow a diadem upon him. This was probably a stage-managed affair, but it backfired when there was applause that he had refused it. He was unable to shake off the idea that he wished to be king, a hateful idea to the Romans.

Never one to sit still, Caesar was planning further conquest in 44. First he was going to attack the Dacians and then go against the Parthians to avenge the death of Crassus at Carrhae. Although the most significant Republican opponents had died in the wars – Pompey himself, Cato, Ahenobarbus, Metellus Scipio and Gnaeus Pompeius – many lesser supporters of the old ways remained. More than sixty were involved in his assassination. The figurehead was M. Iunius Brutus, an intellectual whose attachment to the Republic through his uncle Cato was so great that he had sided with Pompey in the Civil War, despite Pompey having killed his father during Lepidus' uprising of 77. The other leading figure was C. Cassius Longinus. As Caesar prepared to depart to the east, it was obvious that if he was not dealt with in 44, another chance might not arise for several years. It must be understood that although they would style themselves liberators, the assassins were striving to free themselves from the political constraints that Caesar imposed upon them. They were looking to restore the political order that would allow them to continue to gain overseas commands, riches and dignity without being beholden to Caesar.

KEY INDIVIDUALS

M. Iunius Brutus
Dates: 85–42 BC

The figurehead of the assassination plot. His father was killed by Pompey in 77. His mother Servilia was Caesar's long-term mistress. He was raised by his uncle Cato, who informed his deep-seated Republicanism. He died at Philippi.

C. Cassius Longinus
Dates: Died in 42 BC

Second to Brutus in the conspiracy. He was later awarded overall command of the Republican forces of the east by the Senate. He also died at Philippi.

FIGURE 2.7
Caesar.

Rumour of plots certainly reached Caesar, but he dismissed these and any idea of a bodyguard (Plutarch, *Caesar* 57 (PS)). The later sources give portents of his death. Seemingly a soothsayer had warned him that he would be in danger on 15 March – the Ides of March. Nevertheless, and despite feeling unwell that day, Caesar arrived at Pompey's theatre where a Senate meeting had been called. One of the assassins, C. Trebonius or Decimus Iunius Brutus, drew Antony away to one side; another, L. Tillius Cimber, pressed a petition upon Caesar; the other conspirators crowded around him. Cimber pulled his toga off his shoulder and C. Servilius Casca struck the first blow. The remaining assailants stepped in. According to Suetonius, Caesar's dying words 'and you my son' were directed at Brutus.

TOPIC REVIEW

- Collate the methods by which Caesar gained support during and after the Civil War.
- Consider how far some sections of society benefited from Caesar's reforms.
- Discuss whether the assassins were justified in their actions.

Further Reading

Everitt, A. (2001), *Cicero*, London: John Murray.
Goldsworthy, A. (2006), *Caesar*, London: Weidenfeld & Nicolson.
Seager, R. (2002), *Pompey the Great*, 2nd edition, Oxford: Wiley-Blackwell.
Southern, P. (2002), *Pompey the Great*, Stroud: Tempus.
Stockton, D. (1971), *Cicero*, Oxford: Oxford University Press.
Welch. K. & Powell, A. (1998), *Julius Caesar as Artful Reporter*, London: Duckworth.

2.6 The Second Triumvirate

The challenges to the Constitution

- The Aftermath of Caesar's assassination
- Antony against the Senate
- The Second Triumvirate
- Octavian's successes; the unification of Italy
- Victory at Actium and in Egypt.

The means by which politicians achieved success and their importance in the breakdown of the Republic

- Land bills, largesse, games and donatives.
- Antony and Octavian's military commands.
- Army and veteran support.
- Political marriages.

The roles and importance of individuals in the breakdown of the Republic

- Antony
- Cicero
- Lepidus
- Sextus Pompeius
- Octavian

The prescribed sources for this subheading are:

- Cicero, *Second Philippic* 88–97
- Cicero, Selected Letters Nos 113, 114, 118 (*ad Atticum* 14.1, 14.12, 15.11)
- Appian, *The Civil Wars*, 3.43–3.51, 3.74–75 3.80–81, 86–94, 5.12–5.13, 5.127–132
- Suetonius, *Deified Augustus* 26–8
- Plutarch, *Antony* 54–6

- Denarius of Brutus 43–42 BC
- Denarius of Antony 43 BC
- Denarius of Octavian and Antony 39 BC
- Denarius of Octavian with Agrippa 38 BC

As we have seen, politicians used various methods to influence events, with more or less success. These methods included largesse, corn doles, donatives, bribery, intimidation and violence. Ultimately, when Octavian's successes are considered in this topic, it will be seen that he followed the actions of many who had gone before him. However, in at least two cases (the way he treated the Italian communities and his association with the military), he was better at doing so than many of his predecessors.

KEY INDIVIDUAL

M. Antonius, Mark Antony

Dates: 83–30 BC

Accomplished soldier who served Caesar in Gaul, he was Consul with Caesar in 44 and continued as head of state after the assassination. Fought Octavian and the Senate in 43, but formed Second Triumvirate with Octavian and Lepidus thereafter. Defeated by Octavian at Actium in 31, he committed suicide in Egypt the next year.

AFTERMATH OF CAESAR'S ASSASSINATION

There was a bemusement on the part of the assassins who expected to be warmly received by a public who had been 'freed'. In fact the masses had greatly benefited from Caesar's largesse and soon confined the conspirators to the Capitoline Hill (Appian, *The Civil Wars* 2.120). Antony secured the support of M. Aemilius Lepidus, who held the position of Master of Horse, which gave him troops close to Rome. Antony also acquiesced when P. Cornelius Dolabella assumed the consulship made vacant by Caesar's death. Both were former lieutenants of Caesar. The Senate debated whether to honour the assassins or condemn them. Antony pointed out that most of them either had benefited, or stood to benefit from magistracies already designated by Caesar. If they honoured the assassins, then they condemned Caesar, and by default they then invalidated his decisions and disadvantaged themselves. The Senate agreed, and a general sense of amnesty prevailed so that the conspirators came down from the Capitoline. Soon after, Antony presided over Caesar's funeral, purposefully inflaming the populace who had all benefited from Caesar's largesse, most recently as a result of his will. There was a huge outpouring of grief among the common people against the assassins (Cicero, *Philippics* 2.88–91 PS). Antony quickly secured Caesar's will and access to his papers, together with his wealth. He began to pass off his own decisions as those of Caesar. Cicero, unable to hide his distaste for Antony, was appalled:

PS

> I am afraid that the Ides of March will have given us nothing except a feeling of happiness and recompense for our hatred and grief. . . . O deed that was noble, yet incomplete! You know how much I love the Sicilians and how I declare that I am honoured to have them as my clients. Caesar gave them much – and I did not object, though making them Latins was intolerable. But anyway, look how Antony has received a large sum of money and established a law passed in the assembly under the dictator, under which the Sicilians are Roman citizens – something never mentioned when in his lifetime.
>
> Cicero, *ad Atticum* 14.12 = SL 114 (LACTOR 7, B177c)

Depending on their allegiances individual politicians looked to either Caesar's former lieutenants or the liberators and Pompey's surviving son Sextus to re-establish order (Cicero, *ad Atticum* 14.1 = SL113 PS). Despite Cicero's encouragement, the liberators realised that they had misjudged the mood of the Republic. Brutus and Cassius were keen to leave Rome, but they were still serving as praetors. The Senate proposed that they take a new command over the corn supply, allowing them to leave the city prior to going on to

Denarius of Brutus (Figure 2.8)

Date: 43–42 BC

Obverse: Head of Brutus, inscription L PILAET(orius) CES(tianus) who was Brutus' supporter who minted the coin, BRUT(us) IMP(erator)

Reverse: Pileus (a freedman's hat) between two daggers, inscription EID MAR (Ides March)

Significance: Brutus revels in the assassination of Caesar and the supposed freedom that has brought

View it here: 508.3.1 in Ghey, Leins, Crawford, *Roman Republican Coins in the British Museum* (online catalogue: http://www.britishmuseum.org/research/publications/online_research_catalogues/rrc/roman_republican_coins.aspx)

FIGURE 2.8
Denarius of Brutus
43–42 BC.

their already allocated pro-praetorian provinces. Antony now sought to adjust the pro-magisterial provinces, taking those already awarded to Brutus and Cassius for himself and Dolabella. This did not go down well. Cassius saw the corn commission as an insult and vowed to go directly to the east. Brutus was all for returning to Rome in the name of the Republic. Cicero, who was present at a family conference, cautioned against this. Brutus was persuaded to go to the east also (*ad Atticum* 15.11 = SL 118 **PS**). Once in the east, Brutus was free to revel in the achievement of the Ides of March, as the denarius minted by him shows (Fig 2.8).

ANTONY AGAINST THE SENATE

With confusion among the liberators, Antony seemed to be in command of the situation. However, he had failed to account for Caesar's nominated heir and great-nephew, the eighteen-year-old Octavian. Arriving at Rome, Octavian chastised Antony for being conciliatory towards the assassins, and more critically for not distributing Caesar's property according to his will. Antony simply dismissed the youth as an upstart. Further disputes arose over the honours that were to be bestowed on the dead Caesar at upcoming games. At the same time there was sufficient resurgent Republicanism to make Antony less sure of his position. He used the comitia tributa to take the strategically important Cisalpine Gaul as a future province, already held by one of the assassins Decimus Iunius Brutus.

As Antony prepared to move troops to Cisalpine Gaul, Octavian began to raise men in Caesar's name. This was of course illegal, but Pompey had done the same for Sulla, and

KEY INDIVIDUAL

Octavian
Dates: 63 BC–AD 14

Heir to Caesar, he worked with senatorial forces against Antony at Mutina. Subsequently formed Second Triumvirate with Antony and Lepidus. Finally defeated Antony at Actium. Went on to become first Emperor Augustus.

PRESCRIBED SOURCE

Title: *Second Philippic*

Author: Cicero

Date: 44 BC

Significance: A vitriolic attack on Antony's morality and administration of Rome. The prescribed section deals with embezzled funds and Antony's recognition of the Galatian king Deiotarus' territories in exchange for cash

Read it here: OCR source booklet

Octavian recognised immediately that if he was to be a major player, he needed military might. What is incredible is that he thought he could avenge his adoptive father and continue as his political heir at such an early age. Two of Antony's legions deserted for Octavian because of Antony's mean donatives, harsh discipline and not a few financial inducements, gifts promised by Octavian (Appian, *The Civil War* 3.43–8 **PS**). Aware of Antony's approach, the previously appointed governor of Cisalpine Gaul, Decimus Brutus, had holed up at Mutina, so this became Antony's first objective (Appian, *The Civil War* 3.49 **PS**).

Now the Senate courted Octavian, he was able to muster forces in Caesar's name that they could not (App 3.75 **PS**).

> . . . for which reason the Senate had previously called in the help of Octavian against him. Although Octavian knew this he desired nevertheless to take the lead in humbling Antony.

> Appian, *The Civil Wars* 3.51

The attitude of the Senate is summed up in a quip of Cicero's that the boy ought to be praised, raised up and then got rid of (Appian, *The Civil War* 3.50 **PS**). This sort of attitude would not endear Cicero to Octavian and would later prove to have been a significant mistake, once Antony and Octavian had made their peace. Before Antony had departed to muster troops, he and Cicero had verbally attacked each other in the Senate. This caused Cicero to retire to compose the Second Philippic, a full-blown attack on Antony and his morality, accusing him of public extortion and private licentiousness (*Philippics* 2.92–7 **PS**; *ad Atticum* 14.12 = SL 114 **PS**). In old age, twenty years after Catiline, Cicero looked to reassert himself as the grand old man of the Republic; few other ex-consuls remained alive as a result of the Civil War and even fewer optimates. There followed another dozen Philippics attacking Antony at every opportunity.

FIGURE 2.9
Denarius of Antony 43 BC.

PRESCRIBED SOURCE

Denarius of Antony (Figure 2.9)

Date: 43 BC

Obverse: Head of M. Antonius, with lituus (a symbol of an Augur), inscription M ANTON(ius) [IMP]

Reverse: Laureate head of Julius Caesar with jug (a symbol of an Augur), inscription CAESAR DIC(tator)

Significance: Antony links himself to Caesar, so diminishing Octavian's claim to be Caesar's political heir

View it here: 488.1.1 in Ghey, Leins, Crawford, *Roman Republican Coins in the British Museum* (online catalogue: http://www.britishmuseum. org/research/publications/online_research_catalogues/rrc/roman_ republican_coins.aspx)

The Senate conferred pro-praetorian imperium upon Octavian and he departed to campaign against Antony with the consuls for 43, A. Hirtius and C. Vibius Pansa. Antony minted coins claiming the legitimacy of his position. In the denarius issued by him (p. 136) he associated himself with Caesar in order to diminish Octavian's claim to Caesar's name. Mutina was besieged in mid-December; after several battles in April 43, with Hirtius dead and Pansa dying, Antony escaped to Transalpine Gaul. Here, after some procrastination and posturing on both sides, and largely because of the sentiment of Caesar's veteran legions who crossed to Antony ahead of their commander, Lepidus and other supporters of Caesar re-joined Antony. From this period onwards, soldiers became increasingly important in deciding the fate of generals. As a result, Antony was militarily significant again.

The Senate at Cicero's suggestion awarded Decimus Brutus a supplicatio of an unprecedented fifty days. Appian says that so great was Cicero's hatred of Antony that he acted out of all proportion; in so doing he completely ignored Octavian and this would be his undoing (Appian, *The Civil War* 3.74 **PS**). Octavian could not honourably deal with Decimus as one of Caesar's assassins. He further recognised that if Cassius and Brutus returned to Italy, he would become irrelevant. As a result, Octavian began communicating with Lepidus and Antony (Appian, *The Civil War* 3.80–1 **PS**). Meanwhile, the Republicans at Rome were trying to prise Octavian's troops away from him with donatives. Octavian sent centurions ahead to demand the consulship. When they were rebuked by the Senate, he followed Caesar's example and crossed into Italy. The Senate panicked and promised to pay the troops, but soon reneged on the deal. When Octavian arrived at Rome, the few Republican soldiers that existed went over to him and the Senate was seen to be impotent. He withdrew just outside the city while he was elected consul at the age of twenty. Again it is the soldiery that are instrumental in deciding who gained authority (Suetonius, *Deified Augustus* 26 **PS**; Appian, *The Civil War* 3.86–94 **PS**).

THE SECOND TRIUMVIRATE

Octavian met with Antony and Lepidus on an island near Bononia on 27 November 43. They made a formal alliance voted through the comitia plebis tributa by the tribune P. Titius, that they should be triumvirs for the restoration of the Republic, with authority to make laws and nominate magistrates for five years. The triumvirs divided the Roman provinces between them: Antony retained Further and Cisalpine Gaul, Lepidus took Narbonese Gaul and Spain, and Octavian held Africa, Sicily and Sardinia, which was the weakest position strategically. Italy was shared. The east was of course in the hands of the Republicans.

To wage war in the east, money was essential, and to placate veterans, land was required. Therefore the triumvirs posted up proscriptions so that 300 senators and 2,000 equestrians were deprived of their lives and estates. Among those proscribed was Cicero, paying the price for the Philippics. Antony requested not only that his head, but also the hands that had penned the speeches, be cut off and displayed. With Cicero dead, our understanding of the period is significantly reduced. Although Plutarch, Suetonius and

ACTIVITY

Read Appian, *The Civil War* 3.86–94 **PS** to consider the effectiveness of donatives in securing the loyalty of the army.

Study questions
With reference to the sources:

1. Were the liberators naive in thinking that they could restore the Republic?
2. Was Cicero foolish to attack Antony?

Appian offer accessible and concise accounts of the period, this far they can be often be cross-referenced to letters and speeches of Cicero. For the period to Octavian's eventual success, we have no first-hand evidence.

In the late summer of 42, Cassius and Brutus marched into Greece, and camped at Philippi. Here they lost two engagements and their lives. With their deaths, the Republican cause was over. There would be further conflict, but any suggestion that the old self-interested aristocracy could re-establish themselves was gone. After the victory, Octavian had a difficult job, with as many as 100,000 veterans to settle. Antony was to go east and find the funds to pay for these settlements. However, in doing this, Antony would make the same mistake as Pompey had done in the 60s, in that while he was absent, Octavian would be the face of the Triumvirate in Italy.

OCTAVIAN'S SUCCESSES

Through the following decade, rival claimants to power and several military adventures repeatedly put the relationship between Antony and Octavian under pressure. Three times – at Brundisium in 40, Misenum in 39 and Tarentum in 37– the pair met to work out their differences. In so doing they postponed the inevitable clash between them. The sources concentrate on the military aspects of the period and do not dwell on how Octavian won over Italy – but win it over he did.

Octavian began the process of settling veterans in 42. The towns that lost land to this process sent deputations to Rome. The veterans and serving soldiers were heavy-handed with the civilians and contemptuous of Octavian, knowing that he needed their support to remain in power. There was street fighting and widespread discord (Appian, *The Civil War* 5.12–13 (PS)). In 41, Antony's wife Fulvia and his brother Lucius fostered a short-lived rebellion in the name of the Republic. This is named the Perusine War after Perusia where a winter siege took place. Octavian won through, and although he spared Lucius and Fulvia, he killed another 300 senators and equestrians, providing him a little of the much-needed land to redistribute to the veterans. Antony was at first unaware of the rebellion, but later returned to make his peace at Brundisium. After protracted negotiations the two triumvirs redistributed the provinces between them so that Octavian gained all of the west and Antony the east. Their peace was sealed with a political marriage; Fulvia had died soon after Perusia so that Antony was free to marry Octavian's sister Octavia (Virgil's fourth Eclogue celebrates their future offspring).

After Philippi, Lepidus was marginalised because he was thought to have tried to cut a deal with Pompey's youngest son Sextus Pompeius. He was only allowed Africa as a sphere of influence. Sextus had been granted imperium in Sicily and Sardinia by the Republican government at the time of Mutina. Sextus blocked the trade routes to Rome and brought about a grain shortage and famine. Taxes raised to fund a new war against Sextus caused civil unrest, and Octavian and Antony were attacked trying to quell the Plebs' anger. The triumvirs had no option but to negotiate with Sextus so that he received five years' imperium over the corn-producing islands when they met at Misenum. This only brought a year's peace. After a first disastrous naval campaign against Sextus in 38,

PRESCRIBED SOURCE

Title: *The Civil Wars*

Author: Appian

Date: Early second century AD

Significance: The prescribed sections deal with events during the Second Triumvirate. After Cicero's demise, Appian becomes the chief source for the period. He is believed to have followed the lost histories of the contemporary Asinius Pollio

Read it here: OCR source booklet

Denarius of Octavian and Antony (Figure 2.10)

Date: 39 BC

Obverse: Head of Octavian, inscription CAESAR IMP(erator)

Reverse: Caduceus, inscription ANTONIUS IMP(erator)

Significance: Octavian and Antony affirm their *amicitia*

View it here: 529.2.1 in Ghey, Leins, Crawford, *Roman Republican Coins in the British Museum* (online catalogue: http://www.britishmuseum.org/research/publications/online_research_catalogues/rrc/roman_republican_coins.aspx)

FIGURE 2.10
Denarius of Octavian and *Antony* 39 BC.

Octavian handed over military matters to his lieutenant Agrippa. Agrippa was the most prominent of several of Octavian's supporters, who were content to be subordinate to him. They were not of the established political order and would not have enjoyed such power under the traditional constitution. As a result they were very loyal. Antony returned to meet with Octavian at Tarentum in 37. Antony offered Octavian ships in exchange for troops. Octavian was now sure of Agrippa's military talents and not inclined to accommodate Antony. Only the intervention of Octavia averted a crisis, and the Triumvirate was renewed for five more years. Meanwhile, Agrippa revitalised and trained Octavian's navy, and in 36 directed a three-pronged campaign against Sextus, ejecting him from the island. Sextus fled to the east where he was killed, possibly on Antony's orders.

The war against Sextus had required Lepidus to land forces in the west of Sicily. After the victory he attempted to take the island for himself, but his troops were tired of war and deserted to Octavian. Octavian spared him, only allowing him to retain his position as *pontifex maximus*. However, Octavian faced a bigger challenge from the soldiers themselves who, having seen some colleagues resettled after Philippi, now revolted. Octavian had no land to give them and little money to buy them off. He was compelled to exact money from the unfortunate Sicilians, with which he bribed the majority, giving them an additional two years' pay and the promise of more money when they were discharged. Only the longest serving were discharged and resettled (Appian, *The Civil War* 5.127–30 **PS**).

Finally Octavian could compete with Antony's military reputation. He was granted an ovation and, among other honours, the sacrosanctity of a tribune. This was one of the mechanisms through which he would ultimately hold power. He set up a golden statue of himself in the forum with an inscription that proclaimed that order had been restored by land and sea (Appian, *The Civil War* 5.130 **PS**). The propaganda worked: Appian's

KEY INDIVIDUAL

Sextus Pompeius
Dates: 67–35 BC

The younger son of Pompey. He was granted *imperium* at sea by the Republican government. He threatened the grain supply to Rome and forced the triumvirs to accept a treaty at Misenum. Defeated by Octavian in the naval war, he fled and died in the east.

Denarius of Octavian with Agrippa (Figure 2.11)

Date: 38 BC

Obverse: Head of Octavian, inscription IMP CAESAR DIVI IULI F = Imperator Caesar son of the divine Julius

Reverse: M AGRIPPA COS DESIG = M Agrippa Consul Designate

Significance: Agrippa is elevated to near equal status with Octavian

View it here: 534.3.1 in Ghey, Leins, Crawford, *Roman Republican Coins in the British Museum* (online catalogue: http://www.britishmuseum. org/research/publications/online_research_catalogues/rrc/roman_ republican_coins.aspx)

FIGURE 2.11
Denarius of Octavian **PS**
with Agrippa 38 BC.

narrative of the civil wars ends at this point (Appian, *The Civil War* 5.131–2 **PS**). Unfortunately that means that our sources are further reduced.

Octavian's success at home was mostly due to Antony's failures overseas. Plutarch, writing much later under the influence of Augustan propaganda, depicts Antony as an inactive sot, drunk on wine, women and power. Late in 37 he set off on the Parthian expedition which was poorly conceived with uncertain strategy. About 32,000 Roman soldiers perished, although the fact that anybody survived at all was down to Antony's leadership and resolute character.

When news of Antony's Parthian defeat arrived at Rome, Octavia sought permission to go to her husband. Octavian approved, according to Plutarch, in the hope that she would be dishonoured and so give him greater cause for complaint. She took 2000 reinforcements with her. By sending so few soldiers, Octavian was also sending a message to Antony that he was now militarily dominant. If Antony wanted more men as promised at Tarentum he would have to deal nicely with Octavian. Antony, however, had settled with and now favoured Cleopatra; he dismissed Octavia. To make matters worse, Antony, despite his Parthian failure, celebrated a triumph in Alexandria for lesser victories he claimed in Armenia. This in itself was unconstitutional – triumphs were celebrated at Rome. Antony went further: he declared that Caesarion, Cleopatra's son by Caesar, was the legitimate heir of Caesar, thereby claiming that Octavian was a usurper. Caesarion was titled King of Kings; his mother was titled Queen of Kings. Antony's children by Cleopatra were also designated rulers of provinces within a new Egyptian empire, despite some of these being Roman holdings (Plutarch, *Antony* 54 **PS**). These events are referred to as the Donations of Alexandria.

With Antony absent, Octavian slowly increased his gravitas in Italy with age and familiarity. In 35 he undertook operations in Illyricum. This kept his forces under arms in preparation for the inevitable showdown with Antony. At the same time this removed the army from Italy and reduced the burden on the countryside. The days of aristocratic Republican government must have been fading from the public memory, particularly thanks to his propaganda machine headed by another close supporter, Maecenas. He was Octavian's literary agent, who at this time sponsored Virgil's *Georgics*, which proclaimed the benefits of rural peace. The Donations of Alexandria caused disquiet at Rome (Plutarch, *Antony* 55 (PS)). Octavian denounced Antony's actions and went on a public relations campaign. He celebrated his successful campaign in Illyricum with building works. Agrippa, who was already an ex-consul, took on the aedileship of 33. The position had lost its attraction since Caesar's dictatorship had made the prestige of providing services to the city less relevant. Agrippa spent a fortune renovating the public water supplies, building a new aqueduct, 700 cisterns, 500 fountains and 170 bathing houses. Supplying so much fresh water was a huge boon to the poor in a city such as Rome. Concurrently he put on a massive set of public games, Octavian's generals from Illyricum celebrated triumphs, and Maecenas opened his own gardens to the poor. The overall effect was to buy the support of the plebs urbana.

VICTORY AT ACTIUM AND EGYPT

The myth of Actium is something that Octavian subsequently worked up throughout the early years of the principate. Cleopatra was demonised as an exemplar of all that was bad with the east. She was supported by exotic easterners who sought to dethrone Rome; clearly she had to be stopped. Antony was not the enemy; he had simply been corrupted after five years in the east. According to the tradition, Antony was consistently portrayed as a debauchee. For instance, according to Plutarch (*Antony* 56 (PS)), on his way to Actium he delayed at Samos to enjoy pleasures and festivals. Predictably, Antony's own propaganda barely survives. He did publish a pamphlet on sobriety, because his drinking was thought to be damaging his image. Also Caesar's former agent Oppius wrote a pamphlet denouncing Caesarion's paternity. Therefore Antony's recognition of Caesarion as Caesar's heir must have been an issue for some at Rome.

Antony crossed to southern Greece in early 32. At this time Octavian sought an oath of allegiance from the Italian people, that they accept him as leader in the war against the east (*Res Gestae* 25; see p. 7). This is reported in *Res Gestae* published after Augustus' death in AD 14, an account of the deeds that Augustus achieved in his lifetime. It was inscribed outside his mausoleum, but a copy survives from Asia Minor. It is propaganda plain and simple. It is to be noted that he gained an oath from all Italy, not just Rome. Octavian was completing what the Social War had begun, and including all Italians as Romans. In particular he was reaching out to the propertied classes – the equestrians. If war was coming, then for them Octavian was to be preferred, rather than the old Republican aristocracy who had impacted on their business interests in the east and their farms in Italy. Finally, at the end of 32, Octavian declared Antony no longer fit to rule and declared war on Cleopatra, her advisors, even her hairdresser, but not Antony. This was war against an eastern exotic, not another civil war.

Antony found himself trapped in the bay of Actium in the summer of 31. With his army beset by malaria and dysentery Antony needed to move, either by sea or by land. The propaganda, picked up by later authors has Antony simply acquiescing to Cleopatra's will in preferring to fight at sea. This is nonsense, since in choosing to fight on land or sea, he was faced with choosing the lesser of two bad options. If he fought at sea and lost, at least he could make good his escape. The accounts of the battle itself cannot be fully reconciled. One cannot be sure, but it seems most likely that the action was not going Antony's way and Cleopatra took up a prearranged agreement to flee if and when the situation demanded. Actium had been a remarkably easy victory but it was soon to be portrayed as the culmination of a great struggle against a foreign eastern enemy, most spectacularly by Virgil (*Aeneid* 8.675–723; see p. 7). There were to be five yearly festivals, a victory arch was erected, the prows of captured ships were displayed at Rome. Actium was not to be forgotten. Antony and Cleopatra survived another year at Alexandria, before they both killed themselves.

Finally, in 29, Octavian possessed great wealth from Egypt, with which he could rebuild Italy, reward his soldiers and buy popular support. In the triple triumphs of 29 – for Illyricum, Actium and Alexandria – every soldier and male citizen received donatives. In 27 Octavian announced to the Senate that he would relinquish his special powers and allow the restoration of the Republic. Soon after he was titled Augustus – the revered one, and made the claim to be princeps – the first citizen (*Res Gestae* 34). He retained control of the most important provinces, and with them twenty-three of the remaining twenty-eight legions under arms. Later in 23, he acquired a greater imperium over the governors of those provinces not directly under his command and if he had not already done so assumed the powers of the tribune (see pp. 7–14).

That Octavian should succeed where others failed is interesting. He used many of the methods that others before him had used including largesse, intimidation and violence. Although his relationship with the army was tempestuous, weathering repeated dissent and mutiny, he always recognised their importance to his rule. He was also incredibly driven, raising troops on his own initiative as Pompey had done, marching on Rome as Sulla and Caesar had done. The proscriptions and the subsequent scale of veteran settlement led to such widespread redistribution of wealth that the old senatorial houses never regained their control of the plebs urbana. After Octavian's ten years as a triumvir in Italy, the Italian people had become accustomed to him. Where he was different from the old political establishment was that he elevated individuals to be his closest advisors who were not of the aristocracy, such as Agrippa and Maecenas. They would have stood no chance within the confines of the traditional constitution and so were loyal to him. Neither did Octavian ever lose sight of the importance of image, the message displayed on his mausoleum proudly delivered spin from beyond the grave:

> At the age of nineteen, on my own initiative and at my own expense I raised an army by means of which I restored liberty to the republic . . .
>
> *Res Gestae* 1–2

Further Reading

Alston, R. (2015), *Rome's Revolution*, Oxford: Oxford University Press.

Everitt, A. (2001), *Cicero*, London: John Murray.

Goldsworthy, A. (2006), *Caesar*, London: Weidenfeld & Nicolson.

Goldsworthy, A. (2011), Antony and Cleopatra London: Weidenfeld & Nicolson.

Keaveney, A. (2005), *Sulla*, Abingdon: Routledge

Seager. R. (2002), *Pompey the Great, 2nd edition*, Oxford: Wiley-Blackwell.

Southern, P. (2002), *Pompey the Great*, Stroud: Tempus.

Stockton, D. (1971), *Cicero*, Oxford: Oxford University Press.

Tatum, J. (1999), *The Patrician Tribune*, Chapel Hill: University of North Carolina Press.

Taylor, D. (2013), *Cicero and Rome*, London: Bloomsbury Academic.

Welch, K. & Powell, A. (1998), *Julius Caesar as Artful Reporter*, London: Duckworth.

PRACTICE QUESTIONS

1. Read Appian, *The Civil Wars* 3.86, and 5.127–8.

   How useful are these sources for our understanding of the importance of the army to Roman politicians?

   [12]

2. 'Without Cicero's view we would have little understanding of the Late Republic.'

   How far do you agree with this statement?

   You must use and analyse the ancient sources that you have studied as well as your knowledge to support your answer.

   [36]

2.7 Social and Economic Relationships and Their Importance in the Breakdown of the Republic

TOPIC OVERVIEW

Social and economic relationships and their importance in the breakdown of the Republic

- The social and economic standing of: Senators, and Equestrians including the publicani
- The changing role of the rural and especially the urban poor – the plebs
- Patron-client relationships
- Inequality in wealth
- Land bills, corn doles and largesse
- The reaction of possessors of ager publicus to land reform
- Migration of the rural poor to Rome
- Spartacus' slave revolt.

The roles and importance of individuals in the breakdown of the Republic

- Sulla; Lepidus; Pompey; Cicero; Crassus; Catiline; Caesar; Cato; Clodius; Octavian

The prescribed sources for this topic are:

- Sallust, *Histories* [3.34] {3.48M}
- Sallust, *The Catiline Conspiracy* 14 16 20 31, 33
- Cicero, *in Catilinam* II.18–21
- Cicero, *de lege agraria* II.7–10
- Suetonius, *Deified Julius* 38–42.

If faced with the question, 'What caused the fall of the Roman Republic?', a valid answer might focus on the ambition of certain individuals. Certainly a desire for glory was a significant factor in the motivation of individuals such as Pompey, Caesar, Cato, Clodius and Cicero. Yet the methods that these individuals employed often played on the needs of the poor and the social divisions in Roman society. There is a school of thought that marries political and military history with prominent individuals. According to this view, without these individuals, or some other version of them, the Roman Republic would have just continued happily along its way. This is the 'Great Man' theory, which requires a significant individual to bring about change. Contrary to this is the 'long term' view, which has change happening almost imperceptibly slowly over centuries, because of climatic, geographic, ethnographic and demographic pressures. According to this view, one could consider the forced conscription of farmers to fight wars and their replacement by slaves, which brought about a demographic shift. Equally, the huge inequality in wealth that caused the plebs urbana to call out for more land, more corn and more money created an economic engine for change. As to which was responsible for the end of the Republic, the truth lies somewhere between the different views. There were certainly demographic and economic pressures, but great men acted as catalysts to effect or oppose the change that was necessary. As we have seen, Octavian became the face of government that the people chose to be associated with, not the established political classes.

SOCIAL AND ECONOMIC RELATIONSHIPS

Social and economic standing of the orders and the changing role of the poor

In Topic 2.1, the stratification of Roman society was explained. Society was divided according to this wealth. At the very top was the senatorial order, which governed the state. They did this according to the principle that leadership was incumbent on them as the richest people and originally gave freely of their time as public servants. Senators were drawn from the equestrian order. By the late Republic there were few significant differences between patrician and plebeian members of the senatorial order. The distinction was more a case of class and belonging, so that the patrician Catiline was able to denounce Cicero as a mere provincial, while Cicero struggled to find enough evidence to prove Catiline a revolutionary. The only practical bar to patricians was access to the comitia plebis tributa and the **tribunate**. That Clodius, was so keen to be a tribune and so effective in using the position to his advantage should not detract from the fact that he was very rare.

> **tribune/tribunate** the office of the tribune of the plebs. Responsible for defending the rights of the people, it had become an important office for aspiring politicians

To be an equestrian required assets to the value of HS 400,000. From agricultural land an equestrian might expect at least a 5 per cent return that equalled an income of HS 20,000 a year. Most equestrians' wealth was in land. They also provided the business classes of Rome and engaged in foreign trade. As a result it fell to the equestrians to provide financial direction. The largest ventures went to the publicani, the corporations that bid for public contracts. The sums involved were huge, so that no single individual could afford to pay for a contract; but the capacity to make money was also huge. Equestrian money lenders caused a credit crisis in Italy in the middle 60s by calling in debts; this in turn made Catiline's policy of cancelling debts so attractive (Sallust, *Bellum Catilinae* 14 (PS), 20 (PS), 33 (PS); Cicero, *in Catilinam* II.18–21 (PS)). Soon after, the **publicani** realised that in hope of great profits they had overbid for the tax contract in Asia, and sought a re-negotiation. Generally, however, the activities of the equestrian business men go unreported because economics was not part of Roman historiography, which instead dwelt on politics and by extension warfare. However, the equestrians' interests were similar to the Senate's and, despite the two instances of friction just mentioned, ordinarily both orders would agree. Cicero's political philosophy of *concordia ordinum* was really acknowledging what was normal.

As well as providing leadership, the richer members of society, senators and equestrians had traditionally taken it upon themselves to serve their community and look after the poor. The normal patron-client relationship required the patron to represent the interests of the poor within their community. Patrons expected a morning visit and greetings from their clients. This was in turn rewarded with a small daily gift of sustenance, money or food. This system was hierarchical, and many patrons were themselves clients of more powerful men. Political families such as the Metelli and the Claudii could expect daily throngs outside their doors.

The great divide in Roman society was between the Senate and equestrians together and the poor. The poor were very much poorer. In Topic 2.1 it was shown that the poorer an individual was, the less say they had in the *comitia centuriata*. At the lowest level, they were relegated to a single voting century. Similarly, the poorest members of society were unlikely to be represented in court. The poor farmer should have been better off than the city dweller. He could feed himself and because people always need food, he should have been able to make a profit. Again it was shown in Topic 2.1 that because of the requirement for citizen farmers to serve in armies overseas, many farms were not properly looked after. Then the ready supply of slaves captured in overseas wars allowed the rich to buy agricultural workers to farm not only their own land, but as much *ager publicus* as they could get hold of, as *possessores*. As the estates of the rich spread, there was a tendency to encroach on the land of poor neighbours, especially if fathers or sons were absent fighting Rome's wars. The lot of the failed farmer is seen in Manlius' complaint that poor farmers were compelled to work for their creditors if, after they had relinquished their land-holdings, they still owed money (Sallust, *Bellum Catilinae* 33 **PS**).

The result was net migration to Rome as the rural poor upped sticks and moved to live on hand-outs at Rome. Once at Rome, they swelled the ranks of the *plebs urbana*. Caesar, as dictator, doubled army pay to HS 900. The army was a relatively attractive proposition even before the pay rise, therefore a poor man at Rome can be expected to have only earned about the same: HS 500 if unskilled, maybe as much as HS 2,000 a year for a craftsman. As an equestrian earned at least HS 20,000, he was ten to forty times better off than a poor man at Rome. In contrast, many poor men did not have regular work. The inequality in wealth was massive and a catalyst for change.

One final thing that compounded Rome's social and economic woes was Spartacus' slave revolt which, although it began with gladiators, drew support from the working population of the slave estates. Crassus defeated Spartacus, but not before Italy had been ravaged by a marauding band of 120,000 slaves. They could have more easily plundered the poor farmer than the rich, but the poor farmer would have been less able to recover from a loss of stored food or damaged property. Also, in the aftermath, who was to say who was free and who was slave? Many poor Italians would have been pressed into slavery to re-stock the *possessores*' farms.

Land bills and the reaction of the possessors, corn doles and largesse

Individual politicians responded to these demographic and economic pressures in one of two ways. The optimates looked to defend the existing system that allowed them to continue to enjoy the magistracies and pro-magisterial commands that brought wealth and glory. In contrast the populares attempted to secure the votes of the plebs through land bills, debt relief, corn doles and largesse. These in part restored the social imbalance. There was little altruism among the populares, however; they sought glory and prestige as much as the optimates.

Land grants were the traditional reward of soldiers; land grants could also return the urban poor to the countryside. Sulla rewarded his men with land belonging to those communities that had sided with the regimes of Cinna and Carbo, in particular those in Etruria. Immediately after Sulla's death, Lepidus proposed that land confiscated by Sulla should be restored. It was in support of this that Etruria revolted. Later Sulla's veterans would join together with the very people that they had dispossessed to support Catiline in the hope of debt relief (Sallust, *Bellum Catilinae* 16 **PS**, 33 **PS**). When Cicero opposed Rullus' land bill, he was repaying his optimate backers, many of whom as possessores of large estates stood to lose out (Cicero, *de lege Agraria* II.7–10 **PS**). Writing much later, in 44 BC, Cicero made his own view, and probably that of many reasonably well off Romans, quite clear when he asked: how it was fair that a family that has worked land for generations be deprived of it in favour of someone who had done no work. This encapsulates the problem of redistributing ager publicus: somebody had to lose out. Piso Frugi and Flavius tried to sponsor land bills for Pompey's veterans; where they failed Caesar succeeded. After the civil wars Caesar had huge numbers of troops from both sides to settle (Suetonius, *Deified Julius* 38–42 **PS**). Octavian faced the same problem with each successful military campaign through the 30s. Although it was a long-time happening the cumulative effect of land bills was a rebalance in wealth. Whether a land owner was paid or proscribed, and even if each individual land allotment was but a small part of the total estate, then the reciprocal effect was that the gap between rich and poor narrowed.

Corn doles

In establishing a subsidised supply of corn at a fixed price, Gaius Gracchus was prising the support and votes of the plebs urbana away from prominent political families and associating them with himself. If he had not done so they would not have starved, they would have simply gone back to hand-outs from the political families. The number of recipients was reduced almost immediately after Gaius' death and Sulla abolished the dole completely. Lepidus unsuccessfully sought to bring it back, but it was left to the consuls of 73, M. Terentius Varro and C. Cassius Longinus, to achieve this (Sallust, *Histories* 3.34 = 3.48M **PS**). In 62, Cato as tribune increased the number of recipients (Plutarch, *Caesar* 8). This might not be expected from such a traditionalist. However, in the immediate aftermath of the Catiline conspiracy this was probably an attempt to quell popular disquiet. Cato would have gained some popular renown from this, but he was soon overshadowed by Clodius who as tribune in 58 made the dole free to 320,000 recipients. Caesar as dictator actually reduced the number of recipients to 150,000, but this was at the same time as resettling many urban poor and carrying out a huge public works programme that would have provided work for those that remained at Rome (Suetonius, *Deified Julius* 41 **PS**).

Largesse

The political classes increasingly engaged in conspicuous largesse beyond the normal patron client relationships to buy the favour of the plebs. Any excuse to show off was acceptable. As aedile Caesar put on extensive funeral games ostensibly for his father, but he had died twenty years before. Funeral games were particularly useful because they allowed the use of gladiators – always a favourite of the plebs. Crassus as consul in 70 provided a dinner for the whole population of Rome and gave sufficient gifts that they could live for three months. Fifteen years later, and by now the much richer man, his co-consul Pompey held elaborate games at the opening of his theatre. When hoping to secure a second consulship by standing in absentia, Caesar spent huge sums on games in honour of his deceased daughter; he also gave freeborn citizens a Gallic slave each. Accompanying Caesar's triumphs, there were huge public feasts for the whole populace, with donatives of HS 400 and gifts of wheat and oil to every citizen at Rome (Suetonius, *Deified Julius* 38–9 **PS**). Even after his death, Caesar practised largesse; he bequeathed HS 300 to every Roman citizen. Octavian was also conspicuous in superintending games that honoured Caesar. Octavian's lieutenant Agrippa took the position of aedile, and spent huge sums on public works at Rome. In particular the aqueducts, cisterns, fountains and baths that provided the poor with sanitation.

INDIVIDUALS

Of the above responses to demographic and economic pressures, more were carried out by popularis than optimate politicians. They did not do so out of the goodness of their hearts. And when these moves were opposed by the optimates, there was no deep philosophical or ideological reason to do so. Generally all politicians were motivated by the desire to attain high honour, dignity and glory – in a word, ambition. Political office conferred dignity in itself: from political office came pro-magisterial imperium and the opportunity to wage, and to win a war, and then to celebrate a triumph. These were the highest honours; Rome was a competitive and militaristic society. The Roman army was all-conquering, so the prizes of empire were glittering at this time. The most competent leaders that Rome produced were successively lured away from solving the social inequality at home by the opportunity of overseas victory and glory: Sulla in 87, Pompey throughout the 70s and 60s, Caesar in the 50s and again in 44. Only Octavian, who was the least military-minded of them all, could see that equal power and prestige might be achieved by resolving the issues at home.

Yet these politicians were also beset by personal jealousies, often unfairly pursued or arising out of trivial matters. Both Crassus and the optimates wanted to set up Piso in Spain as a foil to Pompey. Lucullus thwarted Pompey because Pompey had usurped his command against Mithradates. Lucullus persecuted Clodius over the Bona Dea scandal because Clodius had fostered a mutiny among his men in Armenia. Then when Cicero did not lie, or at least stay silent in the subsequent court case, Clodius drove him from Rome. Hatred of each other provoked Clodius and Milo to fight through the city's streets, killing many as they went. Pompey was the least consistent of all the players in his policy, tacking from optimate to popularis and back again. His motivation was simple jealousy, or maybe political naivety or insecurity.

> In fact Pompey, from the time when he first took part in public life, could not brook an equal at all. In undertakings in which he should have been merely the first he wished to be the only one.

> Velleius Paterculus 2.33

Only very occasionally did an individual act for the good of the state. Sulla did, although to the disadvantage of the poor and with the accompanying proscriptions that brought their own brutal social upheaval with them. Yet at least he recognised that the system was broken and sought a means of fixing it – in his case by shoring up the powers of the Senate. Caesar as triumvir began to do so, but the confines of a single year in office only allowed him to resolve the most pressing issues. As dictator he was able to do much more with a programme of social engineering and economic reform. He changed the composition of the Senate. He granted citizenship to Cisalpine Gaul and Latin rights to Sicily. This answered a desire to belong on the part of Italian peoples. Debt relief and rent rebates have already been mentioned, as has a massive programme of resettlement and public works that found employment for many poor (Suetonius, *Deified Julius* 41–2 **PS**). Caesar was the first great reformer. He was inclusive and generous, but his very generosity would be his undoing. Octavian was less generous with his political opponents and more carefully controlling of his power, yet with longevity came acceptance. Slowly through the 30s he managed to alleviate debts, minimise taxation and provide public works at Rome. He continued what Caesar had begun, opening up politics to the provincials and protecting the business interests of the equestrians of Italy. Octavian's social reform was coupled with the near extinction of the old political classes through the civil wars. Ultimately people wanted peace and prosperity, and Octavian had (with some difficulty) provided these.

TOPIC REVIEW

- Consider how far the ruling classes perpetuated the problems of the poor.
- Discuss why there were so many land bills between the Gracchi and Caesar.
- Consider whether Caesar recognised that the poor deserved better.

Further Reading

Alston, R. (2015), *Rome's Revolution*, Oxford: Oxford University Press.

Brunt, P.A. (1982), *Social Conflicts in the Roman Republic*, London: Chatto & Windus.

PRACTICE QUESTIONS

1. Read Appian, *The Civil Wars* 1.7–8. **CW**

   How useful is the source for our understanding of the problems faced by the Italian poor and
   the Roman state in the late Republic? [12]

2. 'Social inequality was the most significant factor in the demise of the Roman Republic.'

   How far do you agree with this statement?

   You must use and analyse the ancient sources that you have studied as well as your
   knowledge to support your answer. [36]

Introduction to The Flavians, AD 68–96

This Depth Study focuses on the interplay of political, military, social, economic and religious factors that affected the reigns of the Flavian dynasty resulting in a different type of principate to that of the preceding Julio-Claudian dynasty. The topics in this Depth Study are all interrelated, and learners should be encouraged to see the connections between different topics to deepen their understanding of the period.

The premature death of Nero, leaving behind him no designated successor, had the potential to create a constitutional crisis. The ending of the Julio-Claudian Dynasty could have led to a resurgence of the Senate and popular democracy, but Rome had by now become so used to the Principate that no consideration was given to changing the system. Instead the period 68–69* became one of civil war, as various generals attempted to seize political power by exercising their control of the legions.

After the vicissitudes of this war, the Flavians, headed by Vespasian, emerged victorious and established themselves as the second dynasty of the Roman principate. This Depth Study investigates the actions and motivations of this family as they sought to demonstrate that one could be a Caesar without being a Julio-Claudian.

The various topics cover the reigns of Vespasian and his two sons, Titus and Domitian, who would govern and guide the Roman world between 69 and 96. The choices that these

---

EXAM OVERVIEW   **H407/22 SECTION B**

Your examination for the Flavian emperors, in Section B of your paper, will require you to show knowledge and understanding of the material you have studied. This component is worth 48 marks – 12 based on AO1 skills, 12 on AO2 and 24 on AO3.
In this section, you will answer two questions:

- a 12-mark stimulus question focussing on an issue relating to a historical event or situation, where you will need to assess the source's utility; and
- one of two essay questions, each worth 36 marks. The questions will require you to use, analyse, and evaluate source material to address issues in the question. The essays will target one or more of the themes listed.

---

* In this component, AD will not be given unless needed for clarity.

individual emperors made allow us to understand more fully not only the challenges of being an emperor, but also the way in which posterity viewed the Julio-Claudian dynasty, as the Flavians consciously chose to emulate or ignore aspects of their predecessors' work.

VESPASIAN

Titus Flavius Vespasianus had been a successful military officer under the Julio-Claudian emperors, serving in Britain and finally being appointed by Nero to deal with the revolt in Judaea in 66.

As the first emperor of a new dynasty he faced numerous difficulties, not least because he had come to power after a period of intense civil war. However, he himself was suspect. Tacitus tells us that his reputation was doubtful (*Histories* 1.50 PS) and that he was 'the first emperor to ever change for the better'.

Indeed until 70, the only real successes he had enjoyed had been military in nature. While Vespasian had served as aedile in 38, the Emperor Gaius had stuffed mud down his tunic (Suetonius, *Vespasian* 5.3 PS; Cassius Dio, *Roman Histories* 59.12.3) making him appear a ridiculous figure. As a praetor (*c.* 40) he cut a pathetic and servile figure, making overtures to Gaius as often as possible (Suetonius, *Vespasian* 2.3). During his proconsulship of Africa (*c.* 62–3), he had been so unpopular with the locals that they had once even pelted him with turnips in the market at Hadramentum (Tacitus, *Histories* 2.97; Suetonius, *Vespasian* 4.3 PS).

Therefore, on his accession, Vespasian had much to overcome. The fact that he did so successfully, establishing his dynasty on good grounds, is testimony to the inherent character of the man, entailing that retrospectively he was viewed as a model emperor: Suetonius claims that Vespasian left nothing undone 'to first shore up the foundations of the commonwealth . . . and then to embellish it artistically' (*Vespasian* 8.1 PS).

FIGURE 3.1
Vespasian.

Born: AD 9
Accession: 69
Died: 79

TITUS

Titus Flavius Caesar Vespasianus Augustus succeeded his father to the principate on 24 June 79. Having cut his teeth as a dashing young military officer, taking a leading role in the Judaean campaign begun by his father, Titus acceded to the imperial throne as the elder son of an established imperial family.

The success of Vespasian's reign, to say nothing of Titus' own charm, ensured a smooth transition for the thirty-nine-year-old. Popular support was with him and the lack of any significant opposition for the past ten years, aside from the obstinacy of his own brother, Domitian, should have led to a long and stable reign.

However, fate once again intervened, as it had done in the reign of Augustus with the deaths of several would-be-successors, and Titus enjoyed power for a little over two years. His brief reign is perhaps more famous for the eruption of Vesuvius than anything that Titus himself did. However, his reign does highlight the qualities which would be judged as being crucial for an emperor to be remembered well in posterity.

FIGURE 3.2
Titus.

Born: 39
Accession: 79
Died: 81

FIGURE 3.3
Domitian.

Born: 51
Accession: 81
Died: 96

DOMITIAN

The last of the Flavian emperors, and younger son of Vespasian, Domitian would rule for longer than his father and his brother combined. Although perhaps never expected to rule in his own right, he had always been a significant figure within the dynasty, if for nothing other than the added stability he provided. Ultimately, following the early death of Titus, his presence was needed otherwise the dynasty would have been remarkably short-lived.

Domitian has tended to be a polarising figure, not only among his contemporaries, but also among scholars of the period. The contrast between his being perceived as a tyrant and his demonstration of his capacity as a meticulous and forthright administrator is particularly interesting. It highlights the biases of our source material more pointedly than perhaps any other emperor.

KEY DATES

AD **9 (17 Nov.)**	Birth of Vespasian
38	Vespasian serves as plebeian aedile
39 (30 Dec.)	Birth of Titus
c. **40**	Vespasian praetor
42	Vespasian commands the Second Legion Augusta in Germany
43	Vespasian takes part in Claudius' invasion of Britain
43–7	Vespasian campaigns in SW Britain, including the capture of the Isle of Wight, for which he is awarded triumphal ornaments
51 (24 October)	Birth of Domitian
51 (Nov.–Dec.)	Vespasian serves as suffect consul
c. **62–3**	Vespasian serves as proconsul of Asia
66	Vespasian appointed to deal with the revolt in Judaea
68 (8–9 June)	Fall of Nero
69 (15 January)	Otho overthrows Galba
69 (14 April)	Vitellius' forces defeat Otho's at the Battle of Bedriacum
69 (19 April)	Vitellius recognised as Emperor by the Senate
69 (1 July)	Vespasian proclaimed Emperor in Egypt

69 (3 July)	Vespasian proclaimed Emperor in Judaea
69 (24–5 Oct.)	Flavian forces defeat those of Vitellius at Cremona
69 (20 December)	Vespasian's troops take Rome
69 (21 December)	Full imperial powers conferred on Vespasian
70 (21 June)	First ceremony for the rebuilding work on the Capitol
70 (autumn)	Vespasian returns to Rome
70 (Aug.–Sept.)	Titus captures Jerusalem; Great temple burned
71 (June)	Triumph of Vespasian and Titus in Rome
71 (1 July)	Titus awarded tribunicia potestas and imperium proconsulare maius
71	Titus takes command of the Praetorian Guard
c. 71–2	Exile of Helvidius Priscus
73–4	Vespasian and Titus hold the census for the first time in 26 years
c. 74–5	Execution of Helvidius Priscus
75	Dedication of the Temple of Peace
75	Formal extension of the pomerium
c. 76	Completion of the rebuilding work of the Capitol
77 (late summer)	Agricola arrives in Britain
79 (24 June)	Death of Vespasian; accession of Titus. Vespasian is deified
79 (24 August)	Eruption of Vesuvius and destruction of Pompeii and Herculaneum
80	Titus inaugurates the Colosseum
80	Fire of Rome
81 (13 Sept.)	Death of Titus
81 (14 Sept.)	Accession of Domitian
82 (Jan.–Feb.)	Domitian returns coinage to Augustan standard
82–3	Domitian's Rhine expedition against the Chatti
83	Domitian celebrates a triumph for the Chattan War
83 (late)	Battle of Mons Graupius
84–5	Dacian successes against the Romans in the First Dacian War

85	Domitian assumes perpetual censorship
85 (Apr.–Sept.)	Domitian devalues coinage to the Neronian standard of 64
85 (post Sept.)	Second devaluation of coinage
86	Domitian's Second Dacian War
86	Inauguration of the Capitoline Games
88	Celebration of the *Ludi Saeculares*
89 (1 January)	Revolt of Saturninus
89	First Pannonian War
89	Senate voted for the *Equus Maximus*
92 (May)	Second Pannonian War
93 (23 August)	Death of Agricola
96 (18 September)	Assassination of Domitian

3.1 The Year of the Four Emperors: The Establishment of the Flavian Dynasty AD 68–69

TOPIC OVERVIEW

- The failures of Galba, Otho, and Vitellius and the reasons for these failures
- The actions of Vespasian and his supporters
- The means by which Vespasian gained the principate, including his use of military, political, financial, and popular support
- Religious aspects to Vespasian's accession
- The role of the army, Senate, people of Rome, and provincials in the events of AD 68–69 and the accession of Vespasian.

The prescribed sources for this topic are:

- Josephus, *The Jewish War*: 4.592–600; 4.601–7
- Suetonius, *Galba* 11–17, 19, 22
- Suetonius, *Otho* 5–9
- Suetonius, *Vitellius* 8, 10–12, 15
- Suetonius, *Vespasian* 4–7
- Suetonius, *Titus* 4–5
- Tacitus, *Histories* Book 1: 1–14, 18–22, 27–8, 33–6, 41–3, 46, 50–3, 62, 74–8, 86, 89
  - Book 2: 1–2, 4–7, 74–5, 79, 83–6, 90–91, 100–1
  - Book 3: 47–8, 71, 84–6
  - Book 4: 2–4

The period upon which I embark is one full of incident, marked by bitter fighting, rent by treason, and even in peace sinister. Four emperors perished violently. There were three civil wars. . . However, the period was not so barren of merit that it failed to teach some good lessons as well.

PS

Tacitus, *Histories* 1.2–3

Tacitus' remarks here say much about the period of Roman history covered by his *Histories*. While its narrative survives only to Book 5 (i.e. midway through AD 70), his description is certainly most applicable to the run-up to and events of AD 69, the Year of the Four Emperors.

Study question

Tacitus should be familiar from the *Annals* in the Period Study. As a reminder, read p. 14.

What traits does Tacitus display as a historian in the *Annals* and how do these manifest in the passage quoted above?

PRESCRIBED SOURCE

Title: *Histories*

Author: Tacitus

Date: *c.* AD 109

Genre: Prose history

Significance: Factually accurate, but often biased, this is the fullest surviving account of the troubled years of 68–9

Prescribed sections: Book 1: 1–14, 18–22, 27–8, 33–6, 41–3, 46, 50–3, 62, 74–8, 86, 89; Book 2: 1–2, 4–7, 74–5, 79, 83–6, 90–1, 100–1; Book 3: 47–8, 71, 84–6; Book 4: 2–4, 10

Read it here: Tacitus, *Histories*, trans. Wellesley (London: Penguin, 1991)

The year 69 is perhaps the most remarkable one in the history of Rome, with the landscape of political power in both city and empire changing forever. Tacitus summarises the situation well: for the first time power could be sought by those not based in Rome itself and an emperor could be appointed by might rather than right (*Histories* 1.4 **PS**).

Following Nero's suicide, having been declared an enemy of the state on 8 June 68, the Roman Empire descended into civil war. The Roman world had not seen a crisis of this nature since the last days of the Republic, where the forces of Octavian and his rival Mark Antony vied for supremacy. Ultimately Titus Flavius Vespasianus would emerge victorious, establishing the Flavian Dynasty. However, 69 reveals much of the socio-political change since Augustus' foundation of the principate, not the least of which was the now central importance of the army in both the creation and maintenance of an emperor's power.

As we saw in the Period Study (pp. 78–9), Nero's death was intimately linked with his failure to respond adequately to the revolt of Gaius Julius Vindex, to whom the first of our Four Emperors was allied: the elderly governor of Spain, Servius Sulpicius Galba. His troops hailed him as imperator on 9 June 68.

Vindex' revolt ended at the battle at Vesontio (see p. 76) and this could also have marked the end of Galba's move for the imperial throne. Even though he himself was not present, he had clearly aligned himself with the rebellion of Vindex in its aims for the removal of Nero. However, Galba was now committed to his course. News was brought by the freedman Icelus that the Praetorian Guard and Senate had also proclaimed Galba emperor, so, trusting also to support from Otho (see p. 161) in Lusitania, he set out for Rome at the beginning of July.

However, Galba overestimated the security of his position: perhaps, given his experience under the Julio-Claudians, he felt that the public acknowledgement of the Senate was enough to guarantee his position. If so, he was very mistaken. Moreover, his old-fashioned military discipline was very much at odds with the majority

KEY INDIVIDUAL

Galba
Dates: 3 BC–AD 69

Governor of Spain from 60.
Galba was something of a relic of a bygone age: notorious for being a tough military disciplinarian, and the antithesis to Nero. Tacitus records Galba's famous remark that he 'select[ed] his troops, [he] d[id] not buy them' (*Histories* **1.5** **PS**).

of the army at this time, whose commanders tended to be more avuncular and indulgent.

Galba's march to Rome from Spain was slow and Tacitus' narrative of the journey is dominated by executions (*Histories*, 1.6 (PS)), such as of Clodius Macer and Fonteius Capito, on the suspicion that they were plotting against Galba. He also disposed of Nymphidius Sabinus, the Prefect of the Praetorian Guard, who had attempted to seize the principate himself, only to be prevented by his own troops, who were actually keen to ingratiate themselves with Galba (Suetonius, *Galba* 11 (PS)).

Likewise Tacitus also tells us that, in addition to the freedman Icelus (on whom see Suetonius, *Galba* 22 (PS)) – whose very status would have irked the senatorial classes – Galba was also in the sway of individuals who were rather less than ideal:

> Old and feeble, Galba was dominated by Titus Vinius and Cornelius Laco. The former of these was the most vicious of men, the latter the most idle. Between them, they saddled the emperor's reputation with crimes that caused public revulsion, and then ruined it altogether by an indolence that earned contempt.
>
> Tacitus, *Histories* 1.6

Suetonius (*Galba* 14 (PS)) gives exactly the same assessment of the over-influence of these individuals. Thus, by the time that Galba actually arrived in Rome, most likely in late September, much of whatever initial popularity he had enjoyed had been eroded (Suetonius, *Galba* 12–13; 15 (PS); Tacitus, *Histories* 1.7–11 (PS)). He was generally regarded as strict, uncompromising and – most crucially from the army's perspective – miserly. Suetonius records Galba's refusal to give a bonus to the troops who had supported him and his dismissal of Praetorians whom he suspected had been bought by Nymphidius, when he sought the throne (*Galba* 16 (PS)).

PRESCRIBED SOURCE

Title: *Galba*

Author: Suetonius

Date: AD 121

Genre: Prose biography

Significance: Character-driven assessment of the brief reign of Galba; his later biographies such as this are characterised by rather anecdotal stories rather than documentary evidence

Prescribed sections: 11–17; 19; 22

Read it here: *Suetonius: The Twelve Caesars*, trans. R. Graves (London: Penguin 1957)

donative a handout of money to the soldiers of Rome, the frequency and scale of which could assure the loyalty of the troops

The significance of Galba's refusal to pay the **donative** cannot be overemphasised, as it highlights not only that he was out of touch with recent military practices, but also the fact that increasingly the loyalty of the soldiers went to the highest bidder, something all emperors had to realise from now on.

Study question

Galban coinage

Given his rather stern image, it is important to see how Galba strove to present himself, with perhaps the most ubiquitous of all forms of imperial propaganda: coinage. Many of his designs were later reused by Vespasian.

FIGURE 3.4
Denarius of Galba, 68.

Obverse: laureate head, globe at point of bust; 'Galba, emperor'
Reverse: Roma, helmeted and in military dress, advancing with Victory on globe & transverse spear; 'Rome rising again'

FIGURE 3.5
Denarius of Galba, 68–69.

Obverse: laureate head; 'Servius Galba, emperor'
Reverse: Concordia standing, holding olive branch and cornucopia; 'Harmony of the provinces'

FIGURE 3.6
Denarius of Galba, 68.

Obverse: laureate head, globe at point of bust; 'Galba, emperor'
Reverse: Roma standing holding spear, foot on globe; 'Rome victorious'

Note that all these coins were minted in Spain, reinforcing that province as
the heart of Galba's power.

- Looking at these examples, what messages was Galba trying to convey to
  the Roman people about his rule?
- Why may he have chosen these particular messages?

KEY INDIVIDUAL

Otho
Dates: AD 32–69

Orchestrated the
assassination of Galba and
replaced him as Emperor
on 15 January AD 69.

However, by far Galba's greatest failure was never to believe that others would try to do
what he had, that is, seize the imperial throne. In particular, he grossly underestimated
the ambitions of his erstwhile ally, the governor of Lusitania, Marcus Salvius Otho.

Otho most likely 'tied himself to Galba's wagon' along with many others (Tacitus,
Histories 1.12 **PS**) from the belief that the elderly *princeps* (Galba was already seventy-
one at the time of his troops declaring him emperor), who was also childless, would have
to declare a successor (Suetonius, *Otho* 5 **PS**). Tacitus similarly notes that adoption was
Otho's growing ambition (*Histories* 1.13 **PS**).

However, Otho would be greatly disappointed: Galba selected Lucius Calpurnius Piso
Frugi Licinianus (Suetonius, *Galba* 17 **PS**; Tacitus, *Histories* 1.14 **PS**), a descendant
of Pompey the Great and Crassus the triumvir, who had recently returned from exile. On
10 January 69, Galba headed to the Praetorian camp and declared that Piso would be
his successor, following the precedent set by Augustus (*Histories*, 1.18–20 **PS**).

The reaction of the troops was underwhelming, but the situation could have been
saved if Galba had been more generous. Tacitus observes that his 'old fashioned rigidity
and excessive strictness' meant he was unable to see the result in the form of the troops'
lukewarm response.

Otho, by contrast, was popular with the Praetorians (Suetonius, *Otho* 8 **PS**), partly
because he had gone some way to cultivate their loyalty, and was seen as similar to Nero.
Now, with his personal ambitions dashed with regard to legitimate succession, Otho
resolved to seize the principate by violence. His action was swift, made expedient by the
burgeoning unpopularity of Galba (*Histories*, 1.21–2 **PS**; Suetonius, *Otho* 6 **PS**).

Galba's end came on 15 January 69, only five days after his adoption of Piso. The
brief chain of events began as he was offering sacrifice in front of the Temple of Apollo

Palatinus (*Histories*, 1.27). Otho made excuses to leave and headed immediately to the Praetorian camp for proclamation as emperor, although the support that he received there was far from universal:

> Their mood may be summed up thus: a shocking crime was committed on the unscrupulous initiative of few individuals, with the blessing of more, and amid the passive acquiescence of all.
>
> Tacitus, *Histories* 1.28

In many ways, this summary statement from Tacitus could symbolise the whole of 69, if not the entire period of the principate itself. The majority of the Roman people were followers, not leaders, often acting – at whatever level, from public rioting by the plebs, to assassinations and coups plotted by the elite – only when the status quo was no longer beneficial or tolerable. Perhaps this degree of apathy among the people as a whole contributed to the rise of the military's political significance in the making and breaking of emperors (Tacitus, *Histories* 1.46 PS).

The events of the day unravelled quickly and with a great deal of confusion (Tacitus, *Histories* 1.33–6 PS; 1.41–3 PS). When news of Otho's proclamation as emperor by the Praetorians became known, Galba and Piso returned to the palace. They stayed there until reports of Otho having been killed at the Praetorian camp began to filter through – one member of the imperial bodyguard, Julius Atticus, even claimed to have committed the deed (Tacitus, *Histories* 1.34–5 PS), although Galba's retort to this, 'Who gave you the order, my man?', again reinforces Galba's lack of the common touch (see also Suetonius, *Galba* 19 PS).

Galba thereupon set out with Piso into the forum, where both were killed by the soldiers whom Otho had sent out to secure the city. Thus the brief reign of Galba was brought to an end by violence perpetrated by one whose ambition could not be checked. Tacitus pithily summarises the standard sentiment on Galba:

> . . . so long as he was a subject, he seemed too great a man to be one, and by common consent possessed the makings of a ruler – had he never ruled.
>
> Tacitus, *Histories* 1.49

ACTIVITY

Use your prescribed sources to create a timeline of Galba's reign, highlighting his chief failings noted by the authors.

OTHO'S REIGN AND THE CHALLENGE OF VITELLIUS

Otho was not alone in having imperial ambitions: in Germany another player had entered the political games of 69: Aulus Vitellius.

The majority of the sources paint him a negative light: Suetonius states that he was 'stained by every sort of baseness as he advanced in years' (*Vitellius* 4), but we should not be surprised by this tradition, given that he would ultimately be defeated by the ensuing Flavian dynasty, who would doubtless wish to vilify their opponent.

In mid-December 68, Vitellius had been sent by Galba to take up the position of governor of the Lower Rhine, a post that had been vacant ever since Galba had executed Fonteius Capito. This would be a fateful decision by the elderly princeps, even though he seemed to have considered Vitellius in no way a threat:

KEY INDIVIDUAL

Aulus Vitellius
Dates: AD 15–69
Appointed by Galba in 68 to be the commander of the legions of Lower Germany. His career had previously been unspectacular, with a consulship in 48.

PRESCRIBED SOURCE

Title: *Vitellius*

Author: Suetonius

Date: 121

Genre: Prose biography

Significance: Character-driven biography of the brief reign of Vitellius; his later biographies such as this are characterised by rather anecdotal stories rather than documentary evidence

Prescribed sections: 8, 10–12, 15

Read it here: *Suetonius: The Twelve Caesars*, trans. R. Graves (London: Penguin 1957)

. . . Galba had openly stated that a glutton was the sort of rival whom he feared least and he expected Vitellius to cram his belly with the fruits of the province.

Suetonius, *Vitellius* 7

However, once again, even though Vitellius himself would have perhaps been unlikely to stir up insurrection independently, Galba had failed to account for his lack of popularity with the army at large and the officers of the legions of Mainz and Colonia, in particular Fabius Valens and Caecina Alienus, both of whom held tight to a personal enmity towards Galba.

Thus, on 1 January 69, while Galba was being sworn in as consul, the legions at Mainz refused to swear allegiance to him. Valens immediately set to work and rushed to Colonia, encouraging the soldiers of the First Legion to swear fealty to Vitellius. They duly did so (Suetonius, *Vitellius* 8 **PS**), being hastily followed by the legions stationed at Mainz on 3 January. Tacitus notes their eagerness for action (*Histories* 1.62 **PS**).

It should be emphasised at this point that the politics of Rome, for so long dominated by the affairs of the city, now moved towards a more global scale, with the provinces beginning to exert an increasing influence on the direction of the empire as a whole.

So, in January 69, the confusing situation existed of an incumbent emperor at Rome (Galba), a usurper in Germany (Vitellius), and a would-be assassin (Otho). Tacitus gives us a markedly moralising judgement on the latter two, following Galba's death:

> In Rome, public opinion was nervous . . . Here then were the two most despicable men in the whole world by reason of their unclean, idle, and pleasure-loving lives, apparently appointed by fate for the task of destroying the empire.

Tacitus, *Histories* 1.50

On 16 January 69, Otho had been invested with all the trappings and titles of Emperor, although it must be said that the Senate were not wholly committed to Otho. They may

ACTIVITY

Study Tacitus, *Histories* 1.51–3.

Summarise the situation among the German legions at the outset of Vitellius' rebellion, paying especial attention to the character details of Vitellius, Caecina and Valens.

EXPLORE FURTHER

For candidates wishing to explore the narrative of these months more fully, the best text remains as follows:

Wellesley, K., (2000), *The Long Year: AD 69*, 3rd edition, London: Routledge.

KEY PEOPLE

Arval Brethren

An ancient priesthood revived by Augustus who were increasingly focussed on honouring the emperor and imperial family.

Acts of the Arval Brethren stone plaques commemorating the rituals of the Arval Brethren, essentially cataloguing imperial rites and details of the various reigns

---

have been worried about potential reprisals should Vitellius – whose rebellion was by now known of in Rome – prove victorious. This may account for the absence of imperially minted coinage from the early part of 69. The two men themselves seemed unsure of how to deal with one another, exchanging offers of bribes and ultimately accusing each other of 'debauchery and wickedness'. According to Tacitus, 'here at least both were in the right' (*Histories* 1.74 **PS**).

While the uncertainty of the situation even extended to both men despatching assassins for the other (*Histories*, 1.75 **PS**), probably the most significant aspect of the conflict between Otho and Vitellius is the split in the army's support between the two. The alliances of the various legions and their commanders soon became of prime importance as it was increasingly apparent that war was inevitable. The whole of the East and Africa had declared for Otho, while Spain sided with Vitellius. The latter was also supported by Narbonese Gaul, Aquitania, Lugdunese Gaul, Belgica, Raetia and Britain, in addition to his own Rhine legions. The last significant number of provincial legions, those of Pannonia, Dalmatia and Moesia, declared for Otho (for a full account of the provincial dispositions see Tacitus, *Histories* 1.76–8 **PS**). Otho also enjoyed a surprisingly consistent loyalty from the Praetorians, the vast majority of whom remained in his camp until the very end.

Overall the two were fairly evenly matched. However, Vitellius had the distinct advantage of having the core of his support near at hand. Moreover, Otho had other issues to face aside from military disadvantage. The manner in which he had seized the principate, through assassination and coup, could not be forgotten, even by Otho himself:

> Otho is said to have been haunted that night by Galba's ghost in a terrible nightmare; the servants who ran in when he screamed for help found him lying on the bedroom floor.

> Suetonius, *Otho* 7

Moreover, he must have been struck by the futility of his action, given the timing of the rebellion of Vitellius.

A further issue that blighted Otho was his similarity, at times something he openly exploited, with Nero. The last of the Julio-Claudians has been traditionally viewed as a polarising figure for the Roman world, enjoying support from the lower classes while alienating the upper classes. Otho was in a similar position as he struggled for legitimacy. We therefore see him using the period between January and March to attempt to write himself into the fabric of the principate as Augustus had established it. The **Acts of the Arval Brethren** attest to his many civil and priestly investitures during this period.

Ultimately, however, all the legitimacy in the world would not aid Otho with a hostile army bearing down on Italy. For a while Otho strove to win public and provincial support, Vitellius – guided and prompted by Valens and Caecina – had sent legions towards the capital. The political uncertainty of the time is highlighted by Tacitus:

> Men had to constantly attune their attitudes and expressions to the latest rumour: it would not do to appear too upset by bad tidings and insufficiently gratified by good. But it was above all when the senate was assembled in the chamber that the task of steering a course between Scylla and Charybdis presented a continual hazard.
>
> Tacitus, *Histories* 1.85

This reinforces just how subservient and subject the Senate had become. Tacitus also notes that given the focus on war and military preparations, the deprivations and suffering of the ordinary people within the city were on the increase (*Histories* 1.86 **PS**; 1.89 **PS**), again highlighting the upheaval of the period.

Valens and Caecina, leading elements of the armies of Lower and Upper Germany, respectively, had set out in mid-January and were fast approaching Italy. Otho could no longer count on the arrival of the legions from Pannonia and Dalmatia arriving in time to prevent their further advance. It was strategically imperative for Otho to attempt to prevent the forces of Valens and Caecina from joining up: Valens, leading 40,000 men had approached Italy through the Western Alps, whereas Caecina – with 30,000 men – had passed through Alpis Poenina (Great St Bernard Pass). Both were aiming for Cremona. Thus Otho set out with all the troops available to him, perhaps some 25,000 men, which included the Praetorian cohorts who, while largely untested in battle, were phenomenally loyal.

Otho did enjoy some success in these initial forays against the Vitellians: Placentia (modern Piacenza), held by Vestricius Spurinna, fended off a siege by Caecina. Caecina also failed to execute an ambush along the Via Postuma, but managed to convince his troops that the ensuing Othonian victory was hardly significant. However, despite these victories, the rather ebullient mood of his troops, and the personal enmity between Valens and Caecina, Otho ultimately failed to prevent the uniting of the Vitellian armies. Now came the key decision of the campaign for Otho: whether to engage the joint Vitellian forces or to engage in a delaying campaign in the hope that his Dalmatian forces might yet arrive to swing the numbers towards a more even standing.

Before relating Otho's debate and decision, Tacitus summarises the relative demerits of the two rivals (*Histories* 2.31). He is clear that Otho had never managed to distance himself from the inglorious manner in which he had acquired the principate and suggests that Vitellius, though a glutton, was preferable to the cruel and unscrupulous assassin Otho.

The decision reached was that an immediate confrontation was necessary. This was to be the First Battle of Bedriacum, on 14 April 69. Tacitus' account (*Histories* 2.39–45) is by far the fullest available, but even this is somewhat confused. Far more interesting is his observation prior to the battle on the contemporary Roman attitude to power:

> From time immemorial, man has had an instinctive love of power. With the growth of our empire, this instinct has become a dominant and uncontrollable force.

Tacitus, Histories 2.38

Given the numerical superiority of the Vitellians, unsurprisingly they emerged victorious. Suetonius is critical of Otho's decision to fight, asserting he would better have stayed on the defensive yet was nervous, hasty or could not control his troops (*Otho* 9 **PS**).

Suetonius is almost characteristically unflattering and vague here, far more so than Tacitus. However, both authors do give Otho a great degree of dignity in his final decision to commit suicide, upon receipt of the outcome of Bedriacum.

Thus came the end of our second emperor of 69, a character who – while vilified by many in life – nevertheless acquired a certain dignity and prestige in death:

ACTIVITY

Study Tacitus, *Histories* 2.32–3 on the various arguments for and against engaging the Vitellians.

Draw up a summary of the strengths and weakness of both armies.

Study question

On the basis of your knowledge, from the outset of the principate in 27 BC, how convincing do you find Tacitus' observation of enmity between senate and people?

Give examples from the sources to justify your opinion.

EXPLORE FURTHER

Otho's decision to commit suicide may seem strange given that most of his army had survived and was willing to fight, with reinforcements likely to arrive soon. Study Suetonius, *Otho* 9–11 and Tacitus, *Histories* 2.46–7.

How useful are these passages in determining the reasons for Otho's suicide? Are there any other possibilities which are not suggested by our authors?

Thus many who had hated Otho while alive loved him for the way he died; and he was even commonly believed to have killed Galba with the object not so much of becoming emperor as of restoring the free republic.

Suetonius, *Otho* 12

One could argue that, in death, Otho acquired a legacy that was far more significant than his brief ninety-five-day reign deserved. This is due in no small part to the fact that his 'noble' death played into the hands of the next individual to bestride the political and martial arena: Titus Flavius Vespasianus (Vespasian).

THE ACTIONS OF VESPASIAN AND HIS SUPPORTERS

As the first of the Flavian emperors, Vespasian is doubtless the key figure of this period, but we also need to be aware of his career prior to this point.

Born on 17 November AD 9, Vespasian's career was fairly typical: Suetonius (*Vespasian* 2) claims that he 'scraped into' the position of aedile, wherein he was openly mocked and humiliated by Gaius (*Vespasian* 5 **PS**). Under Claudius, Vespasian was sent to Britain, at the prompting of the imperial freedman Narcissus, where he distinguished himself as a military commander; this was followed by the proconsulship of Africa (*Vespasian* 4 **PS**) where his rule was 'characterised by justice and great dignity'. However, under Nero his star waned. According to Suetonius, this was primarily due to his unwillingness or inability to fawn over the Emperor's performing skills.

It therefore seemed that Vespasian's career had reached an ignominious end, given Nero's dislike for the man. However, rebellion in Judaea necessitated the appointment of a proven and determined military commander. Thus in 66, Vespasian headed east, accompanied by his elder son Titus to suppress the Jewish revolt.

This distance, both geographical and political, from Rome herself doubtless proved useful to Vespasian in the early part of 69, watching from the sidelines while others scrapped for supremacy. He had, early in 69, despatched Titus to Rome to pledge the fidelity of the eastern legions to Galba, as well as stand for political office himself (Tacitus, *Histories* 2.1–2 **PS**; Suetonius, *Titus* 4–5 **PS**), although upon reaching Corinth the young man had been informed of Galba's murder and Vitellius' uprising. Judging discretion to be the better part of valour, Titus returned to his father. It should also be noted that the troops under his command were perfectly happy to swear allegiance to both Galba and Otho as emperors, which later allowed Vespasian to characterise himself as the avenger of Otho and the Roman state against the usurper Vitellius. Here again, we see the salvation of Otho's memory, which had been begun by the manner of his suicide.

However, Vespasian was nothing if not cautious (Tacitus, *Histories* 2.74–5 **PS**), with our sources giving similar opinions on this matter:

Vespasian . . . was engaged in taking careful stock of the military situation and the forces available to him far and near.

Tacitus, *Histories* 2.74

Title: *Vespasian*

Author: Suetonius

Date: 121

Genre: Prose biography

Significance: Character-driven account of the reign of Vespasian; his later biographies such as this are characterised by rather anecdotal stories rather than documentary evidence

Prescribed sections: 1; 4–19

Read it here: *Suetonius: The Twelve Caesars*, trans. R. Graves (London: Penguin 1957)

When Nero and Galba were both dead and Vitellius was disputing the rule with Otho, Vespasian began to remember his imperial ambitions . . .

PS

Suetonius, *Vespasian* 5

The positive presentation of Vespasian by our authors may well be influenced by the tradition of Flavian authors who doubtless wished to couch Vespasian in the most glowing terms, to differentiate him actively from the other ambitious commanders of 69. This is perhaps most visible in the extensive, even excessive, list of 'omens' that presaged the supremacy of Vespasian (see Study Questions right).

However, aside from the pseudo-religious aspects supporting his nomination, far more telling were several key individuals and groups, all of whom assisted in Vespasian's gaining the principate, namely:

1. Gaius Licinius Mucianus;
2. Tiberius Alexander, Governor of Egypt; and
3. the Moesian, Syrian and Judean legions.

> **Study questions**
> Read Suetonius,
> *Vespasian* 5 and 7 PS:
>
> - List the various omens that Suetonius incorporates into his narrative.
> - How useful is this catalogue in aiding our understanding of the contemporary opinion of Vespasian?

GAIUS LICINIUS MUCIANUS: POLITICAL SUPPORT

Mucianus was at the time the governor of Syria and well-known to Vespasian (Tacitus, *Histories* 2.4–7 PS). It is somewhat frustrating that we know comparatively little of the career of this man who was to be the 'kingmaker' of 69. Tacitus gives perhaps the fullest account of his qualities and demerits, concluding:

> . . . by a supple gift for intrigue he exercised great influence on his subordinates, associates, and colleagues, and found it more congenial to make an emperor than be one.

Tacitus, *Histories* 1.10

PRESCRIBED SOURCE

Title: *The Jewish War*

Author: Josephus

Date: AD 75–9

Genre: Prose history

Significance: Fullest and most contemporary surviving account of the Flavian period. Pro-Roman, and decidedly pro-Flavian, despite being a Jew, his writing tends to have a positive bias towards the administration, but it is by no means consistent

Prescribed sections: 4.592–600; 4.601–7

Read it here: H16–17 in LACTOR 20: The Flavians (London: KCL, 2015)

If Mucianus himself had had ambitions for the principate, then Roman history would have been quite different. Instead, Mucianus chose to support Vespasian (*Histories* 2.76), acting as his partner and contributing much to his campaign (*Histories* 2.83–4).

At the moment of Vespasian's choosing whether to pursue the principate or not, Tacitus gives Mucianus an extensive and persuasive speech, designed to convince Vespasian of the security of his position and the need for him to press on towards the imperial role. We should ask what prompted Mucianus to behave in such a manner. Tacitus indicates that he hopes for reward: 'I shall enjoy such status as you choose to give' (*Histories* 2.77), and Mucianus did indeed enjoy substantial influence under Vespasian until his death *c.* 75. In terms of his military capability, statesman-like demeanour, and unwavering loyalty, Mucianus was the greatest asset in Vespasian's camp and his contribution to the overall success of the campaign cannot be overstated.

TIBERIUS JULIUS ALEXANDER: PROVINCIAL SUPPORT

Although perhaps not as important as Mucianus, Tiberius Alexander, the governor of Egypt was nevertheless a palpable asset for Vespasian. His troops swore allegiance to Vespasian on 1 July (Tacitus, *Histories* 2.79).

The significance of Tiberius Alexander's action can be seen in the fact that it effectively gave Vespasian and the Flavian cause control over Egypt and therefore control over Rome's essential grain supply. This day was henceforth regarded as the first of his reign. Interestingly, Josephus (*Jewish War* 4.616) has Vespasian writing directly to Tiberius Alexander for support, although Tacitus' version makes this move spontaneous upon Tiberius' part. Regardless of the axis, the significance of Egypt's supporting Vespasian essentially guaranteed him victory in the conflict that was to come (Tacitus, *Histories* 3.47–8). Josephus reinforces the significance of this asset:

> Once master of Egypt, [Vespasian] hoped to depose Vitellius, even if things dragged on; for the latter would not be able to hold out if the people at Rome were hungry. Secondly, he wished to join the two legions that were at Alexandria to his other legions. Lastly, he planned to make that country a defence for himself against the uncertainties of fate; for Egypt is hard to enter by land, and has no good harbours on the coast.
>
> Josephus, *Jewish War* 4.605–7 (LACTOR 20, H17)

THE MOESIAN, SYRIAN, AND JUDEAN LEGIONS: MILITARY SUPPORT

The last of Vespasian's three advantages noted above was the support of the army. Josephus (*Jewish War* 4.592–600) provides a fictionalised account of Vespasian's soldiers urging him to become emperor. Vespasian is presented as unwilling to accept this burden (*Jewish War* 4.601–4 **PS**). Motivations for military support were twofold: some legions openly supported him; others despised Vitellius. The sources provide other interesting reasons:

- Mucianus made his own legions in Syria swear allegiance to Vespasian, primarily using the allegation that Vitellius wished to transfer his favoured German legions to Syria (Suetonius, *Vespasian* 6 **PS**), while moving the Syrian legions to the harsher duties in Germany (*Histories*, 2.80);
- The Balkan legions, those in Moesia and Pannonia, almost immediately declared for Vespasian. Their motivation was guilt for their failings in the Battle of Bedriacum (*Histories*, 2.85 **PS**; Suetonius, *Vitellius* 15 **PS**);
- Peer-pressure seems to have induced the troops in Dalmatia to follow the examples of Pannonia and Moesia (ibid.).

The speed of Roman military communication also assisted Vespasian at this juncture, and 'in no time a great holocaust of war had been ignited' (Tacitus, *Histories* 2.86 **PS**).

The support of the military was of great advantage to Vespasian, particularly as these were now the few remaining legions in the empire that had not already committed themselves to the conflict. Vespasian was also aided in this regard by Vitellius' lack of care in dealing with the aftermath of his conflict against Otho. He had systemically failed to bring the legions hostile to him back into the fold, and made this worse by replacing units and officers within the Praetorian Guard to favour his own supporters.

Thus Vespasian, with the support of the East behind him, mobilised for war, despatching Mucianus to lead the invasion of Italy.

ROME UNDER VITELLIUS, HIS FAILINGS, AND THE ENDING OF THE CIVIL WAR

The final aspects of the Year of the Four Emperors unravelled rather than collapsed, with the ensuing six months being dominated by dissent, mutiny and uncertainty. Following his arrival in Rome on 17 July 69, our sources paint a particularly unflattering picture of Vitellius (Suetonius, *Vitellius* 10–12 **PS**; Tacitus, *Histories* 2.87) and his reign. Tacitus, whose account is by far the most detailed available, goes to great lengths to compound Vitellius' actions into a litany of disgrace, culminating in his deceptive boasts that flattered the plebs into offering him the title 'Augustus' (*Histories* 2.90 **PS**).

Once again, Rome's urban plebs is depicted in a less-than-positive way by Tacitus, who is frequently infuriated and disappointed by the fickleness of the mob. Yet he himself is hardly free from bias, to some extent caught between the contrasting forces of his own republican sentiments and his own successful career under the Flavians. Perhaps this is particularly the case with Vitellius, whom Tacitus describes as 'ignoran[t] of all law, human and divine' (*Histories* 2.91 **PS**). He also describes how Valens and Caecina effectively carve up power between themselves and their own supporters.

However, his overriding message is of the failure of the new emperor to control the army (*Histories* 2.93–4). This lack of discipline and authority is perhaps Vitellius' greatest fault as described in the sources. Galba's earlier assessment of the man as a glutton was being proved correct:

> Vitellius himself was bent solely upon spending. He constructed larger stables for his charioteers, filled the circus with gladiatorial and wild-beast shows, and embarked upon a spending spree as if his purse were bottomless.
>
> Tacitus, *Histories* 2.94

The emperor's excesses, while doubtless loved by the mob, were mirrored by others in his court: his freedman Asiaticus profited from his position in the same manner Claudius' freedmen had done (see pp. 58–9), garnering the same level of hostility from our senatorial sources. The scale of the spending was lavish and unsustainable: according to Tacitus, Vitellius squandered 900 million sesterces in just a few months (*Histories* 2.95 **PS**).

Vitellius seems to have consciously ignored the threat posed by Vespasian, with only the most futile attempts to curb popular discussion of the Flavian cause. It was not until the invasion of Italy began in early September 69 that Vitellius seems to have decided upon firm action. He despatched Caecina and the army of Germany to deal with the threat. However, this group of soldiers were hampered by having been in Rome for the preceding months, and now lacked discipline and fighting ability thanks to the licence and inactivity they had enjoyed there.

Yet this was not to be the greatest problem facing Vitellius. The once loyal Caecina, along with the commander of the fleet at Ravenna – Lucilius Bassus – betrayed Vitellius and sided with Vespasian's cause (Tacitus, *Histories* 2.100 **PS**). Their motivations are unclear, at least for Caecina, although the hope for personal profit is undoubtedly present. The principate as it evolved gave ample scope for the opportunistic individual to place self ahead of state and Tacitus suggests fear that a rival would supersede them in Vitellius' affections was no small factor (*Histories* 2.101 **PS**).

The plan failed, however, as Caecina's troops refused to follow his lead. They captured him and halted at Cremona, awaiting the arrival of Valens, who had been despatched by Vitellius to take charge of the situation.

The hammer blow now fell through the actions of Marcus Antonius Primus who, independent of the main Flavian force, moved into Italy with the Danube legions stationed in Raetia and Moesia. Again, personal ambition may have been the motivating force, but such evidence once again highlights the significance of the legions and their individual commanders at this stage of Roman history. Antonius' force encountered the Vitellian legions near Cremona, around 24 October, in what is known as the Second Battle of Bedriacum. This was the final brutal battle of 69, resulting in the defeat of the Vitellian legions.

The road to Rome was now in effect clear for the various Flavian forces and the war itself was virtually over. Valens himself had been captured and executed in Narbonese Gaul while trying to kindle support for Vitellius. However, the situation dragged on, thanks in part to the lack of trust between Mucianus and the unknown-quantity that was Antonius. Also, Flavius Sabinus – Vespasian's own brother – was in Rome, still officially part of the Vitellian administration, with Vespasian's younger son, Domitian, living in the city with him.

In this confused and uncertain period, it should not be a surprise that various battles broke out in the city between the Vitellian and Flavian factions. Some of these were bloody and destructive. In one particular encounter the forces clashed around the Temple of Jupiter Optimus Maximus on the Capitol, resulting in the killing of Flavius Sabinus by the Vitellian faction and the destruction of the temple itself (Tacitus, *Histories* 3.71), according to Tacitus 'the most lamentable and appalling disaster in the whole history of the Roman commonwealth' (3.72).

Hyperbole aside, Tacitus' account of this period highlights the fact that brutality and war had riven the city itself, blighting the capital of the Roman world and leaving a stain that had to be removed.

The end came for Vitellius on 20 December, when the troops of Antonius finally entered the city. Despite some resolute actions of the last of the loyal Vitellian praetorian cohorts, the emperor was overtaken and captured. Although Tacitus gives a fuller account of Vitellius' death (*Histories* 3.84–6 **PS**), Suetonius, having detailed Vitellius' cowardice and self-serving attitude in the days and weeks prior to this point – including a moment when he is almost bribed into abdicating (*Vitellius* 15 **PS**) – seems to take inordinate pleasure in narrating his final, gruesome end.

After this, with Sabinus dead, the soldiers hailed the young Domitian as Caesar on behalf of his absent father. Thus after a year (technically a 'long year', as the conflict spanned 68–9) of civil war, during which the fire of rebellion had blazed in nearly all of Rome's provinces, when legions had staked reputation and future on the declaration of their commanders, Rome now held its breath and awaited the arrival of its new princeps in person (Tacitus, *Histories* 4.2–4 **PS**).

TOPIC REVIEW

- Assess the reasons for the failures of the reigns of Galba, Otho, and Vitellius.
- Examine how Vespasian secured support for his attempt on the throne.
- Analyse the strengths and weaknesses of the rival claimants during 68–69.
- Evaluate the problems Rome faced at the end of the civil wars.

Further Reading

Morgan, G. (2007) *69 AD: The Year of the Four Emperors*, Oxford: OUP.
Wellesley, K. (2000), *The Long Year: AD 69* (3rd ed.), London: Routledge.

PRACTICE QUESTIONS

1. Read Josephus *Jewish War* 4.592–600.

How useful is this passage in aiding our understanding of the popular support enjoyed by Vespasian? [12]

3.2 The Nature of the Principate under the Flavians

- The main features of the reigns of each emperor
- The actions of Vespasian on his accession and the reasons for them
- The development of the role of the princeps under his rule
- The political, economic and social factors and events which influenced the development of the principate
- The ways in which Vespasian's successors developed the role and power of the princeps, including the events of their reigns, and their policies and actions
- Their impact on the nature of the principate and the relationship of the princeps to other organs of government and the different classes of citizens
- The actions taken by each Emperor which affected relations with the Senators, equestrians, ordinary people of Rome and the provincials
- Challenges and opposition including the reasons for these and how effectively they were dealt with
- The role of family members and supporters, and their importance in the course of events.

The prescribed sources for this topic are:

- *Chronicle of 354* part 16
- Dio Cassius, *Roman History*, 66.2, 66.10, 66.12–13, 66.16.3–4; 67.1, 67.4.7, 67.6, 67.8–11.4, 67.12–14.4, 67.17
- Josephus, *The Jewish War* 7.63–74
- Juvenal, *Satire* 4.72–135
- Statius, *Silvae* 3.3.85–110
- Suetonius, *Vespasian* 1, 8–19, 25
- Suetonius, *Titus* 7–8
- Suetonius, *Domitian* 4, 7–13, 16–17, 23
- Tacitus, *Histories* Book 4: 3–4, 4.5–6, 10, 38, 52, 68, 80–2, 85–6
- Tacitus, *Agricola* 44.5–45.2

- *As* of Vespasian's sons as senators, AD 70
- Aureus of Vespasian, AD 69/70
- Inscription AD 69/70
- Inscription from Rome.

At Rome, however, the Senate awarded Vespasian all the usual imperial titles. It felt pleased and confident [. . .and] showed a proper respect. By its decree Vespasian received the consulship with his son Titus as a colleague, and Domitian was accorded the praetorship and the powers of a consul.

Tacitus, *Histories* 4.3

Thus begins Tacitus' account of the Flavian dynasty, which lasted twenty-seven years and comprised the rule of Vespasian followed by those of his sons Titus and Domitian. Vespasian's accession represented a decisive change in the style of Roman imperial rule. Even in the brief excerpt above, certain key trends for Vespasian's reign become evident:

- The Senate, having endured Claudius and Nero, the previous two emperors, then having been used as little more than a rubber-stamp to the desires of the army during 69, were filled with hope of stability.
- Vespasian himself seemed willing to work with the Senate in a manner far more similar to Augustus.
- Most importantly, Vespasian and his sons formed a recognised and overt dynasty immediately (Suetonius, *Vespasian* 25 **PS**).

THE ACTIONS OF VESPASIAN ON HIS ACCESSION AND THE REASONS FOR THEM

The earliest actions of Vespasian mostly concern his desire to cement his family as the dynastic rulers of Rome, which was necessary given the relative obscurity of his family (Suetonius, *Vespasian* 1 **PS**). He focused on this throughout his reign in various ways. One of the most common was coinage (see Fig 3.7 **PS**).

PRESCRIBED SOURCE

As of Vespasian's sons as senators (Figure 3.7)

Date: AD 70

Obverse: Laureate head of Vespasian; 'Emperor Vespasian Augustus'

Reverse: Titus and Domitian; 'Caesar son of Augustus, consul; Caesar son of Augustus, praetor'

Significance: The Flavians are presented as a ready-made dynasty, very much suggesting stability

View it here: H28 in LACTOR 20: The Flavians (London: KCL, 2015)

FIGURE 3.7
As of Vespasian's sons.

PRESCRIBED SOURCE

Law on the Power of Vespasian

Date: AD 69

Genre: Senatorial inscription

Significance: A large bronze tablet, displaying the final section of the bill put before the people of Rome granting powers to Vespasian on his accession

Read it here: H20 in LACTOR 20: The Flavians (London: KCL, 2015)

EXPLORE FURTHER

For more on the Law on the Power of Vespasian, see Brunt, P.A. (1977), 'Lex de imperio Vespasiani', *JRS* 67: 95–116; Crawford, M.H. (ed.) (1996), *Roman Statutes* I; London: no.39.

The use of low-value, and therefore very common, coins to spread the message of dynastic rule spoke greatly for the stability and continuity that the Flavians wanted to communicate: the civil war had ended and prosperity was now returning.

It was this, perhaps more than any other factor, that differentiated Vespasian from the other military leaders of 69, and even more so from Nero: Vespasian embarked on his principate with a very clear idea of what he intended to do with the role. It is important to note that Vespasian did little to affect fundamentally the key powers of the emperor established under the Julio-Claudians. This is clearest in the document Law on the Power of Vespasian **PS**.

This document codifies Vespasian's powers as emperor, spelling out in no uncertain terms that Vespasian wished his rule to be both legitimate and authoritative. One particularly telling section specifies that:

> . . . whatever has been performed, accomplished, decreed or commanded by Emperor Caesar Vespasian Augustus before this statute was proposed or by anyone commanded acting by his order, these things are to be lawful and binding just as if they had been performed by command of the people or commoners.

ILS 244 (LACTOR 20, H20)

The retroactive nature of the document was clearly designed to remove any possibility of prosecution or complaint about decisions that had been made during the Civil War. Perhaps Vespasian was learning from the issues that Augustus had faced as a result of his own actions during the triumviral period.

Indeed, Augustus and others of the Julio-Claudians are consistently deployed for purposes of precedent within the document, with phrases such as '. . . just as it was for [X emperor]' dominating the text. The reasoning here is undeniably logical: as a new emperor, with little to no formal claim, legitimacy was a fundamental requirement for Vespasian. Showing that his reign flowed smoothly from the preceding dynasty allowed him to ease the transition, visibly demonstrating that there would be continuity and preservation of the best from before. This is exemplified by Vespasian's extension of the pomerium, consciously copying an action of Claudius (see Inscription MW 51 **PS**).

It should also be noted that both Gaius and Nero are conspicuous by their absence from the text of the document: just as there were examples to be followed, there were also those to be ignored.

Vespasian himself remained in Alexandria after his declaration as emperor, leaving Rome to be administered by Mucianus and Domitian (Tacitus, *Histories* 4.68 **PS**; 4.80–2 **PS**; 4.85–6 **PS**). The former excelled in the acquisition of money, sparing Vespasian 'inevitable unpopularity by diverting it to himself. His constant motto was that cash formed the sinews of government' (Dio, *Roman History* 66.2.5 **PS**).

Thus Vespasian's notable pragmatism is shown, which was a characteristic of much of his reign. At his accession, this was most evident in the need for 'righting the ship of state'. Rome was unarguably in a sorry state in late 69. Perhaps it was not quite as bad as it had been in 31 BC, at Augustus' accession, but Rome was certainly in dire straits following a bloody and wide-ranging civil war, which itself built on the outrages and mismanagement of Nero. Suetonius gives an idea of the scale of the problem: Vespasian

MW 51 – Vespasian extends the pomerium

Date: *c.* AD 76

Location: Rome

Significance: Boundary marker commemorating Vespasian's extension of the pomerium

View it here: H56 in LACTOR 20: The Flavians (London: KCL, 2015)

Aureus of Vespasian (Figure 3.8)

Date: AD 69/70

Obverse: Laureate head of Vespasian; 'Emperor Vespasian Augustus'

Reverse: Vespasian standing, raising Roma from her knees; 'Rome rising up again'

Significance: Vespasian portrays himself as the driving force in re-establishing and restoring Rome

View it here: H25 in LACTOR 20: The Flavians (London: KCL, 2015)

'had declared at his accession that 40,000 million sesterces were needed to put the commonwealth on its feet again' (*Vespasian* 16 **PS**).

Vespasian was clear that Rome required restoration, and this was his prime concern. The legend of his coinage, 'Rome rises again', is designed to suggest the restorative nature of his principate.

Probably one of the key means at Vespasian's disposal for ensuring this 'restoration' was his building programme. This will be treated more fully in Topic 3.4, but one particular project deserves mention now: the restoration of the Temple of Jupiter Optimus Maximus. Vespasian knew very well that the Romans viewed buildings as vessels of memory. Thus when an emperor erected a building in Rome, its construction was proof of his identity as sovereign ruler of the city. This was even more the case when an emperor restored a building of historic significance.

The Julio-Claudian emperors had largely neglected the Capitoline Temple, preferring the Augustan Forum, with its Temple of Mars Ultor, as the centrepiece of their religious activity, even in the context of triumphs. The Flavian decision to rebuild the temple, re-installing it as the pre-eminent religious structure within the city, was symbolic of Vespasian's rhetoric of restoration. The work also aligned him with republican traditionalism and gave a further source of legitimacy to the more autocratic style of government that would characterise the whole Flavian dynasty. The sources give a very clear impression of the priority which this project enjoyed upon Vespasian's arrival in Rome in October 70: both Dio and Suetonius record that he himself disposed of the first load of soil (Dio 66.10 **PS**; Suetonius, *Vespasian* 8 **PS**).

ACTIVITY

Study Suetonius, *Vespasian* 9–19.
Create a catalogue of the various examples of Vespasian's competence as an emperor. Using your knowledge of the Julio-Claudian period, find parallels from the reigns of Augustus, Tiberius, or Claudius for these actions.

FIGURE 3.8
Aureus of Vespasian.

As we shall see in Topic 3.4, Vespasian's other building projects were similarly motivated by a desire to write the Flavians into the physical fabric of the city, while concurrently establishing a legitimacy for the dynasty as a result.

THE FLAVIANS AND ROME (I): THE PRINCEPS AND THE SENATE

In order to appreciate fully the imperial approach of Vespasian and the subsequent actions of Titus and Domitian, it is useful to look at their relationships with the key groups within Rome. By far the most important of these relationships was with the Senate.

It would be fair to say that the Senate had lost much of its influence by 70, and was no longer the guiding organ of Roman government. However, it still played an important role as an administrative force, with the praetors, aediles, and proconsuls fulfilling their duties. The carefully constructed 'republican' facade of Augustus' reign had now been revealed as little more than the shell that it was, through the destructive actions of Nero and the military dominance of the emperors of 69. We must also remember that senators at this time had never known anything other than the principate, and the events of the Julio-Claudian era had revealed that the Senate itself no longer possessed men of the calibre which could see the body return to its republican role, even if that could occur in theory.

In short, the Senate was ineffective, almost criminally so. But, under the guise of restoration, it was still needed, not least as a source of legitimacy – as it had been for Augustus. However, Vespasian's attitude towards the Senate is indicative that he did wish the body to be useful to him, if not influential.

He reformed the senatorial and equestrian orders, now weakened by frequent murders and long-term neglect, reviewing their membership and replacing undesirables with the most eligible Italian and provincial candidates available . . .

Suetonius, *Vespasian* 9

Suetonius' assessment of the situation is characteristically but frustratingly light on facts. It does, however, demonstrate the significance of the Senate to Vespasian, given his 'Augustan' reforms of the body. Vespasian was similarly keen to curry favour with the order, ensuring their involvement in every topic, kept up to date by his sons if not himself (Dio 66.10.5 **PS**).

His promotion, or **adlection**, of men to the Senate also indicates his wish that the body be efficient, although Tacitus (*Histories* 2.82) would seem to suggest that in 69, some initial elevations were made 'in a bid for popularity'. But even Tacitus remarks on the quality of these individuals.

In order to bring about these promotions, Vespasian adopted the censorship in 73–4, again using a republican office and an Augustan precedent. Evidence suggests that those adlected were of increasingly provincial origin, perhaps to make the Senate more reflective of the wider empire, thus moving the role of the emperor further away from simply being the overlord of an aristocratic urban elite.

Vespasian clearly wished to have a positive relationship with the Senate, although it must be noted that he maintained certain of the imperial freedmen to deal with the

adlection the process whereby individuals were included on the senatorial roll, effectively elevating them as members of that body

PRESCRIBED SOURCE

Title: *Silvae*

Author: Publius Papinius Statius

Dates: Early AD 90s

Genre: Poetry (mainly hexameter)

Significance: A court poet under Domitian, Statius tends to give a very positive view of the Flavian period

Prescribed sections: 3.85–110

Read it here: S9a in LACTOR 20: The Flavians (London: KCL, 2015)

> **Stoicism** a school of philosophy founded in the fourth century BC by Zeno of Citium, marked out by a set of uncompromising theses, including that virtue was sufficient for happiness and that nothing except virtue is good

administrative needs of the empire (Statius, *Silvae* 3.3.85–110 **PS**). There were also notable elements of opposition within the body, in particular the so-called **Stoics**, epitomised by one man, Helvidius Priscus.

Suetonius (*Vespasian* 15 **PS**) and Dio (*Roman History* 66.12.1 **PS**) both give the impression that Helvidius Priscus was a constant voice of discontent within the Senate, and it is evident that something of a clique formed behind him. This reflected the split in the Senate, despite Vespasian's best efforts to mollify it, while still extolling the value of the emperor as the functional head of the government. The republicanism preached by Helvidius and those like him, now more nostalgic than practical, perhaps accounts for Tacitus' generous assessment:

> For Helvidius this day above all others marked the beginning of great offence – and great glory.

> Tacitus, *Histories* 4.4

Whatever glory Helvidius may have gained, in whatever circles, was short-lived: his constant refusal to toe the line resulted in his exile *c.* 75. He became a figurehead for the continuance of this new style of philosophically driven opposition to the principate, preaching a form of *libertas* that could not be sustained under the burgeoning autocracy that would come to characterise the Flavian regime:

> When Vespasian summoned [Helvidius] to tell him not to attend the Senate, he replied, 'It is within your rights not to allow me to be a senator, but as long as I am, I must attend.' 'In that case, go in, but keep silent.' 'Don't call on me to give an opinion, and I'll keep silent.' 'But I must ask for opinions.' 'And I must say what I think is right.' 'But if you speak, I shall have you killed.' 'When did I tell you that I am immortal? You do your job and I'll do mine. Yours is to kill, mine is to die fearlessly; yours to banish, mine to leave without regret.'

> Epictetus, *Discourses* 1.2.19–21 (LACTOR 20, P1j)

KEY INDIVIDUAL

Helvidius Priscus
Dates: Politically active *c.* AD 56–75

The son-in-law of Thrasea Paetus (see p. 78) and a politician very much in his mould. A near-constant voice of opposition in the reigns of Nero and Vespasian, he nevertheless served as a tribune in 56 and as praetor in 70. When Thrasea had been forced to commit suicide in 66, Helvidius was forced into exile. He was recalled by Galba in 68 as part of his own restoration programme. Tacitus, *Histories* 4.5–6 **PS** gives the fullest account of his career.

An idea is certainly harder to kill off than a man, and Helvidius' subsequent execution did nothing to halt the Stoic opposition to imperial autocracy (Dio, *Roman History* 66.13 **PS**). This prompted Domitian – when emperor – to persecute the group as a whole in 93 (67.13 **PS**).

Beyond his issues with the Stoics, senatorial opposition to Vespasian is difficult to establish with any real substance. Suetonius alleges that there were frequent plots to murder him (*Vespasian* 25 **PS**), but gives no details. Dio discusses an alleged plot by Caecina Alienus (who had betrayed Vitellius, see p. 170) and T. Clodius Epirus Marcellus (*Roman History* 66.16.3–4 **PS**), but even this is vague enough to remain enigmatic, with even the date of the plot uncertain.

Overall, we should see that Vespasian's issues with the Senate derived from his difficulties in needing that body to be an effective tool through which to enact his decisions, but wishing to limit their overall effectiveness and influence in any decision-making process. This fledgling autocracy, characterised by the personal vigour that Vespasian brought to the role, would be developed by his sons.

Titus achieved relatively little of consequence with regard to the Senate. This should not surprise us given the brevity of his reign, although Dio does pointedly observe that he never had anyone put to death, whether of senatorial or any status (*Roman History* 66.19.1).

Dio further states that maiestas charges were largely non-existent under Titus, with a near-total lack of tolerance for delatores (see also Suetonius, *Titus* 8 **PS**). However, equally, Titus did little to stem Flavian autocracy. Perhaps he could afford such treatment of political informers precisely as a result of the increasing security of the imperial position.

If Vespasian sought to establish a functional autocracy, which Titus continued, it was Domitian who made such a system a living reality. Nowhere is this more evident than in the creation of a formal imperial court, or consilium.

Throughout the first century, the significance of the court had increased, be it the imperial freedmen of Claudius, or the privileged access to Tiberius as controlled by Sejanus. The creation of a key group of imperial advisors might even be seen as the inevitable culmination of the principate system of government. However, the facade of the Republic had endured: although the centrality of the court in government was realised by all, it was not openly proclaimed. Domitian, however, was more blatant:

> His ever-growing autocracy and preference for a monarchical system of government was paralleled by an open admission of what had long been obvious, that real power resided wherever the emperor was, wherever he chose to establish his court, and nowhere else; that was not necessarily on the Palatine. During the course of his reign, it must have seemed to many that not only was the Senate irrelevant, but also that Rome itself was not perpetually the centre of power. Other emperors had left Rome without unduly disturbing the process of government, but none as often as Domitian, none as openly.
>
> B.W. Jones, 'Domitian and the Court'

Domitian seems to have rarely attended meetings of the Senate, even on those occasions when he was in Rome. In this he differed greatly from his father Vespasian, who assiduously attended these meetings until old age left him unable to do so. In place of formal discussions with the entire senatorial body, Domitian established a consilium, in effect a privy council, comprised of men chosen from both the senatorial and equestrian orders.

The formalisation of such a group as this privy council seems to have almost been calculated to offend senatorial sensibilities. However, in this we must acknowledge the hostile tradition to Domitian in the majority of our sources, especially Tacitus. Conversely:

> If our only evidence for the regime of Domitian were the poems written during it, we should see the imperial court as a benign centre of patronage, literary as well as official, and the scene of a civilised existence carried on against a background of elegant houses and suburban estates.

> F. Millar, *The Emperor in the Roman World*

However, it is difficult to explain away all of the aristocracy's 'terrors' (Tacitus, *Histories* 1.2 **PS**) under Domitian, as undoubtedly there were events that can be characterised by no other word than tyrannical.

Undoubtedly some of the damage to Domitian's reputation resulted from his readiness to accept the information provided by delatores. Tacitus viewed them as a class of men invented to destroy the state, who were never adequately controlled (on which see Tacitus, *Agricola* 44–5 **PS** – armed men surrounding a senate where terrified members passed death-sentences desired by the emperor). This gave rise to a wave of new maiestas trials.

On numerous occasions, Dio accuses Domitian of executing senators, in 83 (67.3.3 **PS**), 84 (67.4.5 **PS**), before 89 (67.9.6 **PS**), in 89 (67.11.2–3 **PS**), 91/92 (67.12.1–5 **PS**), 93 (67.13.1–4 **PS**) and 95 (67.14.1–3 **PS**) (see also Suetonius, *Domitian* 10 **PS**). No real deductions as to number can reasonably be drawn from vague allegations of this sort, but Domitian is consistently seen as toying with the Senate (Dio 67.9 **PS**). Similarly,

ACTIVITY

Study Juvenal *Satires* 4.72–135 **PS**, where the satirist creates an account of a supposed meeting of this consilium, dating to *c.* 82.

Analyse the content of the text and establish the atmosphere that Juvenal wishes to create concerning Domitian's court.

ACTIVITY

Study Suetonius, *Domitian* 8–13 **PS**.

- Catalogue the activities of Domitian as detailed here that may account for hostility towards him in our sources.
- Can we establish any pattern to these actions as the reign progresses?

PRESCRIBED SOURCE

Title: *Domitian*

Author: Suetonius

Date: AD 121

Genre: Prose biography

Significance: Character-driven biography covering Domitian's nature and reign; his later biographies such as this are characterised by rather anecdotal stories rather than documentary evidence

Prescribed sections: 1–17, 23

Read it here: *Suetonius: The Twelve Caesars*, trans. R. Graves (London: Penguin 1957)

FIGURE 3.9
Denarius of Domitian.

---

damnatio memoriae the process whereby the names and achievements of individuals deemed to have been hostile or traitorous to the Roman state are formally removed from public monuments

in the Acts of the Arval Brethren for 22 September 87, reference is made to sacrifices made 'on the detection of the crimes of wicked men', without any indication of the 'wicked men' or of their fate.

Thus we should see that that the proto-autocracy of Vespasian gave way to absolute monarchy under Domitian. A further demonstration of this attitude came in 85 when Domitian established and assumed the duties of Perpetual Censor. Earlier emperors, notably Augustus and Vespasian, had made use of the role of the Censor to overhaul the senatorial lists, but Domitian now embodied the role for life. The fact that this role came to be one of the defining features of Domitian's reign, with all its autocratic impact, is further exemplified by his coinage (Fig 3.9).

Fig 3.9 shows one of a series of denarii, first minted in 85, which proudly proclaimed the censorial power of the emperor. We may also note the presence of Minerva on the obverse of the coin (holding thunderbolt, spear and shield) evoking the personal affinity Domitian felt for this goddess (cf. Dio 67.1.2 **PS**), and his adoption of her as a patron goddess.

It is perhaps telling that, after Domitian's creation of the role of Censor Perpetuus in 85, no subsequent emperor formally assumed it, for thenceforth the specific powers of the role seem to have been acknowledged as having been conferred by the initial grant of imperium. Its most significant powers were control over admission to and expulsion from the senatorial and equestrian orders together with a general supervision of conduct and morals, thus evidently marking out the emperor as the ultimate source of authority. Although Suetonius does not mention the title by name, he devotes three chapters (*Domitian* 7–9 **PS**) to the innovations of Domitian in terms of changes censorial, legislative, jurisdictional and pontifical (making little attempt to separate them), and at 8.3 refers to his 'correction of morals'. It is thus not surprising that shortly after creating the title of Censor Perpetuus, in 86 Domitian followed this with a further honorific, that of 'Dominus et Deus' (Dio, *Roman History* 67.4.7 **PS**).

All this autocratic activity under the Flavians made the Senate less capable of active policy and decision-making. Ultimately, however, despite the undoubted grievances that the contemporary Senate would have felt – reflected in the later sources with phrases such as Tacitus' remark in the *Agricola* that 'most have perished . . . and all the most prominent, by the emperor's savagery' (3.2 **PS**) – we have to remember that Domitian was removed not by any senatorial action, as Nero was, but rather by a conspiracy of his courtiers, those closest to him. The Senate itself did nothing more than indulge in damnatio memoriae following the removal of this 'tyrant' (Suetonius, *Domitian* 23 **PS**). Tacitus perceived a similar passivity of the Senate much earlier in the period: in AD 22 he has Tiberius proclaim about the Senate: 'Ah! Men primed for slavery!' (*Annals* 3.65.3).

THE FLAVIANS AND ROME (II): THE PRINCEPS AND THE PLEBS

If Flavian relations with the Senate were complicated by the emperors' increasingly visible autocracy, the relationship with the plebs was certainly more straightforward. We may be guided here by Juvenal's famous statement (*Satire* 10.81) that all the people required were 'bread and circuses'.

The concept of entertaining the masses was nothing new. It had a prime importance as part of republican electioneering, and the Julio-Claudians also used public entertainment, notably Augustus himself, as he commemorated in *Res Gestae* 22. The Flavians, however, went further. One aspect of this, the construction of key buildings, such as the Flavian Amphitheatre, will be treated in a later section, but other aspects will be outlined here.

The significance of the need for 'bread', politically reflected in the state-sponsored grain supply, was evident to Vespasian at the very outset of his reign. At this time he urgently sent ships to alleviate a Rome that, by the time they arrived, had no more than ten days' provisions (Tacitus, *Histories* 4.52 **PS**).

Tacitus succinctly details the fear among the urban populace about the possible disruption to the grain supply (*Histories* 4.38; 4.52 **PS**), and Vespasian almost immediately savoured the opportunity of being seen as the city's provider. Similarly, Suetonius has him remark: 'I must always ensure that the working classes earn enough money to buy themselves food' (*Vespasian* 17 **PS**).

Thus it was obvious that Vespasian wanted to do much for, and *be seen* to do much for, the urban population of Rome. He re-dedicated the very centre of Rome to spaces designed expressly for the use of the people. The dismantling of parts of Nero's Domus Aurea (Golden House) and the reuse of its land for structures such as the Amphitheatre and the Baths of Titus spoke volumes about the Flavian manifesto: returning the very heart of Rome to its people. Doing so created a powerful propaganda message that the dynasty exploited throughout the period. One could convincingly argue that the Flavians adopted a distinctly populist approach towards the city of Rome. This is not unexpected, especially when we consider the reception that Vespasian enjoyed when he returned to Rome in 70, as recorded by Josephus (*Jewish War* 7.63–74 **PS**) including this noteworthy detail:

> The people, exhausted by the miseries of civil war, were even more eager for his coming. For they believed that they could now finally be freed from their sufferings and could again enjoy their former peace and prosperity.
>
> Josephus, *Jewish War* 7.66 (LACTOR 20, H22)

PS

The desire to maintain this popular support may be observed in the Flavian sponsorship of public games and entertainments. An extensive catalogue is impossible here, but Suetonius notes musical performances in the Theatre of Marcellus (*Vespasian* 19 **PS**); sea fights, gladiatorial contests and wild-beast hunts in the Colosseum (*Titus* 7 **PS**; *Domitian* 4 **PS**); and chariot races and a double battle, with both infantry and cavalry in the Circus (*Domitian* 4 **PS**).

Suetonius uses the emperors' attitude towards games as a virtual index of their success in the role, but other sources (e.g. Martial *On the Shows*) similarly highlight the volume and extravagance of the Flavian popular entertainments, reinforcing the link between public entertainment and popular acknowledgement of Flavian supremacy (see also Dio, *Roman History* 67.8 **PS**).

PRESCRIBED SOURCE

Title: *Titus*

Author: Suetonius

Date: 121

Genre: Prose biography

Significance: Character-driven assessment of the brief reign of Titus; his later biographies such as this are characterised by somewhat anecdotal stories rather than documentary evidence

Prescribed sections: 4–11

Read it here: *Suetonius: The Twelve Caesars*, trans. R. Graves (London: Penguin 1957)

Finally, as a further means of maintaining popular support, the Flavian emperors continued the Julio-Claudian practice of largesse. The cash handouts to the urban populace had been a key propaganda aspect of Augustus' reign, one which the Flavians continued to exploit:

> Divus Vespasian . . . gave a handout of 85 denarii . . .
>   Domitian . . . gave three handouts of 75 denarii . . .
>
> *Chronicle of 354*, part 16 (LACTOR 20, K2)

PRESCRIBED SOURCE

Title: *Chronicle of 354*

Author: Unknown

Date: AD 354

Genre: Almanac

Significance: Although a very late source, nevertheless a useful compendium of information on the Flavians; factual in style, the author appears to be well-informed and comprehensive on the Flavian emperors

Prescribed section: 16

Read it here: LACTOR 20: The Flavians (London: KCL, 2015)

THE FLAVIANS AND ROME (III): THE SIGNIFICANCE OF THE EQUITES

You will have seen in your study of the Julio-Claudians that the equestrians were perhaps those most affected by the creation and continuation of the principate. Having been largely of minor political significance during the Republic, this class had relied on business enterprise for financial and social status. Through this they had acquired skill in and knowledge of the economic practices upon which the empire was built and through which it would expand. Therefore it was inevitable that the new principate would seek to employ and exploit the talents of this group as a means of reinforcing their control. Key positions both within Rome and without became the sole preserve of the eques, such as Praetorian Prefect and Governor of Egypt.

The Flavians certainly did not baulk in their promotion of men of character and ability from the Equestrian Order (see p. 176 on adlection). We should remember that it was the equestrian governor of Egypt, Tiberius Julius Alexander, who was the first formally to proclaim Vespasian as emperor, though some overtures to the equites seem little more than publicity stunts:

> Domitian made sure that the theatre officials no longer condoned the
> appropriation by common people of seats reserved for equites . . .
>
> Suetonius, Domitian 8

In truth, given the promotion of equestrians, it is fair to say that there was a certain blurring of the lines between traditional senatorial and equestrian roles; similarly, equites began to replace imperial freedmen as the trusted and competent administrators within the imperial secretariat.

The fact that equites were employed as key figures in the administration, charged with such prime positions as 'prefect of the corn supply', reveals the great significance of the Equestrian Order to the continued success of the principate. Essentially, these men acted as the will of the emperor, ensuring the tight grip necessitated by the autocratic Flavian regime.

This promotion of equites also had the added bonus of apparently reducing the influence and significance of the imperial freedmen. Claudius' freedmen had been one of the key sources of hostility towards him from the Senate, thus the Flavian employment of equites gave the impression that official hierarchies had replaced private servants, whose monopoly of power and access to the emperor had blighted previous reigns. However, the balance here was difficult to strike, for as noted earlier Domitian's consilium included men from both orders. The presence of equites could here be seen as a slight to senatorial dignity.

Note also that speaking about the equites as a collective is problematic because much of our evidence for their role is not about the order as a whole, but rather the careers of individuals, and much of this is derived from a rather incomplete epigraphic record.

The overall picture of the Flavians is that in nearly every avenue of the empire, whether fiscal administration, provincial control or relations with the various classes of

ACTIVITY

Summarise the careers of three significant equites from the Julio-Claudian period. Explain how we may use these individuals to cast light on the system of the principate.

EXPLORE FURTHER

To develop your understanding of the role of the equites, read these LACTOR 20 sources that detail the careers of leading equestrians: S19–24 (pp. 352–3) and U41–51 (pp. 392–5).

The following is also a very useful article giving an overview of the role of equites under the principate:

Brunt, P.A. (1983), 'Princeps and Equites', in *The Journal of Roman Studies*, Vol. 73: 42–75

Rome, they imbued the role of emperor with a greater degree of autocracy – and more than that, overt autocracy – than had previously been demonstrated. The conclusion that one may reach is that the need for playing the political game of maintaining the facade of a republic, which had dominated the approach of the Julio-Claudians – their success and the judgement of posterity being directly linked to the degree to which they conformed to this expectation – was now no longer so significant for the Flavian dynasty. In effect, the need for conformity was driven by the need for the stability that the princeps alone could provide. This may therefore explain why men such as Agricola chose to subordinate their careers to emperors whom they may have personally disliked, but nevertheless acknowledged as being the guarantors of the security of the state.

TOPIC REVIEW

- Evaluate the measures Vespasian took to ensure that his principate began on a solid foundation.
- Assess to what extent his successors maintained Vespasian's programme.
- Examine how the Flavians engaged with particular elements of Roman society.
- Evaluate if the Flavians brought any fundamental changes to the principate.

Further Reading

Carradice, I. and Buttrey, T.V. (eds.) (2007), *Roman Imperial Coinage: From AD 69 to AD 96. 'The Flavians'* v. 2, Pt. 1; London: Spink & Son Ltd; 2nd revised edition.

Jones, B. (1993) *The Emperor Domitian*; Abingdon: Routledge.

Levick, B. (2005) *Vespasian*; Abingdon: Routledge.

Southern P. (2009) *Domitian: Tragic Tyrant*; Abingdon: Routledge.

Zissos, A. (ed.) (2016) *A Companion to the Flavian Age of Imperial Rome*; Oxford: Blackwell.

PRACTICE QUESTIONS

1. How significant were the equites as a class under the reigns of the Flavians?

   You must use and analyse the ancient sources you have studied as well as your own knowledge to support your answer. [36]

3.3 The Personalities of Vespasian, Titus and Domitian

TOPIC OVERVIEW

- The character of each of the emperors displayed through their words, actions and policies in Rome and in the Empire
- Acts as censors, reform of the orders, taxes
- The importance and use of the army in Rome and in the Empire
- Activities in the Empire dealing with the challenges to Roman rule in Britain, Germany, on the Danube border, and in the East.

The prescribed sources for this topic are:

- Dio Cassius, *Roman History*, 66.3.4, 66.9, 66.12, 66.14.3–5, 66.18–20, 66.24, 66.26.1–4; 67.1–4, 67.6, 67.8, 67.10–11.4, 12–17
- *Epitome de Caesaribus* 11.6–8
- Plutarch, *Life of Aemilius Paullus* 25.3–4
- Suetonius, *Vespasian* 12–19, 23–5
- Suetonius, *Titus* 6–11
- Suetonius, *Domitian* 2–7,12–17
- Tacitus, *Histories* Book 1:1; Book 2.1–2; Book 5:1
- Tacitus, *Agricola* 2.1–3.2; 39.1–3; 40; 41.2–3; 42.1; 43.3–4

- Sestertius of AD 72
- Sestertius of AD 95/6 Rome
- Sestertius of AD 85

In Topic 3.2 (p. 173), we saw that Vespasian made a conscious point of presenting not only himself as a restorative emperor, but also himself and his sons as a stabilising dynasty. However, in actuality, the relationships between the key family members were not particularly harmonious, primarily because of their differences in character. The sources that suggest this, however, are very much informed and framed by both contemporary and historical views of the three emperors. Tacitus himself bemoans these issues with reliability:

Truth, too, suffered in more ways than one. To an understandable ignorance of policy, which now lay outside public control, was in due course added a passion for flattery, or else a hatred for autocrats.

Tacitus, *Histories* 1.1

While we may note that even here Tacitus does not overlook the opportunity for lamenting the collapse of republican politics, his main observation highlights the bias in many of our sources. This is especially marked when considering the personalities of the three Flavian emperors: the basic divide is that Vespasian and Titus (those who became gods) are good, whereas Domitian is largely vilified, which is not wholly deserved.

VESPASIAN'S CHARACTER

Some aspects of Vespasian's character are reflected in his actions (as in Topic 3.2), but our sources move beyond cataloguing the events of his reign to address the nature of the man himself (Suetonius, *Vespasian* 12–19 **PS**). From Suetonius in particular we see two key traits that are emphasised above all others: his wit (often vulgar: *Vespasian* 22 **PS**) and his modesty. Suetonius' frequent examples of Vespasian's sense of humour culminate in:

Nothing could stop this flow of humour, even the fear of imminent death . . .
His deathbed joke was 'Dear me! I must be turning into a god.'

Suetonius, *Vespasian* 24

He is also said to have laughed at the notion that his ancestors were connected with Hercules (*Vespasian* 12 **PS**). The contexts of these humorous outbursts are telling, as they relate to family status and the imperial cult, both crucial in maintaining the popularity and power of earlier emperors.

Vespasian's mockery may suggest that he saw family status and deification merely as useful extras, rather than fundamental necessities to rule. Vespasian had risen on the back of military success and popularity and had maintained his power through the considered actions of a competent statesman. He therefore had little need for the reflected glory imparted by distinguished predecessors and hastily acquired divinity.

Dio complements this picture of Vespasian when he describes the habits of the man:

He spent little of his time in the palace, most of it in the area known as the Gardens of Sallust, where he was happy to receive anyone who wished to see him, not only senators but anyone else as well. He enjoyed meeting with his close friends, even before dawn while he was still in bed; others would greet him in the streets. The palace doors were always open throughout the day; there were never any guards on duty there.

Dio Cassius, *Roman History* 66.10.4–5 (LACTOR 20, C10)

Here Vespasian is avuncular, an emperor with the 'common touch', but also supremely confident in his position. Evidence for opposition or threat to Vespasian is scant at best, so what need was there for guards and barred doors?

One trait that the sources do seem to criticise is his greed. Suetonius focuses much on accounts of Vespasian's (aided by Mucianus, until the latter's death in 75) acquisition of funds (e.g. *Vespasian* 16). However, Suetonius' observations reveal more about his own greed for gossip than about Vespasian's true nature. For this rather negative characteristic is immediately qualified by the acknowledgement of Vespasian's prudent spending of public funds and his generosity towards all classes. Since both imperial and public exchequers had been greatly reduced by the Year of the Four Emperors, we should perhaps not think too harshly of Vespasian in increasing public finances.

So what was Vespasian's nature? Money-grabbing military opportunist? Imperial everyman? Lucky last-man-standing? Inevitably the truth lies between these extremes, with the sources extolling virtues as much as condemning shortcomings, as shown by the example of what he was reported to say about his succession:

> Despite frequent plots to murder him, he dared to tell the Senate that either his sons would succeed him or no one would.
>
> Suetonius, *Vespasian* 25

> Vespasian was greatly distressed [at Helvidius' arrest] and left the senate-house in tears. His only comment was that, 'my son is going to be my successor; no one else.'
>
> Dio Cassius, *Roman History* 66.12.1 (LACTOR 20, C12)

Suetonius is hardly positive, shaping the remark as a pointed reminder to any potential opposition that Vespasian's sons would carry on his work (and most probably avenge him?). It is a veiled threat at the very least. For Dio, however, Vespasian's tone is not easily understood, but perhaps it is to be understood that he feared for the longevity of the imperial stability he had brought, believing Titus the only figure available who could maintain the system. In any case, the two authors interpret the moment very differently, and we must always be prepared to question their judgements and interpretations.

TITUS' CHARACTER

Thus far, we have not focused greatly upon Titus, which may be inevitable given the brevity of his reign – two years, two months and twenty days (Suetonius, *Titus* 11 ; Dio 66.26.4). However, Titus is a very interesting figure, especially from the perspective that he seems to undergo a form of redemption during his reign, as the character of the man is presented very differently pre- and post-accession (Tacitus, *Histories* 2.2). Dio, on the general character of Titus' reign (*Roman History* 66.18–19) suggests he would not have been loved had he ruled for longer. And Suetonius acknowledges that '. . . both as a private citizen and later as his father's colleague, Titus had been not only unpopular but venomously loathed' (*Titus* 1).

The observation that Titus was very much Vespasian's 'colleague' is noteworthy: the two acted as censors in 73–4 and were consul together seven times; Titus also enjoyed tribunicia potestas (Suetonius, *Titus* 6). Thus from the outset, Titus was clearly

FIGURE 3.10
Sestertius of Titus.

promoted as the emperor-in-waiting, the designated successor. This may be observed in the coinage of Vespasian, which featured Titus prominently (Fig 3.10).

Titus also served as the Praetorian Prefect, a notable replacement for this predominantly equestrian position. In this role, he was apparently violent and high-handed (Suetonius, *Titus* 6 PS).

Part of this mistrust of Titus almost certainly derived from the fact that he had been raised at the court of Claudius with Britannicus (Claudius' son by Messalina) and also was part of Nero's coterie of youths. In short, by the time Titus became emperor, although having been a noted military commander (Tacitus, *Histories* 5.1 PS) he had acquired a bad reputation for being cruel, extravagant, lustful and accepting bribes (Suetonius, *Titus* 7 PS).

We therefore need to account for how this man could morph into an emperor who was renowned for clemency, generosity and respectability.

Inevitably, as Dio remarks, the fact that Titus' reign did not extend beyond a 'honeymoon-period' is crucial – even Gaius was perceived as doing well for the first six months of his reign. However, we may also attribute Titus' popularity to his handling of two of the greatest disasters to face any emperor: the eruption of Vesuvius on 24–5 August 79, and the fire in Rome of 80 (Dio, *Roman History* 66.24 PS).

Character is bred in adversity, and nowhere is this more visible than in the manner in which leaders respond to crises. Titus' response to the disasters that faced him was very positively received. He 'showed far more than an emperor's concern', not only issuing edicts, but also using his personal wealth and property to refurbish the damaged public buildings. Suetonius suggests he acted as if from 'the deep love of a father for his children' (*Titus* 8 PS).

The interpretation of these actions, if accurate, indicates the manner by which an emperor may be redeemed by his behaviour – and how far imperial personae may be created and moulded by our authors to suit their own purposes. A contrasting example is found in the account of the fire of Rome in 64. Nero is portrayed as the arrogant arsonist, Titus becomes the beneficent saviour; the latter deified, the former damned.

However, this leads to a further point that must be made when we examine the character of Titus. We need to question the extent to which Titus is elevated in order to allow for the utter denigration and condemnation of his brother and successor, Domitian. Domitian is explicitly likened to Gaius (*Epitome de Caesaribus* 11.6–8 PS) and Nero (Eutropius, *Brief History* 23), two emperors who were deliberately omitted from the Law on the Power of Vespasian (*Lex de imperio Vespasiani*), and has traditionally been reported as the 'black sheep' of the Flavian family. Therefore, we should be aware of the possibility that Vespasian's and, especially, Titus' faults may have been underplayed by the sources in order to blacken the memory of Domitian further (see also Suetonius, *Titus* 9 PS; *Domitian* 2–3 PS).

DOMITIAN'S CHARACTER

We have received a very negative portrayal of Domitian from the vast majority of our sources and the damnatio memoriae promulgated by the Senate following his assassination did nothing to help the matter (on the assassination and other conspiracies, see Dio,

Roman History 67.12–17 ; Suetonius, *Domitian* 15–17). The notable exceptions to this character assassination are the 'court poets' Martial and Statius, who exemplify the excessive flattery highlighted by Tacitus.

But we also have to be aware of the dangers of writing with hindsight. One may consider the famous anecdote about Domitian in 70, when he was a Flavian figurehead in Rome awaiting his father. Domitian is portrayed as on edge (Dio, *Roman History*, 66.3.4), concerned about Vespasian's impending arrival. Both Dio (66.9) and Suetonius (*Domitian* 3) include the detail that he enjoyed stabbing flies with his writing stylus. Dio continues:

> This is hardly appropriate material for a serious historical record, but I feel compelled to mention it, both because it is typical behaviour and therefore a useful indication of his character, and above all because he continued to do this sort of thing after he became emperor.

Dio Cassius, Roman History 66.9.4 (LACTOR 20, C9)

Thus with one gruesome story Domitian may be summed up – or rather, our sources' attitude to Domitian may be summed up. It shows that they saw such incidents in the light of his later reputation. However, many of our major sources have specific personal reasons for condemning Domitian, which must always be considered.

Yet, despite understanding the limitations of our sources, we cannot ignore the fact that Domitian did fundamentally accelerate the autocracy of the emperor. An example of this is his construction of the Equus Maximus.

This giant equestrian statue, situated in the Forum, and associated with the Temple of the Flavians (see Topic 3.4), marked a very different way of presenting the emperor. The best precedent for it would have been Nero's Colossus (see p. 69). The fact that the statue did not survive the damnatio memoriae of Domitian shows not only its prominence, but also his unpopularity.

A further aspect of his character which the sources take great pains to detail is the conflict which he created with both his father and brother, persecuting also their friends

Study question

Using your knowledge of the authors, account for why Tacitus, Dio Cassius and Pliny the Younger would be likely to convey a negative attitude towards Domitian.

PRESCRIBED SOURCE

Sestertius of Domitian (Figure 3.11)

Date: AD 95/96

Obverse: Laureate bust of Domitian, draped and cuirassed; 'Emperor Caesar Domitian Augustus Germanicus, consul 17 times, censor for life, father of the fatherland'

Reverse: Equestrian statue of Domitian; 'By decree of the Senate'

Significance: Commemoration of Domitian as a powerful military leader

View it here: K35 in LACTOR 20: The Flavians (London: KCL, 2015)

FIGURE 3.11
Sestertius of
Domitian 95/96.

(Dio 67.2). We have already seen him apprehensive at the approach of Vespasian to Rome, but both Dio and Suetonius make his hostility toward Vespasian and Titus, in particular, one of the strongest cases against him.

Such a description fits with Dio's overall presentation of the younger Domitian – some twelve years Titus' junior – as the 'forgotten man' of the dynasty, effectively sidelined while Titus was elevated to being his father's colleague, with resentment eating away at him. Yet, although relations within the family may have been complicated, Vespasian's or Titus' active exclusion of Domitian would seem inconsistent with the decidedly dynastic presentation of the Flavians.

Moreover, Domitian did hold the consulship six times (in 71, 73, 75, 76, 77 and 79), replacing either his father or brother and usually taking office around 13 January, thus being **suffect consul** (Suetonius, *Domitian* 2 **PS**). His other honours included the titles Caesar and princeps Iuventutis, along with various priesthoods. But although he was given titles and positions, he had very little real political power. This is perhaps not surprising, given that, as the second son of an elderly emperor (Vespasian was sixty on his accession), he was probably not expected to reign in his own right.

However, the sources do seem to present Domitian as the discordant note within the harmony of the dynasty, taking part in conspiracies (Suetonius, *Titus* 10 **PS**) and feigning love for Titus on his death when 'in fact he could not have cared less for him' (Dio, *Roman History* 67.2.6 **PS**).

Domitian is here tarred with examples of the worst-known offences: the threat of civil war is raised again; he displays a false religious enthusiasm for his predecessor, as Nero did with Claudius; and he is guilty of a hypocrisy to rival that of Tiberius.

Regardless of speculation regarding the relationship between the two brothers, it is clear that Domitian seems to have displayed minimal concern for Titus during his illness of September 81. As the emperor lay dying on 13 September, Domitian made for the Praetorians' camp, promised them a donative and was hailed as emperor (Dio 66.26.3 **PS**).

During his own reign, what becomes apparent is just how similar Domitian was in his focus and energy to Augustus, following the paradigm of the first princeps in almost all aspects of concern: in money, morals, religion, building and entertainment, Domitian was a second Augustus, establishing a firm imperial control over these fundamental areas. The difference between the two is evident in terms of the historical judgement on the two men. However, we should not forget how Tacitus reveals negative attitudes towards Augustus, too (*Annals* 1.9.1–10.7).

It is difficult to move away from the overwhelmingly negative portrayal of Domitian that is transmitted through the majority of the sources. It is perhaps better to judge him on the basis not of what was said about him, but rather of what he did.

> **suffect consul**
> replacement consuls who served the second half of the year, but did not give his name to the year (established by Augustus as a way to increase the number of magistracies)

TAXATION AND FINANCES UNDER THE FLAVIANS

The old adage that 'money makes the world go round' is well-founded, and the financial state of Rome has already been seen to be of prime importance under the reigns of Tiberius, Gaius and Nero in particular. The Flavian dynasty as a whole seems to have acknowledged this fact and placed a great degree of focus on the administration of Rome's finances.

We have already seen that the importance assigned to financial matters earned Vespasian the reputation for greed (Dio, *Roman History* 66.14.3–5 **PS**). However, equally it is demonstrable that this allowed the Flavians to enjoy financial stability for much of the period. The introduction of new taxes within the period is often discussed by the sources:

> Titus complained of the tax which Vespasian had imposed on urinals. Vespasian handed him a coin which had been part of the first day's proceeds: 'Does it smell bad, my son?' he asked. 'No, father.' 'That's odd: it comes straight from the urinal!'
>
> Suetonius, *Vespasian* 23

PS

The benefits of this staunch fiscal policy are readily apparent from the extensive Flavian building programmes (see Topic 3.4), the ability to offer donatives to the troops, and the accumulation of reserves required to respond to the calamities of 79–80. Vespasian also appears to have abandoned the Neronian standard of coinage and hugely reduced the levels of precious metals in coins. This is further evidence for the financial issues that he inherited.

Domitian too was expressly concerned with all matters financial and here the sources present a situation with two distinct and separate sides. Suetonius states categorically that a lack of funds made Domitian greedy (*Domitian* 3.2 **PS**), but then spends several chapters (4, 5, 7 **PS**) detailing the generosity of the emperor in terms of extravagant entertainments, public games (Saecular, Capitoline and Quinquatria), *congiaria*, the restoration of old and construction of new buildings, and even raising the pay of the legionaries from 900 to 1,200 sesterces per year.

But, at *Domitian* 12 **PS**, the tone changes. The positive 'achievements' above seemingly exhausted the treasury and, as a result, property began to be confiscated on any pretext. Domitian resorted to every kind of robbery, including the vigorous exaction of the **fiscus Iudaicus**.

The change seems to have occurred *c.* 85, and is associated with Domitian's devaluation of the coinage. At the outset of his reign, he had restored the precious-metal content to the very high levels established by Augustus, but in 85 reduced this to the Neronian level and maintained that level until the end of his reign (although this was still higher than under Vespasian). It should also be noted that accompanying this reform is a marked increase in the uniformity of the imperial coinage being produced by all the mints, again revealing the degree of detail in Domitian's control.

> **fiscus Iudaicus** tax imposed on those living as Jews but not acknowledging the fact publicly (including converts) and upon those concealing their Jewish birth

So what prompted the changes of 85? Imperial income must have proved inadequate to meet the increasing expenses caused by the army pay rise, the German and British wars (see below), and the various programmes of building work that were still continuing.

Unsurprisingly this new need to acquire funds gave rise to the confiscation of lands and estates (Suetonius, *Domitian* 12 **PS**), as Nero had done, which logically inspired extreme condemnation of Domitian in the sources.

One further economic example from Domitian's reign should also be highlighted here: the much-discussed 'Vine Edict'. Suetonius reports that when a glut of wine coincided with a shortage of corn, Domitian believed that grain farming was being neglected in favour of wine-production. He forbade the planting of vines in Italy and simultaneously set aside the same acreage of land in the provinces for wine-production (*Domitian* 7 **PS**).

The Edict, dating to *c.* 90–1, is yet further evidence for the increasing autocracy of the emperor. Domitian was lampooned as a vine-eating goat (*Domitian* 14.2 **PS**), but this does nothing to reduce its logic, especially given Italy's growing dependence on grain shipments from the Black Sea and Egypt. Similarly, the local elite's mismanagement of crop production in the provinces often resulted in shortages and famine. Thus once again we may see how the hostile source tradition affects our impression of Domitian, even where his policy may indeed have been sound.

CHALLENGES TO ROMAN AUTHORITY: THE PROBLEMS IN THE EAST, BRITAIN, GERMANY AND THE DANUBE

The East – Judaea

The major campaign of Vespasian and Titus was the final suppression of the revolts in Judea (begun in 66 but ended in 70 with the capture of Jerusalem), a province which had long caused problems for Rome. The propaganda and political significance of this campaign will be treated under Topic 3.4, but the logistics of this and the other major Flavian expeditions are discussed here.

The Jewish population had long presented a challenge to the Romans in terms of governance and control – we may consider Philo's *Embassy to Gaius* (AD 39–40) on the Alexandrian Jews – but the province of Judea itself had, for decades, been problematic. Inevitably, Josephus constitutes our fullest account of the situation, but we must once again temper his observations with his pro-Flavian stance. On the other hand, the Jews' combination of political and religious fanaticism, especially when embodied in a militant nationalist movement, did make the province uniquely difficult to handle. Josephus reveals that the Jews initiated trouble on occasion and indeed, in *Jewish Antiquities* 18.1–10, he traces sixty years of problems in the province back to the census of AD 6, which was conducted when Judaea was first treated as a Roman province.

Nationalist movements need something to oppose, and tension between the nationals and the Roman administration built up to a breaking-point. The nationalists saw foreign domination as an unqualified evil, to be resisted, and, unlike the majority of provincials elsewhere, could not recognise the benefits of Roman rule, not even on the material level of aqueducts, for example.

The early 50s AD marked the start of irreversible decline into anarchy. In 66, the province rebelled against Rome, causing Vespasian to be sent there to suppress the situation. Inevitably, once he became princeps, he could not complete the task, leaving it to Titus to bring the 'rebellious' population in line. Dio reinforces the fact that Titus had at first attempted diplomacy to resolve the situation, 'but when this proved unsuccessful, he reverted to military action' (*Roman History*, 66.4.1).

The culmination of the conflict from the Flavian perspective was the destruction of the great Temple in Jerusalem in 70. This moment is presented in a rather contradictory manner by the sources, and not even Josephus is consistent on who was responsible for the destruction. In the *Jewish War* (6.251) he claims that the Temple Guards themselves

EXPLORE FURTHER

Examine the background to the Jewish Revolt by studying the brief account in Tacitus, *Histories* 5.2–13, which details the matter from a decidedly Roman perspective.

were responsible for the conflagration; yet at *Jewish Antiquities* (2.250), notably written in 93/94, he claims that it was Titus who started the fire. This detail once again highlights the issue of Josephus' pro-Flavian stance, at least while writing under Vespasian.

There was potential to demonstrate clemency here for the Roman invaders, but the destruction of the Temple had a symbolic significance. Its destruction, the capture of its wealth and treasures – which were paraded in triumph by Titus (see p. 208) – and the corresponding slaughter of 60,000 Jews in the process (Tacitus, *Histories* 5.13) marked the successful restoration of Roman 'order' to the province. Then insult followed upon injury, with Vespasian redirecting a Jewish Temple Tax of two drachmas every year to his own coffers to fund the rebuilding and upkeep of the Capitoline Temple. Not only is this further evidence for the financial acumen of Vespasian, but it also symbolically represented Roman dominance over the defeated population of Judaea.

Britain

If the campaign in Judaea exemplified the prowess of the Flavians as military commanders themselves, generating auctoritas for Titus, the emperor-in-waiting, the one in Britain provides evidence not only for the capability of individual Roman commanders, but also of the regime's intolerance to auctoritas beyond the immediate imperial family. Once again, there are striking Julio-Claudian precedents for the desire to maintain military glory as the express preserve of the emperors and their kin (see p. 10).

The campaign to subjugate Britain at last is intimately associated with one man, Gnaeus Julius Agricola who, having served in Britain as both military tribune and legionary legate, was appointed governor of the province in 78, where he served until 84. Insurgency on the island was nothing new, with the various tribes and groups within the population alternating between apathy and upset with regularity: as Dio puts it: '. . . war broke out once more in Britain' (*Roman History*, 66.20.1 **PS**). Agricola conducted a thorough campaign, extending Roman power as far as the Moray Firth, with a decisive final victory over the Caledonians at the Battle of Mons Graupius.

The campaign was successful, but Tacitus states that 'Britain was left to fend for itself no sooner than its conquest had been completed' (*Histories* 2.1 **PS**). Almost immediately the successes of Agricola were to be devalued by the actions of Domitian. Tacitus hints at this in the *Agricola* itself, where he notes the fate of similar eulogies of men who were out of favour:

> We have read that it was a capital offence when Thrasea Paetus was praised
> by Arulenus Rusticus, and Priscus Helvidius by Herrenius Senecio, that not
> only the authors themselves but their books were savaged.
>
> Tacitus, *Agricola* 2.1 (LACTOR 20, P11a)

Here Tacitus puts Agricola on a level with Paetus and Priscus, the two symbolic voices of opposition to 'tyranny' in the Flavian Senate, perhaps by exemplifying Roman values and virtues which were absent from the princeps himself (for more on this see Tacitus, *Agricola* 2.3–3.2 **PS**). Thus, by extension, he also implies that his own biography of Agricola serves to illuminate the corruption of Domitian's reign.

Domitian's subsequent treatment of Agricola, whom he recalled in 84 (*Agricola* 39–40 **PS**) almost immediately after Mons Graupius, in fear that he was becoming too famous,

> **EXPLORE FURTHER**
>
> Examine the history of Roman Britain and the campaign of Agricola in great detail in Tacitus' *Agricola*, a biography of the man himself. Does the fact that Agricola was Tacitus' father-in-law, make the text more or less reliable, and why?

PRESCRIBED SOURCE

Title: *Agricola*

Author: Tacitus

Date: AD 98

Genre: Prose biography

Significance: Biography of a leading general of the Flavian period, reflecting the contemporary political situation, but biased thanks to Tacitus being Agricola's son-in-law

Prescribed sections: 2.1–2; 2.3–3.2; 39.1–3; 40; 41.2–3; 42.1; 43.3–4; 44.5–45.2

Read it here: LACTOR 20: The Flavians (London: KCL, 2015)

is one of the most interesting aspects of the British campaign and its aftermath. Tacitus is very clear that Domitian removed Agricola from his command in Britain for little reason other than jealousy over military glory. However, the reality may have been rather different. Agricola had, after all, served for an unprecedented six years in the province. And subsequent revolts in other areas of the empire could have required his skills as general, as Tacitus suggests that 'popular opinion demanded' (*Agricola*, 41.3 **PS**).

However, no subsequent command appeared for Agricola, despite the need for a competent commander (*Agricola* 41.2–3 **PS**), with suggestions of much political intrigue by Tacitus to account for this (*Agricola* 42.1 **PS**). Agricola himself died on 23 August 93 in ambiguous circumstances. Tacitus records rumours of poisoning (*Agricola*, 43.1), although Dio (*Roman History*, 66.20.3 **PS**) states that he was ultimately murdered by Domitian. The latter seems unlikely, however, especially as Tacitus does not mention it.

In his will, Agricola left part of his estate to Domitian. This may seem surprising to modern readers, but it was motivated by fear of reprisal from Domitian rather than loyalty. However, the nuance of Agricola's action was lost on Domitian. Ironically, for the conqueror of Britain, in his action Agricola was mirroring the intentions of the British chieftain Prasutagas, husband of Boudicca, when he left part of his estates to Nero in 60, but which failed to preserve the health and safety of his family.

Thus the campaign in Britain highlights not only the efficiency and ability of the Roman army when under the command of capable officers, but also the fact that Domitian, according to the majority of the sources, could brook no challenge to his authority, especially from a military man. Perhaps this is a result of the socio-political legacy of the Year of the Four Emperors, which reinforced the necessity of the emperor enjoying military *auctoritas*.

Germany – the campaign against the Chatti

Domitian's desire for military glory, perhaps to rival Titus' in Judaea, is best exemplified by the campaign he executed against the Chatti. This was a German tribe that had long been a low-level nuisance to Roman control of the region. Suetonius describes this endeavour as being 'quite unjustified by military necessity' (*Domitian*, 6 **PS**). Dio (*Roman History*, 67.1–4 **PS**) claims that Domitian returned 'without even having set eyes on any warfare'.

However, both sources are problematic, rather than useful accounts of the campaign. Book 67 of Dio exists only in the abridgements and epitomes of Xiphilinus and Zonaras, and likewise, Suetonius is continually under-interested in military matters. It is therefore complicated to reconstruct the campaign in any detail, given the limited and hostile records that survive.

What is clear is the significance which Domitian himself ascribed to the success of this campaign, not only taking the title 'Germanicus' in 83, but also emblazoning his coinage with legends that commemorated his capture of Germany (Fig 3.12).

The fact that this 'victory' roughly coincided with Agricola's at Mons Graupius allowed Tacitus to contrast the two, inevitably judging Agricola's the more significant and worthy, and describing Domitian's success as a 'false triumph' (*Agricola* 39.1–3 **PS**).

Thus, according to the source tradition, if Domitian had hoped that this campaign would bring him military glory, he seems to have fallen short of the mark. This outcome is

PRESCRIBED SOURCE

Sestertius of Domitian (Figure 3.12)

Date: AD 85

Obverse: Laureate bust of Domitian, draped and cuirassed; 'Emperor Caesar Domitian Augustus Germanicus, consul 11 times, censorial power, father of the fatherland'

Reverse: Trophy; to right, German captive standing, hands bound; to left, Germania seated; weapons around the figures; 'Germany captured'

Significance: Domitian issues coinage to celebrate his conquests in Germania

View it here: N25 in LACTOR 20: The Flavians, (London: KCL, 2015)

FIGURE 3.12
Sestertius of
Domitian 85.

unsurprising, given the limited threat that the Chatti posed to overall Roman control of the region. Even the rebellion of Lucius Antonius Saturninus (Dio, *Roman History* 67.11.1–4 **PS**; Plutarch, *Life of Aemilius Paullus* 25.3–4 **PS**), the governor of Upper Germany, who declared himself Emperor at Moguntiacum (probably on 1 January 89), was of little actual threat. The rebel's German allies were unable to cross the Rhine because of a sudden thaw, a phenomenon which Suetonius calls 'an amazing stroke of luck' (*Domitian* 6 **PS**), but the troops of Lower Germany, under the loyal Lucius Maximus, soon removed the threat. Far more significant than either of these was the threat posed by the Dacians under Decebalus.

The Danube

Finally we must examine the conflict against the Dacians, a tribe inhabiting a region that coincides roughly with modern Romania. Dio describes this as 'the greatest war which the Romans waged in this period' (*Roman History*, 67.6.1 **PS**; see also 67.10 **PS**). Under the command of Decebalus, 'a brilliant military strategist' (ibid.), the Dacians fought a campaign against Rome between 85 and 89.

Domitian seems to have played little personal role in this campaign, a fact which Dio ascribes to his being 'physically soft and at heart a coward' (*Roman History*, 67.6.3 **PS**). However, here we must once again acknowledge the hostility in Dio's account, to say nothing of the problems with the text's survival.

Thus, once again, the narrative of the conflict is difficult to reconstruct. This is compounded by the fact that most sources are far later than the events themselves. However, it appears that the Dacians invaded Moesia, perhaps fearing oppression by Domitian (not without foundation given what had happened to the Chatti), but nevertheless breaking a pre-existing peace with Rome. The Dacians enjoyed considerable success, killing the governor of Moesia, Oppius Sabinus, and subsequently defeating the legionary forces despatched by Domitian under the command of Cornelius Fuscus, the Praetorian Prefect. In 86, despite having pushed the Dacians back over the Danube, Fuscus was ambushed and killed.

After a series of further indecisive engagements (Suetonius, *Domitian* 6 **PS**), a peace treaty was agreed between Rome and the Dacian nation under Decebalus, establishing

PRESCRIBED SOURCE

Title: *Life of Aemilius Paullus*

Author: Plutarch

Date: Late first century AD

Genre: Biography

Significance: In one of his parallel biographies comparing lives, Plutarch comments on the confusion in Rome concerning Saturninus' rebellion, although details may be blurred to ensure similarities are more overt

Read it here: P8d in LACTOR 20: The Flavians (London: KCL, 2015)

the latter as a client kingdom which received a stipend from Rome. This was a rather shameful outcome for Rome, although Suetonius suggests that Domitian awarded himself a double triumph for this campaign alongside that against the Chatti (ibid.), along with the usual accompanying celebrations:

> So many honours were voted for [Domitian] that almost all the world, or at least that part of it which he ruled, was filled with gold and silver images and statues of him.
>
> Dio Cassius, *Roman History* 67.8.1 (LACTOR 20, D8)

The significance of this false 'victory' would not manifest until 101–2 when, perceiving the threat of the Dacians, Trajan launched the first of his campaigns against them. This was followed by the Second Dacian War in 106, which saw Decebalus hunted down and the region converted into the province of Dacia, stabilising the region in a manner which Domitian had failed to achieve.

TOPIC REVIEW

- Assess how similar the three Flavian emperors were in terms of their personality.
- Assess how much an individual emperor's personality affects the way he administers the empire.
- Examine how the lack of 'provincial' sources impinges on our understanding of the circumstances beyond Rome.
- Evaluate how reliable our sources are on the characters of the Flavians.

Further Reading

Carradice, I. and Buttrey, T.V. (eds.) (2007), *Roman Imperial Coinage: From* AD *69 to* AD *96. 'The Flavians'* v. 2, Pt. 1, 2nd edition; London: Spink & Son Ltd.

Jones, B. (1993), *The Emperor Domitian*; Abingdon: Routledge.

Levick, B. (2005), *Vespasian*; Abingdon: Routledge.

Southern, P. (2009), *Domitian: Tragic Tyrant*; Abingdon: Routledge.

Zissos, A. (ed.) (2016), *A Companion to the Flavian Age of Imperial Rome*; Oxford: Blackwell.

PRACTICE QUESTIONS

1. 'The lack of opposition to the Flavians is suggestive that their rulership of Rome was positive and successful.' To what extent do you agree with this statement?

   You must use and analyse the ancient sources you have studied as well as your own knowledge to support your answer. [36]

3.4 Propaganda: Its Role in Creating and Supporting the Dynasty

TOPIC OVERVIEW

- The use of propaganda in the accession of Vespasian
- The importance of presentation of the princeps and the achievements of each member of the dynasty
- The ways in which the princeps is promoted including architecture, art and sculpture, coins, inscriptions and literature
- The events and policies of the Emperors, and how and why these are presented
- The use of building projects in Rome and the Empire
- The use of entertainment such as festivals, games, theatrical events, triumphs.

The prescribed sources for this topic are:

- Suetonius *Vespasian* 5, 7, 9, 12
- Dio Cassius, *Roman History*, 66.8–10, 66.15.1, 66.25.1–26.4
- Josephus, *Jewish War* 7.119–25, 7.148–52, 7.158–62
- Martial, *Epigrams* 8.49
- Orosius, *Histories against the Pagans* 7.3.7
- Plutarch, *Life of Publicola* 15
- Silius Italicus, *Punic Wars,* Book 3.593–629
- Suetonius *Titus* 7, 10
- Suetonius, *Domitian* 3–5
- Tacitus, *Annals* 11.11.1
- Tacitus, *Histories* Book 1.10

- As of AD 88
- Aureus
- Aureus of AD 70
- Aureus of AD 71
- Aureus of Septimius Severus AD 201–210
- Denarius of AD 69
- Dupondius of AD 85
- Inscription AD 71 and AD 81
- Sestertius of AD 71
- Sestertius of AD 72
- Sestertius of AD 81/2
- Sestertius of AD 95/96

Having spent the preceding topics detailing the actions of the Flavian emperors, we can now examine how these individuals chose to present themselves.

THE ACCESSION OF VESPASIAN AND THE BEGINNINGS OF THE DYNASTY

In Topic 3.1, we saw how Vespasian's accession was accompanied by a resounding catalogue of omens or remembrances of events from his youth (Suetonius, *Vespasian* 5 PS; Dio Cassius, *Roman History* 66.1.2–4). While these seem to have been overt tactics to legitimise his rule, Vespasian was himself modest and realistic about his position (Suetonius, *Vespasian* 12 PS). Therefore here we shall look at the official pronouncements that accompanied his accession and contributed to the image of princeps which he wished to proclaim.

Both Dio Cassius and Suetonius treat the omens with little to no scepticism or analysis, which perhaps says much about the credulity of Vespasian's contemporaries, or the problems for those authors writing with hindsight. Tacitus is the only author who suggests that such 'omens' were actively prommoted by the Flavians themselves, in stark contrast to Suetonius' assessment: 'it was only after the rise of the Flavians that we Romans believed in such stories' (*Histories* 1.10 PS).

Tacitus' comments on the credulity of the Romans (*Histories*, 2.1 PS) and even of Vespasian himself, as he started to believe these revelations (*Histories*, 2.78.2), are suggestive that Vespasian did see these 'omens' as a means of legitimising his reign in the eyes of the masses. However, we must acknowledge that the acceptance of these events was by no means universal, nor indeed influential. Dio Cassius informs us that when Vespasian entered Alexandria in 69 the Nile overflowed and that Vespasian 'healed' two men by either standing or spitting upon them (*Roman History*, 66.8–10 PS). However:

> . . . despite these signs of heavenly honour, the people of Alexandria gave him no sign of welcome; rather, they totally detested him, so much so that both privately and in public they poked fun and hurled abuse at him.
>
> Dio Cassius, *Roman History*, 66.8.2 (LACTOR 20, C8)

The reason for this is clear: they had hoped for rewards for being the first openly to declare Vespasian as emperor, and these had not yet been forthcoming. Useful though 'religious' aspects were in terms of propaganda, they were outweighed by practicalities such as tax exemptions and demonstrations of largesse. Curiously (as Tacitus, unlike Dio or Suetonius, typically pays little heed to omens and so on), it is Tacitus (*Histories*, 4.81 PS) who informs us that eye-witnesses to these 'miracles' continued to vouch for them long after the event, 'though there [was] now nothing to be gained by lying'.

One further example of religious propaganda regarding Vespasian's accession comes from the account of Josephus. After his personal surrender to the Flavians in 67, Josephus begged an audience with Vespasian, swearing loyalty to him and 'prophesying' his supremacy:

You, Vespasian, are Caesar and Emperor, you and your son here. Bind me tighter, and keep me for yourself, Caesar, for you are master not only of me but also over the land and sea and all of mankind.

Josephus, *Jewish War* 3.401–2

Despite Vespasian's initial reluctance, the historian stresses (3.403) that after a while, he began to believe in this supremacy. Regardless of the accuracy of such a statement, the fact that Josephus essentially served as the Flavians' in-house historian suggests that the regime at least acknowledged the propaganda value of such pronouncements, perhaps especially with the provincial populations of the east, who had long harboured a greater sympathy for such 'divine mandates' on rulership.

Thus, how may we judge Vespasian and his attitude towards these prophecies and omens of his impending greatness? The sources suggest two possible interpretations: firstly, from Suetonius, that he largely scorned them or downplayed their value:

> Vespasian, still rather bewildered in his new role of emperor, felt a certain lack of authority and of what may be called the divine spark . . .

Suetonius, *Vespasian* 7

But from Tacitus in particular comes the suggestion that Vespasian understood the tendency of the masses to believe such signs, and sought to exploit their belief as a means of shoring up his legitimacy.

IMAGING THE PRINCEPS – THE EMPEROR IN ART, COINS, AND LITERATURE: THE PRESENTATION OF THE PRINCEPS

From the very beginnings of the principate, the representation of the princeps in various media had taken on a symbolic quality, reflecting the key messages of the regime in a manner understandable by all. Augustus established this use of art as a medium for conveying imperial power.

Thus the Flavians came into power in a state where such ruler iconography was already well-entrenched, and could be deployed to extol the values of Flavian rule. Much of the imagery of the Flavians in art is known only through their building projects (see below p. 210), which together with the literary propaganda (see p. 203) may have been more appreciable by the upper classes. By far the most expedient means of mass communication, therefore, was coinage.

Vespasian's coinage in the early years of his reign was designed to communicate two key ideas beyond all else: the dynastic stability and the peace that the Flavians would bring to Rome. The first of these ideas is clearly communicated in Figs 3.13 (PS) and 3.14 (PS) (and also Fig 3.10 (PS) on p. 188).

The first coin, issued in AD 69, before Vespasian's return to Rome, stressed that the Flavians were coming as a collective. The designation of Titus and Domitian as **principes iuventutis**, deliberately using the terminology Augustus had used with his adopted heirs

EXPLORE FURTHER

Study the Prima Porta and Via Labicana statues of Augustus, which presented him as military leader and sacerdotal figure, respectively, and Book VI of the *Aeneid*, which effectively places Augustus as the culmination of Rome's destiny.

To read about this Augustan material in more detail, consult:

Zanker, P. (1990), *The Power of Images in the Age of Augustus*: University of Michigan Press.

Do these images establish an imperial identity that was expected of each incumbent?

FIGURE 3.13
Denarius of
Vespasian.

PS

Gaius and Lucius, was clearly intended to persuade the populace that at least the next succession was already established, and the threat of civil war was far away.

This stability is emphasised in the second coin, issued in 71. Here a number of factors need to be registered: firstly, the wealth of titles and terminologies attached to Vespasian's name. Although seemingly excessive and self-aggrandising, they clearly established Vespasian as not only the centre of governmental authority, but also the legitimate inheritor of Augustus' mantle. The consecutive consulships, while potentially a source of consternation to the Senate, were nevertheless indicative of the security and stability which his rule had brought to Rome. The reverse of the coin, with its simple but effective message 'freedom restored', is reminiscent of Galba's coinage, but here has the added

FIGURE 3.14
Sestertius of
Vespasian.

PS

detail of 'by agreement of the Senate', making it clear that the emperor is working cordially alongside the traditional heart of Roman government to establish freedoms for all to enjoy. The significance of such messages for a Roman world that had recently endured the deprivations of Nero and the vicissitudes of the Year of the Four Emperors should not be underestimated.

This stability also manifested in other forms of event and commemoration, such as Vespasian's extension of the pomerium in 75. This event, again mirroring the actions of Augustus and Claudius (see pp. 18 and 58), is commemorated on a series of inscriptions on boundary markers:

> Emperor Caesar Vespasian Augustus, *pontifex maximus*, holding tribunician power for the 6th time, hailed *imperator* 14 times, father of the fatherland, censor, consul six times, and designated for a 7th, and Titus Caesar Vespasian, son of Augustus, hailed *imperator* 6 times, pontifex, holding tribunician power for the 4th time, censor, consul 4 times, and designated for a 5th. Having extended the boundaries of the Roman people, they extended and delimited the *pomerium*.
>
> MW 51 (LACTOR 20, H56)

Again the raft of titles is notable, as is the clear designation of Titus as both colleague and successor, which may have been designed to alleviate something of the negative reputation that Titus had acquired (Suetonius, *Titus* 7 PS). By literally changing the boundary of the city, an action that could only occur after the conquest of foreign lands and during a period without civil unrest, Vespasian was commemorating his and Titus' victories, reinforcing the security of the city and stamping the Flavian dynasty onto the history of Rome.

The second key message of Vespasian's early coinage is the peace which he brought to the Roman world – unsurprisingly important given that his reign came after a period of civil war. The coin in Fig 3.15 was minted at Lyons, showing the spread of this message across the Roman Empire.

PRESCRIBED SOURCE

Aureus of Vespasian (Figure 3.15)

Date: AD 70

Obverse: Laureate head of Vespasian; 'Emperor Caesar Vespasian Augustus, *pontifex maximus*, tribunician power, father of the fatherland, consul three times'

Reverse: Nemesis holding a caduceus over a snake; 'To the peace of Augustus'

Significance: Commemorates the establishment of peace following the Civil War

View it here: H35 in LACTOR 20: The Flavians (London: KCL, 2015)

FIGURE 3.15
Aureus of
Vespasian, 70

Predictably, peace was also commemorated in ways other than coinage, with Rome itself providing a key venue for such propaganda: the Temple of Janus. This ancient structure was the physical means of communicating the condition of peace throughout the Roman world: the doors of the temple were closed when there was no conflict. Augustus proudly records that the senate decreed the doors be closed three times in his reign (*Res Gestae* 13) and we know that Vespasian sent exactly the same message during his own reign:

> But then the city of Jerusalem was captured and overthrown, as the prophets had foretold, and the Jews were eliminated by Titus, who had been chosen by God's judgement to avenge the blood of the Lord Jesus Christ. He celebrated a triumph with his father Vespasian and closed the gates of Janus.
>
> Orosius, *Histories against the Pagans* 7.3.7 (LACTOR 20, H42)

Despite Orosius' fifth-century date, and his decidedly negative Christian views about the Jews, he had access to the complete version of Tacitus' *Histories* and used him extensively as a source for the Flavian period. The closing of the doors of Janus was a message of supreme propaganda value, again building on the best of Julio-Claudian precedents.

Domitian's coinage marks a notable change in direction for the Flavians, with religious symbolism being far more prominent and propaganda messages being centred rather more upon his divine right (see more on his coinage in Topic 3.5).

If Vespasian's coinage, inscriptions, and proclamations harked back to Augustus and Claudius, then Domitian's coinage reflected a far more autocratic Rome, in this case that of Romulus and Remus (Fig 3.16). The coin's date, 85, is significant: the same year in which he declared himself both *Dominus et Deus* and *Censor Perpetuus*. However, even Domitian did not disregard messages designed to reflect the centrality of the emperor to the business of government and activity in Rome.

On Fig 3.17, the addition of *Germanicus* commemorates the campaign against the Chatti (see above, p. 194), while the reference to his consulships again reinforces the governmental authority that Domitian enjoyed. It is notable that this coin is an example

FIGURE 3.16
Aureus of Domitian.

PRESCRIBED SOURCE

Dupondius of Domitian (Figure 3.17)

Date: AD 85

Obverse: Head of Domitian, radiate; 'Emperor Caesar Domitian Augustus Germanicus, consul 11 times'

Reverse: Annona (Corn-supply) seated with a bag of corn-ears; to right, small figure standing and in the background, stern of ship; 'Imperial corn-supply; by decree of the Senate'

Significance: Reinforces Domitian's care for the corn supply for Rome

View it here: K85 in LACTOR 20: The Flavians (London: KCL, 2015)

---

of a *dupondius*, a lower-value coin worth ½ HS. The corn supply would resonate more with poorer citizens, who were more likely to possess this coin than the aureus (100 HS) or denarius (4 HS).

FIGURE 3.17 Dupondius of Domitian.

Likewise Domitian was still keen to use his coinage to popularise the dynastic nature of his family, even celebrating his wife, **Domitia**, on coinage, such as the sestertius of 81/82 (Fig 3.18 **PS**).

As well as putting similar Flavian messages on other media (for examples from public monuments such as the Arch of Titus, see p. 208), the written word was also used to great propagandistic effect. We have already seen this in the historian Josephus (p. 168), but

PRESCRIBED SOURCE

Sestertius of Domitian (Figure 3.18)

Date: AD 81/82

Obverse: Bust of Domitia, draped, hair massed in front and coiled in chignon on back of head; 'To Domitia Augusta, wife of the Emperor Caesar Domitian Augustus, son of the deified'

Reverse: Domitia seated, extending right hand to child standing left holding sceptre; 'to the mother of Divus Caesar'

Significance: Domitian issues coinage celebrating his wife and child (the child was born in 73, but died *c.* 83)

View it here: J11c in LACTOR 20: The Flavians (London: KCL, 2015)

FIGURE 3.18 Sestertius of Domitian.

one of the most notable pieces of Flavian propaganda comes from epic literature: Silius Italicus' *Punica*.

Within the prescribed section, the various military endeavours of the Flavians are celebrated, essentially ensuring peace by suppressing threats to the security of the empire. Thus Vespasian will:

> Restrain the Rhine, with vigour rule Africa's shore
> In old age vanquish Judah's palms in war.

While Titus:

> A match for the power he wields: still a boy
> He shall fierce tribes in Palestine destroy.

Finally, Domitian is extolled in the highest terms:

> Yet you, Germanicus, shall surpass your race,
> A boy the gold-haired Teutons dread to face.
> . . .
> O'er happy lands, paternal power he'll wield,
> Both son and sire of gods. So, Romulus, yield
> Your throne, when heavens greet him finally.

> Silius Italicus, *Punica* 3.599–600, 603–4, 607–8, 626–7 (LACTOR 20, H62)

The significance of this section, along with its sycophancy towards Domitian in particular, is telling for the use of propaganda among the educated elite. The focus on their military exploits, whether justified or not in the case of Domitian, emphasises that the dynasty was prepared to ensure peace through force. Successful military exploits were also a key means to gratify the public, maintain the discipline of the legions, and acquire the funds for their extensive entertainment and building programmes.

A similar pointer towards literary propaganda is the fact that Pliny the Elder dedicated his *Natural Histories* to Vespasian, and seems to have ended his (now lost) *Histories* at the apposite point of the Jewish Triumph, despite living eight more years.

ENTERTAINING THE MASSES: FESTIVALS, GAMES, AND TRIUMPHS

We have already noted Juvenal's famous statement that the Roman people's love of spectacle and entertainment meant that all they needed was 'bread and circuses'. The context of the satirist's quip is that in accepting these, they had sacrificed their political power. Tacitus is similarly concerned that the principate had stripped power and decision-making away from the Roman people:

> [Augustus] had enticed the soldiery with gifts, the people with food, and everyone with the sweetness of inactivity . . .

> Tacitus, *Annals* 1.2.1

However true this may have been, they could nevertheless pose problems for the emperors (see pp. 22 and 45 on riots under Augustus and Gaius). Thus the Flavians were all too aware of the expediency of keeping Rome's urban population quietly contented, and of the propaganda value of such action. It was expected that games and entertainment should be at the forefront of the Flavian programme to win the hearts and minds of the urban populace. In contrast with Nero's selfish building-work and pleasure-seeking (see p. 64), the new dynasty sought to return Rome to its people.

The Flavian Amphitheatre (see also p. 211) was a key component in this. Begun by Vespasian in 70, it was one of the first and most significant actions of his reign, and took ten years to construct. It is difficult to conceive of the scale of the games that accompanied its dedication (see Suetonius' brief account in *Titus* 8 **PS** and Dio's lengthy catalogue at *Roman History* 66.25.1–26.4 **PS**).

Dio details 100 days' worth of games and spectacles, including the innovations introduced by Titus in terms of 'bonus prizes' which were thrown out to the crowd. Both the scale and the lavishness of these entertainments speak volumes about the Flavians' desire to ingratiate themselves with the people of Rome. The Amphitheatre was the symbolic centrepiece of their programme. The poet Martial even praises the building above the Wonders of the Ancient World (*On the Shows* 1.7–8).

However, the Amphitheatre and its associated games do not stand in isolation. Indeed, it is Domitian who offered the greatest scope of games to the urban population of Rome. This perhaps accounts for why there was limited popular discontent under his reign, although as we have seen, the senatorial source tradition remained hostile to him.

Suetonius (*Domitian* 4 **PS**) spends much time discussing these various entertainments. One of the most notable was the Capitoline Games, which Domitian himself instituted a new version of – a festival of music, horsemanship and athletics to be held every four years (not five, as stated by Suetonius) in honour of Jupiter Capitolinus. These games established Rome as a cultural capital of the world, enticing artists and poets to the city. They were complemented by Domitian's celebrating the Quinquatrus for Minerva (19–22 March) each year in his Alban villa (*Domitian* 4.4 **PS**). This was accompanied by a smaller set of festal games known as the Alban Games, where we know that Statius won the poetry competition in 90 (Statius, *Silvae* 4.2.63–7). While these games may seem rather 'highbrow' for the urban plebs, and the Alban Games may well have been reserved for a more elite clientele given their venue, we should not limit the average Roman citizen's enjoyment of the arts and culture with our own prejudices. However, the Capitoline Games were also decidedly populist, given that Domitian constructed his famed stadium for the event.

The continuing significance of the Stadium as a venue for athletic games well beyond the Flavian period is attested by Dio (*Roman History* 75.16) for the games of 200, as well as by its featuring on the coinage of Septimius Severus (Fig 3.19 **PS**). The scale of the venue, an indication of the significance of the games held there, may be seen from the fact that the current tourist hot-spot of the Piazza Navona occupies the footprint of the Stadium. Such investment speaks volumes about the importance of these games to the Flavians.

However, Domitian wanted a greater scale of games than even these, but he only had one option: the **Saecular Games**. Augustus' revival of these in 17 BC suggests that there was a precedent for using the games more as propaganda than any real religious

EXPLORE FURTHER
Research the Seven Ancient Wonders, including dates of construction and locations.
  What does this information add to our understanding of the significance of Martial's observation about the Colosseum?

Saecular Games revived by Augustus, these had a pseudo-mythological origin and were held once in a lifetime, more precisely every 110 years (although some emperors, including Claudius, held them to coincide with centenaries)

FIGURE 3.19
Sestertius of
Septimus Severus.

PRESCRIBED SOURCE

Sestertius of Septimius Severus (Figure 3.19)

Date: AD 201–10

Obverse: Laureate head of Septimius Severus, bearded; 'Severus Pius Augustus'

Reverse: Building, in shape of circus; double row of arches, with central arch (featuring statue group?) and another entrance on curve. Inside: runners, wrestlers, standing figures, wrestlers, seated figures; 'father of the fatherland, consul 3 times'

Significance: Given that this coin dates to some 110 years after Domitian's death, it illustrates that some of Domitian's developments retained their popularity

View it here: K51 in LACTOR 20: The Flavians (London: KCL, 2015)

observance. Although Claudius held Saecular Games in 47, Domitian held his in 88, reverting to the Augustan calculation. The games were a means of establishing their reigns as the commencement of new eras in Rome's history.

The commemorative coin in Fig 3.20, again a low denomination as ($\frac{1}{4}$ HS), reinforces the populist value of the celebration. The Reverse shows an enthroned Domitian receiving offerings from the people of Rome. While this may be a ceremony from the festival programme, its portrayal here is designed more to show the supremacy of the princeps.

The final element of mass propaganda under the Flavians is that of the triumph. Under the Republic, these formal processional parades were to honour returning victorious

PRESCRIBED SOURCE

Title: *Annals*

Author: Cornelius Tacitus

Date: *c.* AD 117

Genre: Prose history

Significance: Part of our fullest surviving account of the Julio-Claudian period, *Annals* 11.11.1 is very precise in its treatment of the timings of the Saecular Games, not least because of Tacitus' serving as quindecimviral priest and praetor at the time of Domitian's games

Prescribed sections: 3.55; 11.11.1

Read it here: LACTOR 20: The Flavians (London: KCL, 2015: J4j and L17)

PRESCRIBED SOURCE

As of Domitian (Figure 3.20)

Date: AD 88

Obverse: Laureate head of Domitian; 'Emperor Caesar Domitian Augustus Gemanicus, Pontifex Maximus holding tribunician power for the 8th time, censor for life, father of the fatherland'

Reverse: Domitian seated on platform, approached by two citizens with open sacks; in background; four-column temple; (around edge and on platform) 'Consul for the 14th time; (at the) Centennial Games he received crops from the people. By decree of the Senate'

Significance: Domitian issues coinage commemorating his celebration of the Saecular Games

View it here: L20 in LACTOR 20: The Flavians (London: KCL, 2015)

FIGURE 3.20
As of Domitian.

generals, but Augustus had decreed that only members of the imperial family could enjoy the privilege of a triumph. The Flavian dynasty, since it was built upon military power and success, firmly entrenched the triumph as a means to reinforce imperial power, while at the same time glorifying Rome's successes against the barbarian 'other'.

We have already noted that, immediately upon his return to Rome in 70, Vespasian had personally begun the restoration of the Capitoline Temple, the traditional terminus of the triumph. We have also seen that Domitian was at pains to celebrate a triumph himself for his German and Dacian campaigns, although our sources would suggest that such was unmerited. However, perhaps the key example from the period is that of Titus' triumph for his campaign against the Jews, held in 71, which was the first to be held since Claudius' triumph for the conquest of Britain in 43.

The panel from the Arch of Titus in Fig 3.21, itself a monument of significant propaganda value, gives us an idea of the triumph itself: placards denote defeated tribes; treasures taken from the Temple in Jerusalem are prominent (see also Josephus, *Jewish War*, 7.148–52 (PS)). The arch, established in 82 by Domitian, would be a permanent reminder of the Flavians' success, although a temporary arch had been established in the Circus Maximus for the triumphal procession itself.

That the triumphal parade itself was a moment of significant propaganda value was not lost upon Vespasian and his son. Josephus, in his description of its preparations (*Jewish War*, 7.119–25 (PS)) informs us that:

> When notice was given of the day appointed for the victory procession, not a single person out of the immense population was left in the city. Everyone came out so that there was standing room only, leaving only enough space for the procession to advance.

Josephus, *Jewish War* 7.122 (LACTOR 20, E6b)

FIGURE 3.21
Panel from the Arch of Titus.

The Flavians exploited this spirit by deliberately diverting the processional route through the theatres so that they might be more easily seen by the crowds (ibid. 7.131). All three Flavians, Vespasian, Titus and Domitian, conspicuously rode in the triumphal procession, thus again clearly associating the whole family in its glory. The procession's opulence would convince all but the most cynical of Rome's grandeur and majesty.

The commemoration of the event on coinage was inevitable, as a constant reminder of the Flavians being the guarantors of the security of the empire.

The Jewish Triumph succeeded in inspiring popular enthusiasm and respect upon the emerging dynasty. Domitian, although magnificently adorned and riding with his brother in procession, had played no role in the campaign himself. That the reflected glory clearly

FIGURE 3.22
Aureus of
Vespasian, 71.

PRESCRIBED SOURCE

Aureus of Vespasian (Figure 3.22)

Date: AD 71

Obverse: Laureate head of Vespasian; 'Caesar Vespasian Augustus, emperor, tribunician power'

Reverse: Vespasian standing in *quadriga*, holding branch in right hand and sceptre in left hand, crowned by Victory and accompanied by trumpeter, soldier, and captive; 'imperial triumph'

Significance: Commemorates the glory of the Jewish Triumph

View it here: H41 in LACTOR 20: The Flavians (London: KCL, 2015)

PRESCRIBED SOURCE

Sesterius of Domitian (Figure 3.23)

Date: AD 95/96

Obverse: Laureate bust of Domitian, draped and cuirassed; 'Emperor Caesar Domitian Augustus Germanicus, consul 17 times, censor for life, father of the fatherland'

Reverse: Triumphal arch, showing two archways, surmounted by elephant *quadrigae*; 'by decree of the Senate'

Significance: Domitian issues coinage to attempt to cultivate glory from his own military endeavours

View it here: K23 in LACTOR 20: The Flavians (London: KCL, 2015)

FIGURE 3.23
Sestertius of Domitian.

irked him, kindling a flame of rivalry, may explain why he tried to imitate, if not surpass, the Jewish Triumph with his own processions. The nature of Domitian's triumphs is difficult to establish, especially given the hostile record of our senatorial sources: just because to Tacitus they were a sham (*Agricola*, 39.1 **PS**), does not mean that the contemporary plebs were apathetic or hostile towards them.

That Domitian commemorated the victories with arches is certain, as his coins confirm. But equally evident is that, as part of the damnatio memoriae he suffered, his arches were taken down (Dio Cassius, *Roman History* 68.1.1). Tacitus comments pithily that the Germans had been 'more triumphed over than conquered' (*Germania*, 37.5), highlighting Domitian's concern to use triumphal processions as a means of garnering support and respect. Moreover, once again, the poetry of the period seemed to be at odds with the historical tradition: Martial celebrates:

> Rome now eats with you a banquet of gods' food.
> You promised much, yet how much more you've given us!
>
> Martial, *Epigrams* 8.49.8–9 (LACTOR 20, N49)

PS

Martial elevates Domitian's triumph (both actual and processional) to a mythic status, equating it in line 1 with the Olympian victory over the Giants. It is possible that Martial is mocking the 'victory' of Domitian, but the fact that he states that all of Rome is celebrating along with Domitian suggests, despite later hostility, that Domitian's triumphs received, at the time, as much popular acclaim as that of Vespasian and Titus.

We may conclude that the Flavians were particularly astute in their deployment of public entertainment and celebration to garner popular enthusiasm and reinforce their position as the new rulers of the Roman world. However, such celebrations required a fitting venue, a capital city for a world empire, and the Flavians similarly ensured that Rome acquired a physical quality befitting its status.

PRESCRIBED SOURCE

Title: *Epigrams*

Author: Martial

Date: AD 86–103

Genre: Satirical poetry

Significance:
Contemporary poetic celebration of Domitian's triumph; though probably affected by hyperbole, as satire it must to some degree reflect contemporary viewpoint to achieve its comedic effect

Prescribed sections: 8.49

Read it here: LACTOR 20: The Flavians (London: KCL, 2015)

THE USE OF BUILDING PROJECTS IN ROME AND THE EMPIRE

Thus far we have alluded to several Flavian building projects, such as the restoration of the Capitoline Temple and the construction of the Flavian Amphitheatre (Colosseum). Here we examine some of the remaining wonders that the Flavians established.

Vespasian thought that the physical restoration of Rome was crucial, but he also acknowledged the propaganda value of an imperial building programme. Four modes of 'conversation' can be identified through which Vespasian's buildings asserted the emperor's authority:

1. comparison with pre-Julio-Claudian leaders and traditions;
2. comparison with some Julio-Claudian rulers;
3. declaring the ingenuity of Flavian imperial rule with no historical comparisons; and
4. contrast with other Julio-Claudian emperors.

While some aspects of the building programme were more practical than ostentatious, such as Vespasian's and Titus' restorations of the Claudian aqueduct in 71 and 81, respectively (see the inscription **PS**), by far the most significant to the establishment of the dynasty were those that communicated the four ideals above.

The centrepiece of Vespasian's programme was the Temple of Peace (Suetonius, *Vespasian* 9 **PS**). This was in actuality a large forum complex containing public galleries and a great Library, as well as a central temple, and was a further commemoration of the victories in the Jewish War, not only paid for by the spoils of that campaign, but also becoming a public 'display case' for the treasures from the Temple in Jerusalem (Josephus, *Jewish War* 7.161 **PS**). Notably, the complex repurposed land from Nero's Golden House and its public accessibility consciously contrasted with the former structure.

Like the Capitoline Temple, the Temple of Peace was constructed with a sense of urgency indicating its centrality to Vespasian's principate (Dio Cassius, *Roman History* 66.15.1 **PS**). Along with the pace of its construction (see also Josephus, *Jewish War* 7.158–62 **PS**), Dio highlights that its physical centrality in the heart of the city was designed to mirror the political position enjoyed by Vespasian and his sons. Josephus tells us that the structure was 'beyond all human expectations' (*Jewish War*, 7.158 **PS**). The complex was certainly remarkable, with Pliny the Elder also noting that the Temple of Peace was one of 'the loveliest buildings the world has ever seen' (*Natural History*, 36.102). Perhaps most striking was the collection of artworks that were collected therein:

> [Vespasian] had this temple decorated with masterpieces and great statues. For in the temple were collected and deposited all the works which men had previously wandered all over the world to see, longing to see them one after the other.
>
> Josephus, *Jewish War* 7.159–60 (LACTOR 20, K64)

The complex epitomises the four modes of conversation outlined above:

1. equating Vespasian with Augustus (the complex closely parallels the Temple of Mars the Avenger);
2. commemorating the unprecedented conquest of Jerusalem;
3. elevating Rome itself with a grandeur reflecting its status as an imperial capital; and
4. serving to place Vespasian in stark contrast with Nero.

More than any other structure, the Temple of Peace argued that Rome should be viewed as the centre of the known world, with the Flavians at her head.

In addition to the Flavian Amphitheatre, the Temple of Peace was also complemented by structures such as the Baths of Titus, which again converted an aspect of the Golden House to public use. Similarly, Vespasian made a conscious choice to honour Nero's adopted (and despised) father, Claudius. That he saw Claudius as a positive precedent is stated outright in the Law on the Power of Vespasian. To this end, Vespasian rebuilt the Temple of Claudius on the Caelian Hill, which had been started by Nero's mother Agrippina, but had been almost entirely destroyed by Nero (Suetonius, *Vespasian* 9.1 **PS**).

However, the extreme public generosity of Vespasian's programme would not be consistently maintained: Suetonius deliberately notes that Domitian 'allowed no names to be inscribed on [the buildings he constructed or restored] except his own – not even the original builders' (*Domitian* 5.1 **PS**).

It is this aspect of inscribing his own name upon Rome that differentiates Domitian: if Vespasian's and Titus' buildings were dynastic, then Domitian's are, for the most part, selfish. True, he paid his filial obligations by completing by 90 the Temple of Vespasian that Titus had begun, dedicating the temple to both Vespasian and his now-deified brother. However, even here Domitian may merely have wished to associate with his father's deification. Similarly, his restoration of the Capitoline Temple, following a further fire in 80, may have been to maintain the Flavian connection with this structure established by Vespasian. Plutarch offers another perspective:

> . . . someone brought before Domitian might say something like 'you are not pious or keen to be honoured, you just have an addiction to building; and just like the well-known Midas you want all your possessions to be of gold or marble.
>
> Plutarch, *Life of Publicola* 15 (LACTOR 20, K27)

However questionable Plutarch's notion of Domitian's addiction to building is, it is difficult not to see him as a Midas-figure when we consider the sheer opulence and scale of his palace. Here he flirted with controversy, for in palace-building he aligned himself with the least popular of the Julio-Claudians – Tiberius, Gaius and Nero. However, the expansion and alteration of the imperial palace is entirely in keeping with Domitian's autocratic style of rule. What seems to have mattered more to him than the potential negative impressions he would make within Rome itself, was communication of his power – through an abode worthy of his status as leader of a world empire – to the empire as a whole, as well as to allied parties and potential enemies.

FIGURE 3.24
Map of Rome under
the Flavians.

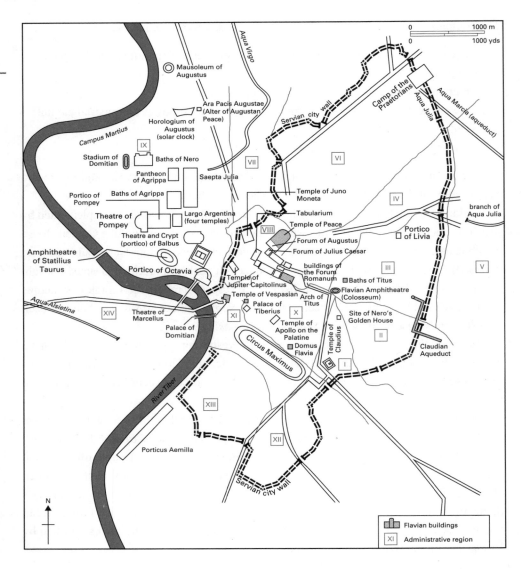

The grandeur of the palace, the Domus Flavia, is hard to understand even from the 3-hectare remains visible today. It is the first Roman structure for which we can identify a specific architect, Rabirius (Martial, *Epigram* 7.56); and the contemporary poets such as Statius (*Silvae* 4.2.18–24) speak using the greatest hyperbole about the building. The variety of building materials, including marbles of various hues, the fact that it included nymphaea, artificial islands, grand reception rooms, vaulted dining areas, sunken gardens and even a miniature circus, is indicative of the power that Domitian sought to communicate.

The palace, dwarfing even the Flavian Amphitheatre, was wholly visible from the Circus Maximus, set beneath it at the base of the Palatine. As the (according to some authorities) 200,000 Romans attended the races, they could not fail to appreciate the supremacy of Domitian. The emperor now possessed and inhabited a building which was expressive of the autocratic governance that would see the principate morph into the dominate.

Further Reading

Carradice, I. and Buttrey, T.V. (eds.) (2007), *Roman Imperial Coinage: From* AD *69 to* AD *96. 'The Flavians'* v. 2, Pt. 1, 2nd edition; London: Spink & Son Ltd.

Jones, B. (1993), *The Emperor Domitian*; Abingdon: Routledge.

Levick, B. (2005), *Vespasian*; Abingdon: Routledge.

Southern, P. (2009), *Domitian: Tragic Tyrant*; Abingdon: Routledge.

Zissos, A. (ed.) (2016), *A Companion to the Flavian Age of Imperial Rome*; Oxford: Wiley-Blackwell.

PRACTICE QUESTIONS

1. To what extent do the building programmes of the three Flavian emperors reflect their personalities?

You must use and analyse the ancient sources you have studied as well as your own knowledge to support your answer.

[36]

3.5 Religion: Its Role in the Principate and Roman Society

TOPIC OVERVIEW

- The status and importance of traditional Roman religious practices and rites in Roman society
- The involvement of the emperors in traditional Roman religion and their reasons for participation
- The impact of the development of religion by the emperors on Roman society
- Development of alternatives to traditional religion including foreign cults
- The role of the emperors in these cults and the reasons for this
- The development and role of the worship of the Imperial family and the Imperial cult in the dynasty
- The attitudes of the emperors toward religion.

The prescribed sources for this topic are:

- *Chronicle of 354*, part 16
- Dio Cassius, *Roman History*, 67.1, 67.4.7, 67.16
- Josephus, *Jewish War* 7.119–25
- Martial, *Epigrams* 9.1
- Suetonius *Vespasian* 7, 9, 19, 23
- Suetonius *Titus* 4–11
- Suetonius, *Domitian* 1, 8, 12, 13, 15, 23
- Tacitus, *Annals* 3.55
- Tacitus, *Histories* 3.74; 4.10, 4.82

- Aureus of AD 82–3
- Aureus of AD 84
- Denarius of AD 71 (Rome)
- Sestertius of AD 71 (Rome)

Ancient religion, as any archaeologist or anthropologist will tell you, is a complex system to investigate. We necessarily lack a shared cultural vocabulary, but also tend to over-simplify the belief systems of ancient cultures, seeing them as enjoying far greater uniformity and cohesion than contemporary systems. With this caveat in place, we shall examine Rome's religious cosmology and practices.

THE STATUS AND IMPORTANCE OF TRADITIONAL ROMAN RELIGIOUS PRACTICES AND RITES IN ROMAN SOCIETY

FIGURE 3.25
Denarius of Vespasian.

Although the term 'traditional' is not unproblematic (see S&C below), the Flavians did make efforts to maintain and promote religious elements that had extensive histories. This may again be seen, for Vespasian at least, as part of his programme of restoration (once more along Augustan lines), for religious practices and institutions tend to be the most conservative elements of a culture and as such may be employed (or exploited) by governments to establish their legitimacy.

The reverse of the denarius shown in Fig 3.25 is decorated with the key ritual instruments of the four traditional priestly colleges. The connection with traditional Roman religion (as well as with Augustan practices) was a significant factor for Vespasian. He needed to confirm his legitimacy, especially given that his associations with the East and Egypt in particular may not have been approved of in all quarters, perhaps even resurrecting memories of Mark Antony. We likewise know that both Titus and Domitian were appointed as priests of all four colleges, suggesting that the dynasty made a conscious effort to acknowledge the significance of traditional cult. This is similarly exemplified by the consistent focus that all three emperors gave to the Capitoline Temple, which became something of a symbol of Flavian traditionalism.

Finally, the fifteenth-century record of an inscription near the Capitol itself (the original stone is sadly lost), reinforces the concern that Vespasian showed for traditional Roman religion: '. . . He preserved the public ceremonies and restored the sacred temples' (MW 151). Again here he deliberately evokes the precedent of Augustus, who famously restored eighty-two temples within Rome (see p. 17). Thus the Flavians, as part of their restoration of Rome, were keen to ensure that they were seen as preservers of religious traditions, enjoying the legitimacy that this perception encouraged.

S&C

The term 'traditional' prompts the question '"traditional" to whom?' Augustus reimagined traditional practices for his own ends, such as when he revised the Sibylline Books (see p. 18), we must bear in mind that 'traditions' are very much contemporary interpretations of historical practices, rather than unwavering repetitions of them.

PRESCRIBED SOURCE

Denarius of Vespasian (Figure 3.25)

Date: AD 71

Obverse: Laureate head of Vespasian; 'Emperor Caesar Vespasian Augustus, Pontifex Maximus'

Reverse: Priestly implements (ladle, sprinkler, jug and augur's staff); 'Augur, Pontifex Maximus'

Significance: Vespasian issues a coin that deliberately echoes one of Augustus' issues to legitimise his position through traditional religious elements

View it here: L1 in LACTOR 20: The Flavians (London: KCL, 2015)

ACTIVITY

Compare Fig 3.25 with the coin of Augustus (LACTOR 17, L1). What similarities are there and what conclusions may we draw from this?

FIGURE 3.26
Sestertius of
Vespasian

ALTERNATIVE RELIGIONS – THE INFLUENCE OF FOREIGN CULTS

Sestertius of Vespasian (Figure 3.26)

Date: AD 71

Obverse: Laureate head of Vespasian, with aegis and globe at point of bust; 'Emperor Caesar Vespasian Augustus, Pontifex Maximus, tribunician power, father of the fatherland, three times consul'

Reverse: Temple of Isis; 'by decree of the Senate'

Significance: Vespasian issues coinage associating him with the cult of Isis

View it here: L24 in LACTOR 20: The Flavians (London: KCL, 2015)

Although the Flavians were keen to preserve Rome's traditions, they were equally conscious that they were the heads of a world empire, not merely the heads of an urban aristocracy. As such, it is telling that during their dynasty foreign cults enjoyed far more respect and tolerance within Rome and her environs than they had under the Julio-Claudians (for their attitudes and actions, see **CW**).

Although the Flavians may have finally succeeded in Gaius' aim of despoiling the Temple of Jerusalem, and continued the long-established ill treatment (or at least suppression) of Jews and Jewish converts in Rome itself, this may be explained by the sheer confusion and mistrust that a monotheistic religion caused among many Romans. A cult that could not co-exist with polytheism was inevitably a source of consternation. The Flavians were far more respectful towards foreign cults that *could* be accommodated by the Roman pantheon.

This phenomenon is observable in Fig 3.26 **PS**, where the association of the emperor with a foreign cult is particularly blatant. The Flavians as a whole seem to have had an association with Isis, with Vespasian and Titus resting at the Temple of Isis before the Jewish Triumph (Josephus, *Jewish War* 7.119–25 **PS**). Likewise Domitian, in 69, had disguised himself as a devotee of Isis in order to escape Vitellius' troops when the Capitoline Temple was set on fire (Suetonius, *Domitian* 1 **PS**).

The cult of Isis had arrived in Rome perhaps as early as 100 BC, receiving greater popular attention during Mark Antony's escapades in Egypt (*c.* 37–31 BC), but had never been officially sponsored or promoted by the state. The cult's popularity grew, peaking in the late first and early second century (Plutarch's *de Iside et Osiride* may have been prompted by imperial enthusiasm for the cult).

The reason the Flavians favoured the cult is difficult to determine: perhaps the Egyptian origins of Vespasian's accession were a prompt for this, but the dynasty's autocratic style of government had a viable model in Egyptian pharaonic kingship. Recent academic work has highlighted the Egyptian stylings of the Flavian dynasty, which in some ways served as a defining characteristic of their rule.

In addition to Isis, the Flavians also displayed a personal connection to the Egyptian deity Serapis. Vespasian visited the Temple of Serapis while in Alexandria (Suetonius, *Vespasian* 7.2 **PS**), as he wished to consult the god on matters of state (Tacitus, *Histories* 4.82 **PS**). There he received a vision from the god that foretold his rule. The story has similarities with Alexander the Great's famous visit to the Oracle of Ammon, but nevertheless suggests that the Flavian connection with foreign cult was one of more personal reverence than political expediency. The only immediate political benefit would have been a symbolic unifying of the eastern and western elements of the empire, which had never co-existed easily.

Indeed, Domitian's favouritism for foreign cults became yet another means for his condemnation in antiquity, with Pliny the Younger remarking that Domitian's banquets were attended by members of foreign cults with accompanying 'obscene behaviour' (*Panegyric to Trajan* 49.8). We have already noted that the Flavians moved away from

Julio-Claudian precedents in their treatment of foreign cults, and the sources show examples of Augustus and Tiberius' treatment of Egyptian cults in particular. Dio (*Roman History* 53.2.3; 54.6.6) records Augustus' persecution of the cult of Isis (his hostility to Egyptian cults probably part of his vilification of Cleopatra) and Tiberius persecuted the priests of the Temple of Isis in Rome, following a scandal, and threw the cult image into the Tiber (Josephus, *Jewish Antiquities* 18.3.4).

Thus the Flavian promotion of foreign, particularly Egyptian, cult within Rome's boundary, including the rebuilding of the Temple of Isis and Serapis, following its being damaged in the fire of 80, was a development unique to their dynasty, laying the foundations for the mass acceptance of the cult to the point where later emperors of the second century would be represented as Serapis in popular imagery.

IMPERIAL FAMILY AND IMPERIAL CULT

The issue of the imperial cult, however, was not new to the Flavian Dynasty: the Julio-Claudians had struggled to find a balance with this aspect of the principate, often veering from one extreme to the other according to their personal preferences (Tiberius' aversion to his worship contrasts with Gaius' deliberate use of the imperial cult to gain the auctoritas that he lacked from other sources). As with so much else, the Flavians seem to have imposed structure on the loosely connected concepts that the Julio-Claudians had engendered. But even here there is a knowing quality to the imperial programme. Vespasian's last words (Suetonius, *Vespasian* 23 (PS)) give a sense that he understood the rules of the game of the imperial cult: a concept to be exploited, but never personally believed.

For various aspects of the imperial cult, Vespasian in particular continued matters in the same manner as had Augustus, with both the genius of the emperor and his household lares featuring in oaths and dedicatory inscriptions, toeing the line of Roman religious conservatism, reflecting society's reluctance to worship a living person. However, in the polytheistic eastern provinces – as ever – there was a greater acceptance of ruler-worship. Thus we see a priest of Vespasian in Pisidian Antioch (MW 132: LACTOR 20, L56), a base for a statue of Titus from Moesia *c.* 80, where he is described as a god while still alive (MW 138: LACTOR 20, L58), and an inscription from Ephesus (MW 139: LACTOR 20, L59) denoting Domitian as a god. The subsequent vandalism of Domitian's name suggests that the original declaration was from his lifetime.

While the Flavians actively promoted their imperial cults in the provinces, which almost certainly won them support, at the same time they further united their rule with the best of the Julio-Claudians (i.e. Augustus and Claudius) through the consolidation of cult practices for the previously deified emperors. The order and structure that the dynasty seems to have incorporated into these practices is exemplified by the rules for emperor-worship at Narbo (the *Lex Narbonensis*: MW 128: LACTOR 20, L57). This inscription indicates that the position of priest of Vespasian was one of great honour, allowing for statues of the individuals to be set up within the temple itself. Thus we may see here that the worship of Vespasian, in Narbo at least, involved a specific priesthood and formal temple, and was clearly taking place while the emperor himself was alive.

FIGURE 3.27
Aureus of
Vespasian, 84.

divi (sg: divus; fem:
diva) the collective term
for the deified members of
the imperial family

**Aureus of Vespasian
(Figure 3.27)**

Date: AD 84

Obverse: Laureate head
of Domitian, with
aegis; 'Emperor Caesar
Domitian Augustus
Germanicus, son
of Divus Vespasian,
consul 10 times'

Reverse: Altar; 'To Imperial
Well-being, by decree
of the Senate'

Significance: Vespasian
issues coinage
commemorating the
dedication of an altar
to his well-being

View it here: K10 in
LACTOR 20: The
Flavians (London: KCL,
2015)

The evidence suggests moreover that the imperial cult in the provinces was extended and homogenised under Vespasian's reign. The extensive publications of Duncan Fishwick (*Imperial Cult in the Latin West*, Leiden: Brill; 3 vols, 1987–2005) suggest that new provincial cults were established in Gallia Narbonensis, Baetica, and Africa Proconsularis, while those of Hispania Citerior, Lusitania, and Tres Galliae were reorganised and regulated in a manner similar to the *Lex Narbonensis*. Therefore, although such practices may have been alien to Rome herself, the formality of the cult in the provinces indicates how useful the imperial cult had become as an aid for ruling the provincial populations.

It was Domitian who moved towards a more overt imperial cult, which again reflected his more autocratic (perhaps pharaonic) style of governance. Again some of this built on the Julio-Claudian precedents, such as celebrating the altars that the Senate had declared on his behalf (see Fig 3.27).

These altars further allowed for the subtle inclusion of imperial cult within Rome herself. The fact that the altar shown on the coin in Fig 3.27 was established 'by decree of the Senate' may be used to argue for the submissiveness of the Senate, or perhaps that the relationship between them and the princeps was not as poor as some sources would suggest.

However, we are also able to see a greater cohesion and organisation of the systems and structures of the imperial cult in Rome under the Flavians. This is especially notable in both the sacral calendar and the place of **divi** (deified members of the imperial family).

Under the Julio-Claudians, the various divi had been treated separately, with accompanying separate cults and a corresponding variety of practice. This is unsurprising given that the honour of state deification was still very much a developing idea under the Julio-Claudians. The Flavian divi, however, were very much treated as a collective, being worshipped in shared temples and with identical practices. These five deified family members were Vespasian, Titus, Julia Titi, Domitian's son who died in infancy, and Domitilla, who was either Vespasian's wife or sister, since both had died before 69.

It is notable that, with the exception of Vespasian himself, all of the Flavian divi were deified by Domitian. This may be because Flavian deifications were more useful to Domitian, who could then draw prestige from a raft of divine relatives. Vespasian had had no familial relationship with the Julio-Claudian divi, which meant that any exploitation of their worship would have been problematic, and so he had left his relationship with the pre-existing imperial cult in a state of flux. That Domitian saw these divine relatives as significant is clear from his coinage.

The aurei in Figs 3.28 and 3.29 (note the high denomination of both) show the infant son of Domitian surrounded by stars (a typical sign of deification) and the deified Domitilla, respectively. These coins are further evidence for the cohesion of the Flavian divi, who are given equal weighting in various media and enjoyed shared temple structures.

There are three separate temples for the Flavian divi known from Domitian's reign: two are dedicated to Divine Vespasian and Divine Titus together; the third is the Temple of the Flavian Family on the Quirinal, which most likely served the cult of all of the Flavian divi, along with their lares and penates. This last structure was actually the family home where Domitian had been born and he converted it into a temple for his family (Suetonius,

Domitian 1.1 **PS**). It was completed *c.* 94. Martial focuses much of his ninth book of *Epigrams* on Domitian and his activities, describing this temple as being:

> . . . the hallowed home which gave the world
> What Rhodes and holy Crete gave to the starry sky.

Martial, Epigrams 9.20.5–6

Here Martial emphatically connects the Temple of the Flavian Family, the birthplace of Domitian, with Crete, the birthplace of Jupiter, which is suggestive that the concept of the 'divine family' is what Domitian wished to promote. Similarly, in *Epigrams* 9.1 **PS** Martial can speak of the 'glory of the Flavian race' (9.1.8) enduring as long as does Rome herself, ensuring that he comments on 'Diva Julia's sweet godhead' (9.1.7) at the same time.

This evidence for the importance of the collective cult of the Flavian divi is underlined by the curious fact that the birthdays of the various Julio-Claudian divi, which had been

FIGURE 3.28
Aureus of
Domitia.

PRESCRIBED SOURCE

Aureus of Vespasian (Figure 3.29)

Date: AD 82–3

Obverse: Head of deified Vespasian, radiate; 'Vespasian Augustus, god'

Reverse: Bust of deified Domitilla, draped, right, hair in long plait behind; 'Domitilla Augusta, goddess'

Significance: Domitian issues coinage to link himself explicitly with his deified family members

View it here: J13a in LACTOR 20: The Flavians (London: KCL, 2015)

PRESCRIBED SOURCE

Title: *Epigrams*

Author: Martial

Date: AD 86–103

Genre: Epigrammatic verse

Significance: Hyperbolised presentation of Domitian as a member of a 'divine' family, which must be used with caution as Martial is prone to excess in terms of both pandering and satirising

Prescribed section: 9.1

Read it here: LACTOR 20: The Flavians (London: KCL, 2015)

FIGURE 3.29
Aureus of Vespasian,
82–3.

consistently and assiduously celebrated after the reign of Augustus (and even during the Year of Four Emperors, according to the Acts of the Arval Brethren), disappear from these documents under the Flavians.

However, this cannot reflect a deliberate break with the past, as if the Flavians were removing the cult of the Julio-Claudian divi: Vespasian readily restored and completed the Temple of Claudius that had been vowed but never fulfilled by Nero (Suetonius, *Vespasian* 9 (PS)), despite there being no need for him to do so. Even the Law on the Power of Vespasian (see p. 174) referred to Claudius merely by his imperial titles, rather than divus, suggesting that Claudius' divine status was by no means secure at the time when Vespasian came to power. It is likely that Vespasian wished to preserve divus Claudius, as he served as a useful precedent for the future deifications of the members of the Flavian family. But aside from Claudius, the only Julio-Claudians who had received lasting deification had been Augustus and Livia, neither of whom could serve as a useful precedent, given their respective uniqueness: the former as the first emperor, the latter deified because of her husband.

Thus the discontinuation of the sacral remembrance of the various birthdays of these Julio-Claudian divi must reflect a change in the treatment of divi as a whole. Perhaps what mattered now was not the individual princeps, but the principate as an institution. The current Emperor drew his authority not from personal charisma, nor special grants of power to himself as an individual, but rather from being the incumbent of what was in effect the highest Roman magistracy. This would account for the unity of cult practice under the Flavians, reflecting not so much the idiosyncrasies of individuals, but rather the continuation of dynastic power that had been legitimately acquired and maintained. Thus, the imperial cult became a reflection of the stability and unity that the Flavians wished to present themselves as having brought to the Roman world.

INVOLVEMENT AND ATTITUDE – THE EMPEROR'S ROLE IN RELIGION

Beyond being an object of veneration himself, the emperor had a significant role to play in Roman religion and its impact on society. The most obvious role of all emperors since 12 BC, when Augustus had assumed the role, was that of pontifex maximus.

While the position was mainly honorific, it did necessarily come with a corresponding degree of moral and religious authority which could be beneficial, especially in terms of the emperor serving as an example for society. We have little material to consider in Vespasian's and Titus' reigns, although the former is credited by Tacitus (*Annals*, 3.55 (PS)) as being influential in his restrained way of life. This may be seen as a counterpoint to the fear and concern at the outset of the Flavian Period (see, for example, the concern over informers in Tacitus *Histories* 4.10 (PS)).

Domitian most certainly used the position of pontifex maximus as part of his programme of moral reform. This is perhaps best exemplified by his punishment of Vestal Virgins who had broken their vows of chastity, such as in the trial of Cornelia, the Chief Vestal, in 91. Pliny the Younger (*Letters* 4.11.6) is clear that in order to pursue this matter, Domitian wished to 'use his rights as pontifex maximus' in order to achieve the

---

PRESCRIBED SOURCE

Title: *Annals*

Author: Tacitus

Date: Early second century AD

Genre: History

Significance: Vespasian is praised for his inherent good qualities, reflecting Tacitus' senatorial outlook and desire in this section to mark a contrast between Vespasian and other emperors

Prescribed section: 3.55

Read it here: J4j in LACTOR 20: The Flavians (London: KCL, 2015)

punishment of having her buried alive, 'since he thought to make his reign memorable by examples of this kind'. Although Pliny wishes to highlight this as an example of Domitian's cruelty, it nevertheless does reflect the fact that he was conscious of punishing those guilty of moral outrages using his official positions.

Domitian does indeed seem to have been genuinely concerned with the beliefs and behaviour of the citizens of the empire. Stern and somewhat forbidding, he appears to have had a personally sincere belief that manifested in actions, with Suetonius (*Domitian* 8.3 **PS**) informing us that he was concerned with the correction of morals. Similarly, in *Satire* 2, Juvenal lampoons Domitian's claim that as Censor he has restored the morals of the state.

Domitian also seems to have held a personal affinity for certain deities, whose cult he promoted. This in itself was not a new concept, as Augustus had presented a connection with Apollo, and had even claimed descent from Venus. Cassius Dio (*Roman History*, 67.1.2 **PS**) claims that Minerva was the deity whom Domitian venerated before all others. This was a sensible choice, if it was a choice: Minerva was one of the Capitoline Triad, that focus of Flavian activity, and had associations with both war and culture. Indeed, Domitian constructed a temple for Minerva in the heart of his Forum, the Forum Transitoria, though sources ascribe both Forum and Temple to his successor Nerva, even renaming the former as the Forum of Nerva. Domitian is also credited with the construction of a Temple of Minerva of Chalcis (*Chronicle of 354*, part 16 **PS**). It is even claimed that Domitian had portents of his own death in dreams, where Minerva, his patron goddess, suddenly withdrew her support and protection from him (Suetonius, *Domitian* 15.3 **PS**; Cassius Dio, *Roman History* 67.16.1 **PS**). It is difficult to ascribe such consistent focus on Minerva to anything other than devout belief, one of the benefits of polytheism being that a deity with similar interests as oneself is readily available.

Domitian also displayed an affinity for Jupiter, whom he regarded as having helped save him during the final struggles between the Vitellian and Flavian forces in Rome in 69. Tacitus (*Histories* 3.74 **PS**) tells us that Domitian established, first, in the reign of Vespasian, a small shrine and altar at the location of his rescue, which was subsequently replaced by a huge temple to Jupiter the Guardian. Martial, as one may expect, provides a number of instances where he speaks of Domitian as Jove (e.g. *Epigrams* 6.10; 9.91), further reinforcing the equivalency between the king of the gods and the princeps.

This desire for primacy was almost certainly what lay behind Domitian's adoption of the title of dominus et deus in 85 (Suetonius, *Domitian* 13 **PS**), with the latter term being fitting for gods proper, not simply the status as a divus. Cassius Dio (*Roman History*, 67.4.7, surviving in the summary by Zonaras **PS**) claims that Domitian was immensely proud of these titles, employing them in state documents, although no examples of this survive for us. However, we may speculate that it was the natural evolution of the near-wholesale deification of members of the Flavian family that Domitian had undertaken.

Following Domitian's assassination, this term of address was immediately rescinded even by poets such as Martial, who had been so praising of Domitian while he lived. The poet claims that such titles of address are more fitting for 'Parthia's turbaned monarchs' (*Epigrams* 10.72.5), which in itself reflects the autocratic programme that Domitian fostered, using his role in religion as an aspect of it.

PRESCRIBED SOURCE

Title: *Chronicle of 354*

Author: Unknown

Date: AD 354

Genre: Almanac

Significance: Although a very late source, nevertheless a useful compendium of information on the Flavians from an author who appears to be well informed

Prescribed section: 16

Read it here: LACTOR 20: The Flavians (London: KCL, 2015)

221

THE IMPACT ON SOCIETY OF THE RELIGIOUS 'DEVELOPMENTS' OF THE FLAVIANS

The necessarily very complicated issue here is hard to assess, given the frugality of our source material and the fact that what we do possess is written by upper-middle-class men, whom we have seen are affected by bias towards or against the Flavian regime. Even the greater acceptance of foreign polytheistic cults into the Roman religious system is difficult to assess, although we may speculate that the provincial populations felt better represented in terms of the social environment of the empire.

That being said, there would certainly have been a significant impact from certain socio-religious decisions of the Flavians, perhaps most obviously the forthright collection of the fiscus Iudaicus (Suetonius, *Domitian* 12.2 **PS**; see p. 191); but those most affected by it have left little by way of useable evidence for our purposes (although the Talmud does record a visit of four rabbis to Rome *c.* 86 to address a proclamation that would have apparently banned Jews from the Empire). This is not substantiated by any Classical source, but it does reflect the unease that Jewish populations may have felt as a result of the Flavians' attitude towards them.

Similarly, as Censor, Domitian could exert considerable influence over society. As Stewart states:

> Domitian exercised a general moral jurisdiction over the behaviour of Roman
> elites and enunciated a moral program that affirmed traditional values, reviving the
> *lex Scantinia* prohibiting male prostitution as well as the Augustan laws.

> Stewart, R. (1994), 'Domitian and Roman Religion: Juvenal Satires Two and Four'

The mention of the 'Augustan laws' refers to the *lex Julia de adulteriis coercendis* and the *lex Julia de maritandis ordinibus* of 18 BC, passed in order to curb adultery within Rome and guarantee the 'purity' of upper-class Roman offspring (see p. 16). The laws were terribly unpopular, not least because the very people governed by the laws – the Senate and equites – were those being ordered to enforce them. All this prompted Augustus to pass them again in AD 9 as the *lex Pappia Poppaea*, this time under the names of the two consuls for that year, rather than under his own (the 'Julia' in the laws' names had designated them his own legislation), in order to shift their stigma away from himself. Ovid (*Amores* 3.4, in particular 36–40) speaks of the sheer folly of trying to prevent adultery in Rome, even going so far as to call the person who is offended by adultery a 'country bumpkin'. Thus, given the unpopularity of such laws a century earlier and their failure at any lasting change, what did Domitian's resurrection of the legislation achieve?

It certainly built upon a Augustan precedent, as did so much of the Flavians' actions, and as such may have served to once again link the two dynasties together, giving both of them a focus of moral behaviour. Or perhaps it was to conceal Domitian's own outrages and faults, in a manner similar to Tiberius' edicts against promiscuous kissing (Suetonius, *Tiberius* 34). If that were the case, then his presentation to posterity reveals it to have been a failure: Juvenal (*Satires* 2.29–33) points out the moral hypocrisy of Domitian in his trying to curb adultery, as he himself was accused of an incestuous affair with his niece Julia, which ended with her dying as a result of 'the abortion that he forced upon her' (Suetonius, *Domitian* 22).

In truth, the impact of this religious and moral legislation of Domitian on Roman society appears to have been minimal, though it may well have given political informants the ammunition to denounce their fellow citizens. Its use by later authors as key evidence detailing the tyranny of Domitian has become far more relevant.

Perhaps the most lasting of the Flavian 'developments' were those that affected the presentation of the princeps and his immediate family. In particular, the cohesion and systemisation of the imperial cult allowed for not only the Flavians, but also the subsequent emperors and their own dynasties to access the prestige and auctoritas of their imperial predecessors, regardless of a lack of blood ties.

TOPIC REVIEW

- Discuss what the key aspects of 'religion' are in this period.
- Evaluate if the Flavian emperors have similar attitudes towards religion.
- Assess how important the Julio-Claudian precedent was in terms of religion.
- Analyse the issues with studying religion.

Further Reading

Augustakis, A. (ed.) (2013), *Ritual and Religion in Flavian Epic*; Oxford: Oxford University Press.
Carradice, I. & Buttrey, T.V. (eds.) (2007), *Roman Imperial Coinage: From AD 69 to AD 96. 'The Flavians'* v. 2, Pt. 1, 2nd edition; London: Spink & Son Ltd.
Zissos, A. (ed.) (2016), *A Companion to the Flavian Age of Imperial Rome*; Oxford: Blackwell.

PRACTICE QUESTIONS

1. To what extent is the Flavian attitude towards religion reflective of other aspects of their reigns?

You must use and analyse the ancient sources you have studied as well as your own knowledge to support your answer.

[36]

DEPTH STUDY 3
Ruling Roman Britain, AD 43–128

Introduction to Ruling Roman Britain, AD 43–128

This depth study focuses on the interplay of political, military, social, economic, cultural and religious factors affecting the complex interactions between the Roman Empire and the British. Beginning with life in Roman Britain before the Claudian invasion, this module will assess the reasons for the invasion of Britain and the profitability of its continued occupation. Literature and archaeology combine to illustrate the efficiency and expediency of the Roman conquest of lowland Britain which seemed only to be halted with the outbreak of the Boudiccan rebellion.

We are fortunate to have the *Agricola* by Tacitus. This shows us, albeit in the best possible light, the military campaigns and social reforms of the governor Gnaeus Julius Agricola, who took the might of Roman arms to the Scottish Highlands. After the departure of Agricola we see a gradual retrenchment in territory and manpower in Britain, to the point where a permanent frontier is established by the Emperor Hadrian, the purpose of which is still debated by scholars.

This depth study examines the literary and material evidence concerning the Roman occupation of Britain, which continued until the early years of the fifth century AD. Roman policy towards Britain and its inhabitants changed over time. We shall examine how far the early depiction from Caesar's accounts changes as Britain becomes a province of the Roman Empire and assess the extent to which the natives benefited from the continued occupation of the island.

EXAM OVERVIEW	H407/23 SECTION B

Your examination for Ruling Roman Britain, in Section B of your paper, will require you to show knowledge and understanding of the material you have studied. This component is worth 48 marks – 12 based on AO1 skills, 12 on AO2 and 24 on AO3.

In this section, you will answer two questions:

- a 12-mark stimulus question focusing on an issue relating to a historical event or situation, where you will need to assess the source's utility; and
- one of two essay questions, each worth 36 marks. The questions will require you to use, analyse and evaluate source material to address issues in the question. The essays will target one or more of the themes listed.

FIGURE 4.1
Map of Roman Britain.

TIMELINE OF KEY EVENTS

55 BC	Caesar's first invasion
54 BC	Caesar's second invasion
AD **43**	Claudian invasion
47	First Iceni revolt
49	Colonia at Colchester established
51	Caratacus is captured
60–1	The Boudiccan rebellion
69	Cartimandua is overthrown
78–84	Agricola's governorship
84	Battle of Mons Graupius
122	The building of Hadrian's Wall begins

4.1 Roman Military Policy towards Britain: Conquest and Expansion

- The relations between Britain and the Roman Empire in AD 43
- The reasons for the Roman conquest of Britain under Claudius
- Factors influencing Roman military policy towards Britain and moves to expand the province and establish a frontier
- Military policy and its effectiveness under the governors of Britain
- Agricola's military campaigns

The prescribed sources for this topic are:

- Dio Cassius, *Roman History*, 60.19.1–22.2, 60.23.1–60.23.6, 60.30.2
- Josephus, *Jewish War*, 2.378, 3.4–5
- Pomponius Mela, *Geography*, 3.49–53
- Suetonius, *Caligula*, 44.2; 46.1
- Suetonius, *Claudius*, 17.1–17.3, 21.6; 24.3
- Suetonius, *Nero*, 18
- Suetonius, *Vespasian*, 4.1–4.2
- Suetonius, *Titus*, 4.1
- Tacitus, *Annals* 12.23, 12.31, 33, 35, 39; 14.29–30, 39
- Tacitus, *Histories* 1.9, 1.59–60, 2.65–66, 3.44
- Tacitus, *Agricola* 13, 16–18, 23, 25–6, 40

- Arch of Claudius
- Aureus of Claudius
- Bronze coin of Cunobelinus
- C. Calventius Celer
- Chester lead water-pipe
- Claudius to the athletes
- Dannicus
- Gaius Saufeius tombstone
- Gold stater of Verica
- M. Petronius tombstone
- Rufus Sita
- Sex. Valerius Genialis
- T. Valerius Pudens

This topic will assess the reasons for the Claudian Invasion in AD 43, and the military narrative of expansion and consolidation up to the departure of Agricola as governor of Britain in 84. It will focus on the policies of Claudius, Nero and the Flavian emperors towards Britain and the Britons.

KEY INDIVIDUAL

Julius Caesar
Dates: 100–44 BC

Roman general. Julius Caesar invaded Britain twice, in 55 and 54 BC, but seemed uninterested in launching a full-scale conquest of the island. After his return to Rome in 49 BC he was victorious in a civil war against his former friend Pompey and proclaimed dictator for life, but was assassinated in 44 BC.

PRESCRIBED SOURCE

Bronze coin of Cunobelinus (Figure 4.2)

Material: Bronze

Date: AD 10–40

Obverse: Head, facing right; CVBOBELINVS REX (King Cunobelinus)

Reverse: Image of a bull butting, head down; TASC(IOVANI FILIVS) (son of Tasciovanus)

Significance: Original, independent evidence for the existence of Cunobelinus

View it here: LACTOR 4: Inscriptions of Roman Britain (5th edn; London: KCL, 2017), A9(iii) (= Mack 246)

ROME'S RELATIONS WITH BRITAIN BEFORE AD 43

Claudius was not the first Roman to visit Britain. Julius Caesar invaded Britain in 55 BC and again the next year in 54. Militarily, Caesar did not achieve much (although he was awarded twenty days of public thanksgiving by the Senate). However, he did manage to forge relationships with certain British tribes, which would provide the backdrop to Claudius' invasion in AD 43.

Caesar's main adversary was Cassivellaunus, who was the leader of the Catuvellauni tribe. We are told by Caesar that Cassivellaunus had killed a rival tribal leader from the Trinovantes tribe and was generally recognised as the ultimate leader of the British resistance to the Romans. During the summer of 54, the Trinovantes submitted to Caesar and swore obedience in the hope of gaining protection against the aggressive Catuvellauni tribe. This triggered the surrender of many tribes to Caesar, and kept the expansionist Catuvellauni tribe at bay. However, by AD 43 the Catuvellauni tribe had managed to dislodge the Trinovantes from their capital at Colchester (see the Bronze coin of Cunobelinus) and had set their sights on another strong and pro-Roman tribe called the Atrebates.

Dio tells us that Verica the king of the Atrebates had been exiled from Britain during a civil war and sought the protection of Claudius in Rome:

> Aulus Plautius, a senator of great reputation, led an expedition to Britain. This was because a certain Berikos [Verica], who had been driven out of the island as a result of civil war, persuaded Claudius to send a force there.

Dio, *Roman History* 60.19.1 (LACTOR 11, p. 37)

Since the time of Julius Caesar, the advantages to the Romans of a conquest of Britain had been debated. According to the poet Horace, the emperor Augustus had contemplated

FIGURE 4.2
Bronze coin of Cunobelinus.

FIGURE 4.3
The tribes of Britain.

PRESCRIBED SOURCE

Title: *Roman History*

Author: Dio Cassius

Date: *c.* AD 230

Genre: History

Significance: A third-century-AD historian who wrote an eighty-volume Roman history

Prescribed sections: 60.19.1–60.22.2, 60.23.1–60.23.6, 60.30.2

Read it here: LACTOR 11: *Literary Sources for Roman Britain* (4th edn; London: KCL, 2012)

KEY INDIVIDUAL

Claudius

Dates: 10 BC–AD 54

Roman emperor.

See Period Study, pp. 52–65. Successor to his nephew Gaius in 41 AD and made emperor by the imperial bodyguard, the Praetorians, Claudius was the first Roman to conquer Britain successfully. He died in suspicious circumstances in Rome in 54 AD and was succeeded by his adopted son Nero.

invading Britain in order to emulate the now deified Caesar, his adoptive father. However, no invasion happened. Upon his death in AD 14, according to Tacitus, *Agricola*, 13 (PS), Augustus told his successor Tiberius that the empire was already large enough and he should avoid embarking upon any sort of conquest.

PRESCRIBED SOURCE

Title: *Agricola*

Author: Tacitus

Date: *c.* AD 105

Genre: History, eulogy

Significance: One of Tacitus' three texts relevant to the study of Roman Britain, the *Agricola* is a eulogy of Tacitus' father-in-law and governor of Britain, Gnaeus Julius Agricola

Prescribed sections: 13, 16–18, 23, 25–6, 40

Read it here: *Tacitus: Agricola and Germania*, trans. H. Mattingley (Harmondsworth: Penguin, 1948)

THE REASONS FOR THE ROMAN CONQUEST OF BRITAIN UNDER CLAUDIUS

So why did Claudius launch an invasion of Britain in 43? The answer is debatable. Dio presents the invasion as a direct response to the pleas of Verica to Claudius, a claim supported perhaps by a gold stater with a vine leaf and Latin wording, illustrating the pro-Roman sympathies of Verica immediately before the invasion. Several British kings had directly beseeched emperors before Claudius, so this was nothing new. The *Res Gestae* mentions Augustus receiving the submission of Dumnobellaunus and Tincomarus (kings of the Trinovantes and Atrebates, respectively) as well as Gaius accepting the surrender of Adminius (brother of Caratacus and Togodumnus), who had been exiled by Gaius' father Cunobelinus in 40 (Suetonius, *Caligula* 44.2 **PS**) and from there the emperor Gaius had launched an aborted campaign against the Britons (Suetonius, *Caligula* 46.1 **PS**). Claudius' willingness to launch an invasion was certainly not felt by the soldiers chosen for the campaign in 43 who, according to Dio, objected to the enterprise.

FIGURE 4.4
Stater of Verica. **PS**

> The soldiers objected to the idea of campaigning outside the limits of the civilised world, and would not obey Plautius until Narcissus, who had been sent out by Claudius, mounted Plautius' tribunal and attempted to address them . . . their mutiny had made their departure late in the season.
>
> Dio, *Roman History* 60.19.2–3 (with omissions) (LACTOR 11, p. 37)

If Verica's exile was only a pretext for the invasion, what was the real motive? It may help to consider Claudius' position as emperor after the assassination of Gaius in AD 41. Claudius did not have the support of the Senate.

An invasion and subsequent conquest of Britain might be the perfect way to demonstrate Claudius' suitability to govern the Empire. Indeed, he would be surpassing

PRESCRIBED SOURCE

Stater of Verica (Figure 4.4)

Material: Gold

Date: AD 15–40

Obverse: Vine leaf; VI to left, RI to right

Reverse: Leaping horseman with spear and shield

Significance: Possible evidence for Verica's support for Rome immediately before the invasion

View it here: LACTOR 4: Inscriptions of Roman Britain (5th edn; London: KCL, 2017), A7 (= Mack 125)

PRESCRIBED SOURCE

Title: *Caligula, Claudius, Nero, Vespasian* and *Titus* from *The Twelve Caesars*

Author: Suetonius

Date: Late first/early second century AD

Genre: Biography

Significance: Important source about Julius Caesar and the first eleven emperors

Prescribed sections: Suetonius, *Caligula*, 44.2; 46.1; *Claudius*, 17.1–3, 21.6; 24.3; *Nero*, 18; *Vespasian*, 4.1–2; *Titus*, 4.1

Read it here: LACTOR 11: *Literary Sources for Roman Britain* (4th edn; London: KCL, 2012)

the achievements of Julius Caesar. If the response of the soldiers to campaigning in a mysterious and frightening place like Britain is to be taken literally, then a military victory there would provide Claudius with more personal glory than anywhere else.

> He sought the honour of a real triumph, and chose Britain as the best field in which to seek this, for no one had attempted an invasion since the time of Julius Caesar.
>
> Suetonius, *Claudius* 17. 1–2 (LACTOR 11, p. 37)

The presentations of Claudius' victory as outlined by Suetonius and Dio add belief to the theory that Claudius invaded Britain for his own glory. Suetonius 21.6 **PS** tells us that Claudius theatrically re-enacted the siege and capture of a British **oppidum**, clad in a general's cloak in order to emphasise the magnificence of his victory, and we are told by Tacitus (*Annals* 12.23 **PS**) that Claudius extended the pomerium in line with the achievements of Sulla and Augustus. An interesting letter of Claudius to some visiting athletes **PS** from AD 46 shows that provincials were making use of the victory to ingratiate themselves to the emperor. The letter indicates that the athletes had awarded Claudius with a symbolic golden crown for the victory over the Britons. Suetonius (*Claudius* 17 **PS**) and Dio (*Roman History* 60.22 **PS**) describe both the scene upon Claudius' return to Rome and the Senate's reaction (see also Period Study pp. 57–8).

The motivation for Claudius' invasion in AD 43 is unclear, as we get no adequate assessment from the ancient sources. The contemporary geographer Pomponius Mela (*Geography* 3.49–53 **PS**) mentions that Claudius had been successful in opening up the island; Pomponius claims this was the motivation for the invasion, but unfortunately he does not elaborate on this point. He does, however, provide a very brief assessment of the advantages of the conquest in terms of the economy and the minerals available, and

> **oppidum** a fortified Iron-Age settlement in Britain

> **S & C** Read the account of the difficulties of Claudius' accession in Josephus, *Jewish War* 19.158–267 (LACTOR 19: Tiberius to Nero (London: KCL, 2011).

Title: *Claudius to the athletes*

Type: One of several letters transcribed on an Egyptian papyrus

From: Claudius

To: The athletic synod of travelling athletes

Subject: Thanks for the gift of a golden crown

Date: AD 46

Current location: Now in the British Museum (111)

Significance: An example of the recognition of Claudius' victory in Britain

Read it here: LACTOR 4: Inscriptions of Roman Britain (5th edn; London: KCL, 2017), B15

Title: *Annals*

Author: Tacitus

Date: *c.* AD 117

Genre: History

Significance: Concerns Rome and the Empire from the death of Augustus in AD 14 to the later years of Nero's reign

Prescribed sections: 12.23, 12.31, 33, 35; 14.29–30, 39

Read it here: LACTOR 11: *Literary Sources for Roman Britain* (4th edn; London: KCL, 2012)

Title: *Roman History*

Author: Pomponius Mela

Date: *c.* AD 40s

Genre: Geography

Significance: Produces a very small work on Roman geography. Writing during the reign of Claudius

Prescribed sections: 3.49–53

Read it here: LACTOR 11: *Literary Sources for Roman Britain* (4th edn; London: KCL, 2012)

Study question
Outline the personal, political and economic advantages to Claudius in conquering Britain.

offers a brief ethnographic assessment of the Britons in line with similar accounts in Strabo and Caesar which would have been easily available to him.

ROMAN MILITARY POLICY TOWARDS BRITAIN AND ITS EFFECTIVENESS

The narrative of the invasion and early conquest period is dealt with more fully by the sources, although there is some debate about the initial landing place. Dio 60.19.4–5 **PS** tells us that Claudius sent over his troops (four legions – about 20,000 men – and an equal number of auxiliary troops) in three divisions, but it is unclear whether he means they landed at three separate intervals or in three separate places. What is clear is that, unlike during the invasions of Caesar, the Britons did not attempt to oppose the initial invasion force.

Eventually the Romans under Aulus Plautius engaged the British at most probably the River Medway in Kent, led by the Catuvellaunian Caratacus and Togodumnus. The latter, according to Dio 60.20.1 **PS**, died at the battle of the River Medway or shortly afterwards.

KEY EVENT

The battle of the River Medway

Date: Summer AD 43

Victorious side: Romans under Aulus Plautius

Losing side: Britons under Caratacus and Togodumnus

Roman auxiliaries defeated the chariots of the Britons; the Second Legion Augusta under future emperor Vespasian (see p. 153) attacked the natives, yet were unable to secure a victory on the first day of fighting. Hosidius Geta attacked on the second day and secured a victory for the Romans, and the Britons fell back to territory north of the Thames (see Dio, 60.20.2–4 **PS**).

Plautius' earliest successes can be attributed to his expert use of auxiliary troops and the actions of Vespasian and his brother Sabinus. After a similar victory at the River Thames, according to Dio 60.21.1–5 **PS**, Plautius became afraid and sent for Claudius, after consolidating what he had already gained, which probably was most of Hertfordshire and below eastwards. The capture of the Catuvellaunian stronghold of Camulodunum (Colchester) is attributed to Claudius' generalship, possibly more evidence of an expedition motivated by the need for personal military glory.

> Crossing over to Britain he joined the troops that were waiting for him at the Thames. Taking over the command of these troops he crossed the river and engaged the barbarians who had assembled to oppose him; he defeated them, and captured Camulodunum, the capital of Cunobelinus. After this he won over a number of tribes, some by diplomacy, some by force, and was saluted as **Imperator** several times, contrary to precedent, for no one may receive this title more than once for any one war.
>
> Dio, *Roman History* 60.21.3–5 (LACTOR 11, p. 39)

PS

After the capture of Colchester, Claudius' actions were quick and decisive; Dio 60.23.1–6 **PS** tells us that Claudius only spent sixteen days in Britain in total before departing back to Rome for his triumph with all treaties ratified as if by decree of the Senate. According to Dio, 60.30.2, **PS** Plautius received a triumph for his part in the victories but Suetonius, *Claudius* 24.3 **PS** states that he received the lesser ovation. The latter is more likely as triumphs were generally not awarded to anyone other than the emperor. Josephus, *Jewish War* 3.4–5 **PS** states that the efforts of Claudius' generals had actually provided Claudius with his triumph, with little credit to be given to Claudius himself.

Title: *Jewish War*

Author: Josephus

Date: *c.* AD 75

Genre: History

Significance: Commander of the Jews during the Jewish Rebellion AD 66–73. Favoured by Vespasian and Titus who rewarded him with Roman citizenship

Prescribed sections: 2.378, 3.4–5

Read it here: LACTOR 19

It was much easier for Claudius to win over various sections of the natives, divided up already by tribal loyalties and even geographical boundaries. We have a fragment of the triumphal arch of Claudius (largely reconstructed and so its precise details are impossible to verify) which refers to the surrender of tribes to Claudius as well as a commemorative aureus from AD 46–7 which shows the arch .

Tiberius Claudius Caesar Augustus Germanicus, son of Drusus, pontifex maximus, in his eleventh year of tribunician power, consul five times, hailed as imperator (22 or 23) times, father of his country; erected by the Senate and people of Rome because he received the submission of eleven British kings, conquered without any loss, and because he first brought barbarian tribes beyond Ocean into the dominion of the Roman People.

Arch of Claudius AD 51 (LACTOR 4, B16)

PS

PRESCRIBED SOURCE

Arch of Claudius

Date: AD 51

Original location: Rome, north of the Campus Martius

Current location: Destroyed; fragments in the Capitoline Museum

Significance: Set up to commemorate Claudius' victory in Britain, with inscriptions referring to the surrender of tribes

View it here: LACTOR 4: Inscriptions of Roman Britain (5th edn; London: KCL, 2017), B16 (= ILS 216)

FIGURE 4.5
Aureus of Claudius showing the arch.

PRESCRIBED SOURCE

Aureus of Claudius (Figure 4.5)

Material: Gold

Date: 46–47

Obverse: Head of Claudius, laureate; TI CLAVD CAESAR AVG P M TR P VI IMP XI

Reverse: Arch of Claudius; inscription on arch DE BRITANN

Significance: Provides an image of Claudius' triumphal arch

View it here: LACTOR 4: Inscriptions of Roman Britain (5th edn; London: KCL, 2017), B14 (= RIC Claudius 33 = BMC Claudius 32)

FIGURE 4.6
Maiden Castle, a **hill fort** in Dorset.

hill fort defensive earthworks

The evidence which supports a three-pronged attack to bring the remaining areas of the south and south-east of Britain under Roman control comes from legionary and auxiliary tombstones as well as the bodies of Britons at oppida such as Maiden Castle and Hod Hill. The Ninth Legion Hispana was sent northwards towards Lincolnshire, the Fourteenth Legion Gemina westwards towards Shropshire and the Second Legion along the south coast. The remaining Twentieth Legion Valeria Victrix remained at Colchester.

Inscriptions among the prescribed sources are from tombstones that provide evidence for the early conquest period:

> To Gaius Saufeius, son of Gaius, of the Fabian voting tribe, from Heraclea, soldier of the Ninth Legion, aged 40, off 22 years' service; he lies here.
>
> > Tombstone found in Lincoln in the Claudio-Neronian period
> > (LACTOR 4, B11)

> Marcus Petronius, son of Lucius, of the Menenian voting tribe, from Vicetia, aged 38 years, a soldier of the fourteenth Legion Gemina, served 18 years, was a standard-bearer and lies buried here.
>
> > Tombstone found in Wroxeter mid-first century AD
> > (LACTOR 4, B13)

PRESCRIBED SOURCE

Inscriptions on the tomb-stones of Gaius Saufeius, M. Petronius, Dannicus, Sex. Valerius Genialis, Rufus Sita

Location: Lincoln, Wroxeter, Cirencester and Gloucester

Date: Mid-first century AD

Significance: Evidence for soldiers that died during the early conquest period

View them here: LACTOR 4: Inscriptions of Roman Britain (5th edn; London: KCL, 2017), B11 (= RIB 255), B13 (= RIB 294), B3 (= RIB 108), B4 (=RIB 109), B5 (= RIB 121)

Dannicus, cavalryman of the *ala Indiana*, from the troop of Albanus, served for 16 years, a citizen of the Raurici, lies buried here; Fulvius Natalis and Fl[avi]us Bitucus (*set this up*) according to his will.

Tombstone found in Cirencester Claudio-Flavian period (LACTOR 4, B3)

Sextus Valerius Genialis, cavalryman of the *ala Thracum*, a citizen of the Frisiavones, in the troop of Genialis, aged 40 years of 20 years' service, lies buried here; his heir had set this up.

Tombstone found in Cirencester Claudio-Flavian period (LACTOR 4, B4)

Rufus Sita, cavalryman of the Sixth Cohort of Thracians, aged 40 of 22 years' service, lies buried here; his heirs had this stone erected according to his will.

Tombstone found in Gloucester mid-first century AD (LACTOR 4, B5)

By good fortune, the archaeological record is supported by the literary. Suetonius tells us about the actions of the Second Legion Augusta under its commander Vespasian. Therefore by the end of Aulus Plautius' governorship in AD 47, most Britain below the **Fosse Way** had fallen into Roman hands.

Crossing with the legion to Britain, he fought the enemy thirty times. He conquered two of the strongest tribes, captured more than twenty towns.

Suetonius, *Vespasian* 4.1–2 (with omissions) (LACTOR 11, p. 39)

> **Fosse Way** the road from Exeter to Lincoln. Acted as the western boundary of Roman Britain during the early conquest period.

KEY INDIVIDUAL

Vespasian

Dates: AD 9–79

Roman emperor and general.

The first emperor of the Flavian dynasty. He became emperor in AD 69/70 by defeating his rival Vitellius in a bloody civil war (see Tacitus, *Histories*, 3.44 PS on the mixed loyalties of the troops in Britain during the Roman Civil Wars of AD 69). Vespasian was responsible for starting the Flavian Amphitheatre (or Colosseum) in Rome. He had experience in Britain before his accession as the commander of the Second Legion Augusta securing the south coast harbours as far as Cornwall (see p. 153).

EXPLORE FURTHER

The website romaninscriptionsof britain.org has very helpful information and images for a range of material evidence from Roman Britain, including some of the prescribed sources.

The second governor of Roman Britain was Publius Ostorius Scapula, an experienced general, an ideal choice to consolidate the gains of Plautius and launch further raids against recalcitrant tribes. However, on his arrival he faced immediate difficulties from the opportunistic Britons, who may have wanted to test the new governor. Tacitus is our main source for the period, and his presentation of the early governorship of Scapula is most favourable.

It is at this point that the Iceni are mentioned for the first time. Tacitus tells us that although they were allied to the Romans as possibly part of those won over by diplomacy by Claudius, they rebelled against this new governor's harsh administration and led a local confederacy against Scapula in the first real test of his governorship. Scapula, like his predecessor Plautius, used auxiliary troops to put down the rebellion, possibly at the hill fort of Stonea Camp in Cambridgeshire which, like Maiden Castle, has evidence of human remains killed in violent struggle with swords.

Wales became the arena for warfare for the next ten years (see map, p. 231). It would prove to be a lot more difficult for the Romans to conquer and subdue than the territory below the Fosse Way. We are told that after a relatively quick and successful campaign against the Deceangli tribe in North Wales, the Romans were faced with armed resistance by the much more formidable Silures tribe. The strength of this naturally warlike tribe, according to Tacitus, was increased due to the ability of their adopted leader, Caratacus, a refugee from the Catuvellauni tribe who were defeated decisively by Claudius in AD 43 (see p. 235). Scapula recognised that he had to control this particular tribe with a legionary garrison, so moved the Twentieth Legion Valeria from Colchester to Gloucester as well as auxiliary units to Cirencester.

Tacitus outlines the difficulty of the task in subduing a confederacy of the Silures and Ordovices, illustrating well the advantage of the Britons in waging war in familiar territory.

> He chose for battle a site that was difficult to approach but easy to abandon, and in every other respect suited his men rather than ours. On one side were high mountains and wherever there was a more gradual incline he constructed a barrier of stones like a rampart. This was behind a river which had no safe crossing-points, and in front of the fortifications armed men had taken up their positions.
>
> Tacitus, *Annals* 12.33 (LACTOR 11, p. 43)

Tacitus does not depict Scapula as a particularly decisive commander and indeed tells us that it was the soldiers themselves who actually demanded that the governor join battle. The Romans' tactical superiority eventually showed and Tacitus records the outcome as a famous victory for the Romans, but is careful not to attribute any of the credit to Scapula (*Annals* 12.35 **PS**).

After this defeat, the Silures regrouped and managed to record a number of victories against the Romans, including killing a legionary commander and eight centurions. Again Tacitus paints a less than positive picture of the end of the governorship of Scapula, who had taken the successes of the Silures after the capture of Caratacus as a personal failure and threatened to exterminate the entire tribe. Tacitus concludes Scapula's governorship by saying that he died from anxiety over waging such a complex war with such a relentless tribe.

There is no break in the narrative, but the archaeological record is unhelpful for the early 50s. Claudius quickly appointed a new governor with an impressive military background. Aulus Didius Gallus had serious reservations about his predecessor's administration of the province. This is unsurprising, bearing in mind Tacitus' earlier comments about Scapula's final years (Tacitus, *Annals* 12.39 **PS**). Gallus manages to defeat the Silures, but Tacitus provides no details of his final battles.

KEY PEOPLE

The Iceni
Territory: East Anglia (see map, p. 231)

Study question
What can we learn from Tacitus' account about the strengths and weaknesses of Scapula as a governor?

After successfully negotiating a civil war against the **Brigantes** (again Tacitus is happy to give the credit to those on the governor's staff), Gallus is replaced in AD 57 by Quintus Veranius, a rapacious governor who we are told 'ravaged' Silurian territory (Tacitus, *Annals* 14.29 **PS**). It is hard to gauge what Tacitus thought about him, as Veranius lasted less than a year as governor, with his cause of death unknown. Tacitus is critical of the governor's flattery towards the new Emperor **Nero** in his will, in which Veranius makes the bold claim that if he had lived for two more years, he would have conquered the entire island.

Tacitus provides us with an account of the attack on Anglesey by Suetonius Paulinus, the fifth governor of Britain, in AD 60. We are told that this governor was greatly admired for his military ability back in Rome, and seemed the ideal candidate to finish off the campaigns of Gallus and Veranius. Tacitus' vivid description of the appearance of the Britons is notable:

> Standing on the shore before them were the enemy forces, a densely packed body of armed men; there were women running among them, dressed in funereal robes like Furies, with hair streaming and with torches in their hands; and round about them stood the Druids, raising their hands to heaven and pouring down terrible curses. . . . After [their defeat] a garrison was set over the conquered islanders and the groves destroyed which had been devoted to their barbarous and superstitious rites; for it was part of their religion to honour their altars with the blood of their prisoners and to consult the gods by means of human entrails.
>
> Tacitus, *Annals* 14.30 (LACTOR 11, p. 47)

The event which is best dealt with by the sources occurs at the same time as Suetonius' subjugation of Mona, the Boudiccan rebellion. A full assessment of what we can learn from the sources about this pivotal event is better dealt with in the key topic on Resistance to Roman Rule (see pp. 265–8).

The period in Britain which coincides with the end of Nero's reign and the **Year of the Four Emperors** is barely dealt with in the literary record. Tacitus is once again the main source for this complicated period, which saw a halt in the expansion of the province and potentially the start of a more conciliatory administration by the governors; a consequence perhaps of the setback caused by Boudicca or the general upheaval caused by the end of Nero's reign and the period of instability which followed. After the expulsion of Suetonius by the government in Rome due to the negative effects of his punitive campaign against the tribes involved in the rebellion of AD 60/61, we are told that the next governor was deliberately appointed as a contrast to his warlike predecessors.

Having just held the consulship in Rome, Petronius Turpilianus in AD 62 embarked upon a policy which seemed sensible when dealing with the aftermath of the Boudiccan rebellion. Consolidating the south was more important than trying to finish off the Silures, and with four legions now stationed in Exeter, Lincoln, Kingsholm and Wroxeter, the area destroyed by Boudicca could be rebuilt and the tribes resettled. Tacitus' judgement on the short governorship of Turpilianus is harsh, bearing in mind the state of the province upon his arrival:

He (Suetonius) was replaced by Petronius Turpilianus, who had just completed his consulship. Turpilianus neither aggravated the enemy, nor was he himself provoked, and he dignified this lazy inactivity with the honorable name of peace.

Tacitus, *Annals* 14.39 (LACTOR 11, p. 54)

In AD 67, during the reign of Turpilianus' successor, Trebellius Maximus, the Fourteenth Legion Gemina was withdrawn from Britain by the Emperor Nero, although it would briefly return (see Tacitus, *Histories* 2.66 **PS**). This move demonstrates military policy towards Britain during the mid–60s. As the expansion into Wales and potentially into Yorkshire had been abandoned, four legions stationed in Britain would have been seen as a waste of resources. The Twentieth Legion Valeria Victrix was moved to Wroxeter to fill the gap left by the Fourteenth Legion Gemina, and the Second Legion Augusta was moved to a legionary base in Gloucester. These movements illustrate the successes of Turpilianus and Maximus in aiding the recovery of southern Britain after the Boudiccan rebellion. Tacitus, *Histories* 1.59–60 **PS** mentions a rebellion with the troops due to inactivity led by the legate of the Twentieth Legion, Roscius Caelius. Tacitus' assessment of Trebellius once again seems over-simplistic.

There was, however, a serious mutiny; for the troops, accustomed to campaigns, got out of hand when they had nothing to do. Trebellius fled and hid to escape his angry army. His honour and dignity compromised, he now commanded merely on sufferance. By a kind of tacit bargain the troops had licence to do as they pleased, the general had his life; and so the mutiny stopped short of bloodshed.

Tacitus, *Agricola* 16

During the Year of the Four Emperors in AD 69, Tacitus, *Histories* 2.65 **PS** states that Vettius Bolanus was sent to Britain by the emperor Vitellius, but with no particular mandate. A province which Suetonius, *Nero* 18 **PS** tells us that Nero apparently had considered abandoning entirely did not feature high in the priorities of a newly appointed emperor engaged in a civil war back in Rome. We are told by Tacitus that Bolanus adopted the same policy of Trebellius Maximus but with less resentment from the legions, who may have been pleased that they were not directly involved in the civil wars in Rome.

The British army remained quiet. During all the civil strife which followed, no other legions conducted themselves more correctly, whether this was because, at such a distance, they were divided from the rest of the world by the Ocean, or because, hardened by frequent fighting, they hated the enemy rather than each other.

Tacitus, *Histories* 1.9 (LACTOR 11, p. 54)

Expansion north only resumed due to a resumption of the struggle between Cartimandua and Venutius in Brigantia. As with the Boudiccan revolt, this is dealt with better in the key topic on Resistance to Roman Rule, but its consequences again affected Roman military policy in Britain. From this moment, focus on the province would relate to conquest and expansion. Brigantia's size and location provided Rome with great danger

---

KEY EVENT

Year of the Four Emperors

Date: AD 69

After the suicide of Nero, four individuals were declared emperor one after another during bloody civil wars: Galba (9 June 68–15 January 69), Otho (15 January 69–16 April 69), Vitellius (16 April AD 69–22 December AD 69) and Vespasian (1 July 69–23 June 79).

Study question

Why does Tacitus seem overly critical of Petronius and Trebellius compared to his treatment of other governors?

PRESCRIBED SOURCE

Title: *Histories*

Author: Tacitus

Date: c. AD 105

Genre: History

Significance: The *Histories* deal with the Civil Wars in AD 69 to the death of Domitian in 96

Prescribed sections: 1.9, 1.59–60, 2.65–6, 3.44

Read it here: LACTOR 11: *Literary Sources for Roman Britain* (4th edn; London: KCL, 2012)

and so decisive action needed to be taken quickly. This crisis needed a different type of governor, so in AD 71, Bolanus was replaced by Petilius Cerialis, who was no stranger to Britain. Cerialis had been the legate of the Ninth Legion during the time of Boudicca's rebellion and had recently quelled the rebellion of the Batavians, a tribe in Germany. The new emperor of Rome, Vespasian, saw Cerialis as the ideal governor not only to deal with the crisis in Brigantia but also to lead a general expansion of the province now that the south had been successfully settled. Evidence of this change in policy can be seen with the arrival of the Second Legion Adiutrix in the same year as Cerialis' arrival as governor, increasing the legions available to the governor back to four. Josephus, *Jewish War*, 2.378 admires the effectiveness of the four legions during this time in having subjugated and held the entire island.

Epigraphic evidence shows that this legion replaced the Ninth Legion, which in turn was moved northwards into Brigantia, based at Malton and then York.

> Titus Valerius Pudens, son of Titus, of the Claudian voting tribe, from Savaria, a soldier of the Second Legion Adiutix Pia Fidelis, in the century of Dossennius Proculus, aged 30 years, of 6 years' service; his heir set this up at his own expense; here he lies.
>
> Tombstone found in Lincoln *c.* AD 71–8 (LACTOR 4, B22)

Cerialis seems to fit Tacitus' view of a governor as predominately a military commander, and is credited with the annexation of a large part of the tribal region.

> Petilius Cerealis at once struck terror into their hearts by attacking the state of the Brigantes, which is said to be the most populous in the whole province. After a series of battles – some of them by no means bloodless – Petilius had overrun, if not actually conquered, the major part of their territory.
>
> Tacitus, *Agricola* 17

With the whole of Brigantia under Roman control, the next governor, Julius Frontinus, decided to make the bold move to resume hostilities against the Welsh tribes. These had been abandoned by Suetonius Paulinus over ten years earlier on his hearing of the outbreak of the Boudiccan rebellion (Tacitus, *Agricola* 17). It may be considered rather impetuous that Frontinus did not choose the consolidation of the territory of the Brigantes as his main focus. It seems that he believed that the Ninth Legion in York and the Second Legion Adiutrix in Lincoln could hold the largest tribal area in Britain. Tacitus admired Frontinus for his achievements in Silurian territory, but as Tacitus' purpose was to set the scene for Agricola's arrival quickly, we do not get more than a few sentences about the final conquest of the Welsh; it is thus hard to reconstruct the campaigns.

> But Julius Frontinus was equal to shouldering the heavy burden, and rose as high as a man then could rise. He subdued by force of arms the strong and warlike nation of the Silures, after a hard struggle, not only against the valour of his enemy, but against the difficulties of the terrain.
>
> Tacitus, *Agricola* 17

We do know that during the late AD 70s, the Second Legion Augusta was moved westwards from Gloucester to a new legionary base at Caerleon and the Second Legion Adiutrix once again was moved, this time from Lincoln to Chester (see tombstone of C. Calventius Celer **PS**). With the legions now based in Chester, York, Wroxeter and Caerleon, the focus was perhaps on the conquest of the entire island.

PRESCRIBED SOURCE

Inscriptions on the tombstones of T. Valerius Pudens and C. Calventius Celer

Date: *c.* 71–8

Original location: Lincoln and Chester

Current location: British Museum, London, and Grosvenor Museum, Chester

Significance: Evidence for the movement of the legions in Britain during the conquest period

View it here: LACTOR 4: Inscriptions of Roman Britain (5th edn; London: KCL, 2017), B22 (= RIB 258) and B23 (= RIB 475)

THE GOVERNORSHIP OF AGRICOLA

The governor who receives by far the most attention in our sources is Gnaeus Julius Agricola, governor of Britain from AD 78 to 84. Appointed by the Emperor Titus, who himself had served in Britain as a military tribune (see Suetonius, *Titus*, 4.1 **PS**), we know so much about his life and his achievements due to a close family connection between Agricola and the historian Tacitus. Tacitus was married to Agricola's daughter, and although we should examine the portrayal of his father-in-law in Britain with caution, this connection allows us a unique perspective on the achievements of this particular governor. We have seen that Tacitus' accounts of previous governors reigns are either too small to evaluate or are painted in the worst possible light.

Tacitus in his text chooses to focus on the personality of Agricola which is a natural for a **eulogy**, rather than make any serious attempt to plot the expansion of the province or to justify it. Agricola the man is authoritative, fair, decisive and almost always right; in short, he outshines all of his predecessors. However, careful moderation is needed when assessing the value of the eulogy as a source; it is not so simple as to write off the claims made by Tacitus as **hyperbole**. Tacitus had unparalleled access to Agricola, and his account was probably very accurate. The historian has to read between the lines and assess what happened in Britain in the years after Agricola's recall, then balance this with the claims in the text that Agricola's achievements were significant.

KEY INDIVIDUAL

Agricola
Dates: AD 40–93

Military commander and governor of Britain. Known mostly through an account of his life by his son-in-law, the Roman historian Tacitus.

eulogy a speech or text in praise of a recently deceased person

hyperbole deliberate exaggeration

FIGURE 4.7
Agricola, Governor of Britain.

Study question
Read the *Agricola* (the text) and note the main achievements of Agricola (the man). What is Tacitus' assessment of these?

Agricola's expansion into Caledonia (ancient Scotland) was largely his own achievement, but it could not have been achieved without the successes of Cerialis and Frontinus in conquering and subduing Brigantia and south Wales, respectively, or even the successes of Turpilianus, Maximus and Bolanus in bringing about peace in southern Britain after Boudicca and rebuilding settlements destroyed in AD 60.

Agricola saw action against Boudicca as a Junior Officer and then as commander of the Twentieth Legion Valeria Victrix in the early 70s. This would have made him acutely aware of the necessity to ensure that Wales and Brigantia were completely subdued before embarking upon a Northern Campaign to conquer Scotland. He arrived as governor at the very end of the summer of AD 78 and immediately launched a campaign against the troublesome Ordovices in North Wales. We are told by Tacitus that they had successfully destroyed a squadron of auxiliary cavalry and their success had stirred the Silures. Tacitus shows the actions of the new governor as decisive and exemplary:

> The summer was now far spent, the auxiliary units were scattered all over the province, and the soldiers assumed that there would be no more fighting that year. . . . In spite of all, Agricola decided to go and meet the peril. He concentrated the legionaries serving on detachment duties and a small force of auxiliaries. As the Ordovices did not venture to descend into the plain, he led his men up into the hills, marching in front himself so as to impart his own courage to the rest by sharing their danger, and cut to pieces almost the whole fighting force of the tribe.
>
> Tacitus, *Agricola* 18

The island of Anglesey, the focus of Suetonius Paulinus in AD 60, was duly conquered and thus the conquest of Wales was completed. A legionary fortress was built to control northern Wales at Chester and was occupied by the Second Legion Adiutrix; a lead water-pipe **PS** from here has been excavated, bearing the name of the governor. Tacitus describes Agricola's reticence in accepting a triumph with more detail than the Anglesey campaign itself:

> Yet he did not use his success to glorify himself. He would not represent his action as a campaign of conquest, when, as he said, he had merely kept a defeated tribe under control. He did not even use laurel-wreathed dispatches to announce his achievement. But his very reluctance to admit his title to fame won him even greater fame: for men gauged his splendid hopes for the future by his reticence about an exploit so remarkable.
>
> Tacitus, *Agricola* 18

FIGURE 4.8
Chester lead water-pipe.

By AD 81, Agricola had reached the Forth–Clyde line, and Tacitus (*Agricola* 23 **PS**) tells us that this could have been a sensible frontier for the province (over sixty years later the Roman emperor Antoninus Pius would build 'the Antonine Wall', indicating the Forth–Clyde line as the limit of the province). However, Agricola's decision to expand further is attributed to glory and valour rather than impetuosity or poor-planning.

Tacitus tells us about Agricola's use of the fleet in reconnoitring (making a military observation of) the harbours of Caledonia. He notes that this simultaneous assault both by land and now by sea caused great alarm to the natives, who apparently were 'stupefied' as their last hope of safety in retreating across the sea had been removed from them. Their response was to launch an attack in AD 83 on an auxiliary fort.

> The natives of Caledonia turned to armed resistance on a large scale – though the facts were exaggerated, as the unknown always is, by rumour. They went so far as to attack some of our forts, and inspired alarm by their challenging offensive. There were cowards in the council who pleaded for a 'strategic retreat' behind the Forth, maintaining that 'evacuation was preferable to expulsion'.
>
> Tacitus, *Agricola* 25

Agricola, however, advocated counter-attack, lest the enemy surround him with greater numbers. Tacitus focuses on the tactical brilliance of Agricola in dividing his troops into three divisions so as to avoid an ambush (*Agricola* 25 **PS**). However, these tactics weakened a detachment of the Ninth Legion, which was subjected to a night attack. Tacitus gives a vivid account of the attack, but is again selective in his praise for Agricola's leadership.

> The fight was already raging inside the camp when Agricola was warned by his scouts of the enemy's march. He followed close on their tracks, ordered the speediest of his cavalry and infantry to harass the assailants' rear, and finally made his whole force raise a shout. Dawn was now breaking, and the gleam of the legions' standards could be seen. Caught thus between two fires, the Britons were dismayed, while the men of the ninth took heart again; now that their lives were safe they could fight for honour. They even made a sally, and a grim struggle ensued in the narrow gateways. At last the enemy were routed by the efforts of the two armies -the one striving to make it plain that they had brought relief; the other, that they could have done without it. Had not marshes and woods covered the enemy's retreat, that victory would have ended the war.
>
> Tacitus, *Agricola* 26

This near disaster apparently encourages the soldiers to be even bolder in their expansion and focus on the complete subjugation of the entire island. The main show-piece of Agricola's campaigns in Scotland is the Battle of Mons Graupius in AD 83, a discussion of which can be found in Topic 4.3, pp. 272–3.

Tacitus does not give an adequate assessment of Agricola's actions in Britain after his victory at Mons Graupius. We are told that Agricola handed Britain in a peaceful state over to his successor, Sallustius Lucullus, of whom there is virtually no evidence except a reference in Suetonius, *Life of Domitian*, to his execution around AD 90.

Two-thirds of those that fought for the Caledonians at Mons Graupius escaped to the highlands and, although pursued by Agricola, were never defeated. Archaeology shows

Chester lead water-pipe (Figure 4.8)

Date: AD 79

Inscription: '(Made) in the ninth consulship of the emperor Vespasian and in the seventh of Titus, acclaimed imperator, in the governorship of Gnaeus Julius Agricola'

Current location: Grosvenor Museum, Chester

Significance: Evidence for Agricola's campaigns in north Wales

View it here: LACTOR 4: Inscriptions of Roman Britain (5th edn; London: KCL, 2017), B21 (= RIB 2.3.2434.1)

KEY EVENT

The Battle of Mons Graupius

Date: AD 83

Victorious side: Romans under Agricola

Losing side: The Caledonians under Calgacus

A victory over a similar number of Britons by the auxiliary units, with the legionaries held back in reserve, under the leadership of Agricola in an unknown territory in north-west Scotland. It was the final battle against the Caledonians and a resounding victory for the Romans.

Study question
What are the difficulties in using Tacitus, *Agricola* to understand the major events in Britain from AD 78 to 84?

a significant number of forts in the area above the Forth, possibly garrisoned to protect against another battle. Tacitus claims that due to the end of the campaigning season, Agricola decided to abandon any further plans, being satisfied, we assume, that he had achieved his aim of the complete conquest of Britain. Agricola was removed as governor of Britain in AD 84 due to the apparent envy of Domitian and any further operations were suspended until the new governor arrived.

> Agricola, meanwhile, had handed over the province to his successor in a state of peace and security.
>
> Tacitus, *Agricola* 40

Study question
What are the strengths and weakness of Tacitus as a source on the governorship of Agricola?

KEY INDIVIDUAL

Domitian

Dates: AD 51–96

Roman emperor

The last of the Flavian emperors and son of Vespasian. Popular with the people but despised by the Senate, he was assassinated in AD 96 in his palace in a conspiracy. He is almost exclusively criticised and condemned by the sources.

TOPIC REVIEW

- Review the factors that may have influenced the decision by Claudius to invade Britain in AD 43.
- Discuss why the Romans were so successful at defeating the Britons during the early conquest period.
- Explain how Roman policy towards Britain changed after AD 61.
- Analyse the significance of the achievements of Agricola as governor of Britain.

Further Reading

Hill, S. and Ireland, S. (1996), *Roman Britain*, Bristol: Bristol Classical Press.
Ireland, S. (1996), *Roman Britain, A Sourcebook*, Abingdon: Routledge.
Maxfield, V. A. and Dobson, B (1995), *Inscriptions of Roman Britain*, LACTOR 4, London: KCL.
Rathbone, D. and Rathbone, Y. (2012), *Literary Sources for Roman Britain*, LACTOR 4, London: KCL.
Salway, P. (ed.) (2002), *The Roman Era*, Oxford: Oxford University Press.

PRACTICE QUESTIONS

1. 'Agricola achieved more than other governors in Britain.' How far do you agree with this statement?

   You must use and analyse the ancient sources you have studied as well as your own knowledge to support your answer. [36]

4.2 Frontier Policy: Consolidation and Retrenchment AD 85–c. 128

This topic will focus on the period after the campaigns of Agricola up to and including the building of Hadrian's Wall. There is very little literary evidence to reconstruct precisely the reasons why the Romans decided to abandon Scotland and demark the limits of the province with Hadrian's Wall. We rely almost exclusively on archaeology, which reveals the various changes to frontier policy AD 85–c. 128. We then have to deduce the motivation of these changes in policy by what was most likely, but by no means most certain.

Title: *Agricola; Histories*

Author: Tacitus

Prescribed sections:
Agricola 23;
Histories 1.2

Read it here: *Tacitus: Agricola and Germania*, trans. H. Mattingley (Harmondsworth: Penguin, 1948); LACTOR 11: *Literary Sources for Roman Britain* (4th edn; London: KCL, 2012)

THE CHANGES TO FRONTIER POLICY AFTER *AGRICOLA'S* GOVERNORSHIP INCLUDING RETRENCHMENT

The written sources for the period AD 85–*c.* 128 are virtually non-existent. Even the building of Hadrian's Wall merits only one sentence in the literary record. Therefore, we have to rely almost exclusively on archaeological remains. We must judge what was probable rather than what was definite. **Tacitus**, *Agricola* 23 **PS** did tell us that the Forth–Clyde line seemed to some an appropriate place to halt the expansion. However, as we have seen, Agricola's conquest of Caledonia and the circumnavigation afterwards implies that full conquest of Britain was the aim.

The most exact proof of this came in the building of a full legionary fortress (although it was quickly abandoned) for the Twentieth Legion Valeria Victrix at Inchtuthil **PS**, north of the river Tay, supported by auxiliary forts further north; the obscure Sallustius Lucullus' attempt to close off the glens in the highlands.

PRESCRIBED SOURCE

Inchtuthil fort (Figure 4.9)

Built: *c.* 82

Location: North of the river Tay in Scotland

Significance: Short-lived fortress at the northern limit of Roman expansion in Britain

PRESCRIBED SOURCE

Title: *Domitian* from *The Twelve Caesars*

Author: Suetonius

Date: Late first/early second century AD

Genre: Biography

Significance: Important source about Julius Caesar and the first eleven emperors

Prescribed section: 12.1

Read it here: *Suetonius: The Twelve Caesars,* trans. R. Graves (Harmondsworth: Penguin, 1957)

Tacitus' *Histories* 1.2 **PS** state that Britain was completely conquered and immediately let go. We must assess why there was such swift retrenchment after so much effort to control the highlands. Perhaps the answer lies in profitability. Suetonius, *Domitian* 12.1 **PS** refers to the emperor's financial constraints resulting in reducing the number of troops across the Empire. Perhaps the idea of controlling the highlands of Caledonia seemed unnecessarily unprofitable to Domitian. In addition, urban settlements were expanding in the south-east, and London was becoming a fitting capital of the province.

Also, *Agricola* or Domitian may have been motivated by the same desire for personal glory which galvanised Claudius to launch the initial invasion. However, the occupation of the whole of Britain would be impractical and unprofitable. In addition, there were problems elsewhere in the empire. Shortly after *Agricola's* departure as governor of Britain in *c.* AD 87, the Second Legion Adiutrix was withdrawn from Britain and sent to Moesia (modern-day Romania) to assist with the First Dacian War. Henceforth only three legions would occupy the province. It was logical and probably necessary to keep

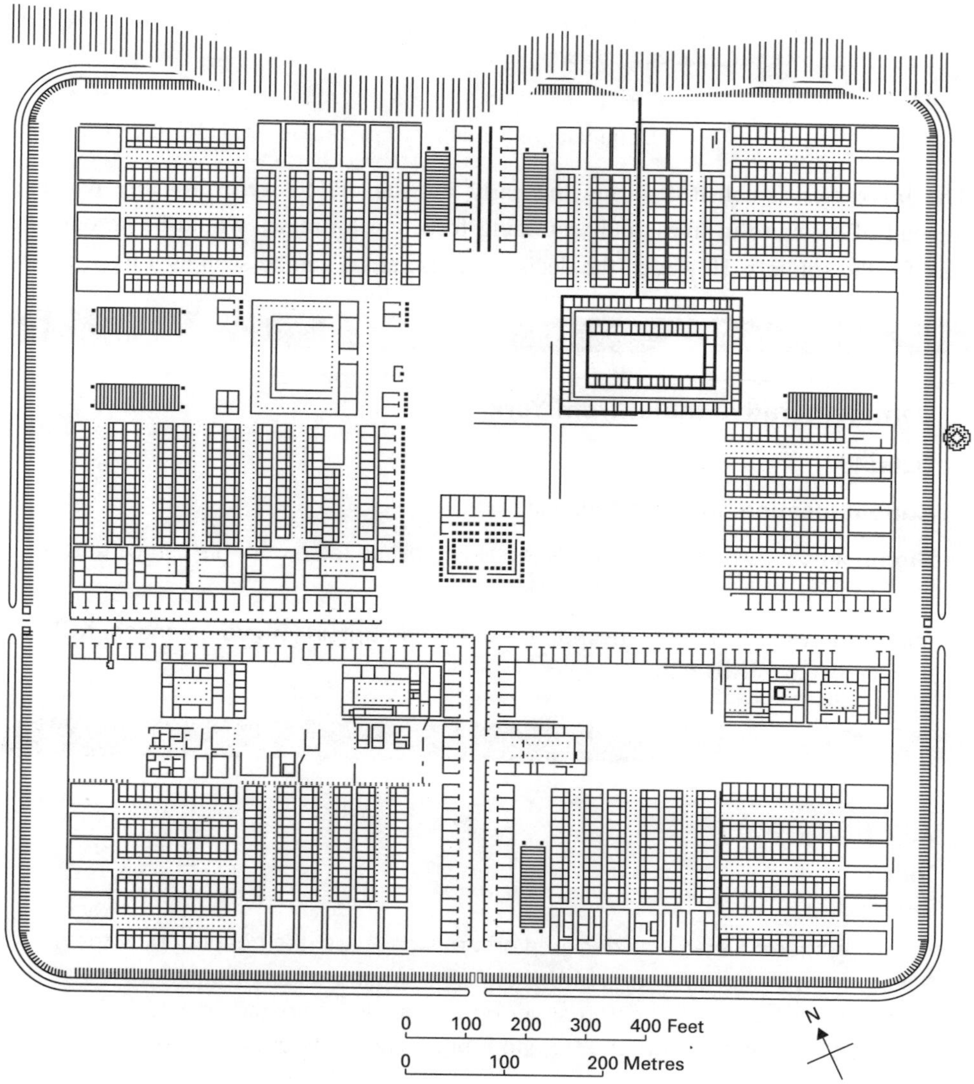

FIGURE 4.9
Plan of Inchtuthil. **PS**

control over the still recently subjugated Welsh tribes and Brigantia. Therefore the twentieth Legion Valeria Victrix was moved to Chester to replace the Second Legion Adiutrix, Inchtuthil and the glen forts were abandoned and destroyed.

By the start of the second century AD, the large lowland forts of Dalswinton and Newstead had been reconstructed and enlarged to house detachments of the legions and auxiliary cavalry. This shows that the territory immediately south of the Forth–Clyde line had far from been abandoned.

A new emperor in AD 98, Trajan, decided to make the legionary fortresses at Caerleon, York and Chester permanent using stone rather than timber structures.

> For the Emperor Caesar Nerva Trajan Augustus, son of the deified Nerva, conqueror of Germany, high priest, with tribunician power, father of the country, consul for the third time, the Second Legion Augusta (erected this)
>
> Caerleon stone of Trajan (LACTOR 4, C1)

> The Emperor Caesar Nerva Trajan Augustus, son of the deified Nerva, conqueror of Germany, conqueror of Dacia, pontifex maximus, in his twelfth year of tribunician power, acclaimed imperator seven times, consul five times, father of the country, by the Ninth Legion Hispana.
>
> Commemorative tablet from York (LACTOR 4, C2)

fortress legions are housed in legionary fortresses, large enough for 5,000 soldiers

The **fortresses** established during the early Flavian period were probably reaching the end of their useful lives, and rebuilding forts and fortresses would be an ongoing task for the soldiers. However, the decision to use stone can be seen as a fixed policy

KEY INDIVIDUAL

Trajan
Dates: AD 53–117

Roman emperor. Trajan was declared optimus princeps (the best ruler) by the Senate from the earliest parts of his reign. He is admired as an excellent administrator and military commander by almost all the sources including Tacitus. At the end of Trajan's reign, the Roman Empire was at its greatest size.

to concentrate the legionary forces in the territories subdued in the late 70s, campaigning was over and the soldiers would act as a permanent garrison.

THE STANEGATE ROAD SYSTEM

The Stanegate road which ran from Carlisle to Corbridge (Coria) could be seen as the first '**frontier**' of the post-*Agricola* period. The road itself was built during the *Agricola* push northwards with the fort at Corbridge acting as a supply base for the Scottish campaign. This fort was burnt along with several others below the Forth–Clyde line including Newstead and Dalswinton.

It is unclear whether these forts were attacked and then there was a conscious withdrawal to the Stanegate line, or whether they were abandoned and destroyed by the Romans, with the withdrawal to the Stanegate line premeditated. A Vindolanda tablet 2.291 (PS) from this period shows that the wife of the commander at the fort at Briga (location unknown) invited her sister (the wife of another commanding officer) to celebrate her birthday with her. This implies that this period may have been quite stable and certainly safe enough for the commanders' wives to be travelling to visit one another.

We know very little about the operations of the Stanegate frontier system, but we can deduce that the Agricolan Stanegate had forts at approximately one day's march apart. Around the turn of the second century AD, forts at Haltwhistle Burn and Throp were added to reduce the marching time between the central forts to around half a day. One such fort was Vindolanda, an **auxiliary** fort first for the first cohort of Tungrians (Belgic Gauls) and

> **frontier** a political or geographical boundary. Roman frontiers denote the edge of the Roman Empire

> **auxiliaries** soldiers who fought in the Roman army but were not Roman citizens. They formed the cavalry and light infantry, and were used as specialist fighters. They were always posted away from their own country

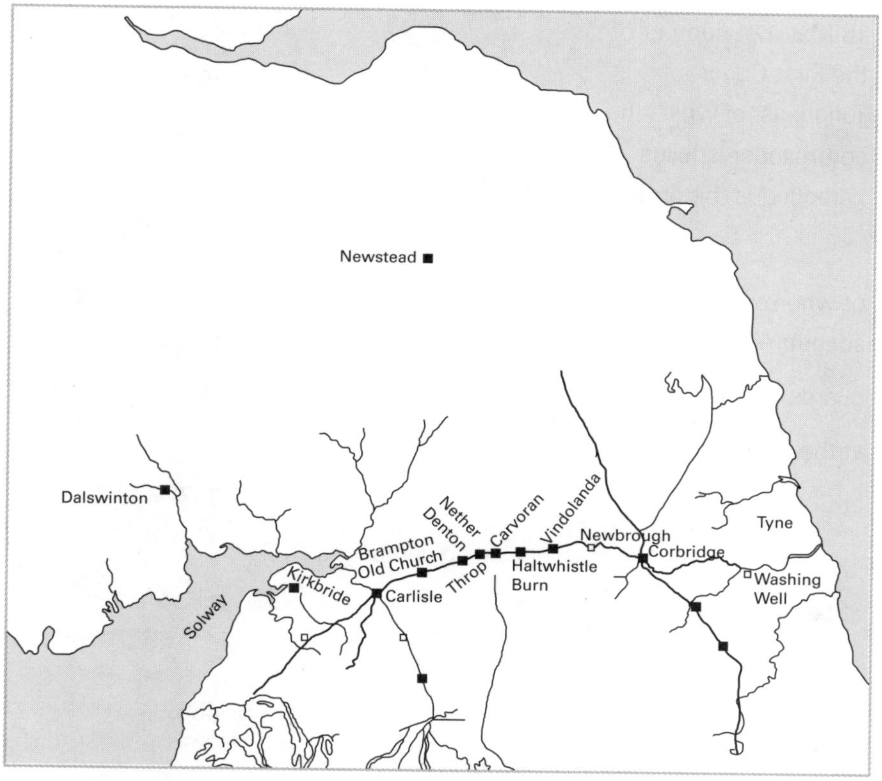

FIGURE 4.10
The Stanegate line and its forts, and the Scottish lowlands.

Study question
What were the strengths and weaknesses of the Stanegate line as a potential permanent frontier?

Vindolanda tablet: Invitation to a birthday party

Date: *c*. AD 100

Original location: Vindolanda

Current location: British Museum

Significance: The invitation to travel to celebrate a birthday indicates that the region was relatively peaceful at the time

View it here: LACTOR 4: Inscriptions of Roman Britain (5th edn; London: KCL, 2017), G10 (= Tab. Vindol 2.291)

Vindolanda tablet: Military strength report

Date: AD 90s

Original location: Vindolanda

Current location: British Museum

Significance: Unique evidence for the numbers of different soldiers at the fort

View it here: LACTOR 4: Inscriptions of Roman Britain (5th edn; London: KCL, 2017), G4 (= Tab. Vindol 2.154)

secondly the ninth cohort of Batavians (Germanic tribe). We can be more certain about the early Vindolanda compared to virtual anything else in Trajanic Britain due to the discovery, in the 1970s, of writing tablets among other artefacts. These were preserved due to the anaerobic conditions caused by the demolition and rebuild of several wooden forts (the clay put down when rebuilding the new fort created a layer preventing oxygen decaying the materials). Over 700 have been discovered and translated already, one of which gives us insight into the occupation of this fort on the Stanegate (see table below **PS**).

18 May, net number of the First Cohort of Tungrians, of which the commander is Iulius Verecundus the prefect,		752
	including centurions 6,	
of whom there are absent:		
guards of the governor		46
at the office of Ferox		
at Coria		337
	including centurions (?) 2	
at London	centurion	1
...		
total absentees		456
	including centurions 5	

remainder present	296
including centurion 1	
from these:	
sick	15
wounded	6
suffering from inflammation of the eyes	10
total of these	31
remainder, fit for active service	265
including centurion 1	

PRESCRIBED SOURCE

Site of Vindolanda (Figure 4.11)

Built: Late first century to early second century AD

Location: Just south of Hadrian's Wall, on the Stanegate road, a line of defence across northern Britain

Significance: Key defensive fort; important archaeological evidence in the form of the Vindolanda tablets has been found here

Find out more here: www.vindolanda.com

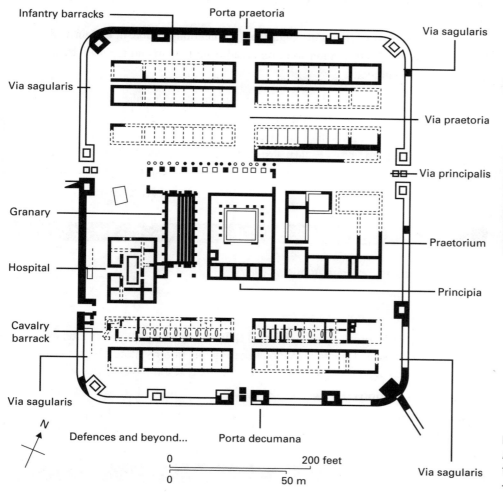

FIGURE 4.11
A plan of the earliest fort at Vindolanda.

EXPLORE FURTHER

The website vindolanda.csad.ox.ac.uk has useful information and images of the Vindolanda tablets that you will study.

The first cohort of an auxiliary unit was normally 800 strong, but there were only 752, and six not ten centurions. The sheer number of absentees illustrates that there was probably limited threat of attack during this period, vindicating the withdrawal of Trajan from the Forth–Clyde line to the Stanegate; in any case, 337 were in Corbridge so were not too far away if needed.

It would be wrong to see Trajan's policy in Britain as reflecting his overall attitude to expansion in the Empire. At the end of Trajan's reign, the empire would be at its largest due to recent conquests of Dacia and Mesopotamia. But the withdrawal first by Domitian to the Forth–Clyde line and then by Trajan to the Tyne–Solway line was caused by prudence in letting go territory impossible to control due to a lack of man power with the removal of troops. The three legions would control the north of England and Wales, and the auxiliary troops would man the frontier line.

HADRIAN'S WALL: ITS HISTORY, FEATURES AND FUNCTIONS

Hadrian, Trajan's successor in AD 117, would establish a permanent frontier in Britain in the form of an impressive wall, eventually built in stone running 80 Roman miles across the Tyne–Solway isthmus.

The SHA (Scriptores Historiae Augustae) **PS** mentions trouble in Britain at about the same time that the Ninth Legion were removed from Britain and replaced by the Sixth Legion Victrix Pia Fidelis.

> When he became emperor, Hadrian at once reverted to an earlier policy and concentrated on maintaining peace throughout the world; for a while those nations which had been subdued by Trajan were rebelling, the Moors also were making attacks, the Sarmatians were waging war, the Britons could not be kept under Roman control, Egypt was hard pressed by revolts, and Libya and Palestine were showing an eagerness for rebellion.
>
> SHA 5.1–2 (LACTOR 11, p. 59)

PS

PRESCRIBED SOURCE

Inscription on the tombstone of Titus Pontius Sabinus

Date: *c.* AD 119

Location: Farrentinum, Italy

Significance: Shows the large number of troops needed in Britain at the start of Hadrian's reign

View it here: LACTOR 4: Inscriptions of Roman Britain (5th edn; London: KCL, 2017), C19 (= ILS 2726)

We are told that the Britons could not be kept under Roman control, but no other evidence can illuminate the nature of the hostilities in Britain at the start of Hadrian's reign. The very detailed career inscription on the tombstone of Titus Pontius Sabinus (PS) states that Sabinus was in command of detachments of 1,000 men from three legions during the British expedition, indicating that the troubles were severe enough to warrant a considerable military response from the emperor. Perhaps the removal of the Ninth Legion could have been as a result of the situation in Britain. The earliest recording of the Sixth Legion Victrix Pia Fidelis is on a pair of altars (PS) set up at a shrine across one of the Tyne bridges. Whatever the meaning of the SHA, Hadrian brought about a successful conclusion to the troubles relatively quickly, as can be seen by coins commissioned in AD 119 and another to commemorate his victories at the end of his reign (see Fig 4.12 (PS)).

PRESCRIBED SOURCE

As of Hadrian (Figure 4.12)

Date: AD 119

Material: Bronze

Obverse: Bust of Hadrian, laureate; IMP CAESAR TRAIANVS HADRIANVS AVG (Imperator Trajan Hadrian Augustus)

Reverse: Britannia seated and holding sceptre, with large shield right; PONT MAX TR POT COS III S C BRITANNIA (pontifex maximus, holding tribunician power, three times consul)

Significance: Commemorates the swiftness of Hadrian's campaign in Britain

View it here: LACTOR 4: Inscriptions of Roman Britain (5th edn; London: KCL, 2017), C4 (= RIC Hadrian 577a)

FIGURE 4.12
As of Hadrian.

KEY INDIVIDUAL

Hadrian

Dates: AD 76–138

Roman emperor. Successor to Trajan who conducted a comprehensive tour of the provinces during his reign. Gave up territory won by Trajan and looked to demark the limits of the empire with frontier systems in Britain, Germany and North Africa.

The SHA is the only source that tells us that Hadrian ordered the building of the Wall. The text tells us that in AD 121 or 122, Hadrian himself visited the province along with a new governor Aulus Platorius Nepos who would have coordinated the building of the wall; we know from inscriptions that the legionary soldiers were the builders:

> So, having reformed the army in an excellent manner, he set out for Britain. There he put right many abuses and was the first to build a wall, eighty miles long, to separate the barbarians and the Romans.
>
> SHA 11.2 (LACTOR 11, p. 59)

PS

> (In honour of) the emperor Caesar Trajan Hadrian Augustus, the Second Legion Augusta (built this) under Aulus Platorius Nepos, governor.
>
> Milecastle 38 building inscription (LACTOR 4, C7)

PS

The wall was begun at Newcastle running westwards to Bowness on Solway with eighty milecastles with turrets every third of a mile. Where possible, a ditch was dug to the north of the wall unless the natural features of the terrain provided a more appropriate barrier, such as steep cliffs. The original wall contained no forts, as the main bases for the troops would still be slightly south on the Stanegate forts.

turret a small watch tower appearing every third of a Roman mile

The **turret** at Peel Gap only has a vantage point southwards and is directly above Vindolanda, implying that the original wall had signalling towers to the forts on the Stanegate. The curtain wall itself was built in stone from Newcastle to the crossing of the River Irthing with the remaining 30 miles or so to the west built of turf. Archaeology has

PRESCRIBED SOURCE

Milecastle 38 building inscription

Date: c. AD 122–6

Original location: Hotbank milecastle

Current location: Great North Museum

Significance: Evidence for the building of Hadrian's Wall

View it here: LACTOR 4: Inscriptions of Roman Britain (5th edn; London: KCL, 2017), C7 (= RIB 1638)

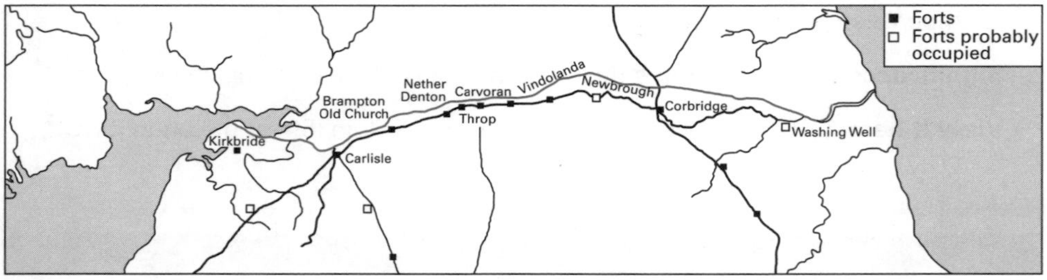

■ Forts
□ Forts probably occupied
Kirkbride
Carlisle
Brampton Old Church
Nether Denton
Throp
Carvoran
Vindolanda
Newbrough
Corbridge
Washing Well

FIGURE 4.13
Hadrian's Wall as originally planned with forts on the Stanegate line.

shown the original foundations were 10 ft wide commonly known as '**broad wall**' but this plan was abandoned and a **narrower wall** of between 6 and 8 ft, possibly due to scarce resources or the need to increase the speed of the building of the wall. It is clear from the narrower gauge of the curtain wall that the **milecastles** and turrets were built earlier as the wall was interwoven to link the constructions. Archaeology can give us a reasonably accurate schedule of the order of the main features of the early Hadrian's Wall. Hadrian's new frontier progressed in this way up until about AD 125, where we can see that forts were added to the wall itself. An inscription from Halton Chesters shows that Nepos and the Sixth Legion Victrix Pia Fidelis were building forts on the wall around three years after the initial foundations were laid.

> For the emperor Caesar Trajan Hadrian Augustus, the Sixth Legion Victrix Pia Fidelis (built this) under Aulus Platorius Nepos, governor.
>
> Halton Chesters dedication (LACTOR 4, C8)

PS

> **broad wall** the foundations for the earliest designs of the wall, 10 ft thick
>
> **narrow wall** the parts of the Wall which have narrower foundations
>
> **milecastle** a small fort every Roman mile for the length of the Wall, large enough for about ten soldiers on sentry duty from a nearby fort. Gateways to the north and south. They run right to left numbers one to eighty

Archaeology shows that the forts at Housesteads, Chesters and Birdoswald were built on existing turrets from the old system. They show that there had been a change of policy on how the frontier system would be manned, as some of the forts on the Stanegate were abandoned about this time. The earlier forts on Hadrian's Wall, however, were built astride the curtain wall in a very offensive position, with three of the four gates built to the north. But this was changed, as we can see from an inscription at Great Chesters which can be dated after AD 128, as Hadrian is referred to as Pater Patriae (Father of the Country), a title not received until then. This fort was built behind the curtain wall in a defensive position.

It was around this time that the impressive **vallum** ditch was added to the south of the wall. The vallum was a huge defensive structure, flat bottomed and deviated between the forts, showing that it was added later on. It was 20 ft wide and 10 ft deep, with mounds on either side. It was situated about half a mile from Hadrian's Wall, creating a sort of military zone to the south of the frontier. The number of crossing points was vastly reduced from every Roman mile to simply the twelve forts, filling in the vallum to access the forts themselves, implying a closed frontier system. Later on, more forts were added

> **vallum** the flat-bottomed ditch running south of the Wall with earth mounds either side. It appears to demark a military zone for the soldiers

FIGURE 4.14
A reconstruction of a milecastle at Cawfields.

PRESCRIBED SOURCE

Halton Chesters dedication slab

Date: *c.* AD 122–125

Original location: Halton Chesters fort

Current location: Great North Museum

Significance: Evidence for ongoing building of forts on Hadrian's Wall

View it here: LACTOR 4: Inscriptions of Roman Britain (5th edn; London: KCL, 2017), C8 (= RIB 1427)

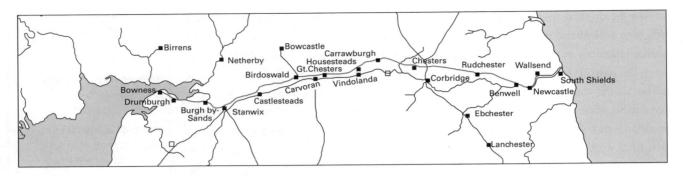

FIGURE 4.15
The forts added to Hadrian's Wall.

such as Carrawburgh which was built over the line of the vallum, implying that the vallum had fallen into disuse relatively soon.

Other changes during the late AD 120s are the extension of the narrow wall by approximately 4 miles from Newcastle to Wallsend and the rebuilding of the western part of the wall from turf to stone. It is unclear why the part of the wall west of the River Irthing had been built in a different material from the eastern part originally. There may have been a lack of good building stone in that part of Cumbria and turf and timber would have been the more usual construction material anyway. Certainly this part of the wall would have been the quickest and cheapest to construct, and the presence of three outpost forts to the north of this segment of the wall could imply a threat from the north in the early period of the frontier system.

The purpose of the wall is hard to define, and although archaeology allows us to see the many modifications made over a relatively short period of time to the frontier, most of the changes still require guesswork. It seems that the frontier system was a work in progress whose focus appeared to shift from offensive to defensive in its design. The SHA tells us that the purpose was to separate the barbarians and the Romans. However, the wall was built with so many gateways that it would be more obvious to see the

FIGURE 4.16
Sestertius of Hadrian.

PRESCRIBED SOURCE

Sestertius of Hadrian (Figure 4.16)

Date: *c.* AD 134–138

Material: Brass

Obverse: Bust of Hadrian wearing a laurel-wreath; Hadrian Augustus, three times consul, father of the country

Reverse: Britannia seated with right foot resting on a rock, with a shield beside her

Significance: Evidence for Hadrian's campaign in Britain

View it here: RIC Hadrian 845

Main Features

S   Marginal mound
    [intermittent]

South Mound

Vallum

North Mound

Wall

Military Way

Postholes

Ditch

N

structure as creating a controlled military zone which monitored movement and possibly trade from one side to another.

We also know that the wall was built by detachments of the three legions but was manned by the auxiliary units, as many inscriptions testify to the men who manned this outpost of the empire. Hadrian's sestertius of *c.* AD 134 **PS** shows that he felt that he had vanquished Britannia and had demarked the line between the Tyne and Solway as the obvious place to cease expansion.

The wall itself is imposing (73 miles long, 15 ft high and 8–10 ft wide) and a true statement to the huge Brigantes tribe, whose settlements show very little Romanisation compared with elsewhere in the province throughout the second century AD. The wall at least prevented any contact between the Brigantes and the tribes of lowland Scotland, who themselves were probably causing problems for the Romans well into the 120s AD. This may be what the SHA referred to with its comment about separation.

> **military way** the road running south of the Wall, which allowed the soldiers to transport goods and information to forts quickly

TOPIC REVIEW

- Review the changes made to frontier policy after Agricola's governorship.
- Discuss the reasons why Hadrian decided to build a permanent frontier.
- Assess the design of Hadrian's wall and what it can tell us about its purpose.

Further Reading

Birley, A.R. (1999), *Tacitus' Agricola and Germany*, Oxford: Oxford University Press.
Breeze, D.J. (2007), *Roman Frontiers in Britain*, London: Duckworth Publishing.
Crow, J. (2004), *Housesteads: A Fort and Garrison on Hadrian's Wall*, Stroud: NPI Media Group.
Johnson, S. (1989), *English Heritage Book of Hadrian's Wall*, London: Batsford.FIGURE 4.8
Bronze coin of Cunobelinus.

PRACTICE QUESTIONS

1. According to the evidence, what was the purpose of Hadrian's Wall?

You must use and analyse the ancient sources you have studied as well as your own knowledge to support your answer.

[36]

4.3 Resistance to Roman Rule

- The reasons for British resistance to Roman invasion and rule
- The nature of the resistance and its effectiveness
- The role of Caratacus against Plautius and Ostorius
- The reasons for the Boudiccan Revolt
- The consequences of Boudicca's actions and the impact of the revolt on Roman policy
- Unrest in Brigantia under Venutius
- The role of Calgacus against Agricola
- The presentation of British leaders by Roman writers: the construct of the noble savage and primitive barbarian

The prescribed sources for this topic are:

- Dio Cassius, *Roman History*, 60.21.1–5, 62.1.1–3.4, 62.7.1–9.2, 62.12.1–6
- Suetonius, *Nero*, 39.1
- Suetonius, *Vespasian* 4.1–2
- Tacitus, *Agricola* 14, 17, 30–2, 37
- Tacitus, *Annals* 12.31, 33–40; 14. 31–8
- Tacitus, *Histories* 3.45

This topic will focus on the extent to which the Britons managed to oppose the Roman invasion effectively. There will be assessments of the nature of the resistance of Caratacus, Boudicca and Calgacus, and the literary creations of these antagonists.

THE NATURE AND EFFECTIVENESS OF BRITISH RESISTANCE TO ROMAN INVASION AND RULE

In common with any other people or nation, the Britons did not like being invaded and conquered. Caesar tells us of concerted British resistance from the tribes in the south-east led by Cassivellaunus, leader of the Catuvellauni, against the Romans in 54 BC. He makes it clear that the Britons, although tactically inferior and with very limited resources, were able to take advantage of their superior knowledge of the terrain and deploy their greater numbers effectively.

The literary sources tend to focus on the British leaders themselves rather than the tribes. Caratacus (Tacitus, *Annals* 12.37 **PS**), Boudicca (Tacitus, *Annals* 14.35 **PS** and Dio, 62.3.1) and Calgacus (Tacitus, *Agricola* 30–2) all come to life in the various narratives. They are often described in precise physical detail, and either motivating their troops or criticising Roman rule in complex and rhetorically brilliant speeches used by the authors as literary set pieces.

The initial invasion would have been bloody. The sources focus on the tactical superiority of the Romans in overcoming the British guerrilla attacks. Remember that the fragment from Claudius' arch refers to 'conquering without loss' (see p. 236). Although it is appropriate to feature such hyperbole on two triumphal arches, one in Rome and one in Gaul, the victory in the south of the island seemed to be relatively quick and decisive.

Dio tells us that the auxiliary troops swam in full armour across the River Medway in Kent and cut down the British chariot-horses. Furthermore, Vespasian and his brother Sabinus won renown in the early battles. Using German auxiliaries, they routed the Britons at the Thames where Togodumnus, one of the two leaders of the British resistance,

---

PRESCRIBED SOURCE

Title: *Agricola; Annals; Histories*

Author: Tacitus

Genre: History, eulogy

Prescribed sections: *Agricola* 14, 17, 30–2, 37; *Annals* 12.31, 33–40; 14. 31–8; *Histories* 3.45

Read it here: *Tacitus: Agricola and Germania*, trans. H. Mattingley (Harmondsworth: Penguin, 1948); LACTOR 11: *Literary Sources for Roman Britain* (4th edn; London: KCL, 2012)

PRESCRIBED SOURCE

Title: *Roman History*

Author: Dio Cassius

Prescribed sections: 60.21.1–5, 62.1.1–62.3.4, 62.7.1–62.9.2, 62.12.1–62.12.6

Read it here: LACTOR 11: *Literary Sources for Roman Britain* (4th edn; London: KCL, 2012)

---

was killed. However, Dio tells us that the death of Togodumnus actually spurred on the natives to resist the invading force with greater determination:

> Because of this, and because even though Togodumnus had perished, the Britons, far from yielding, had united all the more firmly to avenge him; Plautius was afraid to advance further. He proceeded to consolidate what he had gained, and sent for Claudius.

Dio, 60.21.1 (LACTOR 11, p. 39)

Claudius' arrival seems more theatrical than practical (see Dio 60.21.1–5 **PS**). Either way, he concluded affairs within sixteen days and left Plautius with most of Hertfordshire and Essex under Roman control. Suetonius, *Vespasian* 4.1–2 **PS** tells us that Vespasian defeated the Britons thirty times during the early conquest, defeated two tribes (most probably the Durotriges and Dumnonii) and captured more than twenty oppida. Archaeology at Maiden Castle, a hill fort in Dorset, is illuminating in the context of Suetonius' remarks: skeletons with damage indicating violent death have been found that are argued to be the result of Roman attack, though this is disputed.

The scenes at Maiden Castle and elsewhere serve as a clear reminder about the efficiency and brutality of the Roman Army. The Britons themselves had no such thing as a standing army. As we saw in the time of Caesar and during the early months of the Claudian Invasion, the Britons fought in a confederacy of various tribes led by the most warlike leaders. However, as many tribes chose to surrender quickly to the Romans, maybe some preferred the idea of Roman rule and security to Catuvellaunian domination.

Roman and Greek authors constantly mention chariot fighting, but evidence indicates that the chariots were used to carry additional troops in and out of the action or to launch missiles when necessary. They would have been no match for the Roman auxiliary cavalry. It was more likely too that chariot use was confined to the lowlands and used by the nobility, as chariots were expensive and a Celtic status symbol of wealth and power.

There was a lack of the training and discipline among the Britons which was synonymous with the Roman Army. This meant that the Britons favoured surprise attacks and then retreats, drawing the Romans into territory that would benefit their tactics. The sources show that the Britons frequently adhered to tactics which were rarely altered as the battle was lost. Archaeology shows us that the Britons also lacked the equipment to face the legionary soldiers. A long sword and minimal armour seemed to be the main weaponry of a Briton, while elaborate shields were used only by the nobility.

Therefore it is no surprise that resistance, although spirited and sustained, to Claudius' initial invasion force was doomed to fail. But it is wrong to assume that all the tribes south of the Fosse Way were obedient to their new rulers. We are told by Dio that Claudius won over some tribes by diplomacy and others by force, and we assume the

---

KEY INDIVIDUAL

Aulus Plautius

Dates: Mid-first century AD

Roman general who was the first governor of Britain in AD 43 and led the early conquest.

PRESCRIBED SOURCE

Title: *Nero* and *Vespasian* from *The Twelve Caesars*

Author: Suetonius

Prescribed sections: *Nero*, 39.1; *Vespasian* 4.1–4.2

Read it here: LACTOR 11: *Literary Sources for Roman Britain* (4th edn; London: KCL, 2012)

S & C Study what we can learn about the Romans' relationships with the British elite before AD 43 from the finds at Silchester **PS**, Colchester Castle museum and Verulamium museum.

Iceni tribe of Suffolk and Norfolk, which started a rebellion in AD 47, must have been among them.

By AD 47 it was clear that the Claudian invasion force had been briefed to turn Britain into a province. There would be no repeat of Caesar's expeditions of 55 and 54 BC. The Romans were here to stay. But when Aulus Plautius left the island, there was another guerrilla attack on the Roman troops:

> In Britain the propraetor, Publius Ostorius, was faced with a chaotic situation. The enemy had poured into our allies' territory all the more violently because they thought that a new commander, with an unfamiliar army and winter coming on, would not confront them.
>
> Tacitus, *Annals* 12.31 (LACTOR 11, p. 41)

The new governor, Publius Ostorius Scapula, was decisive but his actions alienated even those tribes which had recently been subdued. Tacitus tells us that Scapula disarmed the tribes already conquered and set about consolidating the territory south of the Fosse Way. The Iceni rebelled (not for the last time) in AD 48. It appears that the tribes who had submitted to the Romans under Plautius resented being exposed by the removal of their weaponry. Almost constant warfare between neighbouring tribes would have required the Iceni to be ready for battle at all times, and now they must have felt very vulnerable. Although the rebellion was short-lived, it may have been the beginning of a deeply held hostility against Roman rule which would manifest itself with disastrous consequences a little over a decade later.

We get very little detail about the first Iceni rebellion from Tacitus. The location could have been a hillfort in Cambridgeshire, perhaps Stonea Camp, where bodies have been discovered which had met a violent end. We do, however, get the usual battle narrative of Roman organisation versus British resistance based on use of terrain and superior numbers (*Annals* 12.31 **PS**).

Tacitus mentions more resistance against the Romans from the Brigantes during AD 49. However, absolutely no detail whatsoever is given by the historian. He states that those who had taken up arms were killed and the rest of the tribe settled. The relationship between Rome and Brigantia would be most unstable during the early conquest. Although other Brigantian revolts are much better documented, the severity of this first rebellion can be gauged from Tacitus' comment that Scapula postponed his planned attack on the Welsh tribes in order to focus on bringing the Brigantes into order.

> **KEY INDIVIDUAL**
>
> **Publius Ostorius Scapula**
> **Dates:** Died AD 52
>
> Second governor of Britain who continued the campaign there and succeeded in defeating Caratacus.

CARATACUS

The conquest of Britain until about AD 50 was relatively smooth. Tribes had either submitted and accepted Roman rule or, in opposing it, had been destroyed. As we have seen, even the occasional revolt had been put down relatively quickly by auxiliary troops without much loss on the Roman side. But the conquest of Wales would be far less straightforward. Caratacus reappears back in the narrative (Tacitus, *Annals* 12.33–5 **PS**), but this time as a leader of a Welsh confederacy comprising the Silures and Ordovices tribes. The sources give us no account whatsoever of Caratacus' movements between the battle of the Thames in AD 43 and his re-emergence in AD 50. The comment by Tacitus that Caratacus had matched or defeated the Romans in many battles is puzzling, as he seemingly suffered only two defeats before seeking refuge in Siluria.

Tacitus' account of Caratacus' last stand is vivid and memorable.

> When they reached the rampart and were fighting with missiles, the wounds were mainly on our side and quite a number of men were killed; but our men formed a tortoise-shell formation and tore down the rough and loosely built wall, and in the hand-to-hand fighting the armies were evenly matched. The enemy withdrew onto the slopes of the hills. But there too we broke through their lines; the light-armed troops attacked with their spears, the heavy-armed troops advanced in close formation, and the British troops, unprotected as they were by breastplates or helmets, were put to flight before them. If they stood up to the auxiliaries, they fell before the swords and javelins of the legionaries, and if they turned elsewhere they were struck down by the broad swords and spears of the auxiliaries. It was a famous victory; Caratacus' wife and daughter were taken prisoners and his brothers gave themselves up.
>
> Tacitus, *Annals* 12.35 (LACTOR 11, p. 43)

Caratacus' tour of the tribes of Britain ended rather emphatically when he sought refuge from Cartimandua, Queen of the Brigantes. Caratacus may have naively assumed that all Britons were anti-Roman and put his faith in Cartimandua. He probably considered that an alliance with the Brigantes would be too great a force for the Romans to resist due to its size and position north of the territory already conquered. Tacitus describes the moment that Cartimandua betrays Caratacus to the Romans (Tacitus, *Annals* 12.36 **PS**).

The loss of their leader did nothing to quell the enthusiasm of the Silures in their resistance against the Romans. According to Tacitus, they fought even more vigorously. We are told that a camp commander, eight centurions and the best of the legionaries were killed in an ambush on some Roman forces who were building forts and a foraging party, and the cavalry sent to its aid were routed. Eventually, matters descended into perpetual skirmishing:

> After this there were frequent battles, often taking the form of guerrilla warfare among the passes or marshes, brought on variously by chance or valour; these engagements might be spontaneous or planned, for revenge or booty, sometimes in accordance with the orders of an officer and sometimes not.
>
> Tacitus, *Annals* 12.39 (LACTOR 11, p. 45)

The Silures were proving to be rather unconquerable, but they were finally defeated in battle in AD 52 by Scapula's successor, Aulus Didius Gallus. He was a formidable military commander himself, wining much honour in Roman Crimea before embarking upon the governorship of Britain. Between the death of Scapula and the arrival of Gallus, the Silures had registered their greatest victory yet against the Fourteenth Legion Gemina. We only have information from Tacitus about the conclusion of this campaign against the Silures, and his account is brief. We are told that Gallus exaggerated the enormity of the situation to further his reputation and that he merely drove the Silures off upon arrival. In the *Agricola* we have more to go on, but again it involves Tacitus' own interpretation of the ineffectiveness of Gallus' governorship, who 'merely held what his predecessors had won, establishing a few forts in more advanced positions, so that he could claim the credit of having made some annexations' **PS** (Tacitus, *Agricola* 14 [trans. H. Mattingly, rev. S. A. Handford: London: Penguin).

A close reading of Tacitus' account allows us to see that Gallus' approach to dealing with the resistance of the Silures was not only positive but effective. Not only does he gain control of South Wales, but he was most likely responsible for the building of the Legionary Fortress at Usk. If events in Britain had not conspired against him, Gallus might well have finished the conquest of Wales and established Roman control in that part of Britain.

However, Tacitus mentions the resumption of civil hostilities in Brigantia. Again there are more questions than answers in Tacitus' account of the latest problems within the large state. We are told that Venutius, the husband of Cartimandua, had fallen out with her, and she in turn had captured his brother and family. The enemy (as Tacitus calls them) seem to be the anti-Roman faction of the tribe led by Venutius who seemingly opposed the pro-Roman sentiments of the queen whose status as a woman exacerbated the hostilities. Gallus, aware of the strategic disaster in losing Brigantia to Venutius, responded with swift military action, although Tacitus does not give him credit for the victory (*Annals* 12.40 **PS**).

The Welsh campaign resumed in AD 60 under the leadership of Suetonius Paulinus and the events of the next eighteen months are the best documented by the literary record. After the temporary check on Venutius, the Romans focused on bringing the island of Mona (Anglesey, North Wales) under their control. There is little evidence that this attack was designed to eliminate the power and influence of the Druids. It seems more likely that it was just the next step in the conquest of North Wales, especially as we are told that the island was a sanctuary for deserters.

THE BOUDICCAN REBELLION

Dio 62.8.1 **PS** tells us that the Boudiccan rebellion occurred while Suetonius was subjugating the island of Mona. Tacitus tells us that the governor was informed that 'a sudden rebellion' had sprung up in the south of the province. As we have seen, the Iceni tribe in the previous decade had wavered between openly opposing Roman rule and promoting it in the form of a recognised **client kingdom** (see the chapter on Roman Control, p. 281).

Now a full-scale rebellion had broken out with such enthusiasm and support that the parts of the island recently conquered were in serious danger of falling into the hands of the rebels and the status of Britain as a province of the Roman Empire was in grave danger. The capital of Britain up to this point had been at Colchester, with the main financial seat in London; these are the two cities which Suetonius, *Nero* 39.1 **PS** mentions as being sacked and a large number of their citizens slaughtered. In addition,

> **client kingdoms** pro-Roman tribal areas that were self-governing states but would work in the best interests of the Romans. There were three in Britain: the Iceni (East Anglia), the Brigantes (the North) and the Regni (Sussex)

colonia at Camulodunum
A colony for retired soldiers in Colchester. When the Twentieth Legion was moved to Gloucestershire in AD 49, the Romans converted the Legionary Fortress into a colonia for the veterans

Study question
Why do you think that the Britons regarded the Temple of Claudius at Colchester as 'the stronghold of eternal Roman domination'?

Verulamium (St Albans) was also a strategically important town even by this time, and these three towns would be the focus of Boudicca's wrath. Priorities for the governor were dealing with the rebels and protecting the urban settlements of the south; consequently the campaign against the Welsh was again abandoned.

The cause of the rebellion, according to Tacitus, seemed to be rather specific and personal. It focused on revenge due to the mismanagement of relations with the British nobility rather than a serious attempt to overthrow Roman rule. Tacitus tells us that after the death of Boudicca's husband Prasutagus, the Romans plundered the 'household' and removed property belonging to the Iceni nobility. Boudicca was whipped and her daughters raped. The Trinovantes joined the rebellion quickly as they themselves had been subjected to appalling treatment due to the veterans who occupied the **colonia at Camulodunum** (Colchester).

Tacitus is very clear about the anti-Roman sentiments in East Anglia and makes no attempt whatsoever to sympathise with the Romans in Colchester. He paints them as corrupt, coarse and negligent:

> The soldiers encouraged the lawlessness of the veterans, for their way of behaving was the same, and they looked forward to the same freedom themselves. . . . To destroy the colony seemed no difficult task, as it had no defences; our commanders had paid too little attention to this, thinking more of what was pleasant to look at rather than what the town actually needed.
>
> Tacitus, *Annals* 14.31 (LACTOR 11, p. 48)

Tacitus' account of the rebellion from its causes to conclusion is vivid and detailed, and perhaps we need to treat this version of the rebellion with less caution that the one put forward by Dio who was writing in the early third century AD. This is because of Tacitus' relationship as son-in-law of Agricola, the future governor. Agricola was serving on the staff of the governor in AD 60/61 as Military Tribune and would have been aware of the major events and anti-Roman sentiments of the natives directed at the veterans and the army. So it is perhaps not surprising that Tacitus' account focuses on the resentment caused by the brutality of the Romans, providing a stark contrast to Agricola's fair administration.

Dio's account of the rebellion (of which the prescribed texts include 62.1.1–3.4, 62.7.1–9.2, 62.12.1–6 **PS**) is significantly shorter and far less dramatic than the one put forward by Tacitus. He does not mention Prasutagus' death or the outrages against Boudicca and her daughters. Dio's account paints Suetonius Paulinus as far less of a villain than in Tacitus' version, as he purports that the entire rebellion was the result of financial extortion by the Emperor Nero and his immediate advisors who recalled gifts and loans of money, causing resentment and anger against the Romans.

> But above all the rousing of the Britons, the persuading of them to fight against the Romans, the winning of the leadership and the command throughout the war – this was the work of Buduica (Boudicca), a woman of the British royal family who had uncommon intelligence for a woman.
>
> Dio Cassius, *Roman History* 62.2.2 (LACTOR 11, p. 51)

It is more likely that widespread financial extortion from Rome would have unified the once hostile tribes into working together more than outrages committed against the royal family of one particular tribe. Nonetheless, we expect that the sequence of events in Tacitus' account is more reliable than that in Dio's account and of course the causes as put forward by the two historians can be reconciled as Boudicca almost certainly led the rebellion because it started in Iceni territory after the death of her husband and the cessation of the client kingdom agreement. Similarly the other neighbouring tribes joined forces because of the financial effects of the recalling of the Claudian loans and the general treatment they had been receiving since the colonia at Colchester was established.

The rebellion spread quickly; the rebels were aware of the need for speed as the governor was so far away in Wales. The Romans in Colchester sought refuge in the temple of Claudius, a fitting symbolism as the temple was seen as an emblem of Roman domination over the natives. Tacitus apportions blame for the speed with which Colchester fell into the hands of the rebels to the veterans themselves who neglected to build defensive features due to their indolence and complacency.

> The inhabitants relied on the temple for protection; hampered by those who secretly knew of the rebellion and were confusing their plans, they neither dug a ditch nor built a rampart. Further, the old people and women were not removed, so that only able-bodied men would remain; and when the town was surrounded by a horde of natives it was as if they had been caught unawares in a time of peace.
>
> Tacitus, *Annals* 14.32 (LACTOR 11, p. 48)

The veterans and their families were burnt alive in the temple and the capital of the province fell after a two-day siege. The **procurator** Decianus Catus, who had responded to the revolt by sending just 200 men to combat the rebels, fled to Gaul. Suetonius had sent ahead the Ninth Legion Hispania under its commander Petilius Cerialis from its base at Lincoln in the hope of saving at least London and St Albans. Tacitus, *Annals* 14.33 **PS** tells us that the legion was routed and a large number of legionary soldiers massacred. The procurator who was stationed in London realised the severity of the situation and the likelihood of London falling in the same way as Colchester, and accordingly he fled to Gaul in disgrace.

It seems that the Romans had misread the natives' attitudes to their rule. Claudius' arch refers to the submission of eleven tribes, and the Iceni and the Trinovantes had to be among these. In less than two decades, those willing to accept Roman rule were prepared to fight to the death to destroy it. Even taking into account Tacitus' exaggeration of the events, the behaviour of those in the colonia at Colchester is a microcosm of the mismanagement and arrogance of the Romans more generally in Britain at this time.

Suetonius believed that there was now a genuine risk of losing the whole island, and that he faced political and military ignominy. Just before the final battle, he gave a rousing speech to his own men (Tacitus, *Annals* 14.36 **PS** and Dio.62.9.1–9.2 **PS**), urging them to have confidence even though greatly outnumbered. Tacitus describes the prelude to the final battle focusing on the strengths of both sides, their choice of positions, and emphasising the British expectation of victory (*Annals* 14.34 **PS**).

EXPLORE FURTHER

Outline the different ways that Tacitus and Dio Cassius present the causes of the Boudiccan rebellion. How do you think these differences can be explained?

procurator the financial administrator of a province, of equestrian status, reporting directly to the emperor. In Britain their headquarters was in London, even when Colchester was the capital

KEY INDIVIDUAL

Decianus Catus
Dates: First century AD

Procurator of Roman Britain before the Boudiccan rebellion.

Tacitus, *Annals* 14.37  and Dio 62.12.1–5  give the impression that the battle was brief and one where the heart of the natives would be no match for the tactical acumen of the more experienced Romans. The Romans used javelins and the wedge formation to force the natives (who were superior in numbers) back. The cavalry joined battle quickly and the Britons were either killed or retreated.

The retreat was made difficult by the women and the carts which were on the edge of the battle site. The numbers given by Tacitus were 400 Roman and 80,000 British casualties: this was a comprehensive defeat, especially as Dio.62.8.2  states that Boudicca's army was 230,000 strong; although these numbers are impossible to verify. The fate of Boudicca is different in the two accounts. Tacitus tells us confidently that she poisoned herself, whereas Dio 62.12.6  states that she dies of an illness. The most serious rebellion in Romano-British history was over, yet damage had been done not only to the urban settlements and trade but also to the reputation of the governor. Suetonius was very angry about the events which had robbed him of being proclaimed as the man who had finally managed to complete the full-scale conquest of Wales. The territorial and financial losses weakened the army and – instead of learning the lessons of what caused the rebellion – Suetonius, motivated by pride, was eager for revenge.

> The territory of any tribe which had either wavered in its allegiance, or been openly hostile, was laid waste by fire and sword; but it was famine which caused the natives the greatest hardship, since they had neglected to sow their crops, calling up men of every age to fight, and intending to take over our food supplies for themselves.
>
> Tacitus, *Annals* 14.38 (LACTOR 11, p. 53)

Disagreeing with Suetonius' tactics, the new procurator Julius Classicianus, who had arrived to replace Catus, sent to Rome to ask for Suetonius to be replaced with a new governor who understood how to be sympathetic to the defeated rebels. Classicianus argued that hostilities would not end with Suetonius in command.

CARTIMANDUA AND VENUTIUS

Suetonius eventually lost his position and was replaced by a series of governors to whom Tacitus gives little or no credit. He depicts them as weak and ineffective. As we shall see in the chapter Effects of Roman Rule (p. 292), this period of military inactivity allowed the governors of the 60s time to rebuild the lost cities and repair relations with the locals. The end of Nero's reign and the accession of Vespasian was messy, so Britain received little attention during the period after Boudicca both by the Roman government and the sources.

The governors after Suetonius concentrated on consolidating rather than expansion, and the conquest of Wales was postponed indefinitely. The large Brigantes tribe would remain loyal to Rome so long as Queen Cartimandua kept her position as ruler. However, at about the same time that civil war had ended in Rome and an undisputed emperor had emerged, hostilities broke out again between rival factions in Brigantia. The new governor Vettius Bolanus would have to deal with a situation which could have caused

---

as much damage as the Boudiccan affair did a decade earlier, such was the size and location of the largest tribe in Britain.

The cause of the latest conflict in Brigantia once again stemmed from the marriage of Cartimandua and Venutius, the latter having been shunned for his armour-bearer Vellocatus.

> The power of her house was immediately shaken to its foundations by this outrage. The people of the tribe declared for Venutius: only the passion and the savage temper of the queen supported the adulterer. Venutius therefore summoned his supporters. The Brigantes rallied to him, reducing Cartimandua to the last extremity. She besought Roman protection. Our alae and cohorts fought indecisive battles, but at length rescued the queen from danger. The kingdom went to Venutius; we were left with a war to fight.
>
> Tacitus, *Histories* 3.45 (LACTOR 11, p. 55)

In coming to her aid, the Romans repaid the debt owed to Cartimandua (when she handed over Caratacus almost two decades earlier) and intervened on her behalf.

With Cartimandua removed, the south was no longer protected by the buffer zone of a client kingdom, so Roman policy had to revert to aggression. Vettius Bolanus was replaced by a governor with a more impressive military background and one who had experience of serving in Britain. In AD 71, Petilius Cerialis became governor of Britain and immediately launched a campaign to take control of Brigantia. He moved the Ninth Legion Hispana to York and conquered the Brigantes quickly. We have a very brief account of his exploits in Tacitus, *Agricola* 17 **PS**, with a lack of detail of the final battle.

Tacitus tells us that the accession of Vespasian coincided with a return to expansionism in Britain. After Cerialis and the Ninth Legion Hispana had gained control of Brigantia, Julius Frontinus with the Second Legion Augusta finally brought Wales under Roman control. This event receives no adequate coverage or assessment by the ancient sources, so we have to rely on asides in the Agricola and the archaeology of the fortress in Caerleon to understand the comprehensiveness of the defeat. The period after Boudicca is patchy and Tacitus' comments in this text must always be studied in the context of illuminating the achievements of his father-in-law Agricola.

KEY INDIVIDUAL

Venutius

Dates: First century AD

Husband of Cartimandua. He rebelled against her and took over the rule of the Brigantes after she fled to her Roman allies.

CALGACUS

The most vivid episode in Agricola's northern campaigns is the defeat of the Caledonian leader Calgacus at Mons Graupius in AD 83. Tacitus portrays Calgacus as a figure with the passion and hatred of Boudicca, the magnetism of Venutius and the nobility of Caratacus. He represents the ultimate adversary to Roman rule in Britain, and the location of the battle in the Highlands of Scotland emphasises just how far the Britons have been pushed back to the extremes of Britain.

After a speech by the Caledonian leader and a similar harangue by Agricola, Tacitus begins the narrative of the battle. We are told that the Britons were posted on high ground more to intimidate than anything else. They used chariots like in other battles between the British and the Romans. Tacitus gives specific details about the number of Roman auxiliary infantry and cavalry, but only states that the Romans were greatly outnumbered by Calgacus and the Caledonians. The battle itself began with close combat fighting between the British and the auxiliaries, followed by the cavalry routing the rather ineffective British charioteers. Then Agricola used reserve cavalry late on, which broke the British infantry, and attacked from behind. The battle is described vividly, showing the chaos as the Romans took control due to their natural superiority in pitched battle (Tacitus, *Agricola* 37 **PS**).

Tacitus shows that the resistance of the Caledonians did not amount to much. The numbers, although exaggerated, illustrate that Calgacus and his men were no match for the Romans: 10,000 British were killed compared with 360 Romans. The literary narrative of the conquest of Britain ends with victory at Mons Graupius. Indeed, Tacitus claims that the whole of Britain was completely conquered. It seems that the 20,000 deserters from the battle caused enough alarm for the Romans to begin the permanent occupation of the area with the Legionary Fortress at Inchtuthil. Except for Boudicca, most British resistance took the form of guerrilla attacks on the army foraging for food or in early morning raids on camps. When the army was organised and could face the enemy in pitched battle, there was very rarely a problem and the Romans normally dispatched the natives quite quickly with minimal losses. Calgacus seems more of a literary invention than a real-life adversary. Even in the narrative on Boudicca's rebellion, Tacitus makes it clear that the British victories were more to do with the negligence of the veteran soldiers than the tactical brilliance of the British commander.

Caratacus, Boudicca and Calgacus are all brought to life in the history of Roman Britain by authors who step inside their characters and deliver speeches from their mouths in a stylistic and articulate language, reflecting the probable thoughts and feelings which an oppressed nation may have against their conquerors. There are several speeches including three from Boudicca alone. These speeches are mostly given before the final battle and act as literary set pieces, in the model of Greek historians like Thucydides.

Caratacus is depicted as a noble warrior from the very outset in AD 43. His skill of leadership allows him to be accepted as leader of the Welsh confederacy as he was of his own tribe, the Catuvellauni. The most vivid picture of Caratacus comes from a speech he is reported to have given after his capture in AD 51 in front of Claudius, the Praetorian Guard and the people in Rome. There must have been some record of the event, especially as afterwards we are told that the Senate met to discuss the capture of Caratacus. Tacitus in his position as a senator almost fifty years later would have had access to the 'acta senatus' which detailed the motions put forward and debated in the Senate. Even though the speech itself was a piece of rhetorical style, the general content may be quite accurate. The result of the speech is that Caratacus and his family were pardoned.

The physical appearance of Caratacus emphasises his nobility and standing; he wears decorations and torcs from internal wars from which he had most probably emerged as leader of his tribe. He is unfazed by the situation in Rome and defends his position with words reported by Tacitus that enhance the reputation of the stoical and relentless leader

KEY INDIVIDUAL

Calgacus

Dates: First century AD

Scottish chieftain who opposed Agricola at the battle of Mons Graupius.

of the British resistance to Roman rule, foiled only by trusting the wrong person. Tacitus is able to convey the majesty of the British leader in his attitude to his captors with the words he uses more than his actions:

> If my noble birth and situation in life had been matched by only moderate success, I should have come to this city as a friend rather than a captive, and you would not have scorned to conclude a treaty with one sprung from famous ancestors and holding sway over many nations; my present lot degrades me, just as it brings glory to you. I had horses, men, arms, wealth; is it surprising that I was unwilling to lose them? You may want to rule over all men, but does it follow that all men welcome servitude? But if I had surrendered at once and so become your prisoner, little fame would have attended my fate and your renown would not have shone more brightly; sentence could be passed and everything forgotten; as it is you can preserve my life, and I shall be an example of your mercy for ever.
>
> Tacitus, *Annals* 12.37 (LACTOR 11, p. 44) **PS**

The creation of Boudicca is a complex one. She is portrayed from the beginning of the outset as a noble savage, abused in the most appalling manner by the Romans. Her name is not mentioned once in the narrative of the destruction of the three cities, but as leader she gives the rousing address before the final battle. Dio adopts the exact same literary device in his version of the rebellion, but also includes a physical description of the heroine, either one taken from legend or one made up to fit the occasion (*Roman History*, 62.2.4 **PS**).

Tacitus' speech from the Annals and the one from Dio are roughly equal in length. Tacitus tells us that female commanders were common in Britain and again notes her primitive yet distinguished lineage. She reminds the rebels about the immediate problems of Roman rule with particular emphasis on the physical abuses that the natives are to endure. She tells those gathered about their superior numbers and the necessity to fight for the death. Dio focuses on the notion of freedom versus oppression, and particularly highlights the financial oblivion facing all tribes if the Romans remain. Both speeches seem to reflect their author's view of the causes of the rebellion and have different emphasis on the problems of Roman rule.

> We British are used to women commanders in war. But it is not as the descendant of mighty ancestors that I fight now, avenging lost kingdom and wealth; rather as one of the people, avenging lost liberty, scourging, the violation of my daughters. The lusts of the Romans are gross; they cannot keep their filthy hands from our bodies, not even from the old or chaste. But the gods are at hand with a just revenge; the legion is destroyed which dared to face us in battle; the rest skulk in their camps, or watch for a chance to flee. They will not stand up before the noise and roar of so many thousands, let alone the attack and the hand-to-hand fighting. Think of the number of our troops, think of why you fight — and you must either win on this battlefield or die. That is my resolve, and I am a woman; men may live and be slaves.
>
> Tacitus, *Annals* 14.35 (LACTOR 11, pp. 49–50) **PS**

Experience has taught you the difference between freedom and slavery. Some of you may have been led by your ignorance of which was better, to be taken in by the Romans' tempting promises. But now you have tried both — and you have learned how wrong you were to prefer a foreign tyranny to the way of life followed by your ancestors; you have discovered the difference between freedom in humble circumstances and slavery amidst riches. Have we not suffered every variety of shameful and humiliating treatment from the moment that these people turned their attention to Britain? Have we not been deprived wholesale of our most important possessions, while paying taxes on the rest? Do we not pasture and till all our other property for them and then pay an annual tax on our very lives? How much better it would have been to be traded as slaves once and for all rather than ransom ourselves each year and meaninglessly call ourselves free! How much better to have died by the sword than live and be taxed for it! But why do I speak of death? Not even that is free with them; you know what we pay even for our dead.

Dio Cassius, *Roman History* 62.3.1–4 (LACTOR 11, p. 51)

The speech of Calgacus before Mons Graupius is another good example of the way Roman historians characterised British leaders. Tacitus does say that what he reports is the 'substance' of what Calgacus was reported to have said. Agricola may have been made aware of the preparations for battle from the British side by deserters after Mons Graupius, but its tone is indicative of the way British leaders are characterised. Like the speech of Boudicca, Calgacus reminds his troops that victory against the Romans would mean liberation from slavery. The topography of the battle site and the remoteness of the tribe are emphasised by Calgacus' words, intended by Tacitus to remind readers of how great an achievement Agricola made in defeating such an enemy. Calgacus seems to be aware of the battles of Roman-British history, and reminds his men that they are the most formidable warriors left and superior to all tribes to the south. The Romans believed that civilisation dissipated the further you went away from Rome, and so the Caledonians would prove to be the ultimate test for Agricola and the Roman army. The final words of Calgacus echo the sentiments of Boudicca:

They are the only people on earth to whose covetousness both riches and poverty are equally tempting. To robbery, butchery, and rapine, they give the lying name of 'government'; they create a desolation and call it peace.

Tacitus, *Agricola* 30

In the speech of Calgacus, Tacitus, as in his other speeches, uses his own ideas to create a Roman adversary in an appropriate context. He employs ideas that would be familiar to the Romans, and no doubt Agricola would have cited the remoteness and primitiveness of the Caledonians in describing the significance of his victory. Like the speeches of Boudicca, the speech of Calgacus should be seen as creating a character which befits the narrative.

Despite what Claudius claimed on his arch, there was significant resistance to Roman rule during this period. The resistance took the form of recalcitrant tribes refusing to accept Roman rule, fighting to the death for their liberty, but also as we have seen, tribes

ACTIVITY

Compare and contrast the speeches of Boudicca in the accounts of Tacitus and Dio Cassius.

Study question
Why do Roman and Greek writers use speeches as part of their history?

already subjugated could decide enough was enough and would risk their lives to drive out the Romans from their lands. The writers of the period tended to focus on causes for rebellions and almost always Roman provincial administration was found wanting. Caratacus and Calgacus represent stock leaders of resistance against the Romans, refusing to accept that Wales and Scotland respectively would become part of the empire, leading their men with fanatical speeches and fighting to the end; Boudicca would fight against Roman injustices already apparent in the parts of the province conquered. The writers of the period admired their literary creations and seem at times critical of their own government and officials. The extent to which the writers invent the noble savage or primitive barbarian is debatable; what is clear is that the narrative of the British resistance against Roman rule comes alive due to the words and actions of Caratacus, Boudicca and Calgacus.

TOPIC REVIEW

- Discuss how successfully the Roman invasion of Britain was opposed in AD 43.
- Review the tactics employed by the Britons against the Romans in battle.
- List the causes of the Boudiccan Revolt.
- Discuss how far Roman governance of Britain changed after AD 61.
- Assess how much we can learn from Tacitus about the nature of British resistance against the Romans.

Further Reading

Campbell, D. (2010), *Mons Graupius* AD *83*, Oxford: Osprey Publishing.

Fields, N. (2011), *Boudicca's Rebellion* AD *60–61*, Oxford: Osprey Publishing.

Hobbs R and Jackson R. (2010), *Roman Britain*, London: British Museum Press.

Howarth, N. (2008), *Cartimandua*, Stroud: The History Press.

PRACTICE QUESTIONS

1. Read Tacitus, *Agricola* 37 PS.

How useful is this passage for our understanding of the limitations of the Britons?

[12]

4.4 Roman Control

TOPIC OVERVIEW

- The role and duties of the governor and the procurator in the Roman province
- The effectiveness of these roles in securing and stabilising Roman control
- The reasons for British collaboration with Roman rule
- The use of client rulers (Prasutagus, Cartimandua and Cogidubnus) and its effectiveness
- The role of the Roman Army in dealing with unrest and protecting the province
- The deployment of the army, both legionaries and auxiliaries, within the province
- The army's role in building and patrolling Hadrian's Wall.

The prescribed sources for this topic are:

- Dio Cassius, 62.2.1; 62.12.3–4
- Tacitus, *Agricola* 14, 16–17, 19, 36
- Tacitus, *Annals* 12.32, 14.31–2, 14.38

- An auxiliary standard-bearer
- A beneficiarius at Wroxeter
- Platorius Nepos
- A speculator at London
- Benwell classis Britannica building inscription
- Chichester dedication slab
- Halton Chesters dedication slab
- Julius Classicianus, procurator
- Longinus Sdapeze
- M Favonius Facilis
- Milecastle 38 building inscription
- Silchester baths
- Vindolanda tablet about British cavalry

Governor of Britain a Roman senator appointed by the emperor in Rome to make all military decisions in Britain. He had full authority over the troops as well as holding full executive and legislative decision making in the province

This topic will focus on how the Romans controlled Britain after invasion. It will look to assess the functions of the **governor of Britain** and other officials, and the role played by the army in bringing the natives under control.

As we have seen from the narrative of the history of Roman Britain, its governors were appointed by the emperor and had impressive political and often military backgrounds. We are fortunate to have an inscription from a statue base of Aulus Platorius

Nepos, the governor responsible for overseeing the building of Hadrian's Wall. It is useful in that it allows us to understand the impressive career of one who held the governorship of a rather precarious province like Britain:

> To Aulus Platorius, son of Aulus, of the voting tribe Sergia, Nepos Aponius Italicus Manilianus Gains Licinius Pollio, consul, augur (priest), governor of the province of Britain, governor of the province of Lower Germany, governor of the province of Thrace, legate (commander) of the First Legion Adiutrix, quaestor of the province of Macedonia, curator of the Cassian, Clodian, Ciminian and New Trajanic Roads, a candidate nominated by the deified emperor Trajan, military tribune of the Twenty-Second Legion Primigenia Pia Fidelis, praetor, tribune of the plebs, one of the board of three men in charge of capital sentences, patron, by decree of the councillors.
>
> A. Platorius Nepos, governor *c.* AD 125 (LACTOR 4, F1)

PS

The Governors of Roman Britain during the period

AD **43–7**	Aulus Plautius
47–52	Publius Ostorius Scapula
52–7	Aulus Didius Gallus
57/58	Quintus Veranius
58–61/62	Gaius Suetonius Paulinus
61/62–3	Publius Petronius Turpilianus
63–9	Marcus Trebellius Maximus
69–71	Marcus Vettius Bolanus
71–4	Quintus Petilius Cerialis
74–8	Sextus Julius Frontinus
78–84	Gnaeus Julius Agricola
84–*c.* 89	Sallustius Lucullus
122–5?	Aulus Platorius Nepos

THE ROLE AND DUTIES OF THE GOVERNOR AND THE PROCURATOR IN THE ROMAN PROVINCE

From Plautius to Suetonius Paulinus, and then from Cerialis to Agricola, the focus was on either dealing with recalcitrant tribes or the conquest of new territory. In the cases of Cerialis and Agricola, they had previous experience of campaigning in Britain itself.

Inscription from a statue of A. Platorius Nepos

Date: *c.* AD 125

Location: Aquileia, Italy

Significance: Shows the status of Aulus Platorius Nepos and gives his career details

View it here: LACTOR 4: Inscriptions of Roman Britain (5th edn; London: KCL, 2017), F1 (= ILS 1052)

PRESCRIBED SOURCE

Title: *Agricola; Annals*

Author: Tacitus

Prescribed sections:
Agricola 14, 16–17,
19, 36; *Annals* 12.32,
14.31–2, 14.38

Read it here: *Tacitus:
Agricola and Germania,*
trans. H. Mattingley
(Harmondsworth:
Penguin, 1948);
LACTOR 11: *Literary
Sources for Roman
Britain* (4th edn;
London: KCL, 2012)

They acted as supreme commanders of the troops and were responsible for all tactical decisions. Similarly, the three governors appointed between the disasters in Iceni territory and Brigantia – Turpilianus, Maximus and Bolanus – were all given the task of consolidating the territory south of the Fosse Way and rebuilding the ruined cities. They had recent political experience as consuls, and Maximus had been part of a board of censors in Gaul.

In the Agricola, Tacitus offers his view of all of the military governors from Plautius up to Agricola. However, there is no real assessment of their achievements, and comments are either too vague to be useful or made with scorn to downplay their achievements in relation to his subject matter.

Nevertheless, it is useful for the modern reader to understand what a Roman senator thought about the roles and duties of a governor in a province like Britain. *Agricola* 14 **PS** and 17 **PS** contains a number of Tacitus' comments on the successive governors.

According to Tacitus, the success or failure of a governor in a recently acquired province had primarily to do with how effectively he exercised his military duties, but there are allusions to other duties. Plautius was given credit for the earliest provincial organisation and Scapula for the establishment of the colonia at Colchester. The initial client kingdoms are attributed to Plautius, but developed during the reigns of his successors before breaking down in AD 60. In contrast, his assessment of Turpilianus, Trebellius and Bolanus is over simplistic and not at all sympathetic to the duties of rehabilitation and consolidation of a province after a serious military setback (Tacitus, *Agricola* 16 **PS**).

Tacitus is our main literary source for the period, and his *Agricola* gives us the best insight in Roman literature for the activities of a governor on campaign during the Imperial period. We note that Agricola was appointed immediately after his consulship in Rome and with experience of serving in Britain previously as a military tribune during the Boudiccan rebellion and as commander of the Twentieth Legion during the governorship of Cerialis. In AD 78, Britain desperately needed someone with the career of Agricola to motivate the army, finish off the building of the legionary fortress in Chester and stimulate economic growth before an expedition to face the Caledonians could even be contemplated. We are told that Agricola before all of this had to deal with widespread corruption and indiscipline still prevalent in the province upon his arrival:

He made the contributions of corn and tribute less onerous by distributing the burdens fairly, and put a stop to the tricks of profiteers, which were more bitterly resented than the tax itself.

Tacitus, *Agricola* 19

Agricola had learned from experience the difficulties in trying to wage war far from the main economic settlements of the south when there was potential hostility felt by the natives against their conquerors. Although the governors would have had full control of the army, they would have had little control over the other administrative officials sent to help govern the province. This can be best seen in the dispute between the governor Suetonius Paulinus and the procurator Julius Classicianus in the aftermath of Boudicca's defeat (Tacitus, *Annals* 14.38 **PS**).

> To the spirits of the departed and of Gaius Iulius Alpinus Classicianus, son of Gaius, of the Fabian voting tribe . . . procurator of the province of Britain. Julia Pacata I[ndiana], daughter of Indus, his wife, had this built.
>
> Tombstone of Julius Classicianus (LACTOR 4, B18)

The ultimate power and thus responsibility of the governor made him totally accountable when things went wrong. As discussed in the previous chapter, the rebellion was at least partly caused by an aggressive policy of taxation and the recall of loans. The procurator who was based in London was an equestrian who in theory reported directly to the emperor and had authority in all matters of the economy. Decianus Catus is attributed as cause of the rebellion by Dio (62.2.1), and it is him who the besieged veterans beseech when Suetonius is away once the disaster had reached Colchester.

He acts inappropriately in sending inadequate troops, but the deployment of reserve troops should not have been the concern of the procurator. Perhaps it was more an attempt by Catus to protect London which at that time was the administrative capital of the province. Dio's characterisation of Catus is supported by Tacitus' account of Catus' flight from Britain and indicates that his rapacity was a major factor in inciting the natives to rebellion.

> The procurator, Catus, frightened by this disaster and the hatred borne him by the provincials, whom he had driven to war through his greed, fled to Gaul.
>
> Tacitus, *Annals* 14.32 (LACTOR 11, p. 49)

Perhaps the lack of identity of any of the other procurators of the period implies that they enjoyed a cordial relationship with the governor. Classicianus' judgment regarding the effects of Suetonius Paulinus' punitive campaign against those involved in the rebellion seemed sound enough for the emperor Nero to make a change not only of governor but also of approach to how the province was governed.

PRESCRIBED SOURCES

Tombstones of a speculator at London and a beneficiarius at Wroxeter

Date: First century AD

Original location:
Blackfriars, London, and Wroxeter

Current location:
British Museum and Shrewsbury Museum and Art Gallery

Significance: Evidence for lower-status officers in the army

View it here: LACTOR 4: Inscriptions of Roman Britain (5th edn; London: KCL, 2017), F12 (= RIB 19) and F8 (= RIB 293)

OTHER OFFICIALS

There were other minor officials as part of the governor's staff of which we have some evidence. There is a tombstone from the first century AD which refers to a speculator in London. Speculatores were based near the headquarters of the governor and served as a military police force and scouts.

> To the spirits of the departed, . . . r Celsus, son of Lucius, of the Claudian voting tribe, from . . ., speculator of the Second Augustan Legion, An[tonius?] Dardanius Castor, Rubrius Pudens and . . . s Probus, speculators of the legion (set this up).
>
> A speculator at London, first century AD (LACTOR 4, F12)

Similarly we have a tombstone of a beneficiarius from Wroxeter before the Boudiccan rebellion. It is unclear as to what his role or that of other beneficiarii was as they were soldiers, most probably legionaries, on secondment acting as assistants to the governors and could be deployed how the governor saw fit. Elsewhere in the empire, beneficiarii were responsible for tasks such as collecting corn or supervising the road system, or were involved in the postal service.

> Gaius Mannius Secundus, son of Gaius, of the Pollian voting tribe, from Pollentia, a soldier of the twentieth legion, aged 52 years, served for 31 years, beneficiarius on the staff of the governor, lies here.
>
> A tombstone of a beneficiarius at Wroxeter, possibly before AD 61 (LACTOR 4, F8)

THE SOLDIERS

PRESCRIBED SOURCE

Tombstone of M. Favonius Facilis

Dates: AD 43–9

Original location:
Colchester

Current location:
Colchester Museum

Significance: Tombstone of the centurion of the Twentieth Legion

View it here: LACTOR 4: *Inscriptions of Roman Britain* (5th edn; London: KCL, 2017), B12 (= RIB 200)

There is a copious amount of evidence for the soldiers of Roman Britain. We have huge amounts of inscription evidence from tombstones, to military strength reports, from dedications to graffiti. Archaeology of camps and forts show what soldiers did when on campaign and the skills of the legionaries when not engaged in fighting can be seen in buildings and other constructions. The legions were professional soldiers and the governor's most elite force. There were three or four legions at any given point, stationed in fortresses in strategic locations to help control recently gained territory. Each legion had a commander who was a Roman senator and was assisted by ten military tribunes in charge of the ten cohorts and fifty-nine centurions.

The tombstone of a M. Favonius Facilis shows Facilis in military uniform, carrying a vitis (a vinestick), the staff of office of the centurion.

> Marcus Favonius Facilis, son of Marcus, of the voting tribe Pollia, centurion of the Twentieth Legion; Verecundus and Novicius his freedmen set this up; here he lies.
>
> A tombstone of a M. Favonius Facilis, AD 43–9 (LACTOR 4, B12)

The legionaries themselves were put to good use in suppressing the Britons, as they easily overpowered the weaker and tactically naive natives. These troops were paid the most in the Roman army and received land in the Empire upon discharge. The colony at Colchester, which would go on to incite the Trinovantes to join the Iceni in rebellion, was supposed to accelerate the process of Romanisation in the original capital once the legion that had occupied Camulodunum had moved on. Ironically, given the later revolt:

> This was a strong settlement of veterans intended as a reserve against rebellion and to instil in our allies the habit of observing the laws.
>
> Tacitus, *Annals* 12.32 (LACTOR 11, p. 42)

PS

S & C Choose a number of military inscriptions from LACTOR 4 and research what they can tell us about:

- the origin of troops;
- the lengths of service; and
- the positions and movement of the troops within the province at various times.

The legions were complemented right across the period by auxiliary troops who were normally provincial soldiers serving abroad. During the occupation of Britain, auxiliary units came from Holland, Germany and even as far as the Middle East. Although they were less skilful and more dispensable than their legionary counterparts, they were still highly trained professional soldiers and important to the rapid expansion of the early years of the invasion. The vast majority of the cavalry was made up of auxiliary units (see tombstone of Longinus Sdapeze (ala I Thracum) **PS**, which shows him in scale armour riding over a crouching naked barbarian who has been comprehensively defeated. and the tombstone of an auxiliary standard-bearer **PS**).

There is evidence from the later period that the Britons themselves were recruited to act as cavalry auxiliary to fight for Rome elsewhere in the empire. The author of a Vindolanda tablet seems unimpressed by their ability:

> . . . the Britons are unprotected by armour (?). There are very many cavalry. The cavalry do not use swords nor do the wretched Britons mount in order to throw javelins
>
> Vindolanda tablet on British Cavalry (LACTOR 4, G5)

PS

The legions and their auxiliaries combined well to offer impregnable resistance to the natives. This can be seen particularly well in two battle narratives, one against the Boudiccan rebels in AD 61 and the other against the Caledonians at Mons Graupius in AD 84. Against Boudicca, we see the Roman cavalry defeating enemy cavalry and infantry, while archers for the most part rout the enemy chariots (Dio, *Roman History* 62.12). At Mons

---

PRESCRIBED SOURCES

Tombstones of Longinus Sdapeze and an auxiliary standard-bearer

Date: First century AD

Original location: Colchester and Hexham

Current location: Colchester Museum and Hexham Abbey

Significance: Evidence for the importance of auxiliary (in these cases, cavalry) troops in the conquest of Britain

View it here: LACTOR 4: Inscriptions of Roman Britain (5th edn; London: KCL, 2017), B2 (= RIB 201) and G33 (= RIB 1172)

PRESCRIBED SOURCE

Vindolanda tablet about British cavalry

Date: *c.* AD 97–102/3

Original location: Vindolanda

Current location: British Museum

Significance: Comment by a Roman on the British cavalry

View it here: LACTOR 4: Inscriptions of Roman Britain (5th edn; London: KCL, 2017), G5 (= Tab. Vindol. 2.164)

Classis Britannica the Roman Fleet in Britain. Its base was either Richborough or Dover. It would be used to reconnoitre the waters around Britain as well as transporting supplies for the soldiers by sea

ACTIVITY

Find out more about how the Romans made use of the Classis Britannica in controlling the Empire.

Graupius, the focus is more on the hand-to-hand fighting, with Tacitus contrasting the huge swords and small shields of the enemy with the Roman forces' greater skill and training in such fighting at close quarters. The cavalry are again victorious against the enemy cavalry, although less useful when dealing with the infantry (Tacitus, *Agricola* 36 (PS)).

The Roman army was at first used to conquer and control. Despite guerrilla attacks from time to time, the Britons were largely ineffective in resisting Roman expansion; the army was simply too organised and well trained in battle. The effectiveness of the army in controlling the natives can be seen in several different functions of the army itself. The legionary soldiers were skilled in building and were responsible for the road network, which was initially built for their own communication and supply needs. However, it would in turn make Romanisation and trade easier, as the roads would link the forts to towns and provide merchants with direct access to both.

Important Roman roads included the following:

- Dere Street – from York past Hadrian's Wall to Scotland – used by Agricola on campaign in Scotland to move troops quickly and goods up and down the country
- The Stanegate – Corbridge to Carlisle – used for communications, connected Dere Street with other north-south roads – used to supply Hadrian's Wall
- Watling Street – London to Wroxeter – used by Suetonius Paulinus during Boudiccan revolt
- Fosse Way – Lincoln to Exeter – lined with towns along the way, linked fortresses.

The army would also have assisted with the erecting of administrative, judicial and entertainment buildings, and their regular pay would have boosted the economy in the nearest towns. Veteran soldiers in the coloniae were used to illustrate the benefits of Roman rule and dissuade the natives from rebellion.

Hadrian's Wall was built largely by the legions. We can tell this because of inscriptional evidence from the Wall which details not only the building of various sections, but also exactly who built them (see pp. 283 and 257 for inscriptions from Milecastle 38 (PS) and Halton Chesters (PS)).

The legions were too valuable to be deployed patrolling the various aspects of the frontier system. Therefore, the more numerous auxiliaries were selected to man the Wall. There is a wealth of evidence about the various units stationed on the wall (see Topic 2). There is evidence also for the role of the British fleet in the building of Hadrian's Wall. Since Britain is an island, it was necessary to employ the **Classis Britannica**. The fleet was mainly used to reconnoitre the island and supply troops on campaign with the necessary equipment and food. The fleet was used in the campaigns against the Welsh, Caledonians and even in the earliest conquest period against the tribes in the south-west. We know it was used to help the legions build Hadrian's Wall, as we have an inscription from one of the granaries in a fort.

For the emperor Caesar Trajan Hadrian Augustus, a detachment of the British fleet (built this) under the governor Aulus Platorius Nepos.

Benwell classis Britannica building inscription (LACTOR 4, C9)

FIGURE 4.18
A relief from Trajan's Column, Rome *c.* AD 110, showing the army engaging in construction of a fort. The soldiers were highly skilled at building and construction work.

> **S & C** Study the reliefs on Trajan's column and discuss what we can learn about the Roman Army on campaign.

PRESCRIBED SOURCE

Benwell *classis Britannica* building inscription

Date: *c.* AD 122–125

Original location: Benwell fort

Current location: Great North Museum

Significance: Shows the involvement of the Roman fleet in the building of Hadrian's Wall

View it here: LACTOR 4: Inscriptions of Roman Britain (5th edn; London: KCL, 2017), C9 (= RIB 1340)

The whole of the south-east was practically under Roman control by AD 47, with at least three client kingdoms established among the Iceni (King Prasutagas), the Regni (King Cogidubnus) and the Brigantes (Queen Cartimandua). Presumably, these three client kingdoms were part of those who submitted willingly to Claudius as evidenced by his arch **PS** (see p. 281).

Client kingdoms were a long-standing feature of Roman rule of the provinces and were not unique to Britain. It is likely that in Britain they may have been more of a

KEY INDIVIDUALS

Prasutagas
Date: First half of the first century AD
King of the Iceni and husband of Boudicca, who left his kingdom jointly to Rome and to his daughters in his will, leading to the Boudiccan rebellion.

Cogidubnus
Date: First century AD
Also known as Togidubnus/Cogidumnus. Pro-Roman king of the Regni, who may have lived at Fishbourne Palace.

Cartimandua
Date: Ruled AD 43–69
Queen of the Brigantes, who was loyal to Rome and fled her territory when her husband Venutius rebelled.

ACTIVITY

Make a list of the benefits of client kingdoms for both the Romans and Britons during the period.

temporary measure, providing buffer zones between recently conquered territory and hostile tribes. They were placed strategically in Brigantia (northern England), in Iceni territory (the east coast) and in Regni territory (the south coast). The termination of the formal recognition of the independence of Prasutagus' kingdom upon his death was the catalyst for the Boudiccan rebellion.

> Prasutagus, king of the Iceni, and a man distinguished for the wealth which he had enjoyed for many years, had made the emperor his co-heir together with his two daughters, thinking that by such submission his kingdom and family would be kept from any harm.
>
> Tacitus, *Annals* 14.31 (LACTOR 11, p. 47)

The best evidence of the mutual benefits of client kingdoms can be seen in Brigantia. Cartimandua is repeatedly protected by the Romans against the anti-Roman faction led by her husband, Venutius, and even when she is overrun, the governor Petilius Cerialis came to her aid. Previously she had been the one responsible for the surrender of Caratacus in AD 51 (see p. 264).

The third client king, Cogidubnus, is mentioned by Tacitus as having been presented with certain territories in response for his support for the Roman occupation and his encouragement of Romanisation.

PRESCRIBED SOURCE

Chichester dedication slab

Date: Second half of first century AD

Monument: Altar

Original location: Chichester

Significance: Gives Cogidubnus the title King of Britain

View it here: LACTOR 4: Inscriptions of Roman Britain (5th edn; London: KCL, 2017), F16 (= RIB 91)

> Not only were the nearest parts of Britain gradually organized into a province, but a colony of veterans also was founded. Certain domains were presented to King Cogidumnus, who maintained his unswerving loyalty right down to our own times – an example of the long-established Roman custom of employing even kings to make others slaves.
>
> Tacitus, *Agricola* 14 (with omissions)

The seat of Cogidubnus' power seems to be Chichester, as an inscription has been found illustrating that the British king had acquired Roman citizenship due to his loyalty to the Emperor Claudius, and seems to have been accepted as Rex Magnus (Great King) of the Britons.

> To Neptune and Minerva for the welfare of the Divine House, by authority of Tiberius Claudius Cogidubnus, great king in Britain, the guild of smiths and those who belong to it gave this temple from their own resources, the site having been given by [. . .]ens, son of Pudentinus.
>
> Chichester dedication slab (LACTOR 4, F16)

Client kingdoms were just one way that the Romans tried to control their newly acquired province. Cogidubnus seemed to benefit considerably more than Prasutagus but perhaps control of the south coast was more important for trade than protecting parts of East Anglia.

Client kingdoms existed elsewhere in the empire and so should not be seen as unique to Britain. They provided the Romans with a way of controlling key areas quickly while the army was occupied with the conquest of recalcitrant tribes elsewhere. The south flourished even in the first century AD and this was due to the success of Romanisation not only after the initial bloody struggles but even before AD 43, as certain tribes had enjoyed formal and informal relationships with Rome.

The reference to the submission of British kings in AD 43 and the clear success of the client kingdom relationships with the Regni and Brigantes show that there were certainly those present in Britain who could see the benefits of accepting Roman rule quite quickly and this form of control was equally effective as the deployment of specialist soldiers to conquer and subdue dangerous tribes. The territory of the Atrebates was probably always pro-Roman, as evidenced by early Silchester, which had developed into a Roman provincial town complete with standard amenities even before the Claudian invasion as well as the pro-Roman imagery on the coins of Verica. Tacitus remarks that certain

PRESCRIBED SOURCE

Silchester baths (Figure 4.19)

Date: First century AD

Location: Between Reading and Basingstoke, in Hampshire

Roman name: Calleva Atrebatum

Significance: One of the first Roman public buildings in the town

Find out more here: www.reading.ac.uk/silchester

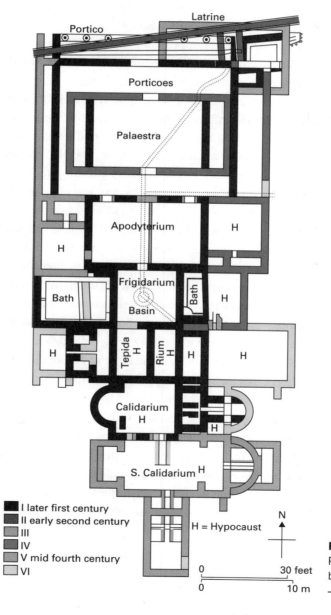

I later first century
II early second century
III
IV
V mid fourth century
VI

H = Hypocaust

N

0   30 feet
0   10 m

FIGURE 4.19
Plan of Silchester baths.

domains were presented to Cogidubnus, and we can safely assume that he eventually had control of several of the old tribes including the Atrebates. The client kingdom of the Regni lasted longer than the other two as it had been more successful. There had been constant trouble in Brigantia between AD 43 and the subsequent removal of Cartimandua, and there had also been a revolt against the Romans led by the Iceni in the AD 40s. Tacitus' remarks concerning Cogidubnus' 'unswerving loyalty' allows us to see the success criteria for client kingdoms from the Roman point of view.

The Roman conquest of lowland Britain was rapid, as the effectiveness of the Roman army made most military engagements quick and decisive. Evidence suggests that the natives were only able to combat the Romans in guerrilla attacks. Even though Caratacus managed to cause considerable trouble for the Romans in the 50s by forming the confederation of Welsh tribes, he was eventually undone by the client kingdom relationship between Cartimandua and Rome.

This episode alone illustrates how the natives underestimated the strategies employed by the Romans to control Britain. The atrocities seen at Maiden Castle provide evidence for the effectiveness of the legions on campaign, and there are many occasions in the early literary record of the auxiliaries being used against British resistance with similar levels of success. Nonetheless, problems arose as soon as the governors decided to expand Roman influence into Wales and the north. The legions were moved and the fortresses that had been left were converted into towns, with the most notable example being the colonia at Colchester. The employment of Romanised elite as rulers of client kingdoms as well as veteran soldiers attracting the wares of Mediterranean merchants was supposed to accelerate the process and allow the legions to expand the sphere of Roman control. The idea was sound although the practice was not. The Boudiccan rebellion showed that the behaviour of the veterans had the opposite effect. Instead of illustrating the benefits of Roman rule, it presented the natives with abuse and, coupled with financial extortion from the procurator, incited the natives to try to expel the Romans permanently and set the occupation of Britain back by almost a decade.

The Romans were successful in securing and then controlling their grip on Britain with the army being the main agents, both in boosting the economy in Britain, building the infrastructure and providing the impetus for trade and in dealing with revolt and resistance. It seems that retrenchment in the 80s and the building of Hadrian's Wall was the Roman statement that the areas already under control were the only ones worth controlling. Even the literary set pieces of the Boudiccan rebellion and the resistance of Calgacus and the Caledonians illustrated that any success in opposing the Roman occupation was only temporary; Boudicca taught the Romans that a more mild-mannered administration was necessary so that the conquest of the north could happen unimpeded. The message that the Roman conquest and occupation would be inevitably successful was accepted by certain tribal leaders from the outset, while more spirited tribes found out the hard way that the Roman military machine was just too organised and too strong to oppose.

Further Reading

D'Amato, R. & Ruggeri, R. (2016), *Roman Army Units in the Western Provinces (1): 31 BC–AD 195 (Men-at-Arms)*, Oxford: Osprey.

De la Bédoyère, G. (2001), *Eagles Over Britannia: The Roman Army in Britain*, Stroud: The History Press.

De la Bédoyère, G. (2013), *Roman Britain: A New History*, London: Thames and Hudson.

Breeze, D.J. (2016), *The Roman Army* (Classical World), London: Bloomsbury.

Richardson, J. (2013), *Roman Provincial Administration*, London: Bloomsbury.

PRACTICE QUESTIONS

1. Read Tacitus, *Agricola* 36 **PS**.

How useful is this passage for our understanding of the effectiveness of the Roman army against British resistance?

[12]

4.5 Effects of Roman Rule

TOPIC OVERVIEW

- Economic exploitation: the extent of Roman influences on the British economy at the time of Claudius' invasion of AD 43
- Evidence for exploitation of economic resources during the Claudian period
- Changes to agricultural production
- Trade and infrastructure, with particular reference to roads
- The impact of the Roman Army on the British economy
- Urbanisation: reasons for the development of towns
- The different types of towns (*coloniae*, *civitates*, *municipia*, *vici*) and their functions
- The development of towns as economic centres during the first century AD
- Leisure and public facilities provided by towns
- Towns as agents of Romanisation
- The emergence of a Romanised elite
- The importance of Fishbourne Palace and its reflection of new cultural tastes and attitudes
- The extent of Romanisation.

The prescribed sources for this topic are:

- Strabo, *Geography* 4.5.1–2, 4.5.4
- Tacitus, *Agricola*, 21
- Tacitus, *Annals* 12.32

- Chichester dedication to Nero
- Fishbourne
- Gold Stater of Cunobelinus
- Mendip lead pig
- Roman Colchester
- Verulamium forum inscription
- Vindolanda tablet of accounts for journey from Vindolanda to York (Bowman & Thomas 185)
- Wroxeter forum dedication

This topic will look at the extent to which life changed for the Britons during the period, using particular towns as case studies. However, it is not possible to assess whether there was a gradual emergence of a distinctive Romano-British culture during the Roman occupation of Britain within the constraints of a period as short as this one. There is so much evidence of urbanisation in Britain that the best way to investigate is to make site visits to a nearby Roman town. The evidence from our period is patchy, as the urbanised settlements were repeatedly built upon with most physical remains dating from the third and fourth centuries AD. The same is the case for villas in the countryside.

THE VALUE OF BRITAIN TO THE ROMANS

Encouraging economic growth and Romanisation was a standard policy of the Romans when administering their empire. The empire was too big for the Roman government to micromanage all matters of government and decision making. Therefore, native elites were given incentives to manage the administration at a local level. There is a wealth of inscriptional evidence of the various magistrates running the old tribal centres in Britain, but this largely dates to the period after Hadrian's Wall when southern Britain had been at least partly Romanised and town life was flourishing. The principle behind Romanisation was to make the Britons as 'Roman' as possible in order to stimulate economic prosperity and prevent rebellion. Therefore, the towns in Britain were designed on the Roman model.

Caesar mentions British society in the 50s BC in his Gallic Wars. He tells us that they had many cattle, used bronze and gold for their coins, and that tin and iron could be found in huge quantities. He more than hints at the mineral worth of Britain and makes the conquest of the island sound potentially lucrative for the Romans.

However, it seemed that emperors before Claudius had little interest in launching a full-scale invasion of Britain, and those who did have plans did not put them into effect. The reasons for this are unclear. Britain may have been seen as too remote to be of value or too difficult to be controlled. This was a view adopted by the Greek historian and geographer Strabo, who was writing in the Augustan period.

Strabo categorically states that there would be no advantage in conquering Britain as there could be no economic gain. He refers to taxation on imports, showing that Britain had some connection with the empire, but refutes any idea that Britain was rich in minerals, although like Caesar he does mention the presence of gold.

> Most of the island is low-lying and wooded, but there are many hilly areas. It produces corn, cattle, gold, silver and iron. These things are exported along with hides, slaves and dogs suitable for hunting. The Gauls however use both these and their own native dogs for warfare also.
>
> Strabo, *Geography* 4.5.1 (LACTOR 11, p. 33)

Strabo himself never visited Britain and it is unclear where he gets his information from to speak so confidently about the unprofitability of the permanent occupation of Britain by the Romans. He would have been influenced by the official line of the day; however,

S & C Using Caesar Gallic Wars 5.12.1–14.5 (LACTOR 11, A15–17) as a starting point, how consistent a view of Britain and the Britons do we get from literary sources?

PS

PRESCRIBED SOURCE

Title: *Geographica*

Author: Strabo

Date: *c.* AD 20

Significance: His Geography was published under Tiberius. A secondary
account based on the work of others intermixed with Strabo's own views
and understanding

Prescribed sections: Strabo, *Geography* 4.5.1–2, 4.5.4

Read it here: LACTOR 11: *Literary Sources for Roman Britain* (4th edn;
London: KCL, 2012)

---

his comments about contact between the tribes of Britain and the empire are verified by
Roman goods found in burials of British tribal leaders before AD 43 for example those
from St Albans and Colchester. Strabo is useful in giving us a more refined version of
British society than we get from Caesar but still one which does not present the reality
of life in towns such as early Colchester , which shows evidence of sophisticated
pre-invasion urban settlement.

> They live much like the Gauls but some of their customs are more primitive and
> barbarous. Thus for example some of them are well supplied with milk but do not
> know how to make cheese; they know nothing of planting crops or of farming in
> general. They are ruled by their own kings. For the most part they use chariots in war,
> like some of the Gauls. Their cities are the forests, for they fell trees and fence in
> large circular enclosures in which they build huts and pen in their cattle, but not for
> any great length of time.
>
> Strabo, *Geography* 4.5.2 (LACTOR 11, p. 33)

There is evidence from the Mendips in Somerset that not only was Britain a rich resource
to be exploited by the Romans but also that Rome was well aware of its economic
profitability even before the Claudian invasion. A lead **ingot** was found 8 km from the
Roman settlement at Charterhouse, a town which probably grew from the presence of the
Second Legion Augusta in extracting the lead and silver from the Mendips.

| **ingot** an oblong block of metal, ready for export |

The date of the lead ingot is AD 49, which shows that the Romans had managed to
exploit the lead and silver resources for export using the army within six years of
invasion, contrary to Strabo's theory of unprofitability.

> Tiberius Claudius Caesar Augustus, pontifex maximus, in his ninth year of
> tribunician power, sixteen times acclaimed imperator, from the British (mines).
>
> Mendip lead pig (LACTOR 4, B17)

Mendip lead pig

Date: *c.* AD 49

Found: Somerset

Significance: A lead ingot which shows how the Romans exploited the metal resources of Britain

View it here: LACTOR 4: *Inscriptions of Roman Britain* (5th edn; London: KCL, 2017), B17 (= RIB 2.1.2404.1)

A ROMAN WAY OF LIFE FOR THE BRITONS

It makes sense now to look at Roman Colchester, Camulodunum, as a test case for the development of towns in our period. Pre-invasion Colchester was like any other tribal capital. Britain before the Romans was a primarily agricultural society, but there is evidence that the Britons were exporting their wares, especially pottery, to the continent. At this time Colchester was the seat of the Catuvellauni, as we can see from **numismatic evidence**.

However, pre-Roman Colchester would not have resembled a town in either the modern or indeed the Roman sense. The natives would have occupied hill forts or low-lying oppida which were well defended, as is the case at Colchester with the man-made

> **numismatic evidence**
> coins used to understand Roman history

Stater of Cunobelinus (Figure 4.20)

Date: *c.* AD 20–40

Material: Gold

Mint: Colchester

Obverse: Ear of corn; CA and MV(LODVNVM) on either side

Reverse: Horse above CVNO(BELINVS)

Significance: Shows that the centre of Cunobelinus' power was in Colchester

View it here: LACTOR 4: Inscriptions of Roman Britain (5th edn; London: KCL, 2017), A8 (= Mack 206)

FIGURE 4.20
Gold stater of Cunobelinus.

dykes. The native Britons would take their families and cattle into these for protection during enemy assault. The chief of the tribe would have his settlement in the centre, but this would probably be no more than an enlarged wattle and daub roundhouse. Excavation has shown that the oppidum at Colchester was an advanced centre of industry and trade for the tribal region. There is no indication that oppida had the central administrative functions of Roman towns and as settlements they were primitive in the context of even provincial urbanisation. Cunobelinus as the King of the Britons would have been the most influential and certainly the richest of the Britons able to import wine, olive-oil and other luxuries from the continent in great quantities. Indeed, earthenware from Gaul as well as Roman **amphorae** indicate that Cunobelinus' tribe was engaged in extensive trade with the Roman world. However, the capital of the tribe would not have resembled at all anything that the Romans would have recognised as a town.

The development of the town at Colchester came as a direct result of the Twentieth Legion's occupation of the fortress built to check the Catuvellauni in AD 43. The soldiers were attractive to foreign and native merchants, being 5,000 men with regular pay to spend their wages on their wares. Civil settlements had developed near the fortress and

> **amphorae** Roman pottery used to store and transport wine and/or olive oil

MODEL 1

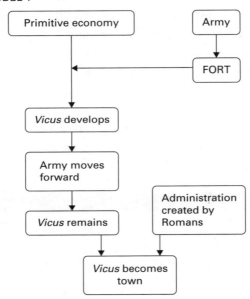

MODEL 2

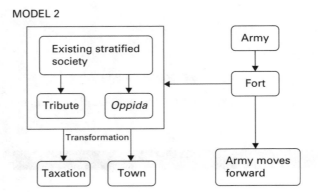

FIGURE 4.21
Two models for the relationship of forts to town origins in early Roman Britain. The Romanization of Britain, Martin Millett, CUP, 2005.

when the army moved on in AD 49, the fortress was converted into a colonia for retired soldiers. Archaeology does not tell us much about the first Roman town in Colchester but we know that there was a temple to Claudius and definitely a theatre but we would expect to have found a forum, basilica and public baths. Roads connecting the colonia to other military settlements and to the coast facilitated the urbanisation process. Similarly, Wroxeter, Exeter and the colonia at Gloucester make use of pre-existing military bases converted into towns. It is unclear how much the colonia was extended beyond the limits of the pre-existing settlement, but a large proportion of agricultural land would have been confiscated from the Trinovantes to support a population of as much as 15,000. This as well as the general treatment of the natives from the new inhabitants of Roman Colchester were causes of discontent, which in turn led to the Trinovantes joining the Iceni for the Boudiccan rebellion. Later on in the period, coloniae for veterans were established at Gloucester for those of the Second Legion Augusta and at Lincoln for those of the Ninth Legion. These would be the only towns in Britain which were the products of a deliberate policy. Other towns grew and flourished due to their positons near the road network and/or how far they were from military bases.

Tacitus, *Annals* 12.32 **PS** tells us that the purpose of the colonia at Colchester was to protect the capital from revolt and encourage Romanisation. The veterans decided to

PRESCRIBED SOURCE

Site of Roman Colchester

Roman name: Camulodunum

Prescribed buildings: Temple to Claudius

Significance: Major town of Britain before the Roman conquest that became a Roman centre of power

> **Study question**
> What does the plan of the developed Colonia at Colchester AD 49–60 tell us about the early development of towns in Britain?

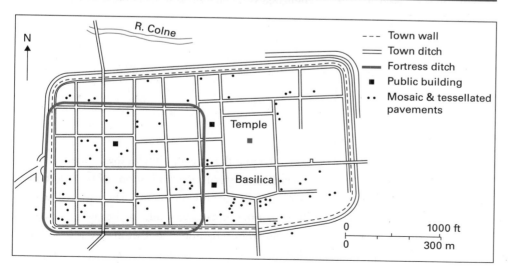

FIGURE 4.22
A plan of the developed Colonia at Colchester, AD 49–60.

remove the pre-Roman defences to create room for the development of the colonia, leaving Colchester totally open to attack. This move was criticised by Tacitus after the events of AD 60. The veterans expected to enjoy their retirement in the Roman style and their wishes would largely have come to fruition due to their attractiveness to potential traders, craftsmen and merchants. Archaeology of the pre-Boudiccan Colchester shows that there were huge amounts of imported **Samian ware**, copious wine and Mediterranean food in huge quantities.

> **Samian ware** high-quality imported red pottery from Roman Gaul

Despite the aim of the colonia to inspire locals to adopt the Roman way of life, Tacitus reports that the veterans' lawless and abusive behaviour encouraged the Trinovantes to join Boudicca and destroy the colonia at Colchester. Another Colchester would be eventually built upon the same site, and so very little evidence of pre-Boudiccan Colchester exists.

We know that there was a concerted effort by the Romans to rebuild much that was lost in AD 60 and to try not only to stimulate the economy in the south, but also to promote a Romanised way of life for the locals. Archaeology shows that there is considerable development of towns in the south in the two decades after the Boudiccan rebellion, with theatres, bathhouses, shops, good housing, and other public amenities being added to the larger urban settlements in the style of a usual Romanised provincial town, such as in St Albans and London. The best evidence for the Romans' policy of urbanisation comes from a very famous passage in Tacitus which highlights the main benefits of Roman rule upon the southern Britons, crediting (rather liberally) Agricola with the entire programme:

PS

> The following winter was spent on schemes of social betterment. Agricola had to deal with people living in isolation and ignorance, and therefore prone to fight; and his object was to accustom them to a life of peace and quiet by the provision of amenities. He therefore gave private encouragement and official assistance to the building of temples, public squares, and good houses. He praised the energetic and scolded the slack; and competition for honour proved as effective as compulsion. Furthermore, he educated the sons of the chiefs in the liberal arts, and expressed a preference for British ability as compared with the trained skills of the Gauls. The result was that instead of loathing the Latin language they became eager to speak it effectively. In the same way, our national dress came into favour and the toga was everywhere to be seen. And so the population was gradually led into the demoralizing temptations of arcades, baths, and sumptuous banquets. The unsuspecting Britons spoke of such novelties as 'civilization', when in fact they were only a feature of their enslavement.

Tacitus, *Agricola* 21

This famous passage reveals a great deal about the direct policy of the Romans towards Britain and the Britons. Tacitus does not use the term 'Romanisation' which is a modern idea; he refers to the process as 'schemes of social betterment'. The use of the word social rather than economic illustrates that the process was intended to win the support of the natives, or at least to distract them from rebellion. The Britons are referred to as 'living in isolation and ignorance and therefore prone to fight'. This is a very simplified

PRESCRIBED SOURCES

Title: *Agricola; Annals*

Date: Late first century and early second century AD

Author: Tacitus

Prescribed sections: *Agricola*, 21; *Annals* 12.32

Read it here: *Tacitus: Agricola and Germania*, trans. H. Mattingley (Harmondsworth: Penguin, 1948); LACTOR 11: *Literary Sources for Roman Britain* (4th edn; London: KCL, 2012)

Roman version of the Britons. Isolation and ignorance must refer to the understanding and adoption of a Roman way of life, as the towns that were being developed during the late 70s AD were hardly isolated – indeed they were the central towns of the south. It is interesting to note that as a Roman, and one who shows sympathy in his writings to the Britons who have been subjected to abuses by the Romans, Tacitus' view is that those who lack elements of Roman civilisation are the ones most likely to engage in direct aggression against the Romans, hence the reference that the 'provision of amenities' would keep them quiet and obedient. Tacitus states that the forums, temples and good housing were built with 'official assistance', which must mean the deployment of the craftsmen from the army who in winter would not be engaged in fighting. The education of the sons of the elite shows not only a policy of the Romans in Romanising the generation born during the Roman occupation, but also hints at the acceptance of Roman rule by the current elite in wanting their children to receive the education that they evidently would not have had. The Britain shown in this passage by Tacitus is one which has willingly submitted to Roman rule and is tangibly enjoying subsequent benefits; far removed from the attitude of the Boudiccan rebels only a generation earlier.

Broadly speaking each major urban settlement would have the same basic layout, access to the main road network and public buildings and amenities. The most important buildings in all Roman towns (except **vici**) were the forum-basilica complexes. The basilica was the main administrative and judicial building of the **colonia**, **municipium** or **civitas** capital. The forum was the central business district of the town, complete with shops and markets.

[For] The Emperor Titus Caesar Vespasian Augustus, son of the deified Vespasian, pontifex maximus, in his ninth year of tribunician power, hailed imperator 15 times, consul 7 times, designated consul for the 8th. time, censor, father of his country, and Caesar Domitian, son of the deified Vespasian, consul 6 times, designated consul for the 7th time, princeps iuventutis and of all the colleges of priests, through Gnaeus Iulius Agricola, governor, the city of Verulamium to mark the building of the basilica.

Verulamium Forum Inscription AD 79 or 81 (LACTOR 4, B24)

S&C Visit the Verulamium Museum and Museum of London if possible. What was the extent of Romanisation in the south by *c.* AD 80?

vici numerous civil settlements which grew near military bases but could exist as small towns in their own right, once the military had moved on

coloniae a town built for retired veterans (Roman citizens), usually converted from a pre-exisiting legionary fortress. Colchester, Gloucester, York and Lincoln were all coloniae

nunicipia a civitas capital which had special status above other civitates. St Albans and probably London were municipia. Its local magistrates would be awarded Roman citizenship

civitates the town from which a tribal area was controlled and administered

---

PRESCRIBED SOURCES

Verulamium (St Albans) and Wroxeter forum inscriptions

Date: AD 79 or 81, and AD 129–30

Current location: Verulamium Museum, St Albans, and Shrewsbury Museum and Art Gallery

Significance: Evidence for the Roman layout of towns with public buildings in central forums

View it here: LACTOR 4: Inscriptions of Roman Britain (5th edn; London: KCL, 2017), B24 (= JRS 46 146–7) and F26 (= RIB 288)

For the Emperor Caesar Trajan Hadrian Augustus, son of the deified Trajan conqueror of Parthia, grandson of the deified Nerva, pontifex maximus, in his fourteenth year of tribunician power, three times consul, father of his country, the civitas of the Cornovii (set this up).

Wroxeter Forum Dedication, AD 129–30 (LACTOR 4, F26)

Each town would have at least one set of public baths. Only the very rich private houses in Roman Britain, such as Fishbourne **PS**, would have had their own private bath suites. Therefore the rest of those who inhabited the town would rely on visiting the cheap public baths built in the style of those found all over the empire. The system of Roman baths involved the bather visiting warm, hot and cold rooms in order to get clean. Archaeology identifies bath suites very clearly from the various rooms and the presence of the hypocaust system used to heat the floor in the hottest room. The quality and size of the baths depended on the importance and size of the different towns, but they were common amenities and the local elites would spend money on building these and other such public buildings in order to increase their own standing within the town.

Urbanised life was accelerated due to the impressive road system, which linked towns to one another as well as to the rural villa estates and military bases. The roads were built very quickly by the army for the army, but the network benefited anyone who wished to make money by selling. For example, farmers could reach all the nearby towns much more easily, and luxury Mediterranean and eastern goods would reach Britain quickly, increasing the likelihood of a Romanised Britain. In addition, existing and new industries could thrive with an infinite amount of new customers. There is a Vindolanda tablet (Bowman & Thomas 185 **PS**) which gives a detailed account of expenditure on a return journey using the road network from Vindolanda to York. It details several items including food, clothing and equipment presumably bought as additional supplies for those serving at Vindolanda. In addition, inscriptional evidence shows that as well as a boom in the British pottery industries, the goldsmith, blacksmith, glassmaking and mosaicist trades flourished, as well as numerous others, including industries in perishable

Vindolanda tablet of accounts for journey from Vindolanda to York

Date: End of first century AD

Original location: Vindolanda

Current location: British Museum

Significance: a record of supplies for a route from York to (and possibly from) Vindolanda

View it here: *Roman Britain: A Sourcebook*, Susan Ireland (2nd edn; London: Routledge, 1996) (= Tab. Vindol 2.291 = Bowman & Thomas 185)

goods such as wool and leather. Although the major part of the British economy depended on farming, as it did pre-invasion, the owners of farms would become extremely wealthy, as can be seen from the emergence of villa estates connected to the nearest towns via roads (see map, p. 227).

AGRICULTURE

Before the Roman occupation, the Britons were farmers. They produced as much as they needed and there was no inclination, nor indeed any mechanism, to sell the surplus. After the invasion, however, huge amounts of corn would be needed to feed the army and we know from Tacitus that contributions of food were required as tribute in the 80s AD. It is unclear how the tribes divided their area up and what the contributions would have been from individual farmers to the tribe. Caesar more than hints at communal living and so it is likely that farms were occupied by several families. It must be stated that the vast majority of inhabitants of Roman Britain would have seen very little improvement or even difference in their lives during the Roman occupation of this period. The town dwellers would be the Britons who saw the most radical changes to their domestic lives.

The emergence of towns and the road system allowed farmers to develop estates and sell surplus quite easily. Roman tools were quickly used by the Britons, such as more effective ploughshares, durable axes and two-handed scythes. Corn-drying ovens and granaries were built so that crops could be stored over winter, making farming more lucrative than ever before. In addition, barns were built of stone, which allowed more livestock to be kept over winter and not culled, so there were more breeding pairs when spring came.

Huge villa estates complete with luxury housing can be found from the last two centuries of Roman occupation in Britain and in this context, the great palace at

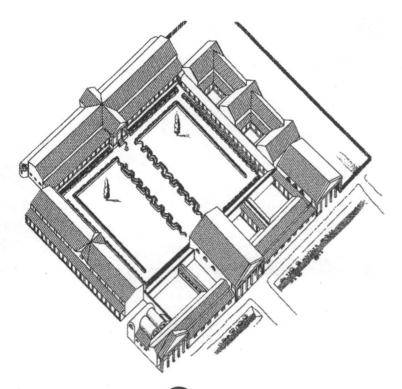

FIGURE 4.23 PS
Fishbourne.

Fishbourne can be seen as an oddity. It is reputed that the client king Cogidubnus resided in the magnificent palace at Fishbourne in the town of Chichester, which had been a Roman town from the earliest time of being occupied by soldiers. We have a very early inscription from AD 59 which documents the public vow from the soldiers for the emperor Nero's safety **PS**. The site was originally no more than a supply-base for the Second Legion Augusta during the early conquest period, but from the time immediately after the Boudiccan rebellion to as late as AD 90, a large palace was built with a colonnaded garden, mosaic flooring and even a bath house complete with hypocaust. There was nothing at all comparable in Roman Britain at that time, and archaeologists are divided as to whether Cogidubnus was indeed the occupier of such a grand palace. Theories that the palace belonged to the governor seem reasonable, but the presence of the inscription from Chichester (p. 282) dating from the time when the palace was most probably built gives us the idea that the palace was supposed to act as a reward for the loyalty shown by Cogibudnus and the Regni tribe to the Romans. With the Boudiccan rebellion so recent, it was perhaps necessary for the Romans to make the benefits of cooperation and acceptance of Roman rule even clearer.

Tacitus' comments in the Agricola about the enslavement of the native population by Romanisation are hard to interpret. By the time of Agricola's governorship, the major urban settlements of the south had been restored after the Boudiccan disaster and the province was peaceful enough that the Romans believed that a full-scale conquest of

---

PRESCRIBED SOURCE

Site of Fishbourne (Figure 4.23)

Date: First century AD

Location: Near Chichester

Significance: Well-excavated palace presumed to be the home of Cogidubnus, the largest Roman private residence in the northern Empire See https://sussexpast.co.uk/properties-to-discover/fishbourne-roman-palace

---

PRESCRIBED SOURCE

Chichester dedication to Nero

Date: AD 59

Location: Chichester

Significance: Evidence for soldiers at Chichester under Nero before the Boudiccan rebellion

View it here: LACTOR 4: Inscriptions of Roman Britain (5th edn; London: KCL, 2017), F17 (= RIB 92)

Scotland was possible. Archaeology from the late first century AD shows that the Roman way of life was being accepted to varying degrees throughout the south. Tacitus' observation that the provision of amenities would encourage the natives to adopt a peaceful and presumably pro-Roman lifestyle seems to have been accurate. There is a wealth of evidence that towns and the countryside thrived due to the money in the province and the road network. Traders and merchants from all around the empire were selling their wares in the marketplaces. Latin was being used among the upper classes, and tombstones of civilians show social and economic mobility. Life had been revolutionised even for the non-elites. Urban settlements resembled towns from the provinces, there was assimilation between Celtic and Roman deities and goods from all over the Mediterranean could be bought in the market places. British society had quickly morphed into a Romano-Celtic lifestyle broadly in line with the experiences of other provincial citizens in the empire. Tacitus' remarks in the *Agricola* that the toga was everywhere seem a fitting metaphor for the adoption of a mutually beneficial Roman way of life. The province would only become richer and more impressive as the Roman occupation continued until AD 410. Art and architecture illustrated a fusion of Roman form with British ideas, and being as Roman as possible seemed to be a proud social and economic statement of the nouveau riche.

The extent to which the natives adopted a Roman way of life was variable. Territory north of Hadrian's Wall was untouched by Roman culture, whereas the original tribal capitals of the south were all Romanised to some degree or another either during this period or in the century that followed. Bath houses, theatres, forums and Roman-style villas can be found all over the country as well as Roman goods and Roman tastes. The army and the road network seem to be the biggest factors in influencing the extent of Romanisation on the province, and although Tacitus implies that Agricola adopted a specific policy of Romanisation, it is doubtful whether such a policy existed. The process was a gradual one and one which started even before the Claudian invasion, where urban settlements were growing in tribal capitals which appeared to have trade links with the continent. For most Britons in the countryside, the only presence of Rome would have been an increased burden on tribute and the adoption of Roman coins and measures. These farmers and farm-workers remained in their ancestral farm communities making use of the old methods and using the old tools. They would not have embraced Latin as Tacitus tells us that the sons of the tribal elite did. They probably spent the entire Roman occupation using their native tongue. It should not be seen that Roman Britain was a thriving urbanised province with great wealth, totally unrecognisable from its late pre-Roman Iron Age existence.

Most material evidence of this distinctive Romano-British culture comes from outside of our time period. However, the development of a people is cumulative and the original plan of the Romans, so put by Tacitus, 'to encourage a people living in isolation and ignorance to adopt a life of peace' was successful. Instead of fighting the Romans, the natives wanted to become Roman. But what cannot be debated is the rapid change and prosperity that the Romans brought to the Britons as a result of their invasion in AD 43. A topic like this can best be understood by visits to Roman sites and museums. Artefacts and plans are primary sources as much as inscriptions and the words of Tacitus.

ACTIVITY

Visit a local Roman town or museum and make a list of evidence which shows that the quality of life of the Britons improved during the Roman occupation.

TOPIC REVIEW

- Assess what the sources tell us about the economic value of Britain to the Romans.
- Discuss how far the Roman invasion and conquest of Britain transformed the life of all its inhabitants.
- Explain how the army impacted the British economy.
- Analyse what the evidence tells us about the importance of Fishbourne Palace.
- Assess how quickly urbanised life developed during the period.

Further Reading

De la Bédoyère, G. (2001), *The Buildings of Roman Britain*, London: Batsford.

De la Bédoyère, G. (2002), *Architecture in Roman Britain*, London: Shire Publications.

Bennett, J. (2001), *Towns in Roman Britain*, London: Shire Publications.

Davies, H. (2008), *Roman Roads in Britain*, London: Shire Publications.

Potter, T. and Johns, C. (1992), *Roman Britain*, London: British Museum Press.

PRACTICE QUESTIONS

1. To what extent did the natives welcome a Roman way of life?

You must use and analyse the ancient sources you have studied as well as your own knowledge to support your answer [36]

What to Expect in the AS Level Exam for the Roman Period Study

This chapter aims to show you the different types of questions you are likely to get in the written examination. It offers some advice on how to answer the questions and will help you avoid common errors.

Your Roman history examination paper is worth 60 marks and 50 per cent of the AS Level. It will ask you questions about the Roman Period Study: *The Julio-Claudian Emperors, 31* BC–AD *68*. The whole examination will last for 1 hour and 30 minutes.

STRUCTURE

There are two sections in the exam, **Section A** and **Section B**. You should answer all the questions in Section A and **one** question in Section B.

Section A

There are two questions:

- **Question 1** is worth 10 marks. It will ask you to demonstrate what you know about an issue relating to one of the content points within one of the five timespans. It therefore has a clear and restricted focus.
- **Question 2** is worth 20 marks. It is a source-based mini-essay question. You will be given prescribed sources on the paper, and asked a question relating to them.

Section B

There is a choice of two questions.

- **Questions 3** and **4** are both essay questions, each worth 30 marks. You are required to answer only one of them. These will be much broader based questions, in which you will be able to use, analyse and evaluate the ancient source material that you have studied in order to answer the issues addressed in the question.

ASSESSMENT OBJECTIVES

There are three Assessment Objectives in the Ancient history AS Level. These are detailed in the table below.

Assessment Objective	Learners are expected to:
AO1	Demonstrate knowledge and understanding of the key features and characteristics of the historical periods studied.
AO2	Analyse and evaluate historical events and historical periods to arrive at substantiated judgements.
AO3	Use, analyse and evaluate ancient sources within their historical context to make judgements and reach conclusions about: • historical events and historical periods studied; • how the portrayal of events by ancient writers/ sources relates to the historical contexts in which they were written/produced.

The weighting that these Assessment Objectives are given in the three question types for the exam is as follows:

Question number	Question type	AO1 marks	AO2 marks	AO3 marks	Total marks
1	Issue	5	5	–	10
2	Source-based mini-essay	5	–	15	20
3 or 4	Essay	5	10	15	30

Each question type is marked according to a distinct marking grid which can be viewed in the specimen papers on the OCR website.

SAMPLE QUESTIONS

This section will examine how to prepare for the question types, and what to expect from them.

Section A: Question 1

As mentioned, this question will focus on one particular area of the specification. An example of such a question might be:

Question: How much did Augustus' building programme reflect the ideals of his principate? [10]

There is plenty of material to discuss here. It is likely that you would suggest that the building programme was the physical embodiment of the Augustan principate. You would want to use the details contained in the prescribed sources, in particular *Res Gestae* chapters 19–21 where Augustus lists the various projects that he undertook. You could mention the famous remark in Suetonius *Augustus* 28, on finding a Rome made of brick and leaving one made of marble. Inevitably the ideas of restoration and renewal will feature in this answer and should be used in a candidate's response. However, candidates could also demonstrate how the ideas of piety and traditionalism also feature in the Augustan building programme.

All in all, therefore, this question requires you to show a good knowledge of the relevant issue, and to draw together this knowledge into a logical set of conclusions.

Section A: Question 2

You will be given one or more than one passage from your prescribed sources, and beneath them will be a question for you to answer relating to them. For example:

> Yet those times were so tainted and contaminated by sycophancy that not only community leaders (whose own brilliancy had to be protected by compliance) but all the consulars, a majority of former praetors, and many pedestrian senators too competed with one another in rising and delivering their foul and excessive suggestions. It is transmitted to memory that, whenever Tiberius went out of the curia, he became accustomed to call out in Greek words in this fashion: 'Ah! Men primed for slavery!' Evidently even he, who disliked public freedom, was averse to such prompt and prostrate passivity from the servile.

Tacitus, *Annals* 3.65.2–3

> Nevertheless with remarkable rivalry on the part of the leaders, there were decrees of supplications at all the cushioned couches and that the Quinquatrus, during which the subterfuge had been disclosed, should be celebrated by annual games; that a golden representation of Minerva should be set up in the curia and an image of the princeps alongside; and that Agrippina's birthday should be included among the disqualified days. Thrasea Paetus, accustomed as he had been to pass over previous sycophancies in silence or with only brief assent, on that occasion made an exit from the senate, thereby providing grounds for danger to himself but not presenting the others with their entry to freedom.

Tacitus, *Annals* 14.12.1

After making this speech, Gaius reintroduced the charge of treason . . . But the next day [the Senate] reassembled and made speeches praising Gaius as a most sincere and pious ruler, since they were most grateful to him for not having put them to death. And for this reason they passed a resolution to offer a sacrifice of oxen to his clemency every year both on the anniversary of the day on which he had made his speech and also on the days belonging to the palace.

Dio Cassius, *Roman History* 59.16.8–10 (with omissions)

Question: On the basis of these passages, and other sources you have studied, to what extent did the Senate become sycophantic under the Julio-Claudian emperors?   [20]

When answering this question, you must of course focus primarily on the three passages given, quoting from them where necessary. From the first passage, you might highlight Tiberius' expressed view that the senators were 'primed for slavery'. You should also try to contextualise this passage somewhat, i.e. that it comes from AD 22, a year that Tacitus characterises as being 'not undisturbed in foreign affairs', and one where the Senate oscillate between not fulfilling their political role and suggesting immense honours to both Tiberius and Livia. The second passage comes from the reign of Nero, in AD 59, and concerns the meeting of the Senate following the announcement of Agrippina's death. Here some discussion of the figure of Thrasea Paetus and his seeming uniqueness in the senatorial body would certainly be required. The final passage is drawn from Dio Cassius on the reign of Gaius. The key term 'maiestas' should be treated here in the discussion of this source material and used as a means of critiquing the Senate's behaviour.

You must of course focus on the question throughout. It asks 'to what extent' so a balanced response is required. The figure of Thrasea Paetus would be a natural starting point for a discussion of senators who are not sycophantic, and this could then move on to a discussion of formal senatorial opposition to the emperors, such as the Pisonian Conspiracy of AD 65. You may also wish to bring in the senatorial opinions of Claudius, such as at the time of his speech suggesting that Gauls be admitted to the senate. It would also be profitable to discuss what factors could have motivated the majority of the Senate to become sycophantic. The best candidates might suggest that the Senate had ceased to be a politically significant organ before the advent of the Julio-Claudians, justifying this statement with either source quotations from outside the prescription or factual knowledge.

It is important to reflect on the reliability of the sources in these passages. The first passage from Tacitus is immediately preceded by a summation of Tacitus' view of the role and nature of history, suggesting that the content of the first passage is used to illumine this. The second passage could be analysed from the perspective of reliability on the basis of the antithesis of Thrasea Paetus to every other senator. Candidates could question how accurate this presentation may actually be, especially considering the republican and senatorial sympathies of Tacitus himself. Dio may be assessed on the basis that he himself is a senator discussing the matter of *maiestas* and is therefore likely to be somewhat affronted by the behaviour of his Gaian antecedents.

Remember too that the question asks you to introduce other sources which you have studied. You may well want to introduce other examples from Tacitus, such as *Annals* 1.7.1 on the 'headlong rush to servitude' that occurred on Augustus' death. Likewise one could employ Dio Cassius 53.11 on the senatorial reaction to Augustus' speech at the First Constitutional Settlement, in addition to the sources pertaining to the Pisonian Conspiracy and others aspects outlined above. As with the sources above, make sure that you reflect on the reliability of any sources you introduce.

Section B: the essay question

Your first task with this question is to decide whether to answer Question 3 or Question 4. Remember that you should answer **only one question**. Read each question carefully. It may be that you are immediately clear which one you would prefer to answer. If so, still check that you have read the question carefully. It is essential that you answer the question given to you on the paper, not a similar question that you have answered before, or a similar question that you would prefer to be on the paper!

Once you have made your decision, try to highlight key words or phrases and focus on them. Let us look at an example:

Question: 'More than any other group, it was key for the emperors to keep the plebs happy, and it just so happened that they were the easiest to appease.' To what extent do the sources support this view?

You must use and analyse the ancient sources you have studied as well as your own knowledge to support your answer. [30]

Let's focus on the key words and phrases here. Clearly, the focus of the essay is the emperors' relationship with the plebs and the means by which they were kept content, so the majority of the essay should be devoted to the discussion and analysis of the sources relating to these ideas. You should also note that the essay covers the entire period 31 BC – AD 68, so you should ensure that your evidence is drawn from across the entire timespan. Also, do not be afraid to note those aspects of the emperors' various reigns that suggest that the plebs were not always happy, for example the tax riots under Gaius (Dio Cassius, *Roman History* 59.28.11).

But the question also states 'more than any other group' and 'to what extent', so you are clearly being asked the level to which you agree, and not just whether you simply agree or disagree. The other groups within Roman society, i.e. the Senate and Equites, should also be discussed and compared with the plebs to come to an informed decision about on which, if any, the emperors placed the most significant focus. You will need to weigh up which relationship was the most important to the emperors. However, here the best candidates have the opportunity to consider the similarities and differences between the political actions of individual emperors. One would also be remiss if a discussion of the importance of the army to the emperors was not included.

Remember too that you will need to think about the reliability of the sources in this period. For example, when we consider the work of the Augustan poet Horace we must consider the extent to which his writing was affected by the idea of Augustan propaganda, such as the focus placed on bountiful harvests and the installation of peace in *Odes* 4.15, and the fact that the poet was gifted an estate in the Sabine Hills by Augustus' literary agent and associate, Maecenas. Also, we have to remember that our sources are predominantly upper-class men, who may be less than useful in our assessing the opinions of the plebs, see for example Tacitus *Annals* 14.14.2.

Above all, plan your answer carefully. Make sure you include a range of evidence and of analysis. Finally, keep your answer focussed to the question asked, and aim to refer back to the key words in the question during your answer.

What to Expect in the A Level Exam

This chapter aims to show you the types of questions you are likely to get in the written examination. It offers some advice on how to answer the questions and will help you avoid common errors.

Your Roman history examination paper will have two sections. **Section A**, worth 50 marks, will ask you questions about the Roman Period Study: *The Julio-Claudian Emperors, 31 BC–AD 68*. **Section B**, worth 48 marks, will ask you questions about your chosen depth study.

The whole examination will last for 2 hours and 30 minutes, and you are advised to divide your time roughly equally between the two sections.

ASSESSMENT OBJECTIVES

There are four Assessment Objectives in the Ancient History A Level. These are detailed in the table below.

Assessment Objective	Learners are expected to:
AO1	Demonstrate knowledge and understanding of the key features and characteristics of the historical periods studied.
AO2	Analyse and evaluate historical events and historical periods to arrive at substantiated judgements.
AO3	Use, analyse and evaluate ancient sources within their historical context to make judgements and reach conclusions about: • historical events and historical periods studied • how the portrayal of events by ancient writers/sources relates to the historical contexts in which they were written/produced.
AO4	Analyse and evaluate, in context, modern historians' interpretations of the historical events and topics studied.

SECTION A

Structure

Section A has two question types, as follows:

- **Essay question** worth 30 marks (Question 1 or 2). You will be given a choice of two essays. You should answer **only one**. You will need to use, analyse and evaluate the ancient source material you have studied in the period study to answer the issues addressed in the question.
- **Interpretations question** worth 20 marks (Question 3). You will be given an unseen extract from an academic historian, writing from the start of the 18th century onwards, related to one of your three prescribed historical debates. You will be asked to analyse and evaluate the extract in the context of the historical debate. You may include the views of other historians, and you should draw on your own knowledge and understanding of the historical event under debate: you will be given credit for knowledge of ancient source material, but only if it is presented in a way which is relevant to the question about the extract.

The weighting of Assessment Objectives for the two question types in Section A is as follows:

Question number	Question type	AO1 marks	AO2 marks	AO3 marks	AO4 marks	Total marks
1 or 2	Essay	5	10	15	–	30
3	Interpretations	5	–	–	15	20

Each question type is marked according to a distinct marking grid which can be viewed in the specimen paper on the OCR website.

Sample questions

Let us examine how to prepare for the question types in Section A, and what to expect from them.

The essay question

Your first task with this question is to decide whether to answer Question 1 or Question 2. Remember that you should answer **only one question**. Read each question carefully. It may be that you are immediately clear which one you would prefer to answer. If so, still check that you have read the question carefully. It is essential that you answer the question given to you on the paper, not a similar question which you have answered before, or a similar question you would prefer to be on the paper!

Once you have made your decision, try to highlight key words or phrases and focus on them. Let us look at an example:

'During the course of the Julio-Claudian Period, the Senate moved from being an effective organ of government to a useless remnant of a bygone era.' To what extent is this statement a fair assessment of the Senate's role under the principate?

You must use and analyse the ancient sources you have studied as well as your own knowledge to support your answer.   [30]

Let's focus on the key words and phrases here. Clearly, the focus of the essay is the role of the Senate and its effectiveness, and you are asked to examine this over the course of the whole Julio-Claudian period. The phrase 'useless remnant of a bygone age' allows for a brief discussion of the role of the Senate in the Republic, and the extent to which this role was now superfluous. Finally, remember that the phrase 'to what extent' means that you are not being asked simply if you agree or not, but about the level to which you agree. You might think that the argument has merit in some ways, but not in others.

In answering this question, you will need to show good knowledge of the relevant sources, and of their strengths and weaknesses, which can lead you to substantiated judgements. You will of course need to know details of the way in which the various emperors worked with the Senate. You will want to bring in the ways in which the Senate were still a useful organ of Roman government. However, you will also want to think about the negative aspects of the relationships between principes and Senate. You will need to weigh up which aspects of the relationship were the most significant in addressing the question.

Remember too that you will need to think about the reliability of the sources in this period. For example it is likely that, in his account of the relationships of Augustus and Tiberius with the Senate, Velleius Paterculus is highly positive, not only because he was a contemporary senator himself, but owed his promotion to praetor to Augustus himself. Moreover, it is hard to know what people may actually have felt at the time itself, as so many of our sources are non-contemporary and are guilty of their own biases (cf. Tacitus, *Histories* 1 for a useful summary).

Above all, plan your answer carefully. Make sure you include a range of evidence and of analysis. Finally, keep your answer focused to the question asked, and aim to refer back to the key words in the question during your answer.

The interpretations question

The interpretations question will be based on one of the three prescribed historical debates relating to this period study. The three prescribed historical debates are:

- the extent to which Augustus actually restored the Republic;
- the characters of Tiberius, Gaius, Claudius and Nero; and
- the benefits of Imperial rule for the inhabitants of Rome.

In the exam, you will be given an extract from an academic historian which will relate to one of these three debates. You will then be asked a question relating to the extract. An example of such an extract and question relating to the first debate above might be as follows:

'The death of Augustus, after forty-five years of personal power and fifty-seven years from the day when he had accepted the legacy of Caesar, was not to pose any problem of succession from a practical point of view. The care he had taken during his lifetime, right from the earliest days of his principate, to put a member of his family constantly in the limelight, with the clear implication that this person was marked out to succeed him, shows how he himself regarded it as natural both that the system he had founded should continue – notwithstanding the provisional character with which he deliberately endowed it by clothing it in legal fictions – and in particular that the principate should remain in his own family. Moreover, it must have appeared natural to the Senate and People of Rome, to Italy and the provinces. After almost half a century of the new regime, the mere fact that people were now accustomed to it was sufficient to remove it from the realm of discussion, if only because it was a lesser evil than the troubled conditions prevailing previously. If we add to this the advantages of a peaceful life in an order of things which the prestige and personal tact of Augustus had managed to overcome mistrust and satisfy sensibilities, it is easy to see why a solid base of universal consent henceforth sustained the Augustan principate, even in its evolution towards the revelation of its own true nature, that of an ever more clearly marked despotism.'

Albino Garzetti, 1974, *From Tiberius to the Antonines: A History of the Roman Empire* AD *14–192; 3*

(a) How convincing do you find Garzetti's presentation on the extent to which Augustus restored the Republic?

You must use your knowledge of the historical period and the ancient sources you have studied to analyse and evaluate Garzetti's interpretation.   [20]

Note that of the 20 marks for this question, 5 are available for AO1, and 15 for AO4. This means that your answer should engage carefully with what Garzetti has said in this passage. There might be a temptation to answer this question very generally, without referring to the detail of what Garzetti has said. So you should aim to read through the extract carefully more than once, and perhaps highlight key points or phrases. Such phrases from the extract above might be:

- 'the care he had taken during his lifetime';
- 'it must have appeared natural to the Senate and People of Rome';
- 'it was a lesser evil than the troubled conditions prevailing previously';
- 'prestige and personal tact of Augustus'; or
- 'an ever more clearly marked despotism'.

There are other phrases which you could also pick out, but those given above open up a range of possibilities for your answer. For example:

- You can reflect on the extent to which you agree that Augustus from the very beginnings of his reign had little intention of restoring a Republic.

- You might think about whether there was any possibility of an end to the principate, despite Garzetti's statement that the system now seemed natural to most people.
- The phrase that Augustus had 'managed to overcome mistrust and satisfy sensibilities' is interesting and could merit much discussion, especially with the events at the outset of Tiberius' reign.
- The references to the various elements of the Roman population could prompt discussion about the extent to which Augustus had satisfied these various groups.

It will also be important for you to draw on your wider knowledge and to introduce other areas of the debate about the extent to which Augustus restored the republic or created a new system. It will also be impressive if you can introduce the views of other academic historians here. For example, some would suggest that there was not even a Republic that could have been restored. We should remember that for much of the first century BC, Rome had been governed by Triumvirates and dictatorships. You may wish to set this view against the views of Garzetti put forward above regarding the situation. You might also wish to talk about whether the republican system was ever actually fit for purpose.

In all that you do, however, you must keep your answer focused on the arguments put forward by Garzetti above, whether you are agreeing with them or challenging them. Remember too that the question asks you 'how convincing'. You do not have to agree or disagree entirely (although you may wish to do so), instead you can think about how much you agree. This gives you plenty of flexibility to examine different perspectives on the debate.

You are not required to know details about the about the historical methods and approach the academic historian used, nor how his or her interpretation may have been affected by the time in which he or she was writing. However, you will be given credit for this approach to evaluation if you do it in a way which is relevant to the question.

SECTION B – DEPTH STUDY (THE BREAKDOWN OF THE LATE REPUBLIC, 88–31 BC)

Structure

Section B has two question types, as follows:

- **Source utility question** worth 12 marks (Question 4). You will be asked to read between one and four of your prescribed sources. You will then be asked a question focusing on how useful this source or set of sources are for telling us about a certain historical event or situation.
- **Essay question** worth 36 marks (Question 5 or 6). This is similar in format to the essay question for the period study (but note that it is worth six more marks). You will be given a choice of two essays. You should answer **only one**. You will need to use, analyse and evaluate the ancient source material you have studied in the depth study to answer the issues addressed in the question.

The weighting of Assessment Objectives for the two question types in Section B is as follows:

Question number	Question type	AO1 marks	AO2 marks	AO3 marks	AO4 marks	Total marks
4	Source utility	6	–	6	–	12
5 or 6	Essay	6	12	18	–	36

As in Section A, each question type is marked according to a distinct marking grid which can be viewed in the specimen papers on the OCR website.

Sample Questions

Let us examine how to prepare for the question types in Section B, and what to expect from them.

The source utility question

An example of a source utility question might ask you to read the passages below and answer the question relating to them:

Citizens of Rome, you are perfectly well aware of the difference between the rights bequeathed to you by your ancestors and this state of slavery engineered by Sulla. I need not, therefore, remind you at length of the many occasions when the plebs took up arms and seceded from the patricians, of the wrongs which led them to this course, nor of how they created the tribunes of the plebs to safeguard all their rights. I have now only to encourage you and to set out at your head upon the path by which I believe we must regain our liberty. I have not overlooked the vast resources of the nobility whose domination I seek to overthrow, single-handed and powerless, clad in but the empty illusion of a magistracy . . . You must surely realize that there is no obstacle on earth that can stop you if you work together. Even when you are apathetic and idle, they fear you. Do you imagine that Gaius Cotta, a consul from the very heart of the ruling clique, had any other motive than fear for restoring a few of the rights of the tribunes of the plebs? Certainly when Lucius Sicinius spoke out about the tribunician powers – and he was the first to dare to – you hardly raised your voices, and he was suppressed; but the nobles learnt to fear your anger before you came to resent your wrongs.

Sallust, *Histories* [3.34] {3.48M} 1–3, 8

After the restoration of the power of the tribunes in the consulship of Pompey and Crassus, this very important office was obtained by certain men whose youth intensified their natural aggressiveness. These tribunes began to rouse the mob by inveighing against the Senate, and then inflamed popular passion still further by handing out bribes and promises, whereby they won renown and influence for themselves. They were strenuously opposed by most of the nobility, who posed as defenders of the Senate but were really concerned to maintain their own privileged position.

Sallust, Conspiracy of Catiline 38

When this was known Caesar addresses his troops. . . . . He complains that a new precedent has been introduced into the state whereby the right of tribunicial intervention, which in earlier years had been restored by arms was now being branded with ignominy and crushed by arms. Sulla he said, though stripping the tribunicial power of everything had nevertheless left its right of intervention free, while Pompeius, who had the credit of having restored the privileges that were lost, had taken away even those that they had before.

Caesar, The Civil War 1.7

Question: How useful are these passages for our understanding of the importance of the office of tribune in late Republican Rome? [12]

Firstly, what does each passage say about the office of tribune? Then how far can we trust each source?

The first source tells us that the office of tribune had been established for the plebs to 'safeguard all their rights'. Yet Sulla curbed the powers of the office when he was dictator. You should demonstrate understanding of the context in which Licinius Macer's speech was given. How through the 70s different politicians sought to restore the powers that Sulla had removed and how Macer was speaking for the full restoration of powers to the office that he himself held at that time (73 BC). Another tribune L Sicinius had been the first to advocate such actions. Macer acknowledges that even the aristocratic Gaius Cotta restored some of the rights to the tribunes, reportedly out of fear of the people. Macer reminds the people that they had had to fight for their freedoms in the past and encourages them to regain their liberty again now. He arguably exaggerates the seriousness of the nobility's domination, and in the face of this, Macer is 'powerless clad in the empty illusion of a magistracy'. As such the source suggests that the people viewed the tribunes as their best means of defence against any malign action on the part of the establishment. It is important to acknowledge that Sallust (who had been a tribune in 52) was hostile towards those members of the aristocracy that he saw as being responsible for the decline in political standards and morality. Furthermore he was unlikely to have been present when the speech was delivered and was so writing up a witness' recollection of the speech.

The second source tells us that the full powers had been restored to the tribunes in the joint consulship of Pompey and Crassus (70 BC). It also refers to it as a 'very important office'. However, it goes onto say that some men had used the office against the Senate and so won renown and influence for themselves. As such, this passage shows us that the office was very attractive to would-be politicians as a way of kick-starting their career, because it was a way of getting themselves known by the plebs urbana and gaining their favour. As far as handing out bribes and promises these refer to the corn dole and acts of popular largesse. Although not in the passage you could make reference to the corn doles of the Gracchi, Cato and Clodius, as well as Clodius' legalisation of the collegia. You should again report that Sallust was hostile towards those who he saw as responsible for the decline in morality which he links to the fortunes of Rome.

The third source is set in the days after the Senate voted that Caesar should relinquish his armies or be considered to be committing treason. When that proposal was put to the Senate, Caesar's lieutenants Mark Antony and Quintus Cassius Longinus had interposed their veto. Subsequently they had been chased from Rome The passage shows us Caesar's reaction to the news. Caesar parades the abuse before his men who as members of the poor would have seen the tribunes as their defenders. He recalls that even Sulla had not dared to remove the right of the veto, so that those members of the establishment, including Pompey, who attacked the tribunes are depicted as being more tyrannical than even Sulla. Caesar probably did give a speech that sought to paint his opponents' abuse of the tribunes in the worst possible light, because it was to his advantage to persuade his men that they were being wronged. However, it is important to point out that because Caesar was able to polish the words that he records to have even greater effect after the event.

Remember that this section is only worth 12 marks, a quarter of the marks for Section B. You should only spend about 15 minutes on it therefore.

The essay question

As mentioned, this question is very similar in format to the essay question in Section A. However, it is worth 36 marks (as opposed to 30 marks in Section A), and so you are expected to spend more time on it and to go into more detail. The assessment objectives are divided in the same ratio as in the Section A essay question. The techniques required to answer this question are the same as in Section A, and you should of course draw as much as possible on the prescribed sources you have studied in your depth study to back up your arguments. Be aware that this question constitutes three quarters of the marks in Section B, and you should therefore aim to spend about 55–60 minutes on it.

SECTION B – DEPTH STUDY (FLAVIANS)

Structure

Section B has two question types, as follows:

- **Source utility question** worth 12 marks (Question 4). You will be asked to read between one and four of your prescribed sources. You will then be asked a question focusing on how useful this source or set of sources are for telling us about a certain historical event or situation.

- **Essay question** worth 36 marks (Question 5 or 6). This is similar in format to the essay question for the period study (but note that it is worth six more marks). You will be given a choice of two essays. You should answer **only one**. You will need to use, analyse and evaluate the ancient source material you have studied in the depth study to answer the issues addressed in the question.

The weighting of Assessment Objectives for the two question types in Section B is as follows:

Question number	Question type	AO1 marks	AO2 marks	AO3 marks	AO4 marks	Total marks
4	Source utility	6	–	6	–	12
5 or 6	Essay	6	12	18	–	36

As in Section A, each question type is marked according to a distinct marking grid which can be viewed in the specimen papers on the OCR website.

Sample questions

Let us examine how to prepare for the question types in Section B, and what to expect from them.

The source utility question

An example of a source utility question might ask you to read the passages below and answer the question relating to them:

> But the fact remains that in the course of his reign Titus never put a senator to death, nor was anyone else executed while he remained emperor. Charges of treason he ruled inadmissible, refusing to try them himself or allow others to do so, insisting that it was impossible to insult or diminish the emperor's majesty in any way.
> 'I never do anything reprehensible,' he asserted, 'and I am indifferent to false slanders. As for emperors who are already dead, if they really are semi-divine and possess supernatural powers, they will avenge themselves, if anyone does them wrong.' he established a number of other measures to render the lives of ordinary citizens more secure and free from anxiety. He issued a decree confirming the right of all recipients of gifts from previous emperors to retain them, thus sparing such people from the trouble of having to petition him individually. He also banished all informers from Rome.

> Dio Cassius, *Roman History* 66.19.1–3

PS

PS

Domitian put many senators to death, including some former consuls; three of these, Civica Cerialis, Salvidienus Orfitus, and Acilius Glabrio, he accused of conspiracy – Cerialis was accused while governing Asia, Glabrio while in exile – but others were killed for the most trivial reasons. Aelius Lamia lost his life as a result of some ill-advised but harmless witticisms made several years previously: when someone praised his voice after he had been robbed of his wife by Domitian, he remarked drily, 'I'm in training'; and then encouraged by Titus to marry again, he asked, 'What You are not wanting a wife too, are you?'

Suetonius, *Domitian* 9

Question: How useful are these passages for our understanding of the differences in the personalities of the Flavian emperors?   [12]

You will want to ensure that you comment on each passage in your answer. You might wish to point out that the first passage deals exclusively with Titus, presenting him very much as the model princeps and containing direct quotation of his own speech, although we should of course query how Dio would have knowledge of this, given his date. Dio also very much concentrates on Titus' relationship and attitude towards the Senate, again reflecting much of his own bias.

The second passage comes from Suetonius' account of Domitian's reign. It would be worth focusing here on how reliable the biographer might be in his research. None the less, some of the information given in the second passage is more precise than Suetonius commonly provides in his accounts, perhaps reflective of the fact that Suetonius lived through Domitian's reign (indeed his birth roughly coincides with the beginning of the Flavian period). However, Domitian is presented as markedly different, almost antithetical, to Titus. It would also be worth commenting on the extent to which the information in both passages is corroborated by other sources: for example, elsewhere in your Prescribed Sources Dio (*Roman History* 66.18.1) claims that Titus' character changed upon his accession. We could therefore ask how this affects our understanding of the material in the first passage.

A further point you may wish to make is the effect of the brevity of Titus' reign, as he had very little opportunity to make mistakes (see Dio 66.18.3–5). Also, inevitably Domitian is compared with Titus and never favourably, so we should also ask how this contrast affects the reliability (and hence the usefulness) of our source passages.

Remember that this section is only worth 12 marks, a quarter of the marks for Section B. You should only spend about 15 minutes on it therefore.

The essay question

As mentioned, this question is very similar in format to the essay question in Section A. However, it is worth 36 marks (as opposed to 30 marks in Section A), and so you are expected to spend more time on it and to go into more detail. The assessment objectives are divided in the same ratio as in the Section A essay question. The techniques required to answer this question are the same as in Section A, and you should of course draw as much as possible on the prescribed sources you have studied in your depth study to back up your arguments. Be aware that this question constitutes three quarters of the marks in Section B, and you should therefore aim to spend about 55–60 minutes on it.

SECTION B – DEPTH STUDY (RULING ROMAN BRITAIN, AD 43–c. 128)

Structure

Section B has two question types, as follows:

- **Source utility question** worth 12 marks (Question 4). You will be asked to read between one and four of your prescribed sources. You will then be asked a question focusing on how useful this source or set of sources are for telling us about a certain historical event or situation.
- **Essay question** worth 36 marks (Question 5 or 6). This is similar in format to the essay question for the period study (but note that it is worth six more marks). You will be given a choice of two essays. You should answer **only one**. You will need to use, analyse and evaluate the ancient source material you have studied in the depth study to answer the issues addressed in the question.

The weighting of Assessment Objectives for the two question types in Section B is as follows:

Question number	Question type	AO1 marks	AO2 marks	AO3 marks	AO4 marks	Total marks
4	Source utility	6	–	6	–	12
5 or 6	Essay	6	12	18	–	36

As in Section A, each question type is marked according to a distinct marking grid which can be viewed in the specimen papers on the OCR website.

Sample Questions

Let us examine how to prepare for the question types in Section B, and what to expect from them.

The source utility question

An example of a source utility question might ask you to read the passages below and answer the question relating to them:

Obverse: VIR(ICA) split by vine-leaf
Reverse: Horseman; Below: C(OMMI) F(ILIVS)
Gold Stater of Verica
Coin date: *c.* AD 20–40 (LACTOR 4) **PS**

Aulus Plautius, a senator of great reputation, led an expedition to Britain. This was because a certain Berikos [Verica], who had been driven out of the island as a result of civil war, persuaded Claudius to send a force there.

Dio Cassius, *Roman History* 60.19.1

He undertook only one expedition, and that a modest one. The Senate had decreed him triumphal ornaments, but he regarded this as beneath his dignity as emperor. He sought the honour of a real triumph, and chose Britain as the best field in which to seek this, for no one had attempted an invasion since the time of Julius Caesar and the island at this time was in turmoil because certain refugees had not been returned to the island.

Suetonius, *Claudius*, 17.1–2

Question: How useful are these sources for our understanding why Claudius invaded Britain in AD 43?   [12]

The best way of approaching a question with multiple sources for commentary is to look at each source individually. Taking the first source we can see that it is dated approximately to the period immediately before the invasion and the gold coin indicates that VIR(ICA) is probably the tribal chief. He is the son of Commius who we know was the leader of the Atrebates tribe, a pro-Roman tribe from Hampshire. There is Latin on the coin 'C(OMMI) F(ILIVS)' and the emblem of a vine leaf possibly indicates at least the presence of continental goods and trade links, if not a general acquiescence to a Roman way of life. The passage by Cassius Dio tells us that Aulus Plautius, one of Claudius' legates, launched an expedition to Britain to try to help restore or take revenge from the ousted Berikos (Verica). We have no details about the nature of his expulsion except that it was as a result of civil war. Clearly Dio indicates that Verica's position had been recognised by Claudius who sort it fit to launch an invasion to help an exiled pro-Roman tribal leader. The coin and this passage are useful in demonstrating that Verica/Berikos had some connection to the emperor in Rome and it does seem likely that Verica/Berikos would have appealed to Claudius to help him in his hour of need. The extent to which this was the casus belli is questionable as we have no further evidence to help us understand the complex relationship between Verica/Berikos and Claudius. The coin at the very least verifies Cassius Dio's claims of the existence of a pro-Roman tribal leader called Verica/Berikos.

The passage by Suetonius perhaps alludes to the Verica/Berikos situation in the final line but not as a direct cause of war. Perhaps Suetonius mentions the situation in Britain only to offer a pretext for invasion; he is very clear in stating that Claudius invaded Britain in AD 43 so as to increase his reputation and receive a real triumph. This passage therefore is clear that Claudius invaded Britain for his own glory and perhaps to surpass the achievements of Julius Caesar. Both Cassius Dio and Suetonius are writing considerably after the event and neither can be sure of the motivation of the long since dead emperor. The Verica/Berikos situation seems likely as both sources mention it and the coin at least supports that Verica/Berikos would have approached Claudius for refuge having been expelled from Britain. It seems unlikely that Roman foreign policy would be dictated by such a minor event and we know from other sources that Claudius acceded to the throne in difficult circumstances only two years earlier. Therefore, the idea that Claudius would use the pretext of restoring/avenging Verica/Berikos to launch a full-scale invasion of Britain to benefit his own reputation seems at least on the surface a plausible one. We know from other passages of Suetonius that Claudius received his triumph and many other honours for the conquest of Britain.

Remember that this section is only worth 12 marks, a quarter of the marks for Section B. You should only spend about 15 minutes on it therefore.

The essay question

As mentioned, this question is very similar in format to the essay question in Section A. However, it is worth 36 marks (as opposed to 30 marks in Section A), and so you are expected to spend more time on it and to go into more detail. The assessment objectives are divided in the same ratio as in the Section A essay question. The techniques required to answer this question are the same as in Section A, and you should of course draw as much as possible on the prescribed sources you have studied in your depth study to back up your arguments. Be aware that this question constitutes three quarters of the marks in Section B, and you should therefore aim to spend about 55–60 minutes on it.

GLOSSARY

Component-specific glossaries will be available on the Companion Website

Acts of the Arval Brethren stone plaques commemorating the rituals of the Arval Brethren, essentially cataloguing imperial rites and details of the various reigns

adlection the process whereby individuals were included on the senatorial roll, effectively elevating them as members of that body

aedile one of six magistrates elected annually; responsible for city maintenance, markets and public games

ager publicus public land owned by the state often worked by Roman citizens

amicitia (pl. amicitiae) a political alliance to serve a particular purpose

amphorae Roman pottery used to store and transport wine and/or olive oil

as (pl. asses) low-denomination coin for everyday expenditures, equivalent to ¹/₁₆ sestertius

auctoritas 'influence', that is the ability of an individual to affect socio-political circumstances without the need for specific official power

aureus the highest value coin, made in gold and equivalent to 100 sesterces

auxiliaries soldiers who fought in the Roman army but were not Roman citizens. They formed the cavalry and light infantry, and were used as specialist fighters. They were always posted away from their own country.

broad wall the foundations for the earliest designs of the wall, 10 ft thick

censor a magistrate responsible for updating and maintaining the census of Roman citizens

civitates the town from which a tribal area was controlled and administered

Classis Britannica the Roman Fleet in Britain. Its base was either Richborough or Dover. It would be used to reconnoitre the waters around Britain as well as transporting supplies for the soldiers by sea.

client kingdoms pro-Roman tribal areas that were self-governing states but would work in the best interests of the Romans. There were three in Britain: the Iceni (East Anglia), the Brigantes (the North) and the Regni (Sussex).

collegium (pl. collegia) clubs made up of individuals often living in close proximity. They fulfilled a social function, often seeing to burial needs. Under Clodius, some became street gangs.

coloniae a town built for retired veterans (Roman citizens), usually converted from a pre-exisiting legionary fortress. Colchester, Gloucester, York and Lincoln were all coloniae.

comitia centuriata the assembly that elected senior magistrates

comitia plebis/populi tributa the assemblies that passed laws and elected junior magistrates

congiarium (pl. congiaria) money (or tokens exchanged for money) given to the plebs, typically at events such as accessions, imperial birthdays or victories

consilium principis a council set up by Augustus to prepare the agenda for the senate, comprising Augustus, the two consuls and fifteen senators; it was reconstituted every six months

consul one of two annually elected senior magistrates, by whose names the Romans dated their years

Curia the assembly house of the Senate

cursus honorum the 'course of offices', the path through successive magisterial offices that senators followed

damnatio memoriae the process whereby the names and achievements of individuals deemed to have been hostile or traitorous to the Roman state are formally removed from public monuments

delatores informants in Tiberian Rome, drawn from any social class, and rewarded with a quarter of the value of the property of those convicted of treason

denarius a small silver coin worth 4 sestertii

dictator originally a magistrate elected during a time of crisis with supreme authority

divi (sg: divus; fem: diva) the collective term for the deified members of the imperial family

donative a handout of money to the soldiers of Rome, the frequency and scale of which could assure the loyalty of the troops

equestrians (Latin: *equites*) members of the second rank of the nobility in Rome, for which there was a wealth qualification. Originally they served as the cavalry of Rome, but eventually took significance as the professional or business class of the Roman world.

eulogy a speech or text in praise of a recently deceased person

factio (pl. factiones) synonymous with amicitia

fiscus ludaicus tax imposed on those living as Jews but not acknowledging the fact publicly (including converts) and upon those concealing their Jewish birth

fortress legions are housed in legionary fortresses, large enough for 5,000 soldiers

Fosse Way the road from Exeter to Lincoln. Acted as the western boundary of Roman Britain during the early conquest period.

frontier a political or geographical boundary. Roman frontiers denote the edge of the Roman Empire.

genius the spirit of a person or place

Governor of Britain a Roman senator appointed by the emperor in Rome to make all military decisions in Britain. He had full authority over the troops as well as holding full executive and legislative decision making in the province.

hill fort defensive earthworks

HS abbreviation for **sestertius**

hyperbole deliberate exaggeration

Imperator a title awarded to generals and emperors victorious in battle

imperial cult the worship of the emperor or his family as divine

imperium general Latin term meaning 'command', 'power' or 'ability to lead', frequently then sub-categorised to reflect the roles of specific magistracies

imperium proconsulare maius literally 'power greater than that of a proconsul': power confirmed that Augustus had the ability to overrule any provincial governor

ingot an oblong block of metal, ready for export

largesse great generosity, often lavish gifts of goods or money

latifundium (pl. latifundia) large estates owned by the rich and staffed with slaves

Latin status municipal rights that allowed individuals to trade and marry with Romans. Originally confined to the area close to Rome, by the late Republic this was a way of elevating a community above that of provincials in the case of Sicily and Transalpine Gaul. Further afield individual towns might enjoy Latin municipal rights. Magistrates in these communities gained Roman citizenship.

laureate wearing a laurel wreath

legate a Roman official placed in charge of a province or region on behalf of the emperor, or a deputy to such an official

lustrum the formal purificatory ritual that officially marked the ending of the census

magistrate an elected official in the Roman Republic and principate

maiestas a charge of treason against the workings of the Roman state, tried in the Senate; the usual punishment was death and confiscation of property

milecastle a small fort every Roman mile for the length of the Wall, large enough for about ten soldiers on sentry duty from a nearby fort. Gateways to the north and south. They run right to left numbers one to eighty.

military way the road running south of the Wall, which allowed the soldiers to transport goods and information to forts quickly

municipia a civitas capital which had special status above other civitates. St Albans and probably London were municipia. Its local magistrates would be awarded Roman citizenship.

narrow wall the parts of the Wall which have narrower foundations

novus homo 'new man': the first member of a family to gain entry into the Senate. Additionally the first member of a family to gain the consulship.

numen the divinity of a person

numismatic evidence coins used to understand Roman history

oppidum a fortified Iron-Age settlement in Britain

optimate (pl. optimates) literally 'the best people', individuals who saw themselves as the defenders of the established order

patricians originally the aristocracy, the title was passed down by birth

Pax Augusta 'Augustan Peace': the concept of the stability and safety that Augustus brought to the Roman world

philhellenism the love of Greek culture

pileus a cap worn by freed slaves

plebeians originally the labouring classes, by the Late Republic the distinction was mostly gone; it was more a question of status

plebs commoners, the ordinary people of Rome

plebs urbana the plebs, or urban poor

pomerium the sacred boundary of the city of Rome

Pontifex Maximus Chief Priest in Roman religion, assumed by Augustus in 12 BC when the previous incumbent died, as was the tradition

popularis (pl. populares) those politicians who played to the needs and wants of the poor in order to secure their political support

possessores those in possession of and working ager publicus but not actually owning it

potestas official political power, typically held by senators occupying positions on the *cursus honorum*

praefectus urbi a role created by Augustus to deal with the day-to-day administration of the city of Rome

praetor one of twelve to sixteen magistrates elected annually; mainly responsible for the administration of justice

Praetorian Guard the cohorts of soldiers who protected the emperor and who were some of the only troops allowed inside the city itself. They enjoyed preferential treatment compared with the rest of the army.

princeps the name adopted to define Augustus' role in his new system of government, first used in 27 BC

princeps iuventutis 'leader of the youth': a title given to both Gaius and Lucius Caesar by Augustus to indicate their potential as successors

principate the new system of government created by Augustus in 27 BC, essentially an autocracy framed in the traditions of the Republic

procurator the financial administrator of a province, of equestrian status, reporting directly to the emperor. In Britain their headquarters was in London, even when Colchester was the capital.

publicani the corporations of equestrians who managed state contracts. They had to pay a fixed price up front to the treasury for their contract. In the case of taxes, they were free to keep a percentage of the revenue collected.

quadrans the lowest denomination (value) of coin

quaestiones perpetuae seven courts established by Sulla that oversaw cases in seven types of crime

quaestor one of twenty magistrates who served as treasurers

quinquennium aureum 'A Golden Five Years', typically applied to the opening of Nero's reign

Republic the system of government that had existed in Rome since 509 BC

Saecular Games revived by Augustus, these had a pseudo-mythological origin and were held once in a lifetime, more precisely every 110 years (although some emperors, including Claudius, held them to coincide with centenaries)

Samian ware high-quality imported red pottery from Roman Gaul

Senate the council of ex-magistrates which advised the magistrates and the people

senatus consultum ultimum (SCU) the last decree of the senate, empowering all magistrates to do whatever they deemed necessary for the preservation of the state

senatus consultum (pl. senatus consulta) (SC) an opinion of the senate arrived at after a debate that directed magistrates or people to follow a particular course of action

sententia a particular style of Tacitus', where his opinion comes at the end of a section

sestertius (pl. sestertii) a Roman coin. Ancient wealth is very difficult to compare, but a poor man may have only earned HS 1–2 a day, while an equestrian could expect at least HS 20,000 a year

Stoicism a school of philosophy founded in the fourth century BC by Zeno of Citium, marked out by a set of uncompromising theses, including that virtue was sufficient for happiness and that nothing except virtue is good

suffect consul replacement consuls who served the second half of the year, but did not give his name to the year (established by Augustus as a way to increase the number of magistracies)

supplicatio (pl. supplicationes) public thanksgiving for a particular victory. The longer the supplicatio, the longer the period of celebration that the people enjoyed and the prestige that the recipient gained.

tribune/tribunate the office of the tribune of the plebs. Responsible for defending the rights of the people, it had become an important office for aspiring politicians

tribunicia potestas nominally the power of one of the ten annually elected tribunes, an office created to protect the interests of the people

triumph a public parade of celebration for a successful military commander who had achieved a notable victory

turret a small watch tower appearing every third of a Roman mile

vallum the flat-bottomed ditch running south of the Wall with earth mounds either side. It appears to demark a military zone for the soldiers.

vici numerous civil settlements which grew near military bases but could exist as small towns in their own right, once the military had moved on

SOURCES OF ILLUSTRATIONS

1.1 Bloomsbury Academic; 1.2 Carole Raddato/Wikimedia; 1.3 CNG (www.cngcoins. com); 1.4 CNG (www.cngcoins.com); 1.5 CNG (www.cngcoins.com); 1.6 Lisa Trentin; 1.7 CNG (www.cngcoins.com); 1.8 Marie-Lan Nguyen/Wikimedia; 1.9 CNG (www. cngcoins.com); 1.10 Bloomsbury Academic; 1.11 CNG (www.cngcoins.com); 1.12 with permission of wildwinds.com; 1.13 Goldberg Coins; 1.14 CNG (www.cngcoins.com); 1.15 CNG (www.cngcoins.com); 1.16 CNG (www.cngcoins.com); 1.17 CNG (www. cngcoins.com); 1.18 CNG (www.cngcoins.com); 1.19 Numismatik Lanz München Auction LA 144 lot 398; 1.20 CNG (www.cngcoins.com); 1.21 CNG (www.cngcoins. com); 1.22 CNG (www.cngcoins.com); 1.23 with permission of Roma Numismatics Ltd romanumismatics.com; 1.24 Numismatica Ars Classica NAC AG, Auction 67, lot 658; 1.25 Bloomsbury Academic; 1.26 Numismatica Ars Classica NAC AG, Auction 100, lot 1774; 1.27 CNG (www.cngcoins.com); 1.28 with permission of wildwinds.com; 1.29 Numismatica Ars Classica NAC AG, Auction 78-I, lot 2131; 2.1 Bloomsbury Academic; 2.2 CNG (www.cngcoins.com); 2.3 CNG (www.cngcoins.com); 2.4 Glauco92/Wikimedia; 2.5 CNG (www.cngcoins.com); 2.6 CNG (www.cngcoins. com); 2.7 Ann Wuyts; 2.8 CNG (www.cngcoins.com); 2.9 CNG (www.cngcoins.com); 2.10 CNG (www.cngcoins.com); 2.11 CNG (www.cngcoins.com); 3.1 shakko/ Wikimedia Commons; 3.2 Bibi Saint-Pol/Wikimedia Commons; 3.3 jastrow/Wikimedia Commons; 3.4 Numismatica Ars Classica NAC AG, Auction 67, lot 127; 3.5 with permission of wildwinds.com; 3.6 with permission of wildwinds.com; 3.7 with permission of wildwinds.com; 3.8 Lisa Trentin; 3.9 with permission of wildwinds.com; 3.10 Numismatik Lanz München Auction LA 125 lot 699; 3.11 Lisa Trentin; 3.12 with permission of wildwinds.com; 3.13 with permission of wildwinds.com; 3.14 Lisa Trentin; 3.15 CNG (www.cngcoins.com); 3.16 CNG (www.cngcoins.com); 3.17 Numismatik Lanz München Auction LA 106 lot 347; 3.18 with permission of wildwinds.com; 3.19 with permission of wildwinds.com; 3.20 CNG (www.cngcoins.com); 3.21 Steerpike/ Wikimedia Commons; 3.22 Goldberg Coins; 3.23 Lisa Trentin; 3.24 Bloomsbury Academic; 3.25 CNG (www.cngcoins.com); 3.26 Lisa Trentin; 3.27 with permission of wildwinds.com; 3.28 Numismatica Ars Classica NAC AG, Auction 59, lot 960; 3.29 Lisa Trentin; 4.1 Bloomsbury Academic; 4.2 with permission of wildwinds.com; 4.3 Bloomsbury Academic; 4.4 CNG (www.cngcoins.com); 4.5 CNG (www.cngcoins.com); 4.6 Last Refuge/robertharding/Getty images; 4.7 Ad Meskens/Wikimedia Commons; 4.8 Lisa Trentin; 4.9 Bloomsbury Academic after Scullard; 4.10 Bloomsbury Academic; 4.11 Bloomsbury Academic; 4.12 CNG (www.cngcoins.com); 4.13 Bloomsbury Academic; 4.14 Heritage Images/Contributor/Getty images; 4.15 Bloomsbury Academic; 4.16 with permission of wildwinds.com; 4.17 Bloomsbury Academic; 4.18 Angus Lamb; 4.19 Bloomsbury Academic after Scullard; 4.20 CNG (www.cngcoins.com); 4.21 Bloomsbury Academic; 4.22 Bloomsbury Academic after Scullard; 4.23 Bloomsbury Academic after Cunliffe.

SOURCES OF QUOTATIONS

Period Study: The Julian–Claudio Emperors, 31 BC–AD 68

11 'the civil wars were now . . .' Velleius Paterculus, *History of Rome*, 2.90.1 PS (LACTOR 17), trans. Wilson, B.W.J.G. (2013) in LACTOR 17: The Age of Augustus (London: KCL, 2003), 60; **18** 'There were no honours left for the gods . . .' Tacitus, *Annals*, 1.10.6, trans. Woodman, A.J. (2004), *Tacitus: The Annals*, Hackett: Indianapolis and Cambridge; **28** 'He had not even appointed . . .' Tacitus, Annals 1.10.7; **46** 'show neither affection nor mercy' *Roman History*, 59.16.5; **46** 'take thought only for [his] own pleasure and safety' *Roman History*, 59.16.6; **46** 'reassembled and made many speeches . . .' *Roman History*, 59.16.9; **47** 'There is nothing surprising in all this . . .' Seneca, *On Anger* 3.19.3; **58** 'One might say that everything Claudius did . . .' Suetonius, *Claudius* 25, trans. Graves, R. (2007) London: Penguin; **68** 'It was an old desire of his . . .' Tacitus, *Annals* 14.14, trans. Woodman, A.J. (2004), *Tacitus: The Annals*, Hackett: Indianapolis and Cambridge: 281; **72** 'pretending to be disgusted . . .' Suetonius, *Nero* 38, trans. Graves (2007): 230; **74** 'a man strong in physique . . .' Dio Cassius, *Roman History* 63.22.1, trans. Edmondson (1992: LACTOR 15): 109; **77** 'There is little evidence for the notion that Nero introduced important innovations in ruler cult' Griffin, M.T., 1985, *Nero*: see pp. 215–20 for her section entitled 'The Nature of a Divine Monarchy'.

DEPTH STUDY 1: THE BREAKDOWN OF THE LATE REPUBLIC, 88–31 BC

89 'There have always been two groups . . .' Cicero, *pro Sestio* 96–7 (LACTOR 7, L7), trans F. Santangelo, LACTOR 7: *Late Republican Rome, 88–31 bc* (London: KCL, 2017); **90** 'Nor should those who promise lands . . .' Cicero, *de lege agraria* ll.10 (LACTOR 7, L5), trans F. Santangelo, LACTOR 7: *Late Republican Rome, 88–31 bc* (London: KCL, 2017); **107** 'Because of this, all influence . . .' Sallust, *Catiline Conspiracy* 20, trans. J. C. Rolfe, *Sallust: The War with Catiline; The War with Jugurtha* (Cambridge, MA: Harvard University Press, 1921, 1931); **108** 'For you, an *eques*, . . .' Q. Cicero, *Commentariolum Petitionis* 13, trans. D.W. Taylor and J. Murrell, LACTOR 3: *A Short Guide to Electioneering* (London: KCL, 1968), p. 29; **110** 'I see two bodies . . .' Plutarch, *Cicero* 14, trans. Rex Warner, *Plutarch: Fall of the Roman Republic* (London: Penguin, 1972) p. 325 [originally Cicero *pro Murena* 51]; **111** 'They devote their whole lives . . .' Cicero, *in Catilinam* ll.22–3 (LACTOR 7, B64c), trans. F. Santangelo, LACTOR 7: *Late Republican Rome, 88–31 bc* (London: KCL, 2017); **111** 'For we are wretched and destitute . . .' Sallust, *Catiline Conspiracy* 33, trans. J.C. Rolfe, *Sallust: The War with Catiline; The War with Jugurtha* (Cambridge, MA: Harvard University Press, 1921, 1931); **112** 'for a long time, as when mothers . . .' Sallust, *Catiline Conspiracy* 53, trans. J. C. Rolfe, *Sallust: The War with Catiline; The War with Jugurtha* (Cambridge, MA: Harvard University Press, 1921, 1931); **114** 'Now elections are in prospect . . .' Cicero, *ad Atticum* 1.16 = SL 10 (LACTOR 7, L15), trans. F. Santangelo, LACTOR 7: *Late Republican Rome,*

88–31 bc (London: KCL, 2017); **115** 'Thus he learned that he . . .' Dio 37.50, trans. E. Cary, *Dio Cassius: Roman History, Volume III Books 36–40* (Cambridge, MA: Harvard University Press, 1914) p. 179; **116** 'For it was not the case . . .' Plutarch, *Crassus* 14, trans. Rex Warner, *Plutarch: Fall of the Roman Republic* (London: Penguin, 1972), p. 130; **117** 'And when he was opposed by his colleague . . .' Plutarch, *Pompey* 47, trans. Bernadotte Perrin, *Plutarch: The Parallel Lives Vol. V* (Cambridge, MA: Harvard University Press, 1917); **118** 'Pompey, my hero . . .' Cicero, *ad Atticum* 2.19 = SL 15 (LACTOR 7, B97c), trans. F. Santangelo, LACTOR 7: *Late Republican Rome, 88–31 bc* (London: KCL, 2017); **119** 'Besides this, the young men . . .' Sallust, *Catiline Conspiracy* 37, trans. J. C. Rolfe, *Sallust: The War with Catiline; The War with Jugurtha* (Cambridge, MA: Harvard University Press, 1921, 1931); **120** 'he thinks of nothing but massacring . . .' Cicero, *ad Atticum* 4.3 = SL 22, trans. D. R. Shackleton Bailey, *Cicero: Selected Letters* (London: Penguin, 1983) p. 70; **121** 'all manner of insults ended . . .' Cicero, *ad Quintum fratrem* 2.3 = SL 25, trans. D. R. Shackleton Bailey, *Cicero: Selected Letters* (London: Penguin, 1983), p.75; **125** 'Asinius Pollio's comment . . .' Suetonius, *Deified Julius* 30, trans. A. Kline; **130** 'However, the Romans gave way . . .' Plutarch, *Caesar* 57, trans. Bernadotte Perrin, *Plutarch: The Parallel Lives Vol. V* (Cambridge, MA: Harvard University Press, 1919); **134** 'I am afraid that the Ides of March . . .' Cicero, *ad Atticum* 14.12 = SL 114 (LACTOR 7, B177c), trans. F. Santangelo, LACTOR 7: *Late Republican Rome, 88–31 bc* ; **136** 'for which reason the Senate . . .' Appian, *The Civil Wars* 3.51, trans. H. White, *Appian: Roman History: The Civil War* (Cambridge MA: Harvard University Press, 1913); **142** 'At the age of nineteen . . .' *Res Gestae* 1–2, trans. F.W. Shipley, *Velleius Paterculus: Compendium of Roman History; Res Gestae Divi Augusti* (Cambridge MA: Harvard University Press, 1924) p. 401; **149** 'In fact Pompey, from the time . . .' Velleius Paterculus 2.33, trans F. W. Shipley, *Velleius Paterculus: Compendium of Roman History; Res Gestae Divi Augusti* (Cambridge MA: Harvard University Press, 1924) p. 123.

DEPTH STUDY 2: THE FLAVIANS AD 68–96

157 'The period upon which I embark . . .' Tacitus, *Histories* 1.2–3, trans. Wellesley (London: Penguin, 1991); **159** 'Old and feeble, Galba was dominated . . .' Tacitus, *Histories* 1.6, trans. Wellesley (London: Penguin, 1991); **162** 'Their mood may be summed up . . .' Tacitus, *Histories* 1.28, trans. Wellesley (London: Penguin, 1991); **162** 'so long as he was a subject . . .' Tacitus, *Histories* 1.49, trans. Wellesley (London: Penguin, 1991); **163** 'Galba had openly stated . . .' Suetonius, *Vitellius* 7, *Suetonius: The Twelve Caesars*, trans. R. Graves (London: Penguin 1957); **163** 'In Rome, public opinion was nervous . . .' Tacitus, *Histories* 1.50, trans. Wellesley (London: Penguin, 1991); **164** 'Otho is said to have been haunted . . .' Suetonius, *Otho* 7, *Suetonius: The Twelve Caesars*, trans. R. Graves (London: Penguin 1957); **164** 'Men had to constantly attune their attitudes . . .' Tacitus, *Histories* 1.85, trans. Wellesley (London: Penguin, 1991); **165** 'From time immemorial, man has had . . .' Tacitus, *Histories* 2.38, trans. Wellesley (London: Penguin, 1991); **166** 'Thus many who had hated Otho . . .' Suetonius, *Otho* 12, *Suetonius: The Twelve Caesars*, trans. R. Graves (London: Penguin 1957); **166** 'Vespasian. . . was engaged in taking careful stock . . .' Tacitus, *Histories* 2.74, trans. Wellesley (London: Penguin, 1991); **167** 'When Nero and Galba were both dead . . .' Suetonius, *Vespasian* 5, *Suetonius: The Twelve Caesars*, trans. R. Graves (London: Penguin 1957); **167** 'By a supple gift for intrigue . . .' Tacitus, *Histories* 1.10, trans. Wellesley (London: Penguin, 1991); **168** 'Once master of Egypt . . .' Josephus, *Jewish War* 4.605–7 (LACTOR 20, H17), LACTOR 20: The Flavians (London: KCL, 2015); **170** 'Vitellius himself was bent solely . . .' Tacitus, *Histories* 2.94, trans.

Wellesley (London: Penguin, 1991); **173** 'At Rome, however, the Senate . . .' Tacitus, *Histories* 4.3, trans. Wellesley (London: Penguin, 1991); **174** 'whatever has been performed, accomplished . . .' *ILS* 244 (LACTOR 20, H20), LACTOR 20: The Flavians (London: KCL, 2015); **176** 'He reformed the senatorial and equestrian orders . . .' Suetonius, *Vespasian* 9, *Suetonius: The Twelve Caesars*, trans. R. Graves (London: Penguin 1957); **177** 'For Helvidius this day above all . . .' Tacitus, *Histories* 4.4, trans. Wellesley (London: Penguin, 1991); **177** 'When Vespasian summoned [Helvidius] . . .' Epictetus, *Discourses* 1.2.19–21 (LACTOR 20, P1j), LACTOR 20: The Flavians (London: KCL, 2015); **178** 'His ever-growing autocracy . . .' B.W. Jones, 'Domitian and the Court'; **179** 'If our only evidence . . .' F. Millar, *The Emperor in the roman World*; **181** 'The people, exhausted by the miseries . . .' Josephus, *Jewish War* 7.66 (LACTOR 20, H22), LACTOR 20: The Flavians (London: KCL, 2015); **182** 'Divus Vespasian . . . gave a handout . . .' *Chronicle of 354*, part 16 (LACTOR 20, K2), LACTOR 20: The Flavians (London: KCL, 2015); **183** 'Domitian made sure that the theatre officials . . .' Suetonius, *Domitian* 8, *Suetonius: The Twelve Caesars*, trans. R. Graves (London: Penguin 1957); **186** 'Truth, too, suffered in more ways . . .' Tacitus, *Histories* 1.1, trans. Wellesley (London: Penguin, 1991); **186** 'Nothing could stop this flow of humour . . .' Suetonius, *Vespasian* 24, *Suetonius: The Twelve Caesars*, trans. R. Graves (London: Penguin 1957); **186** 'He spent little of his time in the palace . . .' Dio Cassius, *Roman History* 66.10.4–5 (LACTOR 20, C10), LACTOR 20: The Flavians (London: KCL, 2015); **187** 'Despite frequent plots to murder him . . .' Suetonius, *Vespasian* 25, *Suetonius: The Twelve Caesars*, trans. R. Graves (London: Penguin 1957); **187** 'Vespasian was greatly distressed . . .' Dio Cassius, *Roman History* 66.12.1 (LACTOR 20, C12), LACTOR 20: The Flavians (London: KCL, 2015); **189** 'This is hardly appropriate material . . .' Dio Cassius, *Roman History* 66.9.4 (LACTOR 20, C9), LACTOR 20: The Flavians (London: KCL, 2015); **191** 'Titus complained of the tax . . .' Suetonius, *Vespasian* 23, *Suetonius: The Twelve Caesars*, trans. R. Graves (London: Penguin 1957); **193** 'We have read that it was a capital offence . . .' Tacitus, *Agricola* 2.1 (LACTOR 20, P11a), LACTOR 20: The Flavians (London: KCL, 2015); **195** 'So many honours were voted . . .' Dio Cassius, *Roman History* 67.8.1 (LACTOR 20, D8), LACTOR 20: The Flavians (London: KCL, 2015); **198** 'despite these signs of heavenly honour . . .' Dio Cassius, *Roman History*, 66.8.2 (LACTOR 20, C8), LACTOR 20: The Flavians (London: KCL, 2015); **199** 'You, Vespasian, are Caesar . . .' Josephus, *Jewish War* 3.401–2, LACTOR 20: The Flavians (London: KCL, 2015); **199** 'Vespasian, still rather bewildered . . .' Suetonius, *Vespasian* 7, *Suetonius: The Twelve Caesars*, trans. R. Graves (London: Penguin 1957); **201** 'Emperor Caesar Vespasian Augustus . . .' MW 51 (LACTOR 20, H56), LACTOR 20: The Flavians (London: KCL, 2015); **202** 'But then the city of Jerusalem . . .' Orosius, *Histories against the Pagans* 7.3.7 (LACTOR 20, H42), LACTOR 20: The Flavians (London: KCL, 2015); **204** 'Restrain the Rhine, with . . .' Silius Italicus, *Punica* 3.599–600, 603–4, 607–8, 626–7 (LACTOR 20, H62), LACTOR 20: The Flavians (London: KCL, 2015); **204** '[Augustus] had enticed the soldiery . . .' Tacitus, *Annals* 1.2.1, trans. Woodman, A.J. (2004), *Tacitus: The Annals*, Hackett: Indianapolis and Cambridge; **207** 'When notice was given of the day . . .' Josephus, *Jewish War* 7.122 (LACTOR 20, E6b), LACTOR 20: The Flavians (London: KCL, 2015); **209** 'Rome now eats with you a banquet . . .' Martial, *Epigrams* 8.49.8–9 (LACTOR 20, N49), LACTOR 20: The Flavians (London: KCL, 2015); **210** '[Vespasian] had this temple decorated . . .' Josephus, *Jewish War* 7.159–60 (LACTOR 20, K64), LACTOR 20: The Flavians (London: KCL, 2015); **211** 'someone brought before Domitian . . .' Plutarch, *Life of Publicola* 15 (LACTOR 20, K27), LACTOR 20: The Flavians (London: KCL, 2015); **219** 'the hallowed home . . .' Martial, *Epigrams* 9.20.5–6, LACTOR 20: The Flavians (London: KCL, 2015); **222** 'Domitius exercised a general . . .' Stewart, R. (1994), 'Domitius and Roman Religion: Juvenal Satires Two and Four'.

DEPTH STUDY 3: RULING ROMAN BRITAIN, AD 43–c. 128

230 'Aulus Plautius, a senator of great reputation . . .' Dio, *Roman History*, 60.19.1 (LACTOR 11, p. 37), LACTOR 11: Literary Sources for Roman Britain (4th edn; London: KCL, 2012); **232** 'The soldiers objected to the idea . . .' Dio, *Roman History*, 60.19.2–3 (with omissions) (LACTOR 11, p. 37), LACTOR 11: Literary Sources for Roman Britain (4th edn; London: KCL, 2012); **233** 'He sought the honour of a real triumph . . .' Suetonius, *Claudius*, 17. 1–2 (LACTOR 11, p. 37), LACTOR 11: Literary Sources for Roman Britain (4th edn; London: KCL, 2012); **235** 'Crossing over to Britain . . .' Dio, *Roman History*, 60.21.3–5 (LACTOR 11, p. 39), LACTOR 11: Literary Sources for Roman Britain (4th edn; London: KCL, 2012); **236** 'Tiberius Claudius Caesar Augustus Germanicus . . .' Arch of Claudius ad 51 (LACTOR 4, B16), LACTOR 4: Inscriptions of Roman Britain (5th edn; London: KCL, 2017); **237** 'To Gaius Saufeius, son of Gaius . . .' Tombstone found in Lincoln in the Claudio-Neronian period (LACTOR 4, B11), LACTOR 4: Inscriptions of Roman Britain (5th edn; London: KCL, 2017); **237** 'Marcus Petronius, son of Lucius . . .' Tombstone found in Cirencester Claudio-Flavian period (LACTOR 4, B3), LACTOR 4: Inscriptions of Roman Britain (5th edn; London: KCL, 2017); **237** 'Dannicus, cavalryman of the . . .' Tombstone found in Cirencester Claudio-Flavian period (LACTOR 4, B3); **238** 'Sextus Valerius Genialis, cavalryman . . .' Tombstone found in Cirencester Claudio-Flavian period (LACTOR 4, B4), LACTOR 4: Inscriptions of Roman Britain (5th edn; London: KCL, 2017); **238** 'Rufus Sita, cavalryman of the Sixth Cohort . . .' Tombstone found in Gloucester mid-first century ad (LACTOR 4, B5), LACTOR 4: Inscriptions of Roman Britain (5th edn; London: KCL, 2017); **238** 'Crossing with the legion to Britain . . .' Suetonius, *Vespasian* 4.1–2 (with omissions) (LACTOR 11, p. 39), LACTOR 11: Literary Sources for Roman Britain (4th edn; London: KCL, 2012); **239** 'He chose for battle a site . . .' Tacitus, *Annals* 12.33 (LACTOR 11, p. 43), LACTOR 11: Literary Sources for Roman Britain (4th edn; London: KCL, 2012); **240** 'Standing on the shore before them . . .' Tacitus, *Annals* 14.30 (LACTOR 11, p. 47), LACTOR 11: Literary Sources for Roman Britain (4th edn; London: KCL, 2012); **241** 'He (Suetonius) was replaced . . .' Tacitus, *Annals* 14.39 (LACTOR 11, p. 54), LACTOR 11: Literary Sources for Roman Britain (4th edn; London: KCL, 2012); **241** 'There was, however, a serious mutiny . . .' Tacitus, *Agricola* 16, trans. H. Mattingly, rev. S. A. Handford: London: Penguin; **241** 'The British army remained quiet . . .' Tacitus, *Histories* 1.9 (LACTOR 11, p. 54), LACTOR 11: Literary Sources for Roman Britain (4th edn; London: KCL, 2012); **242** 'Titus Valerius Pudens, son of Titus . . .' Tombstone found in Lincoln *c.* ad 71–8 (LACTOR 4, B22), LACTOR 4: Inscriptions of Roman Britain (5th edn; London: KCL, 2017); **242** 'Petilius Cerealis at once struck terror . . .' Tacitus, *Agricola* 17, trans. H. Mattingly, rev. S. A. Handford: London: Penguin; **242** 'But Julius Frontinus was equal . . .' Tacitus, *Agricola* 17, trans. H. Mattingly, rev. S. A. Handford: London: Penguin; **244** 'The summer was now far spent . . .' Tacitus, *Agricola* 18, trans. H. Mattingly, rev. S. A. Handford: London: Penguin; **244** 'Yet he did not use his success . . .' Tacitus, *Agricola* 18, trans. H. Mattingly, rev. S. A. Handford: Penguin; **245** 'The natives of Caledonia . . .' Tacitus, *Agricola* 25, trans. H. Mattingly, rev. S. A. Handford: London: Penguin; **245** 'The fight was already raging inside the camp . . .' Tacitus, *Agricola* 26, trans. H. Mattingly, rev. S. A. Handford: London: Penguin; **246** 'Agricola, meanwhile, had handed over the province . . .' Tacitus, *Agricola* 40, trans. H. Mattingly, rev. S. A. Handford: London: Penguin; **250** 'For the Emperor Caesar Nerva Trajan Augustus . . .' Caerleon stone of Trajan (LACTOR 4, C1), LACTOR 4: *Inscriptions of Roman Britain* (5th edn; London: KCL, 2017); **250** 'The Emperor Caesar Nerva Trajan Augustus . . .' Commemorative tablet from York (LACTOR 4, C2), LACTOR 4: *Inscriptions of Roman Britain* (5th edn; London: KCL, 2017); **254** 'When he became emperor, Hadrian at once reverted . . .' SHA 5.1–2 (LACTOR 11, p. 59), LACTOR 11:

Literary Sources for Roman Britain (4th edn; London: KCL, 2012); **256** 'So, having reformed the army . . .' SHA 11.2 (LACTOR 11, p. 59), LACTOR 11: *Literary Sources for Roman Britain* (4th edn; London: KCL, 2012); **256** '(In honour of) the emperor Caesar Trajan Hadrian Augustus . . .' Milecastle 38 building inscription (LACTOR 4, C7), LACTOR 4: *Inscriptions of Roman Britain* (5th edn; London: KCL, 2017); **257** 'For the emperor Caesar Trajan Hadrian Augustus, the Sixth Legion . . .' Halton Chesters dedication (LACTOR 4, C8), LACTOR 4: *Inscriptions of Roman Britain* (5th edn; London: KCL, 2017); **262** 'Because of this, and because . . .' Dio, 60.21.1 (LACTOR 11, p. 39), LACTOR 11: *Literary Sources for Roman Britain* (4th edn; London: KCL, 2012); **263** 'In Britain the propraetor, Publius Ostorius . . .' Tacitus, *Annals* 12.31 (LACTOR 11, p. 41), LACTOR 11: *Literary Sources for Roman Britain* (4th edn; London: KCL, 2012); **264** 'When they reached the rampart . . .' Tacitus, *Annals* 12.35 (LACTOR 11, p. 43), LACTOR 11: *Literary Sources for Roman Britain* (4th edn; London: KCL, 2012); **264** 'After this there were frequent battles . . .' Tacitus, *Annals* 12.39 (LACTOR 11, p. 45), LACTOR 11: *Literary Sources for Britain* (4th edn; London: KCL, 2012); **266** 'The soldiers encouraged the lawlessness . . .' Tacitus, *Annals* 14.31 (LACTOR 11, p. 48), LACTOR 11: *Literary Sources for Britain* (4th edn; London: KCL, 2012); **266** 'But above all the rousing of the Britons . . .' Dio Cassius, *Roman History* 62.2.2 (LACTOR 11, p. 51), LACTOR 11: *Literary Sources for Britain* (4th edn; London: KCL, 2012); **267** 'The inhabitants relied on the temple . . .' Tacitus, *Annals* 14.32 (LACTOR 11, p. 48), LACTOR 11: *Literary Sources for Britain* (4th edn; London: KCL, 2012); **268** 'The territory of any tribe . . .' Tacitus, *Annals* 14.38 (LACTOR 11, p. 53), LACTOR 11: *Literary Sources for Britain* (4th edn; London: KCL, 2012); **269** 'The power of her house . . .' Tacitus, *Histories* 3.45 (LACTOR 11, p. 55), LACTOR 11: *Literary Sources for Britain* (4th edn; London: KCL, 2012); **271** 'If my noble birth and situation in life . . .' Tacitus, *Annals* 12.37 (LACTOR 11, p. 44), LACTOR 11: *Literary Sources for Britain* (4th edn; London: KCL, 2012); **271** 'We British are used to women commanders . . .' Tacitus, *Annals* 14.35 (LACTOR 11, pp. 49–50), LACTOR 11: Literary *Sources for Roman Britain* (4th edn; London: KCL, 2012); **272** 'Experience has taught you the difference . . .' Dio Cassius, *Roman History* 62.3.1–4 (LACTOR 11, p. 51), LACTOR 11: Literary *Sources for Roman Britain* (4th edn; London: KCL, 2012); **272** 'They are the only people on earth . . .' Tacitus, *Agricola* 30, *Tacitus: Agricola and Germania*, trans. H. Mattingley (Harmondsworth: Penguin, 1948); **275** 'To Aulus Platorius, son of Aulus . . .' A. Platorius Nepos, governor *c*. ad 125 (LACTOR 4, F1), LACTOR 4: *Inscriptions of Roman Britain* (5th edn; London: KCL, 2017); **276** 'He made the contributions of corn . . .' Tacitus, *Agricola* 19, trans. H. Mattingly, rev. S. A. Handford: Penguin; **277** 'To the spirits of the departed . . .' Tombstone of Julius Classicianus (LACTOR 4, B18), LACTOR 4: *Inscriptions of Roman Britain* (5th edn; London: KCL, 2017); **277** 'The procurator, Catus, frightened by this disaster . . .' Tacitus, *Annals* 14.32 (LACTOR 11, p. 49), LACTOR 11: *Literary Sources for Roman Britain* (4th edn; London: KCL, 2012); **278** 'To the spirits of the departed . . .' A speculator at London, first century ad (LACTOR 4, F12), LACTOR 4: *Inscriptions of Roman Britain* (5th edn; London: KCL, 2017); **278** 'Gaius Mannius Secundus, son of Gaius . . .' A tombstone of a beneficiarius at Wroxeter, possibly before ad 61 (LACTOR 4, F8), LACTOR 4: *Inscriptions of Roman Britain* (5th edn; London: KCL, 2017); **278** 'Marcus Favonius Facilis, son of Marcus . . .' A tombstone of a M. Favonius Facilis, ad 43–9 (LACTOR 4, B12), LACTOR 4: *Inscriptions of Roman Britain* (5th edn; London: KCL, 2017); **279** 'This was a strong settlement of veterans . . .' Tacitus, *Annals* 12.32 (LACTOR 11, p. 42), LACTOR 11: *Literary Sources for Roman Britain* (4th edn; London: KCL, 2012); **279** 'the Britons are unprotected by armour . . .' Vindolanda tablet on British Cavalry (LACTOR 4, G5), LACTOR 4: *Inscriptions of Roman Britain* (5th edn; London: KCL, 2017); **280** 'For the emperor Caesar Trajan Hadrian Augustus . . .' Benwell classis Britannica building inscription (LACTOR 4,

C9), LACTOR 4: *Inscriptions of Roman Britain* (5th edn; London: KCL, 2017); **282** 'Prasutagus, king of the Iceni . . .' Tacitus, *Annals* 14.31 (LACTOR 11, p. 47), LACTOR 11: *Literary Sources for Roman Britain* (4th edn; London: KCL, 2012); **282** 'Not only were the nearest parts of Britain . . .' Tacitus, *Agricola* 14 (with omissions), trans. H. Mattingly, rev. S. A. Handford: Penguin; **282** 'To Neptune and Minerva . . .' Chichester dedication slab (LACTOR 4, F16), LACTOR 4: *Inscriptions of Roman Britain* (5th edn; London: KCL, 2017); **287** 'Most of the island is low-lying and wooded . . .' Strabo, *Geography* 4.5.1 (LACTOR 11, p. 33), LACTOR 11: *Literary Sources for Roman Britain* (4th edn; London: KCL, 2012); **288** 'They live much like the Gauls . . .' Strabo, *Geography* 4.5.2 (LACTOR 11, p. 33), LACTOR 11: *Literary Sources for Roman Britain* (4th edn; London: KCL, 2012); **288** 'Tiberius Claudius Caesar Augustus, pontifex maximus . . .' Mendip lead pig (LACTOR 4, B17), LACTOR 4: *Inscriptions of Roman Britain* (5th edn; London: KCL, 2017); **292** 'The following winter was spent on schemes . . .' Tacitus, *Agricola* 21, trans. H. Mattingly, rev. S. A. Handford: Penguin; **293** '[For] The Emperor Titus Caesar Vespasian Augustus . . .' Verulamium Forum Inscription ad 79 or 81 (LACTOR 4, B24), LACTOR 4: *Inscriptions of Roman Britain* (5th edn; London: KCL, 2017); **294** 'For the Emperor Caesar Trajan Hadrian Augustus . . .' Wroxeter Forum Dedication, ad 129–30 (LACTOR 4, F26), LACTOR 4: *Inscriptions of Roman Britain* (5th edn; London: KCL, 2017); **301** 'Yet those times were so tainted . . .' Tacitus, *Annals* 3.65.2–3, trans. Woodman, A.J. (2004), *Tacitus: The Annals*, Hackett: Indianapolis and Cambridge.

What to Expect in the AS Level Exam for the Roman Period Study

301 'Nevertheless with remarkable rivalry . . .' Tacitus, *Annals* 14.12.1, trans. Woodman, A.J. (2004), *Tacitus: The Annals*, Hackett: Indianapolis and Cambridge; **302** 'After making this speech . . .' Dio Cassius, *Roman History* 59.16.8–10 (with omissions), trans. Edmondson (1992: LACTOR 15).

What to Expect in the A Level Exam

308 'The death of Augustus . . .' Albino Garzetti, 1974, *From Tiberius to the Antonines: A History of the Roman Empire ad 14–192*, 3; **310** 'But the fact remains that in the course of his reign . . .' Dio Cassius, *Roman History* 66.19.1–3, LACTOR 20: The Flavians (London: KCL, 2015); **310** 'Domitian put many senators to death . . .' Suetonius, *Domitian* 9, *Suetonius: The Twelve Caesars*, trans. R. Graves (London: Penguin 1957); **312** 'Citizens of Rome, you are perfectly well aware . . .' Sallust, *Histories* [3.34] {3.48M} 1–3, 8 trans LACTOR 7 p.12; **313** 'After the restoration of the power of the tribunes . . .' Sallust, *Conspiracy of Catiline* 38, trans S.A. Handford, Penguin p.204; **313** 'When this was known Caesar addresses his troops . . .' Caesar, *The Civil War* 1.7, trans A.G. Peskett, Loeb p.12; **315** 'Aulus Plautius, a senator of great reputation . . .' Dio Cassius, *Roman History* 60.19.1, trans. Edmondson (1992: LACTOR 15); **316** 'He undertook only one expedition . . .' Suetonius, *Claudius*, 17.1–2, Suetonius: *The Twelve Caesars*, trans. R. Graves (London: Penguin 1957).

INDEX

In this index the page numbers given for Prescribed Sources refers to the Box Features only.